BENEDETTO CROCE AND ITALIAN FASCISM

Benedetto Croce and Italian Fascism

FABIO FERNANDO RIZI

UNIVERSITY OF TORONTO PRESS
Toronto Buffalo London

© University of Toronto Press Incorporated 2003
Toronto Buffalo London
Printed in Canada

ISBN 0-8020-3762-3

Printed on acid-free paper

Toronto Italian Studies

National Library of Canada Cataloguing in Publication

Rizi, Fabio Fernando, 1935–
    Benedetto Croce and Italian fascism / Fabio Fernando Rizi.

    (Toronto Italian studies)
    Includes bibliographical references and index.
    ISBN 0-8020-3762-3

    1. Croce, Benedetto, 1866–1952.   2. Italy – Politics and
government – 1922–1945.   3. Fascism – Italy – History – 20th century.
4. Anti-fascist movements – Italy.   I. Title.   II. Series.

    B3614.C74R59 2003   945.091′092   C2002-905726-4

University of Toronto Press acknowledges the financial support for its
publishing activities of the Government of Canada through the Book
Publishing Industry Development Program (BPIDP)

This book has been published with the help of a grant from the Humanities
and Social Sciences Federation of Canada, using funds provided by the
Social Sciences and Humanities Research Council of Canada.

University of Toronto Press acknowledges the financial assistance to its
publishing program of the Canada Council for the Arts and the Ontario Arts
Council.

To my parents, Maria Vittorioso and Pelino Rizi,
my wife, Joan,
and our children, Margaret and Richard

Contents

Preface ix

Introduction 3

1 The Background to National Politics, 1866–1920 12
2 From Giolitti to Mussolini, 1920–1922 35
3 From Critical Benevolence to Opposition, 1923–1924 50
4 'Continuous and Resolute Opposition,' 1925 80
5 New Forms of Opposition, 1926 104
6 Towards a New Definition of Liberalism, 1927–1928 123
7 The Defence of Liberal Italy, 1926–1928 140
8 The Lateran Pacts, 1929 155
9 'Faith in the Future and Courage in the Present,' 1930–1940 171
10 Cultural Activity as Political Opposition, 1930–1940 196
11 Difficult Choices, 1930–1940 213
12 The Fall of Mussolini and the Kingdom of the South, 1940–1944 233
13 The Elder Statesman, 1944–1952 246

Conclusion 261

Notes 269
Bibliography 295
Index 313

Preface

This book is the result of a revision and a re-elaboration, with new documents, of a dissertation defended in December 1999 at York University in Toronto. I would like to take this opportunity to express my gratitude to all the people and institutions whose help and assistance made possible both enterprises.

A scholarship from the Mariano A. Elia Chair in Italian Canadian Studies at York University encouraged a research trip to Italy. In Rome, the hospitality of my friend Filippo Taddei and the cordiality of his family allowed a much longer stay than would otherwise have been possible and turned the research into an enjoyable and fruitful experience.

Giovanna Colombo of Milan, Giacomina Calcagno of Genoa, Tiziano Vanola of Toronto, and my uncle Italo Fallavollita of Sulmona at various times sent valuable bibliographic material from Italy. Alda Croce graciously donated to the University of Toronto her father's diaries, *I Taccuini di Lavoro*, previously published in a private edition of six volumes. Mariolina Franceschetti of the Italian Cultural Institute and Robin Healey of the Robarts Library facilitated the arrival and cataloguing of these books in Toronto.

The Resource Sharing Centre of York University and the Archivio Centrale dello Stato in Rome provided an efficient and friendly service. Mario Giacobbi of Italbook and Mario Ciccoritti of Librital used their expertise to locate and order several books published by small and obscure Italian publishers.

William Irvine of York's Faculty of Graduate Studies, history program, was the director of my dissertation. He had to read several long versions before the final result was achieved, bravely enduring the ordeal without complaining. In each session he showed admirable patience and offered astute advice which removed obstacles and smoothed the project along.

At different stages, Stephen Hellman of York's political science department, and Modris Eksteins of the University of Toronto history department, read the dissertation with great attention and made remarks about the whole work which gave me a real boost, like an espresso stretto after a summer siesta.

During a seminar on modern European history at the University of Toronto School of Graduate Studies, John Cairns asked me to read the essays on Croce written by Denis Mack Smith and Chester M. Destler, starting the *causa causorum.* In fact, however, the new opportunity rekindled an old passion, which had begun in my native farming community of Corfinio, in a valley of Abruzzi, and was further nourished in the Liceo Classico Ovidio of Sulmona.

A subvention from the Aid to Scholarly Publication Programme of the Humanities and Social Science Federation of Canada has helped finance the publication of this book. Deserving of *vivi ringraziamenti* are Ron Schoeffel of the University of Toronto Press for his encouraging kindness, the official readers for their prompt and positive responses, and my editor, Curtis Fahey, for reading the manuscript with great attention and making numerous changes which improved the work considerably.

Rocco Capozzi, graduate coordinator and associate chair of Italian studies at the University of Toronto, at regular intervals during these last years, spent many hours patiently listening to my problems and providing sympathy and advice, plus an inordinate amount of apple fritters and cups of coffee, enough to drown both of us.

Among those who have shown interest in this project and made a contribution, none was more generous with his time and with his advice than Alexander De Grand of North Carolina State University. His encouragement came at crucial times and provided me with the confidence to carry the work to a positive conclusion. My debt of gratitude to him is simply enormous.

I hope that the final product meets with the approval of all those who have been 'present at the creation,' despite the traces in its pages of a residual 'Crocianite,' as a friend in the know once labelled my boundless admiration for the author of the *Philosophy of the Spirit.*

At this stage, a few words are in order about my former employer. The Toronto Public Library has a special place in my heart. Its employment policy made it possible for a young Italian immigrant to earn a living, learn a new language, continue his education as a part-time university student, and, *dulcis in fundo*, find a wife within the venerable walls of the old Toronto Reference Library building. Much of my professional work was carried out at the Dufferin/St Clair Library as 'Italian Librarian.' In that branch I had the good fortune to work alongside a group of congenial and helpful friends, who were able to take the pressures of modern life in stride. 'The Duffies' knew the art of turning coffee breaks and lunch hours into relaxed and lively conversations, often touching on history and politics. Among that charming group, I owe a special mention to Beth Rodger and, now with great sadness, the late Nancy Wade Stadler, two outstanding librarians and delightful friends.

I also have to confess my debt of gratitude to my wife, Joan. Without her literary skills, technical help, and constant moral support, neither the dissertation nor the book would have seen the beginning or the end.

Finally, an editorial note. This book upper cases the names of discrete political groups and parties (such as Socialist, Communist, and Fascist) and lower cases the names of the ideologies they represented (socialism, communism, and fascism). An exception concerns the term 'liberal' or 'Liberal.' The Liberal Party of Italy did not exist until 1922; until then, 'liberals' were individuals sharing a broad set of values rather than members of a political party. Accordingly, while this book uses the term 'Liberal' to refer to members of the Liberal Party from 1922 on, it uses 'liberal' for the earlier period. Of course, 'liberal' is also the spelling of choice, regardless of period, in such phrases as the 'liberal state.' The same logic applies to 'Nationalist' and 'Democrat.' The upper case 'Nationalist' is used to denote members of the Italian Nationalist Association, which merged with the National Fascist Party in 1923; and, similarly, 'Democrat' denotes not an intellectual orientation but members of specific organizations, such as the National Democratic Union, Giustizia e Libertà, and the Party of Action. Such are the intricacies of Italian politics, in Croce's time no less than in ours.

BENEDETTO CROCE AND ITALIAN FASCISM

Introduction

Benedetto Croce was one of the greatest European intellectuals of the twentieth century, and one of the few Italians to have made an original contribution to modern philosophy. With the frequent publications of his books and the regular presence of his own bimonthly periodical, Croce dominated the Italian literary landscape for more than fifty years, at the end leaving a mountain of books, impressive in both quantity and quality. He brought a new vitality to Italian culture that assured the revival of idealism and undermined the dominance of positivism.[1]

His ideas introduced different methods of critical analysis, providing new concepts in literature and historiography. At the same time, Croce offered successful examples and fruitful applications of his theories, putting into practice his ideas in literary criticism and historical interpretation. Some of his books became popular and a few even achieved the status of best-sellers. Croce's intellectual and social influence on Italian society gave him a position of moral leadership that transcended the narrow world of scholarship, especially during the Fascist regime. When political parties were banned and freedom of expression suspended, Croce emerged as the custodian of the Risorgimento liberal tradition and became the symbol of the resistance to the dictatorship of Mussolini.[2]

Croce's anti-fascism, greatly praised in his time, was challenged and even denigrated after the war by his political opponents, from the left and from the right; today it continues to be celebrated, once in a while, at the appropriate anniversaries. But his political activities of that time have received only episodic attention and have not been narrated in full detail. This lack of critical investigation has left an impoverished image of Croce's anti-fascism. When it is remembered, Croce's contribution to the struggle against Mussolini's dictatorship is often reduced to the writing of two historical books and the making of one speech in the Senate, as if he did nothing else of political importance during those years.

Given Croce's central position in Italian intellectual life, scholars naturally paid greater attention to his cultural activity than to his political involvement. As a result, despite scholarship filling library shelves on Croce's philosophical ideas, misunderstandings about his political activities still persist and inaccuracies about his social life are often repeated. Rectifying these shortcomings of the existing literature on Croce is the aim of this book, one that is facilitated by the presence of documents not available in the past.

After the First World War, Croce's place in Italian political affairs was no longer marginal. He was a senator for many years and had a close relationship with the liberal elite that ruled Italy before fascism; in two crucial moments of Italian history he was a member of the cabinet. In 1920, when fascism became a major force in Italian political life, he was minister of education under Giovanni Giolitti; in 1944, as a member of the Pietro Badoglio cabinet, he was among the protagonists who shaped the new democratic life of Italy after the fall of Mussolini. Above all, during the Fascist regime, especially after the death of Giolitti, Croce assumed the role of leader of the opposition.

Croce's cultural and political activities cannot be neatly separated and considered as if they were two discrete entities. More often than not they went together, one influencing the other. A better knowledge of Croce's involvement in social and political events allows us to appreciate his ideas and his intellectual evolution. Many of Croce's political essays, cultural polemics, and historical books originated in passionate contemporary interests and had as their constant aim the revitalization of the liberal tradition of the Risorgimento. This is particularly true for the Fascist period. Under Mussolini's dictatorship, Croce's political and cultural activities coincided. He employed his books and periodical as instruments to express his political ideas, to manifest his opposition to the Fascist regime, and to combat the political and cultural ideals that Mussolini was promoting.

Political passions and ideological motivations have also greatly influenced the opinions of Croce's critics, either when they challenged his philosophy or questioned his politics. After the Second World War, old and new adversaries called into question Croce's political position during the Fascist regime and accused him of having been a progenitor of fascism, an early supporter of Mussolini, and even a tepid opponent of the dictatorship after 1925. In those turbulent years, both Croce's philosophical ideas and his liberalism were not only subjected to scholarly criticism but quite often were dismissed outright and condemned as an expression of the conservative forces and agrarian interests that had dominated the history of Italy from the Risorgimento to the Fascist adventure.[3]

Marxist intellectuals were among the first to criticize the philosophy and the personality of Croce, as part of a well-devised political and cultural strategy. The opening shots were fired by Palmiro Togliatti, leader of the Italian Communist Party. In 1944, while both were members of the Ivanoe Bonomi cabinet, Togliatti, in the very first number of his periodical, *Rinascita*, claimed that under Mussolini's dictatorship Croce had enjoyed 'a curious position of privilege' and established 'an open collaboration' with fascism against communism and Marxist philosophy. As a result of that tacit collaboration, and as a reward for his anti-communism, Croce had been allowed by the authorities to direct, 'once in a while,' 'timid arrows' against the Fascist regime. The same accusation was made in the 1960s by Emilio Sereni, the rigid custodian of Marxist orthodoxy in the Italian Communist Party.[4]

By attacking and weakening Croce's authority, Togliatti sought to establish the hegemony of Antonio Gramsci, whose *Letters* and *Quaderni* were being published in those years to great acclaim. From then on, Marxist writers began to compare the personality and career of Croce with that of Gramsci, stressing the differences, not mentioning the affinities, and preferring to ignore the continuous dialogue of Gramsci with Croce, as it appears both in the *Letters* and in the *Quaderni*.[5]

In 1954 Gaetano Salvemini, the great historian and anti-Fascist democrat, expressed reservations of a different nature about Croce's political activities. He recognized the positive role that Croce had played in the struggle against fascism and praised his personal courage, adding even, to avoid any misunderstandings, that 'Italians should never forget the gratitude that they owe to Croce for his resistance to fascism from 1925 to 1943.' Yet he also stressed Croce's 'ambiguity' and enumerated his shortcomings, following – and also enlarging – the pattern set by Denis Mack Smith in his earlier essays on Croce.

Salvemini drew three conclusions from his long list of Croce's personal contradictions and political ambiguities. First, born into a family of great landowners, Croce always maintained the mental attitude typical of the landlords of southern Italy and, like all of them, was a conservative on social and political questions. Secondly, the general nature of Croce's philosophical and political ideas encouraged 'quietism.' Finally, and most important for Salvemini, the opposition of Croce to the Fascist regime was a passive resistance and limited to cultural activity. Despite its moral and educational value, that kind of opposition could not be compared to and should not be confused with the active resistance and the political actions of the young men of *Giustizia e Libertà* and the militants of the Communist Party, who risked persecution, jail, exile, and even death. In Salvemini's vivid dictum: 'There is a difference between Buddha, contemplating his navel, and Christ who dies on the cross.'[6]

The criticism of Italian writers found a favourable echo among American and British historians, and sometimes it was even anticipated by them. In the new atmosphere, the old admiration of Charles Beard, Carl Becker, and Robert Collingwood for Croce's ideas and politics was replaced by a new animosity reflecting feelings created by the war.

In 1949 and again in 1952, the American historian Chester McArthur Destler questioned both the political past of Croce and his intellectual honesty. He argued in the *American Historical Review* and the *Journal of Modern History* that Croce's opposition to fascism began only in 1925. Until that year, Croce had been a progenitor of fascism, an inspirer of Mussolini, and an open supporter of the Black Shirt regime in its formative years. For Destler, Croce's contribution to the revival of idealism and to the demise of positivism had weakened the moral basis of liberal democracy. His criticism of the concept of causality had introduced relativism in morality and presentism in history, creating confusion and uncertainty in ethical and historical judgments. As a champion of the essential amorality of politics and economics, Croce had created the climate in which an aggressive nationalism and later, fascism, could thrive.

In Destler's view, from 1914 to 1919 Croce also helped to undermine Italian liberalism and to damage constitutional democracy with his Machiavellian conception of politics and his insistence that force alone was the basis of the state and international relations. During the war, his emphasis on struggle and ridicule of pacifism, his constant criticism of democratic ideals, and his condemnation of Wilsonian internationalism helped to lay a substantial portion of the intellectual foundations of Italian fascism. After the war, not only was Croce an early admirer and supporter of Mussolini, but once the Fascists achieved power, he praised the government's policies, was not alarmed by the increasing violence or the emerging dictatorship, approved the new anti-democratic electoral law, and finally gave a vote of confidence to Mussolini after the muder of the young Socialist leader Giacomo Matteotti. More damning than anything, during the Matteotti crisis, Croce remained 'favourable

to a durable dictatorship' and gave 'open and public support to Mussolini's bid for permanent power at the time.' Destler even claimed that,
after the Liberation of southern Italy in 1943, Croce, in a new edition of
his occasional writings, altered critical parts of his original newspaper
interviews of 1923 and 1924, with the aim of toning down or even denying that 'he either supported or sympathized with Mussolini.'[7]

Among English-speaking historians, Denis Mack Smith, with three
essays written between 1947 and 1973, has provided the longest account
and the most detailed criticism of Croce's political activities and his relations with fascism. He maintains that in political affairs, by reason of
family background and personal inclination, Croce always favoured conservative solutions. He also argues that Croce's philosophy was an invitation to contemplation rather than action and failed to offer the tools for
a timely appraisal of the dangers of fascism. Smith attempts to show that
Croce made a contribution to the ideological system of Mussolini and to
the political ideas of fascism. His own ideal of the state was not too far
removed from the Fascist conception of the ethical state. Many Fascist
intellectuals, in fact, regarded Croce as their spiritual father and, for his
part, Croce admired the patriotism of Fascist leaders. Croce rejected
British empiricism as too pedestrian and instead greatly admired German authoritarian ideals, and, like Mussolini, he did not have much use
for the principles of 1789. For Smith, Croce and Mussolini had a great
deal in common. Both shared an undue enthusiasm for Georges Sorel,
Machiavelli, and Marx. Both looked askance at humanitarian democracy, despised moralism in politics, and disliked Freemasons. Croce's
doctrine of politics as force and his separation of morality from politics
prepared the terrain for fascism and offered a justification for the violence of the Black Shirts.

Smith also claims that Croce displayed 'an armchair view of politics'
that did not allow him to recognize danger. Before the First World War,
Croce renounced socialism, wrote for a conservative paper, and became
head of the conservative forces in Naples; he welcomed the Libyan war
and was pro-Germany in 1914, always maintaining animosity against the
left-wing parties. After the war, Croce 'volunteered' to write for the
Nationalist periodical *Politica*, approved Giolitti's alliance with fascism,
and not only participated in the Fascist congress in Naples in 1922, but
'fervently' applauded Mussolini's speech on that occasion. Once fascism
achieved power, Croce justified the victory of the Black Shirts, 'voted
full powers' to the new government, agreed to be on the editorial board
of the filo-Fascist periodical *Nuova Politica Liberale*, supported the poli-

cies of Mussolini, approved the new electoral law, and hoped that the Fascist list would obtain a strong majority in the elections of 1924.

Before the Matteotti affair, Smith believes, Croce sensed the cultural disease of fascism but remained blind to the dangers of its politics; for him, fascism was a mere parenthesis in the history of Italy and a malaise imported from abroad. Smith recognizes that, after 1925, Croce changed significantly, evolving from 'a conditional supporter of fascism' to 'the leading anti-fascist' among those Italians who did not choose emigration and exile. But even after that date, Croce's actions left something to be desired, had relapses, and in general were more patriotic than consistent. Croce voted against the authoritarian laws, but in 1931 he advised university teachers to take the oath of loyalty to fascism. He refused to collaborate with the famous *Enciclopedia Italiana* more out of professional jealousy than for political reasons. He sided with the Spanish republic during the civil war and was critical of the Munich agreement, but in 1935 he sent his senator's medal as his contribution to Mussolini's colonial war and then 'welcomed the incorporation of Ethiopia into Italy.' When Italy entered the war in 1940, Croce, 'with some reluctance,' 'stood by his fellow countrymen' just as he had done in 1915 and 1935, wishing well to the Italian army according to the old axiom: my country right or wrong.

Smith concedes that, in the later years of fascism, Croce showed considerable personal courage and became the conscience of the nation in its resistance to totalitarianism: in that period, Croce's books and his periodical remained one of the few free voices to be heard in Italy. But Smith also claims that Croce's historical writings contained much political propaganda, 'relied on imagination rather than scholarly research,' and twisted the evidence, 'inventing and exaggerating facts' and presenting a false idealization of the Risorgimento in order 'to reinforce the eulogy of liberal patriotism.' In particular, Croce's two most famous books, *History of Italy* and *History of Europe*, 'were intended as a consolation to the opponents of the regime' and have to be regarded as a 'splendid apology of liberalism,' but some parts of them were more appropriate to polemical pamphlets than to historical analysis. Those two books did nothing to explain the causes of fascism and the weakness of the liberal state, muddying rather than clarifying the concepts of liberalism, democracy, and fascism. In the end, they 'did not assist the political education of the nation,' leaving young Italians as confused as before.

For Smith, in conclusion, the anti-fascism of Croce was only intellectual and never became a political force; perhaps it even helped to deter many people from more active opposition. The political sacrifice of Giacomo Matteotti 'contributed more to the creation of an anti-fascist myth' than the books written by liberals. Croce's activities were in fact discounted and ignored by the regime; the authorities left him in peace and recognized that his opposition was harmless because of the conservative nature of his ideas and the restricted circulations of his writings. For many reasons, Croce's opposition was even useful to the Fascist regime, first of all as an advertisement abroad of Mussolini's tolerance and then because Croce himself, on account of the foreign royalties earned by his books, was, in Smith's cryptic expression, 'a considerable dollar asset'![8]

During all this time, Croce did not lack defenders.[9] From 1950 until our time, against Italian and foreign critics, a long list of Italian scholars have come to Croce's defence, stressing his positive and relevant contribution to Italian culture and to the struggle against fascism. Sometimes reservations expressed in the 1950s have turned into a fuller admiration in the 1990s, reflecting the changed political passions. This evolution seems quite evident in the recent writings of Norberto Bobbio and Eugenio Garin.[10]

From different points of view, Carlo Antoni and Raffaello Franchini, Federico Chabod and Walter Maturi, Vittorio Enzo Alfieri and Alfredo Parente, Vittorio De Caprariis and Giovanni Sartori, Aldo Garosci and Leo Valiani, and Giuseppe Galasso and Gennaro Sasso have shown that Croce's idealism and historicism, with his postulates of dialectic and distinction, his insistence on freedom and creation as attributes of the human spirit, had little in common with the ideological system of fascism, assuming that there was one or that Mussolini had a coherent and well-defined conception of reality. These writers also argue that Croce found in his philosophical concepts and in his ethical values the elements to reject Fascist ideals and the reasons to fight the dictatorship of Mussolini, as well as to condemn the regime's racial policy. It was, after all, the nature of his own liberalism that compelled Croce to refuse the claim, put forward first by Giovanni Gentile, that fascism was the heir of the Italian Risorgimento and the political realization of philosophical idealism.[11]

However, despite the evident need, little attention has been paid to the nitty gritty of Croce's political activities. Even the few general biographies that exist have been concerned more with his cultural contributions than with his political participation. As a result, no book, either in

Italian or in English, has analysed in detail Croce's political involvement. In English, the now outdated essays of Denis Mack Smith and the short biography of Cecil Sprigge have remained without successors. In French, an intelligent analysis of Croce's personality by Charles Boulay stops at 1911. In Italian, there is the reliable, but general, biography by Fausto Nicolini. Only Croce's activity as minister of education in Giolitti's cabinet has received close, if questionable, attention. Gennaro Sasso has provided valuable information and analysis in books and essays, often in long notes in his philosophical works. Raffaele Colapietra has made an original attempt, not completely successful, to show the reciprocal influence between Croce's ideas and the political society of his time. A few good essays on some aspects of Croce's politics have appeared in *Rivista di Studi Crociani* and in other scholarly publications with a small circulation. Political information and biographical notes can be found dispersed in various books, dealing with Croce's literary production. But we are still a long way from a full account of Croce's political activities and a detailed narration of his social life.

This book tries to fill the gaps in Croce's biography and to give a fuller vision of his political personality. It deals with Croce's practical life and with his direct participation in political events. The aim is to offer a better understanding of Croce's involvement in Italian politics, trying in particular to clarify the nature of his political actions during the years of the Fascist regime. For this purpose, greater attention has been paid to Croce's political activities from 1920 to 1929, especially from the March on Rome to the concordat between the Italian state and the Roman Catholic Church. For the period from 1930 to 1940, I examine only particular episodes, in order to provide a fuller appreciation of Croce's position and activity during the Fascist regime and his relations with the opposition movements. From 1940 to 1944, I have stressed Croce's participation in the fall of Mussolini and the leadership role he played in the so-called Kingdom of the South, until the liberation of Rome.

Two general chapters, a beginning and an end, so to speak, have been added in order to offer a more complete view of Croce's personality and political activity to North American readers. Throughout the book, attention has been paid to certain events in an effort to illuminate Croce's so-called 'ambiguities,' which have caused controversy and still generate confusion and misunderstandings.

In the central part, a year-by-year approach is used in an attempt to show the connections, and the reciprocal influence, that existed between Croce's cultural and political activities. In a study of Croce's personality and career, it is simply impossible to ignore his philosophy; when necessary, his general political ideas and philosophical concepts are mentioned, but only to clarify his political actions.

During this research, I have read Croce's major philosophical and historical books and paid close attention to his biographical essays and occasional writings, which are dispersed in several volumes. The publication of Croce's correspondence is still in process but it has been possible to consult most of his letters, which have appeared in the national edition of his works or in other editions and publications. The six volumes of Croce's diaries, *Taccuini di Lavoro,* did become accessible in Toronto after their publication in a private edition. Several folders, where the authorities during the Fascist regime had collected the reports of the police, and personal letters involving Croce, his family, and his friends have been consulted in the National Archives (Archivio Centrale dello Stato) in Rome.

These last documents make it evident that the political authorities regarded Croce as an enemy of the regime, while the diaries reveal that Croce was deeply concerned with political events during the Fascist period and was closely involved with the leaders of anti-fascism in Italy and in exile. It is no longer possible to view Croce as an Olympian philosopher, serenely contemplating the unfolding of the universe. Croce's liberalism demanded participation and personal responsibility, and his life was coherent with his concepts.

The documentation points to a clear conclusion: Croce's initial benevolence to Mussolini was quite short-lived and full of reservations, and his opposition to fascism was not passive and limited to culture, as his critics have maintained, but was active indeed, finding expression both in cultural and in political fields. With his writings, Croce defended the liberal heritage of the Italian Risorgimento and inspired his readers to remain faithful to democratic ideas. Through his trips and his correspondence, he kept in touch with the exiles and was able to maintain ties to small but influential dissident groups, located throughout Italy and dedicated to keeping alive the flame of freedom.

Not only as a thinker, but also as a defender of freedom and a fighter in the struggle against fascism, Croce belongs, to borrow Carlo Antoni's expression, to 'the castle of the great spirits' of the Italian nation.

CHAPTER ONE

The Background to National Politics, 1866–1920

Benedetto Croce was born 25 February 1866, five years after the unification of Italy under liberal institutions, the crowning event of the Italian Risorgimento, which would change the course of Croce's life and shape his future political ideas. Once his ancestors had been successful shepherds in the remote province of Abruzzi, but at the time of his birth Croce's family had long since moved away from that bucolic corner of Italy, acquired lands, wealth, and reputation, and belonged to the upper classes of Naples. His grandfather graduated from the University of Naples, held important positions in the judicial system, and married into the provincial aristocracy, finally ending his career as a judge of the Supreme Court of the Kingdom of the Two Sicilies.

Croce's father did not take part in the conspiracies of the Risorgimento, and did not embrace liberal ideas, but remained faithful to the old order and loyal to the Bourbon monarchy. As a result, during his childhood, Croce rarely heard mentioned without criticism and sarcasm the events of the Risorgimento and the names of the new leaders; instead, his parents often defended the reputation of the former king and queen and lamented the liberals' criticism of the good old days.[1]

Despite the influence of his family, in high school Croce began to build the pantheon of his own Risorgimento heroes. Attracted by their fame, he read the essays on Italian literature by Francesco De Sanctis and the passionate poems of Giosuè Carducci. The works of De Sanctis put Croce into early contact with the philosophy of Hegel and Vico and with the cultural tradition of southern Italy. In the political arena, De Sanctis offered Croce the example of constitutional opposition, liberal and democratic at the same time, demanding changes without nostalgic appeals to the past and without questioning the basic tenets of the new order.[2]

Religious Crisis and Family Tragedy.

At the age of thirteen and in a college run by priests, Croce had a religious crisis and lost faith in a transcendent God, experiencing periods of pain, remorse, and even shame, unable to reveal the event to his parents or to discuss it with his teachers. In time, Croce developed a totally humanistic conception of reality and a vision of human life without any metaphysics. But despite the rejection of a traditional religion, and the denial of any reality outside the human spirit, Croce never became antireligious. In later years, he criticized the policies of the Catholic Church and defended the lay character of the state, but he always remained respectful of religious life and was sensitive to religious feelings. Often Croce expressed his ideas, especially on questions of morality, in Christian terms and used Catholic precepts, talking and writing almost like a father of the church, as a priest was once prompted to say. Some of Croce's best friends were Catholics; a few priests and prelates had cordial relations with him. His wife was a practising Catholic, and their marriage, in 1914, was celebrated in a church. Croce allowed his four daughters to have a Catholic education, and he left them free to find their own way, respecting their conclusions. Throughout his long life, Croce retained a strong sense of religion, a religion without God no doubt but one with an inner voice no less demanding.[3]

While Croce was still in the midst of his religious crisis, a natural disaster shattered his family life, depriving him of the presence and affection of his parents. On the evening of 28 July 1883, Croce's father, mother, and sister were killed by an earthquake at Casamicciola on the island of Ischia, where they were spending the summer holiday. Croce himself remained buried under the ruins of the hotel until the morning hours, unable to move but hearing the voice of his father calling for help. When he was finally freed by soldiers, the doctors found that he had suffered a broken arm, a fractured leg, and bruises over all his body.

That catastrophe remained in Croce's mind forever and left a deep impression. The tragedy caused moral anguish and psychological scars which never disappeared, but he rarely mentioned it even to his closest friends. The disaster gave Croce a tragic vision of life and a dramatic sense of personal destiny. The presence of death appears frequently in his writings and in his meditations, and so does the need for periodical self-examination, often expressed in the form of philosophical soliloquies which have the sound and the intimacy of a prayer and a confession. To his acquaintances and friends, Croce showed a sunny disposition and an Olympian calm, but his diaries and private correspondence reveal a man subject to anguish and black moods, demonstrating that the positive attitude evident in his ideas and personality were not gifts of nature but precarious conquests, reached after inner struggle. Depression reappeared frequently in Croce's life and was able to interrupt his work for days, especially during natural disasters in which friends were involved or in national emergencies when the destiny of the fatherland was at stake.[4]

The Roman Period

After the tragedy, in the fall of 1883 Croce and his younger brother moved to Rome to live with Silvio Spaventa, their father's cousin, who agreed to become their guardian. The period of time that Croce lived in Rome, from his own admission, was the most unhappy of his life, entirely spent without friends or social amusements but often with the desire for death and contemplation of suicide. Once in Rome, Croce enrolled at the university in the Faculty of Law. However, he was a rather distracted student, neither interested in the subjects he had chosen nor greatly impressed by the intellectual level of his teachers. Unable to establish a working relationship with his teachers, bored by their lectures, Croce preferred to spend his time alone in libraries, following his personal inclinations and doing independent research. During the 1884 academic year, Croce did not write any examinations; the following year he did not rejoin the university: he never graduated, causing grave disappointment to his uncle. In later years, Croce was often called professor, received many honorary degrees, and became a member of prestigious academies, but he remained a man without formal academic qualifications.

The Roman period has some importance in Croce's political and mental evolution. A former Liberal patriot, Silvio Spaventa was one of the most respected members of Parliament and one of the leaders of the opposition. He had been a minister of the Destra Storica, the group of liberals, followers of Cavour, who had ruled Italy from 1861 until 1876, when they were defeated by a coalition of democrats, former republicans, and disgruntled liberals led by Agostino Depretis. Spaventa's house was a gathering place for political leaders, university professors, and newspapermen. It was there that Croce met for the first time Antonio Salandra, the future liberal-conservative premier, and the Marxist philosopher Antonio Labriola. From then on, Labriola would be Croce's mentor, guiding his philosophical and political education.

In Rome, for the first time in his life, Croce came into contact with national issues. Unlike the traditional atmosphere and domestic concerns prevailing in his family, every evening in Spaventa's house he heard discussions of philosophical, legal, financial, and political subjects affecting the business of the nation. Instead of blame, this time he heard praise for Cavour and Destra Storica mixed with scathing invectives against the government of Depretis and the practices of 'transformism,' that peculiar Italian political phenomenon, often necessary, which results in the sudden and continuous absorption of the opposition into the government ranks.

Among the friends of Spaventa, discussions often touched on the very nature of liberalism and democracy and the differences that separated the two movements and generated different policies. Through these discussions, Croce came into contact with the ideas of liberalism and conceptions of the liberal state. He helped his uncle with correspondence and even did some historical research for his political speeches and his legal writings. Years later, Croce recognized that Spaventa's personality offered him a model to be admired. Here was a man of action and of study, holding rational and passionate beliefs at the same time, familiar with political problems and philosophical issues; a liberal ready to defend the rights of citizens under the law, and an Hegelian willing simultaneously to entrust to the state the promotion of the public good; a believer in free trade but also an advocate of the nationalization of the railways.

Under the influence of Spaventa, Croce began to elaborate his own brand of liberalism, moderate in politics but based on idealistic philosophy, supported by a dialectical conception of history and able to balance freedom and good administration, progress and conservation. Spaventa taught Croce that the liberal state required control of public education but at the same time assured freedom of expression and respected private belief. Also, more than any other politician of his times, Spaventa preached the separation of state and church and fought for the independence of the courts and the autonomy of the civil service against political and government interference.[5]

Return to Naples

Unhappy with his situation and unwilling to attend university, Croce asked his uncle for permission to return to Naples and there to live an independent life by himself. Once in Naples, he became a busy academic, spending the entire day doing research in the city archives and in public and private libraries. He joined the local historical society and attended the meetings of the old Pontanian Academy, contributing often to the publications of both organizations.

In Naples, Croce established a special relationship with Giustino Fortunato, a respected liberal parliamentarian and author of important studies on the 'Southern Question,' a man pessimistic by nature but indefatigable in defending and promoting the interests of southern Italy, inside and outside Parliament. Fortunato adopted a paternal benevolence towards Croce, urging him over the years to enter national politics while also suggesting his name for less demanding public offices. In Fortunato's residence, where the Neapolitan political intelligentsia regularly gathered, Croce met Francesco Saverio Nitti, the future prime minister and one of the most progressive politicians of liberal Italy. Nitti was still a young professor of finance at the University of Naples, but he already possessed a boundless faith both in his own abilities and in technocratic solutions. Despite their different personalities, the two young men established a warm friendship, that lasted a lifetime, surviving wars, exile, and dictatorship.6

Once Croce left Rome and returned to Naples, in 1886, and became free of Spaventa's guardianship, he had to look after the administration of his land possessions. For a few years, he was compelled to undertake inspections of his properties, to make decisions on cultivation, and to enter into negotiations with tenants. He valued the heritage of his family, but Croce cannot be regarded, then or later, as a gentleman farmer, let alone a typical and traditional southern Italian landlord. He did not have the practical inclination to be a landlord, and, as he confessed later, always organized his business to have as little trouble as possible, leaving the care and supervision to others. As soon as his brother rejoined him in Naples, abandoning a military career, Croce entrusted to him the direction of their economic affairs and devoted all his energies to studies and cultural activities, following his natural avocations.

Much has been said about Croce's wealth and possessions. Wealth, however, not only allowed Croce to live a life free of economic concerns but also permitted him also to be generous with people in need. He built and then shared with other scholars a remarkable private library, supported the publication of various cultural periodicals, and financed the printing of books written by his friends. Often he helped friends, sometimes even strangers, to the dismay of Labriola. But, despite economic independence, Croce lived a rather Spartan existence throughout his life. He never indulged in luxuries and sometimes avoided even comfortable things, instead spending long hours in his room 'as a tenacious and silent worker.'

In reality, from an early stage, not the enjoyment of wealth but the requirements of study shaped Croce's days, with a monastic division of time from eight in the morning until midnight. In his adult life, work became for Croce a new religion, almost a daily devotion to an inner god. The diaries show on many occasions that work, and even the simple routine of work, was used by Croce as a therapeutic exercise to maintain or regain equilibrium, to fight the returning pains of anguish, to avoid the dispersion of energies, and to overcome the temptation of self-indulgence. In all his life, wealth provided a shield of protection. No doubt it offered opportunities, too, but primarily it was work that gave harmony and value to Croce's life.[7]

Marxism, Socialism, and Non-conformity

By the early 1890s, Croce had acquired the reputation of a scholar of great erudition. He had done research and written essays on particular aspects of Neapolitan history, and he had learned the major European languages. But often he was not satisfied with his work, feeling the need for a different direction and a deeper understanding of history. The times were posing new problems and creating different conditions. Italy's society and economy were undergoing great change. The increased pace of industrialization and emigration created social unrest and political agitation. In 1892 the Socialist Party was founded and in 1894 the Sicilian peasant leagues were crushed by Francesco Crispi, the energetic and erratic prime minister, whose colonial adventures and financial scandals added to the uncertainties of the times.

The critical mood of Croce was sharpened by the continuous advice he received from Antonio Labriola, who kept suggesting books and authors to read, continually urging him to pay deeper attention to philosophical problems and political issues, and generally to abandon erudition for more serious studies. On his own, Croce wrote two critical essays, trying to define and clarify the nature of history and the nature of art and their relation to philosophy and science. Then in 1895 came a turning point, when 'Marxism entered my life.' That year, at his own expense, Croce became editor and publisher of Labriola's essays on Marxism and historical materialism. The reading of those essays gave a new direction to Croce's intellectual interests, creating a profound enthusiasm for philosophy and politics. In the next few months, Croce read 'with inflamed mind' all the available works of Marx, Engels, and other socialist writers, Italian or German. He also made an intensive study of the economists of the classical school so as to be better able to appreciate and criticize the economic theories and social prescriptions of Marx. Helped by Labriola, Croce borrowed papers from Engels himself and entered into correspondence with Georges Sorel in France, Eduard Bernstein in London, and Karl Kautsky in Germany. In a short time, Croce produced several essays on historical materialism and Marxist economy, and his writings, to Labriola's annoyance, became part of the revision of Marxism, started in the German Social Democratic Party by Bernstein, who maintained that capitalism could be gradually transformed and workers could obtain their ends through democratic means.

Croce's enthusiasm for Marxism did not last long and practically came to an end in 1900. Croce and Labriola had a different approach to Marx and Marxism. For Labriola, Marx was the prophet of a new world and of a new faith; Marxism provided a general vision of life and represented the ultimate philosophy. For Croce, Marxism was just another philosophy to be used for his own needs, in the hope of finding solutions to his personal and intellectual problems. Marx, for Croce, was a revolutionary genius, a vigorous political mind, providing sharp tools for the working classes but not absolute truths or scientific laws. Also, for Croce, the proletariat was an historical movement, and as a protagonist of modern society it could not be identified with Marxism or even with socialism. Socialism did not necessarily need Marxism for the realization of its goals, and a socialist society could not be regarded as the final solution to all the problems of the human spirit.

At the end, Croce reduced Marxism to a canon of historical interpretation, a guide for historians and politicians to pay special attention to the role of economic factors both in the past and in the present. But Marxism remained a fundamental moment in Croce's intellectual development and made a lasting contribution to his philosophical system. As a result of the importance given to economic factors by Marx, when Croce, in future years, elaborated his philosophy of the spirit, to the traditional three categories of the beautiful, the true, and the good, he added a fourth: the useful, under which he included political and economic activities, and in general all those human actions that are the result of the volition of the individual. In this way, practical activity was given the same dignity as intellectual and artistic creation. Marx compelled Croce to make a systematic study of philosophy and to deal in depth with the heritage of Hegel and the dialectic. From Marx, Croce acquired the conception of life as a continuous struggle and also a sense of historical realism and political concreteness.[8]

The study of Marx not only influenced Croce's philosophical develop-ment, it also generated a strong interest in Italian political affairs and even an emotional involvement in the socialist movement. Until then, Croce had had little sympathy for traditional Italian politics and was repelled by 'the current Italian liberalism.' But because of his study of Marx and interest in the socialist movement, everything seemed to change, 'as when a man falls in love for the first time.' Socialism appeared as a liberating force, capable of generating a renovation of the present social order and of creating a new public morality. 'I seemed to breathe a new faith and a new hope in the vision of a regeneration of mankind, redeemed by work and in work.' In reality, Croce was never a member of the Italian Socialist Party; he never asked for a membership card, nor did he run for public office under its banner. But the general public identi-fied him as a member, and even Filippo Turati, leader of the Socialist Party, once referred to him as comrade, a mistake that Antonio Labriola, with more direct knowledge, never made. For him, Croce remained only 'half radical, half socialist and half Marxian.'

However, for a while Croce had strong and emotional sympathies for socialism. He publicly supported the leaders and the policies of the Socialist Party and the general aims of the movement. He was in corre-spondence with Socialist leaders, helped Socialist members in economic difficulties, and wrote essays for Socialist papers. He made a large contri-bution to the founding of the Socialist national paper, *Avanti!*, in 1896. When a convocation address by Labriola was censored by the govern-ment and the university authorities failed to defend academic freedom, Croce, at his own expense, published Labriola's speech. When Turati was arrested in 1898, in the atmosphere of panic created by the food riots in Milan, Croce wrote him a letter of solidarity, condemning the proclamation of the state of siege and the creation of special tribunals. After the government curtailed the activity of the opposition press, he tried to organize, with other liberal friends, the publication of a periodi-cal 'to defend or to regain freedom of expression.'

As had been the case with Marxism, Croce's passionate involvement with socialism had a lasting influence on his political outlook. Even when Croce lost enthusiasm for Marx and for socialism, and criticized the shortcomings of the Socialist Party, he continued to have a natural sympathy for the socialist movement, regarding it 'as a beneficial movement of civilization and progress.' When he wrote *History of Italy* in 1928, he described socialism as beneficial to Italian culture and society. For Croce, the proletariat was a creation of modern society; as such it could neither be stopped nor rejected but had to take its rightful place in Parliament and in the political realm.

For these reasons, Croce never had the fears about socialism that were typical of a Antonio Salandra or even a Giustino Fortunato. He continued to hope that the proletariat would imitate the bourgeoisie in its fight against the aristocracy and the *ancien régime*, displaying the same moral energy, the same cultural intransigence and political ability. In his writings Croce often seemed to holdout to the new movement the example of the Destra Storica in 1860, 'a national liberalism, moderate and revolutionary at the same time,' a movement capable of destroying the old order and building a new one, avoiding chaos and anarchy, and willing to preserve historical continuity.[9]

From 1892 to 1900, not only was Croce critical of the political establishment and sympathetic to the Socialists, but his personal conduct was that of a rebel against the prevailing social conventions. To protest against the policies of the government and the conduct of the king, he often refused to take part in official ceremonies at which his presence was required by his status and family connections. During these years, Croce showed interest in the women's movement, contributed to feminist periodicals, and even joined a league against 'white slavery.' More important, for twenty years Croce was romantically involved with a young woman of 'Byzantine beauty.' From 1893 until 1913, the year of her death, Croce and Angelina Zampanelli lived as man and wife, though the relationship was never formalized; they travelled and attended social functions together, despite the establishment's disapproval of such unorthodox arrangements.[10]

The Giolittian Era, 1900–1912

With the new century a new era began in Italy, characterized by economic progress, social reform, and a more democratic political course. After the turmoil and the uncertainty of the 1890s, the ruling classes rallied around the new king, Vittorio Emanuele, and accepted the leadership of Giovanni Giolitti, who created a broad political consensus that lasted until 1914. Even Sidney Sonnino, the leader of the conservative forces, abandoned his program of reaction and in general accepted the new order.

During this period, Croce's political position changed and evolved, the radicalism of his youth disappearing as he returned to a more moderate liberalism. In his memoirs of 1902, Croce had been rather clear in the indication of his political orientation: 'sympathy for socialism' and 'adhesion to the liberal and radical movements.' However, in an addition to those memoirs, written in 1912, political movements were no longer mentioned; instead, Croce expressed a cultural aspiration. His aim was 'to continue the work for the formation of a modern Italian consciousness,' which had to be 'not socialist, and neither imperialist nor decadent' but able 'to recreate in a new form that of the Italian Risorgimento,' which had meant love of fatherland and faith in freedom, conciliation of nation and humanity. More than a political agenda, this was a cultural program – a program that inspired Croce's work during these years and that in fact he had already in part realized.

The Giolittian era was one of the most creative periods in Croce's life. From 1902 to 1914, at regular intervals, he produced the fundamental texts of his philosophical system. In future years there would be continuous revisions, new elaborations, sometimes even relevant modifications, but the foundations remained in place. It is a system of complete immanentism and total humanism, a celebration of the freedom and creative energy of the human spirit in all its activities, a philosophy to satisfy the need to understand the reality and the desire to make the world a better place. Near the end of his life, Croce called his philosophy 'absolute historicism,' to indicate that history is the only reality for the thought and action of man. As a summary of Croce's philosophy we could repeat one of Vico's great axioms: this world of ours has been created by man and can be understood and changed by man. In many ways, in fact, this philosophy was a reform of Hegel's idealism and Vico's historicism, accepting the dialectic but rejecting metaphysics and teleology.

One of the characteristics of Croce's philosophy was the particular accent he gave to the distinctions among categories of the spirit. Faithful to the secular tradition of Italian philosophy, he reaffirmed the autonomy of the individual forms in the activity of man and in the circularity of the spirit, chief among them being the fundamental distinction between thought and action, theory and practice, morality and politics. In Croce's historicism, the distinction avoids the danger of relativism and moral indifference: it makes affirmations either true or false and actions good or bad. In the words of Carlo Antoni: 'For Croce ... evil remains evil and never changes into good even if history or providence makes use of it, error remains error even if it stimulates the spirit to reach the truth ... the ugly remains as such even if it provokes the desire of beauty ... pain remains such even if life overcomes it.' In the unity of the spirit, then, the distinction has the special function of recognizing the proper individuality of each category and also assigning to every form of human activity its own moral requirements and responsibility.[11]

Croce's books and ideas had a great influence on Italian culture, especially his theory of art as lyrical expression and history as contemporary history. The young, both of the right and of the left, were deeply affected by his ideas. Croce's achievements were greatly helped by the friendship of, and the fruitful collaboration he enjoyed with, Giovanni Gentile, then at the beginning of his university career but already displaying a precocious philosophical maturity. In practical matters, Croce's work was made much easier by the reciprocal trust and cooperation he was able to establish with the publisher Giovanni Laterza, a shrewd businessman and a man of strong convictions. It is, however, only a polemical exaggeration to talk of 'Croce's fifty years of cultural dictatorship.' Far from enjoying an unchallenged hegemonic position, throughout his life Croce found himself in opposition to the dominant culture of the time and outside the academic establishment. Rather than being the lay pope of Italian culture, as Gramsci called him, not without some justification, Croce was more simply 'a teacher without a university chair,' fighting against positivism in the Giolittian age, fascism and Gentile's 'actualism' under Mussolini, and Marxism after the war, not to mention the ever present Thomism of the Catholics.

La Critica

The most important instrument for the diffusion of Croce's ideas was the periodical, *La Critica*, which began publication in 1903 under Croce's direction and with Gentile's collaboration. Croce proved to be a brilliant editor and Gentile a formidable polemicist. *La Critica* appeared with regularity every two months for more than forty years and enjoyed a good circulation for a scholarly paper, reaching more than 1,500 readers, with many foreign subscriptions. *La Critica* was an attractive publication, appealing for the power of its ideas, the variety of its essays, and the number and timeliness of its book reviews. The journal soon became a tool of reference for all those involved in scholarly research.

La Critica offered a coherent, hard-hitting cultural program; its aim was 'a reaffirmation of the dialectical synthesis' and 'a reawakening of the philosophical spirit.' The periodical promised to fight against 'all the superficial people' who despised philosophy and to oppose without quarter 'all the mystical and reactionary movements, and the Jesuitical and Voltairian currents.' Finally, Croce and Gentile hoped to rekindle the philosophical 'ideals that had animated the generation of 1860' and that had been abandoned later for positivism, scientism, Darwinism, nihilism, and mysticism.

The reference to 'the generation of 1860' showed that the periodical, besides philosophical concerns, had political aspirations and wanted to show the beneficial efficacy of freedom in all aspects of society. Croce's main expectation was to generate an intellectual and cultural renovation, but he was also hoping that this renovation would prepare the ground for a new political awareness and the emergence of new forces, which could bring a new vigour to the political life of the nation. Often, philosophical essays and literary criticism appearing in La Critica had political implications and involved criticism of or disagreement with political movements. In particular, Croce constantly aimed his arrows against the nationalist and decadent poet Gabriele D'Annunzio, futurism and clericalism, and, in general, those irrational currents that, after the war, in many cases, coagulated into the Fascist Party.

But Croce also waged a relentless battle against what he used to call, with disdain, the 'Masonic mentality.' By this he meant less the actual members of the Masonic Order than the democrats and the radicals who appealed to the Jacobin tradition and shared positivist ideas. All of these, according to Croce, possessed an abstract mentality, lacked an historical sense, and had a mechanical conception of life that they borrowed from the mathematical sciences and tried to apply to social questions and moral problems. From 1910, this criticism also included socialism, which, in Croce's view, had abandoned the original dialectic of Marx, acquired a determinist idea of progress, and now shared the materialistic spirit of the bourgeoisie. In this new form, he believed, socialism no longer offered a new vision of reality or the hope of a different society, let alone 'the regeneration of mankind.'[12]

Political Activities

In the Giolittian era, compared to his cultural production, Croce's presence in political affairs was rather limited and without national impact. However, it is fair to assume that at this stage Croce had more admiration for the personal austerity and the political integrity of Sonnino than for the prosaic manners and the pragmatic ways of Giolitti. One has also to remember that, viewed from Naples, the economic program of Sonnino seemed to promise a more balanced development of Italian society, more equitable to agriculture and southern interests and less slanted towards the commercial and financial requirements of northern industry.

But Croce's lack of enthusiasm for Giolitti cannot be compared to the militant antagonism of Gaetano Salvemini, a radical democrat, author of a polemical book attacking Giolitti's electoral practices. Even during this period, Croce maintained an open mind, in general supporting Giolitti's social reforms but opposing specific acts of government policy. In 1902 the Zanardelli–Giolitti government proposed a divorce law; Sonnino and Salandra opposed it, while Croce approved the project and campaigned for it, joining a Pro Divorce Committee in Naples that tried to counter the pressures of Catholic organizations. It is worth noting the difference between Croce's and Salandra's position on this occasion. For Salandra, at stake was the stability of the family, which he regarded as the bulwark of a cohesive society and a unified nation. For Croce, in contrast, divorce involved freedom of choice, and at stake was the lay character of the state.

In 1908 Gentile applied for a teaching position at the University of Naples, but despite his academic credentials the appointment was given to somebody with lesser qualifications but with the right family and political connections. Immediately Croce wrote and published at his own expense a polemical pamphlet, in which he denounced 'the dishonesty in the life of Italian universities' and the favouritism that governed the appointment of university teachers.

In 1912, just after the end of the Libyan war, Giuseppe Prezzolini, the editor of the periodical *La Voce*, was brought to trial and accused of having damaged the reputation of the army. In a series of articles for his periodical, Prezzolini had brought to light some racy actions of a few cavalry officers that the military authorities and the political establishment felt it better to keep secret. Croce was among the few public figures who came to Prezzolini's defence, appearing as a character witness at the trial and then defending the right of every citizen to criticize and to scrutinize the activities of the army or any other branch of government.[13]

In 1903 Croce stopped his collaboration with the Socialist papers and began an association with *Il Giornale d'Italia* that lasted until 1925, when the paper was taken over by a Fascist editor. Until then, this paper was the mouthpiece of the conservative forces opposed to Giolitti's policy. Founded in 1902 by Sonnino, it was edited by Alberto Bergamini, a gifted and innovative newspaperman who opened the paper to cultural debate. Croce was not a shareholder in this paper, as has often been implied, but at regular intervals he published literary essays in its pages. The political significance of Croce's contribution to *Il Giornale d'Italia* should not be exaggerated. During this period, Croce also wrote for other newspapers, and, more important, he encouraged and supported in various ways the influential *La Voce* of Prezzolini in 1908 and *L'Unità* of Salvemini in 1912. Different in editorial content and in the personalities of the publishers, the three publications had in common the rejection of Giolitti's political system but also a desire for social and cultural renovation.

Croce's involvement with these papers had political implications, of course, but it was also influenced by personal relations and the social conventions of the times, which were in general less marked by ideology than they would be after the war. Occasionally, in fact, even the Marxist Antonio Labriola wrote essays and articles for the conservative *Il Giornale d'Italia*. On specific issues, the editorial position of the papers often contrasted with the personal views of its writers. For example, while Croce defended Prezzolini during his legal difficulties, Luigi Federzoni, the future Nationalist leader, led a campaign against him in *Il Giornale d'Italia*. Similarly during the Libyan war, Salvemini opposed the war while Croce supported it.[14]

In 1910 Croce was made a senator during one of Sonnino's short-lived governments. Under the Albertine Statuto, Italy's constitution, the Senate was not an elective body. Senators were appointed by the king at the recommendation of the prime minister, and then had to be confirmed by the Senate itself. Croce's real sponsor had been Giustino Fortunato, who had tried to effect the appointment two years before, and failed, with Giolitti. It was rumoured then that Croce lost the nomination because of his unconventional marital status, his earlier support for socialism and Socialists, and his recent polemical criticism of Giolitti's minister of education. This time, the presence in the government of Salandra, and the old friendship between Fortunato and Sonnino, clinched the outcome. His position in the Senate certainly increased Croce's social prestige, but it did little for his political influence. Though, with his usual diligence, he took part in the most important meetings, he remained only minimally involved in parliamentary activities. Certainly, he displayed little partisanship, always casting his ballots with an open mind. In 1912 he voted for Giolitti's new electoral law, which practically established universal male suffrage in Italy. Never an enthusiast of colonial adventures, Croce nonetheless supported the Libyan war and then approved the Treaty of Lausanne, which put an end to the hostilities between Italy and Turkey, while Sonnino and the nationalists opposed the peace and continued to call for more expansion.[15]

Croce acquired senatorial dignity not because he was a famous philosopher but *per censo*, that is, because he was a rich man who devoted time and energy to community work and public affairs without compensation, especially as a government appointee in charge for some time of the city's elementary and junior schools. Croce's participation in municipal politics illuminates his political orientation and even party preference. In Naples, Croce was active in cultural associations, the Dante Society, and academic institutions. But he also showed an early concern for ecological problems and fought for the protection of the city's artistic heritage, often lamenting the neglect of historical buildings and the disappearance of public green spaces. Twice, in fact, in 1901 and 1914, Croce was directly involved in municipal elections, and both times he supported an alliance of liberals and Catholics opposed to left-wing bloc made of democrats, radicals, and socialists.

In the elections of 1914, Croce was president of the electoral committee of the moderate alliance, wrote its electoral platform, and even made public speeches. Finally, in 1914, as a result of the changing political atmosphere and social agitation, a new political organization was created in Naples, the Liberal Monarchical Association, and Croce was elected its president. 'Monarchical' was the descriptive label used by the moderate liberals, followers of Sonnino and Salandra, while the friends of Giolitti were called 'Liberal Democrats' and the 'Democrats' were those who supported the more progressive policies of Francesco Nitti.[16]

This development represented a definitive choice for Croce. From now on, he regarded himself as an exponent of the liberal movement and spoke as a member of the bourgeoisie. A moderate liberalism reflected both his personal inclinations and his historical training; it expressed his respect for tradition, his preference for concrete and specific solutions, his opposition to generic and general social reforms, and his rejection of a demiurgic conception of politics. But liberalism was for Croce not only a political movement, it was also the expression of his philosophy, and since this philosophy was based on a dialectical conception of reality, Croce's liberalism could assume positions and include features that his more moderate or conservative friends could neither share nor support.

The First World War

With the First World War, Croce's participation in national politics began. When the great powers declared war, the Italian government proclaimed neutrality, which was approved by the great majority of the Italian people and supported by the entire liberal establishment in Parliament. Neutrality has been the first choice of Italian governments in modern times. But geographic position, economic interests, and political reasons make that choice hard to maintain when all the major European powers are involved. In the case of 1914, the political unanimity did not last long; soon the policy of neutrality was challenged both inside and outside Parliament. A movement arose for Italian intervention in the war, and parties and public opinion were split between interventionist and neutralist factions.

When the interventionists began their agitation to win public support, Croce became one of the most prominent leaders of the neutralist movement; he helped to organize the association of the neutralist forces, Pro Italia Nostra, and then gave financial support to the weekly periodical of the association, *Italia Nostra*, for which he also wrote several articles. Croce's neutralism cannot be confused with the pacificism of the Socialists, but in many ways it was similar to the position of Giolitti. Opposed to the demagogic agitations of the interventionists, Croce, like Giolitti, rejected an absolute neutrality and did not exclude a priori Italian participation in the war if national interests required it. Until such a political necessity became evident, however, he saw no need to increase public passion and social unrest or to urge government and Parliament to make a hurried decision.

Croce's position, clear on the general question, showed some incongruities and was open to criticism on specific issues. He, like the majority of Italian political leaders, was not psychologically prepared to face a sudden war of European proportions after many years of peace, and he would have preferred the continuation of the status quo. At the beginning, Croce's neutralism was more sympathetic to Germany than to France. He was reluctant to break the old and tried alliance for a new and uncertain one which had assembled nations with different interests and diverging ideals. He even believed that Italy's interests lay with the Central Powers, and regarded an intervention against Germany as an act of betrayal. Though he certainly had no sympathy for Austria and its obtuse policies, he had strong ties with German culture and allowed these feelings, for a while, to interfere with his political judgment. Despite his proclaimed realism, while war was raging, he continued to contrast German historicism with French Jacobinism, Latin superficiality with Teutonic seriousness. He was aware of German imperial aspirations but seemed more concerned with the desire of England and Russia for expansion in the Mediterranean and the Adriatic. He regarded speculation about the consequences of German victory on the European balance of power as idle fantasy and a waste of time.

But other reasons for Croce's neutralism were more solid and better reflected the reality of Italian society. He was convinced that the majority of Italian people did not want a war and that only a minority was agitating for intervention. After the Libyan experience, he also considered the Italian army unprepared for a new and sudden war against old allies. Moreover, he feared that Italy did not possess the material resources and moral stamina to endure the sacrifices that a modern and protracted conflict required. Above all, he was frightened by the political consequences of possible defeat. He remembered well the military defeat at the battle of Adowa in Ethiopia in 1896, and feared the dangers that could follow another such disaster. And recently, in June 1914, social and political agitation against the military policy of the government had renewed doubts about the cohesion of Italian society and shown the fragility of national unity.

During the neutrality period, Croce directed his criticism against both the Democratic and the Nationalist interventionists, and especially against D'Annunzio. He accused the nationalist poet of wanting the war not for Italian interests or for love of the fatherland but from a spirit of adventure, for the fulfillment of turbid passions, almost for sexual gratification. He contrasted the present position of the nationalists with the ideals of the Italian Risorgimento, and pointed to the noble passions of Giosuè Carducci and Giuseppe Garibaldi, who fought for the freedom and independence of other nations, not for their conquest. At the same time, Croce also accused the Democratic interventionists of abstract idealism, misplaced humanitarism, and naive internationalism; they called for war in the interests of democracy and the principle of nationality, but in so doing they ignored the needs of the Italian people. Against the public demonstrations of the interventionists, Croce defended the right of Giolitti, as leader of the parliamentary majority, to force a vote in Parliament on the destiny of the country.[17]

When Italy declared war on Austria in May 1915, Croce stopped his campaign for neutrality, accepted the decision with fatalism, went to Rome, and, as senator, voted full powers to the government. During the war, he was involved both at a personal and at an official level in providing social assistance to the families of soldiers in economic need. But these social activities were not enough to satisfy his sense of responsibility or to consume all of his energy. As always, even in the new circumstances created by the war, his main efforts were devoted to cultural activity. In the middle of the war, Croce 'hoped, feared and trembled,' like any other good patriot, but he also tried to keep alive a scholarly tradition and to give an example of scientific independence of mind. He argued that, in time of war, military necessities had priority but other works had to be carried out as well, for the good of the country once peace returned. He decided to continue his work as if the war were not taking place, refusing to be distracted by military worries and above all trying not to acquire a 'warrior mentality.' Also, on questions of science, in conformity with his philosophy, he made a clear distinction between the duty of the citizen and the duty of the scholar, 'between the responsibility towards the fatherland and towards the truth.'

From 1915 to 1918, Croce's cultural activity was guided by three principles: he defended the independence of science, reasserted the common heritage of European peoples, and defended the authority of the state. During the war, Croce fought a constant battle against propaganda, which tried to turn literature into a tool of war. He especially criticized those men of letters and science, Italian or European, who spread lies and calumnies against other nations and other intellectuals, often reversing their previous beliefs, and began that malignant habit which Julien Benda later called 'la trahison des clercs.' Croce defended the integrity of science and warned against the danger of putting culture at the service of political expedience or of military and economic interests.

In all his political writings, later collected into the book *Italy from 1914 to 1918*, Croce also defended the common heritage of the European peoples and the contribution of all nations to the character of European civilization. To French and German scholars who had carried war into science and literature, making disparaging remarks about each other's national character and contrasting their cultures and civilizations, Croce recalled the reciprocal and beneficial influence that each nation had received from the other. To the Italian nationalists, and even to some Democrats, who liked to blame Hegelian philosophy for German imperial aspirations, Croce pointed out that during the Italian Risorgimento some of the greatest Italian patriots had been scholars of German idealistic philosophy.

Besides those two themes, Croce defended with equal fervour the authority of the state and the idea of force in politics. Against the Democratic and Socialist ideologies and their humanitarian internationalism, Croce reasserted the role of power in political relations. In this polemic Croce never separated the concept of force from morality, nor did he ever identify force with violence, but the emphasis was put on force and much less was said on morality. Years later, after Mussolini had achieved power, even Croce himself had to recognize that the passion with which he defended the concept of force and the authority of the state may have been excessive. He allowed that he had dwelled too much and for too long on that argument, and in doing so 'perhaps had made a mistake.'[18]

During the war, compared to his cultural work, Croce's direct interventions in political affairs remained rather limited and can be characterized as patriotic and liberal. Throughout the conflict, Croce praised the decision of the German Social Democratic Party, which in general supported the government's war effort, and criticized the policy of the Italian Socialists, with their slogan 'not to sabotage and not to support.' The policy of isolation, imposed by the 'maximalist' faction on the Socialist Party, against the protests of Turati, proved fatal both to socialism and to democracy during and after the war.

Croce also praised the army for giving moral cohesion to the Italian people, through the education and the discipline it imparted to millions of peasants. However, unlike many other literati, he did not participate in the exaltation of military leaders which celebrated their personalities without restraint and often invoked them as saviours of the country against the intrigues of political parties.[19]

Even during the disaster of Caporetto, where the Italian army had suffered a huge defeat, Croce defended freedom of expression and the right of every citizen to question the policies of the government and the leadership of the generals. Croce regarded that disaster as 'worse than a mortal illness in the family,' and the news from the front gave him pain and anguish, lasting for days. For the occasion, he wrote a short message to the Italian people, inviting all citizens to fight against the invading enemy with resolution and unity. In the same message, there is also a veiled criticism of the Socialist Party and its pacifist propaganda. Despite this polemical spirit, for Croce, Caporetto was part of a long historical tradition that included the military defeats at Novara, Custoza, and Adowa, and revealed the moral and political weakness of the old Italy, weakness that the ideals of the Risorgimento had not yet been able to overcome.

Others preferred to put the blame on Socialist propaganda and on the defeatism of the soldiers. In the polemics that followed Caporetto, Umberto Cosmo, a Democratic teacher at the University of Turin, dared to put forward a different opinion. In a series of articles published in *La Stampa* of Turin, he pointed out that at Caporetto military mistakes had been made and there had been disagreements among the generals, and concluded that it was rather unfair to blame the Socialists and the soldiers and to absolve the military officers in charge. The Nationalists of Turin staged a press campaign against Cosmo, demanding his removal from the university, an immediate inquiry into his political activities, and a trial before a military tribunal. Croce came to the aid of the beleaguered Cosmo, defended his patriotic intentions, rebuked in public his main accuser, another colleague at the university, and finally wrote a letter of reference on his behalf to the tribunal. In the end, Cosmo was not prosecuted and did not lose his teaching position.[20]

Croce and the Post-War World

Victory in November 1918 was a pleasing moment for Croce but did not cancel the pain of Caporetto. The most responsible Liberal leaders felt pride in the achievements of the army and in the endurance of the Italian people. For all of them, the war had been an historical trial, the crowning event of the Risorgimento: Italy had acquired the rightful status of a great power. Victory, however, did not give Croce the sense of national exaltation then common to the elite and to the general public. His thoughts dwelled on the defeated enemies, to the destruction of old empires, to the death and ruin common all over Europe. Croce's mind was agitated not by dreams of territorial expansion but by the difficulties of the future. He felt a great deal of nostalgia for the old and familiar world that the war had destroyed or greatly undermined. For that reason, he asked the scholars returning from the front to shed the prejudices acquired during the war, work for European cooperation, and revive the ideas and traditions that were the common heritage of all European peoples before the cataclysm of the war.[21]

Croce, like most of the Italian leaders, was not pleased by the results of the peace conference in matters concerning Italy and was disappointed with the Treaty of Versailles in general. He did not approve of a punitive peace that offended the sensibilities of the defeated peoples. He disliked U.S. President Woodrow Wilson's intransigence towards Italian requests and expressed solidarity with Vittorio Emanuele Orlando, when the hapless premier returned home after Wilson's unfortunate appeal to the Italian people over the heads of the Italian delegation in Paris.

On the vexing question of the eastern borders, however, Croce showed more moderation than many others and was ready to accept, as he wrote to Gentile, 'the request of the military and naval experts,' 'that is the vital interests of our State.' But the experts were as bewildered and divided by the problems as the majority of Italian people. General Armando Diaz regarded the possession of Dalmatia as a defensive liability, while for Admiral Paolo Thaon de Revel those mountains were essential to assure mastery of the Adriatic Sea.[22]

Croce's feelings after the war, and his opposition to nationalist agitation, found expression in the letters he wrote to his German friend, Karl Vossler, professor of Romance literature at the University of Munich. Reopening the correspondence after the interruption caused by the war, Croce expressed his pain at the material and spiritual ruin brought by the conflict. He hoped now for a period of peace and for a common effort of reconciliation among European nations. He longed for the creation of 'a new scientific brotherhood' among European intellectuals, free of the poison of nationalism and war propaganda. After years of fighting and destruction, Croce wished that every man recognized that 'the world now needs a period of reciprocal tolerance, Christian charity and love.' At a time when many Italian writers were inflamed by D'Annunzio's Dalmatian adventures and his military occupation of the city of Fiume, Croce assured his friend that he was preaching instead and practising 'a sort of Christian humility,' as a necessary preparation to the difficult times ahead, during which there would be a great need of 'calm,' 'reason' and 'good will.'[23]

The desire for international cooperation may appear to contrast with Croce's involvement with the periodical *Politica*, founded in 1918 and published by the Nationalist leaders Francesco Coppola and Alfredo Rocco, Mussolini's future minister of justice. In that involvement, short though it was, both Gramsci and Denis Mack Smith have seen a sign of Croce's affinity with nationalist ideology. Nothing can be further from the truth. The episode had little political significance and has to be regarded as an accident of friendship. Coppola was a Neapolitan like Croce, and the two had cordial personal relations. He asked Croce to contribute articles to the periodical, which, he assured him, would be a review of political science and philosophy, offering 'a larger vision' than the program of the Nationalist Party.

Croce's opposition to the ideology of nationalism was well known and of long standing. Even on this occasion, before sending his first essay, Croce repeated to Coppola his criticism of the Nationalists' 'political exaggeration' and their penchant for 'decadent literature.' During the first months of 1919, Croce sent *Politica* only six short articles, most of them written long before Coppola made his request, and then appeared almost simultaneously in other papers; none of these essays shared the political views of the Nationalists and one even took a position that starkly contrasted with theirs. In any event, the collaboration did not last long. When *Politica*, contrary to Coppola's assurances, became in 1919 the official organ of the Nationalist Party, Croce immediately stopped any further dealings with the periodical and announced his decision, with some bitterness, in letters to the press and to his friends. But in the ideologically charged atmosphere after the war, Croce was more than 'a little unwise,' as he himself wrote years later, to associate his name with well-known Nationalist writers. His collaboration gave prestige to one of their publications and was bound to create confusion among the general public, not to mention future historians.[24]

Essays on Southern Italy

But Croce's brief and occasional contribution to *Politica* cannot be used to confuse his patriotism with the chauvinism of the nationalists, or to disregard the gulf that separated Croce's ideas from the ideology of nationalism. For Croce, the nation was an historical creation, while for the Nationalist ideologues the nation was the result of natural forces, geographic elements, and ethnic heritage. In 1919 no nationalist reader could share the ideas and the feelings expressed in Croce's *Montenero-domo*, a history of the ancestral village in Abruzzi from whence his forefathers had moved to Naples. Standing in the public square, looking at the surroundings, Croce felt almost a stranger to the buildings and the lands that once had belonged to his ancestors. He concluded that perhaps man, rather than 'filius loci,' is 'filius temporis,' belonging less to a place than to the universal spirit.

Croce's general political ideas in this period were even better reflected in the historical essays that he devoted to the Poerio brothers, the liberal patriots, who had been active under the Bourbons in the first half of the nineteenth century. The essays, written in 1917 and 1918, were published in 1919 in book form under the title *Una Famiglia di Patrioti*. In the reconstruction of their lives, Croce not only paid tribute to the Poerios' personal qualities and political activities but implicitly proposed their program and ideas as an example to contemporary Italians. During the passions generated by the war, Croce confessed that he had been attracted 'by their genuine and refreshing personalities' and had wanted to contrast their frank and sincere nature with 'the charlatanism and the vulgar nationalist demagoguery.'[25]

To meet the challenge of modern times, Croce, following in the footsteps of the Poerios, regarded as necessary an alliance between the liberal bourgeoisie and the people. The historical experience had taught the Poerios that 'from the combined energy of those diverse forces, something great for the welfare of Italy would have been generated.' Moreover, to avoid the failures of the past, the program of the new liberal movement had to be not an imitation of foreign models but something born from the 'needs and the customs of the people.' At the same time, the new liberal leaders, to be successful, had to refuse 'geometric government,' oppose the 'abstractness of Jacobinism,' avoid 'the vacuities of the nationalists,' and, above all, show 'a tenacious faith in free institutions.'[26]

Outside Italy, for a concrete example of a modern party able to perform the functions of a ruling elite, Croce looked with sympathy to the German Social Democratic Party; he approved its policies and lauded its achievements. In this period, Croce was full of admiration for the constitution of the Weimar Republic.

These sentiments, expressed in private letters and public writings, reflect Croce's political aspirations in this period. It is also significant that in 1919 he agreed to become president of the Association for the Interests of Southern Italy, the organization founded by Fortunato and Umberto Zanotti Bianco and devoted to building public libraries, technical schools, and day-care centres in the southern provinces. Finally in 1919, after the resignation of Orlando, Croce voted for the Nitti government, and in 1920 he participated in the last Giolitti cabinet as minister of education.

Those were the two Liberal leaders and the last two governments that tried without success to solve the problems created by the war, to revitalize Liberal institutions and to meet the aspirations of the new times. The tragic failure of those attempts should not obscure the fact that Nitti and Giolitti, in their different ways, along with Croce and the majority of the Liberal leaders, wanted to provide democratic solutions to the problems afflicting Italian society after the war.

CHAPTER TWO

From Giolitti to Mussolini, 1920–1922

The First World War destroyed ancient empires and changed the course of European history, creating the social and economic conditions for revolution in several nations. The realities brought by the war compelled people to change personal habits and to acquire new political beliefs or to abandon old aspirations. New and more radical movements were born; Socialist parties became more militant; revolution and subversion grow more appealing, even fashionable; violence learned in the war spread to all aspects of civil society; strikes became endemic and were called on the least pretext. The mood of rebellion challenged traditional assumptions and undermined liberal institutions, greatly weakening in the process the old ruling elites, which had matured before the war.

The Giolitti Cabinet

In Italy, the political strife and the social agitation that followed the end of the war and the conclusion of the peace conference were made more difficult and almost intractable by the results of the general elections, which were held within a system of proportional representation. The elections of 1919 were a disaster for the liberal groups; almost two-thirds of their candidates went down to defeat. However, they were a triumph for the Socialist Party and for the Catholic Popular Party. The forces and classes excluded from the process of the Risorgimento came back into the political life of Italy as protagonists, claiming the right of full citizenship. Separated by ideology and program, together the two parties controlled Parliament, and no majority could be formed without the participation of one of them. The liberal elites, for their part, lacked a modern organization in the country and so had been unable and unprepared to meet the challenge of national parties and the requirements of mass politics. Now the old leaders had lost their freedom of manoeuvre in Parliament and their monopoly of power in the cabinet. More ominous for the future, the ideals of the Risorgimento and the institutions shaped by those ideals were rejected by the Socialists, in the name of internationalism and a future proletarian revolution, and questioned by the Popolari, as supporters of the Catholic Popular Party were called, who appealed to a different tradition and to an outside authority.

Furthermore, the Socialists made the situation more complicated for the Liberal leaders and, at the end, fatal for themselves. On principle, they refused to assume ministerial responsibility, and even to support with their votes in Parliament any coalition government. At their 1919 national congress in Bologna, against the reformist wing, led by Filippo Turati, the radical or 'maximalist' majority affirmed the old revolutionary creed and continued to preach the violent conquest of power, the dictatorship of the proletariat, and the establishment of a socialist republic, meanwhile ordering the parliamentary group to reject government collaboration with bourgeois parties. The Socialists' policy of intransigence and isolation weakened the position of Nitti and Giolitti, their natural allies, but above all it nullified their parliamentary strength and reduced the Socialist Party to watching with fatalism the unfolding of events.[1]

Amidst these new fears and old resentments, it became difficult to find a stable majority in Parliament and to form a lasting government around a coherent program and under a strong personality. The fifth Giolitti cabinet was the last attempt by the liberal groups to restore the authority of the state and to bring financial problems under control while devising at the same time acceptable solutions to social agitation. Giolitti formed a centre-left coalition, supported by the Liberal and Democratic groups and by the Catholic Popular Party. To broaden the appeal of his government, he brought into the cabinet independent personalities with national prestige. Benedetto Croce, as minister of education, and Carlo Sforza, as minister of foreign affairs, were two of them.

Croce did not know Giolitti personally, nor had he been a supporter of Giolitti's political system before 1914. During the war he had even written a protest against one of Giolitti's rare political interventions. Always reluctant to accept political burdens, Giolitti's invitation, when it came, created some consternation in Croce's mind and produced conflicting feelings. Yet, encouraged by his wife, Croce accepted the offer, especially when the old statesman appealed to his patriotism and to his sense of duty. In their first meeting, Giolitti stressed the dangers of the current situation by pointing out that 'Italy was in such trouble that all of us have to make efforts for her salvation, though I am not sure we shall succeed.'[2]

Once in his new position of responsibility, Croce discharged his obligations with his customary punctuality, and without even interrupting his studies. But the new work did not give him much joy, and his feelings of uneasiness were reinforced by the political conditions then prevailing in Italy and in Europe. 'The public events,' he confessed, to his German friend, Karl Vossler, 'not only of our nations but of the entire world, frighten me.'In this condition of spirit, Croce carried his new duties 'without that joy, which is generated by ... hope in the present and in the near future.'[3]

Minister of Education

The ministry did not last long enough for Croce to make a personal and long-lasting impact on the future of education in Italy. Despite the enthusiastic help of Gentile and the support of other experts, he was not able to implement a coherent program. The few reforms he proposed to Parliament were rejected or defeated in committee, often for reasons that had little to do with education policy. In the parliamentary debates Croce revealed a good knowledge of the problems of Italian education, as they affected in different ways teachers, students, and school buildings. But the debates also showed that he was not attuned to parliamentary niceties, nor politically adept at winning votes and gaining support for his proposals.

Croce's practical actions as minister and his speeches show that he had an aristocratic idea of education. Following his austere conception of life, Croce wanted to restore discipline in the administration of schools and to reintroduce severity in studies at all levels, hoping to give a new direction to the entire system. To reach that objective he made several proposals, chief among them being state examinations, *l'esame di Stato*. For Croce and later for Gentile, this had to be the main instrument to achieve the selection of students, to control the performance of teachers, and to maintain the authority of the state in public and private schools alike.

The importance given to national-standard examinations indicate clearly that, for Croce, the primary aim of education, especially of higher education, was the creation of a worthy cultural elite. On the other hand, Croce's major speech in Parliament showed that he was aware of the changed nature of Italian society created by the war, and of the new needs required by the economic and technical transformation brought about by industrialization. On that occasion he promised to continue the fight against illiteracy, reduce the number of classical lyceums, increase technical institutes, hire more teachers, build more schools, and repair old buildings. Above all, he accepted the necessity of lengthening the years of obligatory schooling from five to eight; children would thus be required to remain in school until the age of fourteen, up the current age of eleven.

During the parliamentary debates and question periods, Croce often expressed sympathy with the proposals of his scientific colleagues in the Senate and agreed with their arguments to increase scientific and technical education. But the financial constraints of the day and cabinet solidarity compelled Croce to tone down his program and to postpone some of his proposals until better times arrived. In agreement with the general policy of government to reduce the national debt, Croce concentrated his efforts on controlling expenditures under his administration, 'proposing and promoting economies' with a puritanical zeal and 'opposing useless expenses.' In so doing, he generated great resentment among employees and even among his collaborators.[4]

As a member of the cabinet, Croce had influence on the general policy of the government. Giolitti himself recognized that 'this philosopher has much good common sense.' The civil servants' partial strike during the elections of 1921 was practically handled by Croce alone, and he displayed, on this occasion, an unsuspected talent for negotiation and publicity. In internal affairs, Croce always defended the authority of the state and critized the disorder created by the strikes and the attendant violence. He supported and admired Giolitti's moderation and cool behaviour during the occupation of the factories; and a few months later, inside the cabinet, he approved of Giolitti's tough instructions to all the prefects ordering them 'to apply the sanctions of the law' against all violence.[5]

As minister of education, Croce pushed for the restoration of scientific and intellectual cooperation among European scholars. Inside the cabinet, he supported Giolitti and Sforza during the negotiations over the Treaty of Rapallo, which brought to an end the hostilities between Italy and Yugoslavia as well as D'Annunzio's adventure in Fiume.[6]

Croce proved also to be a strong advocate of Giolitti's social program. A good example was a brief speech he gave, in September 1920, to the national meeting of the Sociatà Filosofica Italiana during the heyday of the occupation of the factories in Milan and Turin. In this speech Croce seemed to answer indirectly the criticism of the industrialists and in particular of Luigi Albertini, who was waging in his paper, *Corriere della Sera*, a relentless campaign against Giolitti's alleged surrender to the trade unions. Against those who criticized the government's policy and accused the bourgeoisie 'of weakness, meekness, suicide and resignation to its death,' Croce defended 'the historical sense of the government and of the ruling elite.' He asserted that the times were mature 'for profound social transformation,' and that 'the changes after the war were not only necessary but also beneficial.'[7]

Croce's participation in the Giolitti government was an important stage in his intellectual and personal development, offering him new experiences which 'are useful to the studies themselves,' as he said in a letter to Giolitti. Ministerial experience allowed Croce to understand better the nature of politics and led him to share Giolitti's conclusion that 'to achieve better order in a country,' it was necessary to find 'accord between the ends and the means.'[8]

Admiration for Giolitti and his policies, probably compelled Croce to read Giolitti's memoirs, published at the end of 1922, with warmer sympathy. The fruit of this new critical disposition became evident when Croce wrote his *History of Italy from 1871 to 1915* a few years later. In that book, Croce, changing many of his previous views, offered a positive assessment both of the Giolittian era and, more generally, of the historical left. Observation of Giolitti's actions at close range gave Croce a better appreciation of Giolitti's personality and a deeper understanding of his political inspiration. Critics continued to accuse the old premier of 'simple empiricism,' but Croce now recognized that Giolitti's policy was instead characterized by a 'constant and dominant line,' inspired by 'faith in freedom' and guided by 'the effort to bring Italy to the same level as other modern European nations.'[9]

Admiration for Giolitti is also evident in Croce's memoirs of 1944. By then, Giolitti had become for Croce the symbol of the ideal Liberal politician, almost the incarnation of the Poerios' ideals, needed by the times and appropriate for a confident and progressive bourgeoisie. Croce was deeply impressed by Giolitti's 'quick intuition and common sense,' as well as by 'his great political wisdom,' 'his sure judgment,' and 'the steadiness of his will' – all traits required in the man of action. Croce also admired Giolitti's demeanour and social program: the absence of recriminations 'towards loyal adversaries,' his 'scorn for war-profiteers,' and his constant willingness to protect the working class. Above all, Croce admired Giolitti's sense of the state, his respect for Parliament, his display of authority, and his determination and ability to maintain essential order without using violence, as shown when he brought to an end the occupation of the factories or solved the Adriatic question.[10]

The Elections of 1921

In the spring of 1921, Giolitti made a capital error that proved fatal to liberal institutions and put an end to his political career. Believing that the resolution of the Fiume question, and the peaceful ending of the occupation of the factories had increased the government's popularity, he advised the king to dissolve Parliament and call early elections. From these elections Giolitti hoped to obtain a stable majority and then to be in a stronger position to form a new government, supported by a chastised Popular Party or even by a more reasonable Socialist Party, now free from its Communist wing. With the aim of weakening both the Socialists and the Popolari, the old leader encouraged the formation of national blocs, an electoral alliance consisting of the Liberals, the Democrats, and a new protagonist in Italian politics, the Fascists.

During the Giolitti government, especially after the end of the occupation of the factories and the bitter and violent agrarian strikes in the Po valley, fascism became a major force in Italian political life. The elections of 1919 had been a humiliating rejection for Mussolini. After those elections, fascism continued to be a small movement without a clear political objective, made up of a few thousand restless veterans, 'interventisti' of 1915, and 'arditi' (shock troops) of the war, plus 'futuristi' intellectuals grouped around Mussolini and his newspaper. But between the fall of 1920 and the spring of 1921, the Fascist movement changed completely in nature, organization, and ideology. Hitherto an urban phenomenon, fascism now became an agrarian organization. Its base of support moved from the cities to the countryside; its centre of influence, and sometimes even control over its direction, shifted from Milan to Bologna. In this new and more violent incarnation, fascism increased its strength and became widespread, especially in central Italy. Fascist squads began the onslaught against the Socialist organizations in the Po valley, leaving ruin, death, and fear in the aftermath.

Faced by a new movement unleashed by the passions created by the war and the turmoil that followed its conclusion, Giolitti resorted to old tactics which had been successful in the past, or which at least seemed to him to have been successful then. As he had done before with other movements, the old leader tried to absorb fascism into the constitutional life of the nation, hoping to blunt its radicalism and to channel its ambition. But in dealing with fascism and with Mussolini during the elections of 1921, and later, the Liberals made fatal mistakes. They failed to realize that fascism was a new kind of beast, with a voracious appetite, and unlike the old movements would be difficult to pacify or to satisfy. Moreover, not for the last time, the Liberal leaders also made a dangerous miscalculation, underestimating the ability and the ambition of Mussolini.

While the electoral results did not change the parties' standing in Parliament very much, they did introduce a new dynamic into political life. The elections increased the prestige of Mussolini and gave new impetus to fascism.[11]

In the elections of 1921, Croce was in a rather awkward position. He was an independent member of the government, but he was also a personal friend of Nitti, the leader of the opposition. During the campaign he did not make any speeches, nor did he participate in the organization of the national blocs. He was among the few ministers who remained in Rome throughout the election period, minding the government's affairs. After the election, Giolitti resigned, having failed in his gamble. Ivanoe Bonomi, the new premier, made a futile and rather lukewarm attempt to retain Croce in his cabinet. But Croce refused and returned to Naples, devoting his energy full-time again to his studies. Croce's attendance in the Senate did not stop entirely, but it became more sporadic. The letters of this time to his closest friends did not offer comments on political events, nor did they mention the violence of the Fascist squads, perhaps because the city of Naples was the least affected by political violence.

But Croce, even if he wanted, could not be completely removed from the turmoil of the times. During the summer of 1922, at the suggestion of the French-Belgian art historian Jacques Mesmil, Croce wrote a letter to Mussolini in favour of Luigi Fabbri, a teacher and an anarchist, who was being persecuted by the Fascists of Bologna and was in danger of having his house and his valuable library burned. Mussolini replied with a deferential letter to Croce, promising an end to the harassment of the unfortunate teacher. The library was spared any further damage, but the anarchist found it advisable to leave the country soon after.[12]

The Fascist Congress in Naples

In October 1922, a mere week before the March on Rome, Croce was invited, with other Neapolitan senators, to attend as a guest the congress of the Fascist Party, held in Naples. Various accounts have been given of Croce's reaction to Mussolini's speech; many accusations have been made against him because of his presence in that gathering, his extemporaneous remarks being changed, enlarged, and turned into damnable offences and even indictable crimes. It was traditional at such gatherings to invite local personalities. Two years before, for the same reason, Croce had been present at the congress of the Catholic Popular Party, and Don Sturzo, the leader of the party, as a sign of respect, had even invited Croce to sit at the head table, where he remained silent. In his memoirs of 1944, Croce explained that in October 1922 he accepted the Fascist invitation, went to the San Carlo Theatre, sat in the box reserved for senators, and heard the speech of Mussolini, 'believing it useful, and in a certain way, even dutiful to acquire a more direct knowledge of a political party, the importance and force of which was growing in Italy day by day.'[13]

It is, in fact, essential to keep in mind the political strength and the organizational force of the National Fascist Party, as it was known by now, in order to understand the political situation of Italy in October 1922 and to appreciate the policy of the Liberal leaders during that year and particularly that fateful month.

Mussolini's speech at San Carlo, like others in other cities during the summer and fall of 1922, was meant to reassure the silent majority of Italy and to win over the moderate forces of the establishment. In Naples, Mussolini said much that would please Croce, and little that would worry or offend him, or a democrat like Salvemini, for that matter. Mussolini assured his audience that he desired to put an end to violence and achieve national pacification. He gave the impression that a coalition government with five Fascist ministers could be an acceptable solution to him. To this government he gave an historical mission, almost the completion of the Risorgimento. 'The question is to bring into the liberal state, which has accomplished great things, and which we are not forgetting, all the vigour of the new Italian generations, which were born from the war and from the victory,' adding, at the same time, that the state should not reject the working classes but must 'protect their just interests.'[14]

But Mussolini's speech was only one aspect of the gathering, and Croce missed the other part, which was even more important. That weekend more than forty thousand Black Shirts and twenty thousand workers poured into Naples. Most were armed and later paraded with military discipline. To his faithful, gathered in the public square, Mussolini spoke a different language, used a different tone, and promised different solutions. He did not mince words: 'Either they will give us the government or we will take it by marching on Rome.' Once there, he said, 'we will grab by the throat this miserable political class.'[15]

The presence of such a large number of armed people and the behaviour of Mussolini revealed both the strength of fascism and the different nature of the new political movement. By October 1922 the National Fascist Party had become a mass party and without a doubt was the strongest in the country. It had a membership of more than three hundred thousand members, and was still growing, not only in central and northern Italy but also in the south. Above all, besides the regular party organizations common to other mass parties, the Fascist Party had a military apparatus. In 1922 fascism was able to undertake military expeditions like a regular army. It was capable of mobilizing thousands of Black Shirts and of terrorizing entire provinces, unmolested by public authority, and sometimes even helped or protected by them.[16]

Because in 1922 fascism was strong and armed, it was no longer possible to suppress it without the use of the army. That, however, meant the possibility of a civil war, with unforeseen and frightening consequences for the monarchy, the bourgeoisie, and the ruling classes. For this reason, during the summer of 1922, all Liberal leaders tried to negotiate with Mussolini, hoping that he would accept a coalition government, and be satisfied with a junior position. The king expressed the general feeling when he wrote to Premier Luigi Facta: 'The only effective means of avoiding dangerous shocks, is to associate fascism with the government through legal means.'[17]

None of them ever contemplated an anti-fascist coalition, and all shared the illusion that it was possible to normalize fascism, to break its impetus or to control its revolutionary ambitions. Few of the leading politicians, from the right or from the left, realized in 1922 that Italy was on the threshold of a dangerous venture, or understood the true nature of fascism. Perhaps not even Mussolini at this time had a clear, coherent program pointing straight to a dictatorial and totalitarian regime. Years later, Palmiro Togliatti, in his Moscow lessons on fascism in 1936, remarked: 'It is a mistake to believe that fascism started in 1920, or even from the March on Rome in 1922, with a definite plan, devised in advance, of a regime of dictatorship, as afterwards the regime became organized with institutional transformation from 1925 to 1928.'[18]

Croce's Position before the March on Rome

Croce shared the political views of the other Liberal leaders; his position was no different from that of Giolitti, who stated that 'a new party has appeared in Italian politics. It has to take that place to which the number of its followers gives it the right; but in legal ways, the only ones which can give a true and lasting authority to a party in our constitution.' In his 'Autobiographical Notes' of 1934 and 1944, Croce gave an explanation of his position. He believed that fascism had to be brought into the government because it seemed beneficial that 'new and younger forces [be] introduced into Italian political life, to give a new vigour to the political class, which the long war and the postwar period had impoverished and worn out.' Croce, like other Liberal leaders, did not fear that Fascists could or would destroy the institutions created by the Risorgimento, because in his mind he regarded fascism only as 'an episode of the war period, a youthful and patriotic reaction, which would disappear without causing much harm, and perhaps leaving something good behind.'[19]

In those fatal months, Croce shared the illusion, common to all political leaders, that national institutions were safe and that freedom was not in mortal danger. 'It never crossed my mind that Italy would allow freedom to be snatched from her hands: that freedom, which had cost so much effort and so much blood, and which my generation regarded as a conquest lasting forever.'[20]

Years later, Croce recognized the reasons for that mistake. 'Men of my generation were used to judge things with a mind accustomed to the peaceful events of parliamentary disputes,' and even in 1922 they 'hoped and believed that the political crisis would be milder than it turned out to be in reality.' They took freedom for granted as 'a pacific possession' and believed that liberal institutions, 'developed by our fathers,' 'could never again be subverted, certainly not destroyed and vilified' by veterans of the war fought in the name of the Risorgimento. Because he had harboured those hopes, Croce recognized that he could not avoid the charge that he had shown 'little sagacity' and been guilty of 'easy optimism and not enough political foresight.'[21]

Some of the leading Liberals were even older than Croce. The war had not produced new leaders among the liberal elite; instead, it had created more divisions and bitter resentment in their ranks. The old leaders, moreover, had not changed with the changing of Italian society. Set in their ways, they were not prepared to deal with the passions and the demands generated or increased by the war. Expert parliamentarians, they lacked the qualities required by mass politics and were not attuned to the aspirations of the new emerging classes. More than sagacity the Liberals needed new blood and a modern political party, able to organize and mobilize their existing and potential supporters.

The March on Rome

On 28 October 1922, rather than waiting for parliamentary coalitions, the leadership of the National Fascist Party organized the March on Rome and boldly attempted to achieve political power with a popular insurrection. Faced with a challenge against the state, the Liberal leaders showed a lack of unity and political determination. When the king refused to employ the army against the insurrection, and the offers of coalition under a Liberal leader were rudely spurned, Mussolini was invited to Rome and asked to form his own coalition government. The royal invitation first, the vote of Parliament later, gave to the new government a constitutional character, despite its extra-parliamentary origin. Many people believed that the crisis was over, wisdom had prevailed, a solution had finally been found without a bloodbath, and now the new coalition government would return the country to normal times.

Benedetto Croce shared these hopes, or, more accurately, these illusions. When Mussolini appeared before the Senate, he spoke with deference to the institution and avoided the arrogance and threatening tone he had employed in the House. As a result, the senators, reassured by his manner, gave him almost unanimous support. It is certain that Croce in the Senate, like Giolitti in the House, voted for the motion of confidence in Mussolini's government. Certainly, that vote expressed a benevolent expectation, even a positive disposition, but it should not be regarded as an uncritical adhesion to fascism or as an abdication of liberal principles, at least not for Giolitti, nor for Croce, nor even for the fledgling Liberal Party, whose national council in those days invited the new government and Parliament 'to safeguard freedom in all its forms.'[22]

Typical of this attitude of hope and reservation was also the behaviour of the Liberal Association of Naples, (La Monarchica Liberale), to which Croce belonged and which he had helped to establish before the war. In a meeting called after the March on Rome, like thousands of other associations throughout Italy in that period, it sent a telegram of support to Rome, wishing the new government well. But in the same meeting the majority of the membership first rejected a motion offering full support to fascism and applauding the insurrection and Mussolini, and then adopted another one reaffirming the values of liberalism, expressing faith in liberal institutions, and pledging loyalty to the monarchy.[23]

Croce's Position after the March

The March on Rome is not mentioned in Croce's diaries. This is not surprising. Until 1925 the diaries had only an intellectual purpose; they chronicled books read and essays written, and were not concerned with political matters. But, on rare occasions, political events and feelings generated by them did make a sudden appearance. At the time of Caporetto, for example, the invasion of the fatherland and the defeat of the Italian army caused Croce mental anguish, which took the form of sleepless nights and distraught days. Nothing of the kind happened in October 1922. Evidently, for Croce, Mussolini's March on Rome was of a different order than the rout of Caporetto. The diaries, however, do register heated political discussions during those fateful days, without mentioning names or assigning paternity to opinions expressed. Those discussions in his house, during weekend gatherings, left Croce tired and upset and 'with my head deafened.' In that period Croce was deeply involved in writing and researching the book that became *The History of the Kingdom of Naples*, one of his masterpieces. Political events and the debates that they generated probably interfered with this project, causing unwelcome intellectual distraction.

In the absence of direct mention in the diaries, a good place to find Croce's reactions to the March on Rome and its aftermath is the correspondence of Giustino Fortunato, an old and trusted friend with whom Croce was then in constant touch, especially on account of historical research for his new book. Fortunato despised fascism, opposed violence, condemned the March on Rome, had no faith in the new leaders, did not trust Mussolini, and despaired of the future. Had he been able to overcome his illness, and been strong enough to travel to Rome, he would have voted against Mussolini's government in the Senate 'with a resounding no.' In his letters Fortunato lamented that 'in these sad and dark days,' he remained, 'almost literally alone in the entire city of Naples,' condemned 'to think and to grieve' while 'all are raving with joy, applauding what has happened and is happening.' Later, in a sad letter to Gaetano Mosca on 18 November 1922, Fortunato confessed that sometimes he had 'the sensation of dreaming,' 'since even B. Croce has approved and approves of Mussolini.'[24]

Fortunato returned to this subject in later years; writing in 1924 to Turati and in 1925 to Salandra, he reminded them that 'in November 1922, in my house I had a disagreement with Croce about the victory of fascism.' Luigi Russo, a younger but equally trusted friend of Croce, and faithful to him during the Fascist period, writing in 1953, confirms that Croce and Fortunato clashed in November 1922 about the meaning of the March on Rome and its implications for the future of Italy: 'I witnessed a truly dramatic row, a stormy exchange between Croce and Fortunato.' While Fortunato lamented, with his proverbial pessimism, that the March was 'the end of the Bourgeoisie,' Croce 'invited him not to forget what Marx has said: violence is the midwife of history.'[25]

The contrast between Croce and Fortunato opens a window into the mindset of the old ruling elites of southern Italy and shows the different role that moral and economic interests played in their political choices, at least among those of them who had deep ties with the ideals of the Risorgimento. Government policy favoured landowners now. Both Croce and Fortunato were landlords of long standing, but in their discussions and disagreements there was no mention of economic policy or agrarian questions. In different ways political aspirations and intellectual ideas were of paramount importance for both of them and overshadowed economic considerations of a personal nature.[26]

In the name of those liberal ideas, Croce had a different quarrel in the house of Fortunato with another common friend. That same Sunday, as Russo reports, Francesco Torraca affirmed that 'had Francesco De Sanctis been alive, he too would have been a Fascist.' Torraca was a former pupil of the Neapolitan literary critic but now had become 'an enthusiast of Mussolini.' Croce immediately rejected Torraca's affirmation, expressing his resentment and disapproval with some acrimony and strong words, in the belief that more than 'literary taste' was involved in their disagreement.[27]

With his claim, Torraca was making a direct link between fascism and the Risorgimento. De Sanctis, with Spaventa, was one of the tutelary deities of Croce's moral and intellectual pantheon. At stake, then, was the interpretation and the heritage of the Risorgimento. To support a coalition government, to admire even the audacity of a modern *condottiero*, was one thing, to surrender the ideals of liberal Italy to fascism was a different matter altogether. From this early date until 1924, as we will see, Croce remained hopeful about Mussolini government while expressing criticism of fascism as a cultural and ideological movement.

The reasons for Croce's political benevolence towards Mussolini and the new government after the March on Rome can be found in his memoirs written in 1944. First, Croce shared 'the general feeling of trust and relief' 'which spread throughout Italy' when it became known that Mussolini had formed a coalition government, supported by Liberal and Democratic parties, in which their ministers held important positions.[28]

Secondly, on various occasions, Mussolini proposed to restore the authority of the state and stressed his opposition to violence and disorder, even when they were the work of Fascists. Croce tended to accept the reassurances of his friends, who described Mussolini to him 'as a man of the people, impetuous, even violent, but generous and devoted to the fatherland.'[29]

Above all, for Croce and other Italians, the presence in the new government of General Diaz and Admiral Thaon de Revel, 'trusted by the nation and faithful to the King,' was 'a pledge of security.' Having allowed the two top officers of the armed forces to serve in the new positions, and given his past reputation, the king – Croce and others believed – 'would never allow the liberal constitution to be destroyed or diminished.' Certainly, Croce was not alone in the assumption that the king, 'as head of the Armed Forces, the Army and the Navy, which were faithful to him, held in his hands the key to the situation.'[30]

In placing such faith in the king, Croce and other liberals made a fatal mistake in those chaotic times, one that they were to repeat in 1924. Their memories of the successful outcome of the crisis that had shaken Italy at the turn of the century lulled then into complacency and false expectations. They had forgotten that, even in the past, freedom had been first defended in Parliament and fought for in the country by the press and by popular movements.

Besides these reasons, which explain the attitudes of political leaders and the general public alike, Croce was pleased with Mussolini's coalition government because of the presence in the cabinet, as minister of education, of his old friend Giovanni Gentile. Croce and Gentile had been responsible for the revival of Hegelian philosophy in Italy. Under their vigorous attacks, the old positivism had been mortally wounded and a new cultural landscape had been established. Gentile, more than Croce, was familiar with the problems of education and the needs of Italian schools; he also had the temperament to carry out a general reform. In his new position of power, much more than Croce under Giolitti, Gentile was in a position to implement the pedagogy of idealism and to transform Italian schools, giving them coherence and a new direction.[31]

For Croce, Gentile was 'the right hand man at the right place,' and many other Italian intellectuals – Liberal or Democrat or even anti-Fascist – felt the same way. For them, too, the presence of Gentile in the government and his educational reforms inspired a great deal of expectation that obscured other weighty considerations and transcended political reservations.

Nevertheless, despite his confidence in the moderation of Mussolini, and his friendship with Gentile, Croce refused to accept any official position in the new administration. He declined to be named vice-president of the National Council of Education when Gentile offered him the position, which would have made him the most important figure in the administration of Italian schools after the minister himself. In his memoirs of 1944, Croce explained his decision, writing that 'there was in myself a secret instinct of reluctance, which compelled me to refuse all offers of political office.'[32]

More than a political reservation, this refusal once again revealed Croce's reluctance to take time away from studies for political activity, for which he felt, with some justification, he did not possess the natural predisposition. In 1922 or later, Croce probably would not have refused a call from Giolitti. But only the direct appeal and the authority of 'the old servant of the state,' 'a man venerable for age and experience,' could have succeeded in bringing Croce back to public life.

Not only did Croce not accept any official position offered to him by the new government, he also refused to have a personal meeting with Mussolini, despite several requests made by common friends. To these emissaries Croce replied that he had 'no reason not to esteem Mussolini,' and he certainly 'wished him well in his work,' but a meeting between the two of them would be useless because Croce and Mussolini were 'for social environment, for family and for cultural formation of a different origin.' Their lack of a common outlook, Croce was convinced, would make a meeting between him and Mussolini awkward, almost a dialogue of strangers.[33]

This episode, and the reasons given by Croce for refusing the meeting, shows another handicap which the old establishment had in coping with the new environment. Giolitti, too, had difficulties in his dealings with Luigi Sturzo, a Catholic priest and leader of the new Popular Party: their meetings were often strained or ended on a sour note. The old liberal elite was divided by political outlook and personal ambitions but shared common values, which made it possible, or at least easier, to maintain cordial personal relations despite political disagreements. The war had accelerated social change and brought to the fore new ideas and new leaders. Even styles, tastes, and manners created a barrier between the old and the new. Mussolini, a man in the know, caught this new mood quite well in one of his speeches, when he remarked that 'the people who fought the war have instincts, passions, aspirations and hopes, which are unknown to the people who did not fight the war.'[34]

The new politicians acted in different ways and used novel methods, and the old leaders, well mannered and well educated, often had difficulty coping with them. Unprepared for modern times, they would be out-manoeuvred by the brashness of the young generation. In 1922 and again in 1924, the calm behaviour of Giolitti, unperturbed by events, was not a match for the energy and the audacity of Mussolini, his ambition neither restrained by tradition nor hampered by moral inhibition.

CHAPTER THREE

From Critical Benevolence to Opposition, 1923–1924

After the March on Rome and the creation of a coalition government, neither the present nor the future appeared in a clear light. For all the players, the clarification had still to come, the Fates holding their secrets. In 1923 and 1924, there were few signs of an impending revolution or of a future completely different from the past. As Giorgio Candeloro recognized correctly in his work: 'In those two years, neither the anti-Fascists nor the allies of fascism, nor the Fascists themselves had a clear sense of the institutional transformation which would be realized from 1925 to 1928.'[1]

During the first months of his administration Mussolini, for his part, showed signs of prudence and even restraint. Despite occasional intemperate language, and the usual reference to 'the inexorable rights of the revolution,' he seemed sincere when he struck a moderate tone. Even the new police force, recruited only among Fascist elements and placed under Mussolini's direct command, could be regarded as a necessary instrument first to curtail the freedom of the Fascist squads and later to bring their violence to an end. For the most part, the government continued to act in traditional fashion, with more energy perhaps but usually respecting existing laws. A decree to limit the freedom of the press, after the protest of Salandra, remained unpublished and was not applied, at least for the time being. By a vote of Parliament in November, and by royal assent in December 1922, the government was given not 'full powers,' as many historians have claimed, but merely the authority, for a year only, from January to December 1923, to issue orders-in-council for the reorganization of the civil service and the finances of the state. These laws increased the power of government and gave a more authoritarian character to its actions, but were in keeping with an established tradition and fell within the limits provided by the Albertine Statuto. The extra powers were used, with good results in general, by Gentile to implement his reform of education, and especially by Alberto De Stefani, the new minister of finance, to dismantle economic controls introduced during the war and to apply his free-market theories to the national economy and to the administration of the state.

Croce's Support of Anti-Fascists

Despite some worrisome developments, in 1923 there was some reason to hope for a return to normal political life. Still, acts of violence continued, and Croce protested, both in public and in private, against the recurrence of political persecution. In the first months of 1923 he wrote a letter to *Il Giornale d'Italia* lamenting 'the daily torments' and the 'frequent insults' inflicted by Fascists on the name and the reputation of Nitti, 'and rectifying false statements and showing my distaste for the ignoble accusers.' In normal times, writing a letter to the editor of a paper does not have great significance, but in those days it could be dangerous. Courage was needed to be associated with a man despised by Fascists and regarded as an enemy of the new regime. In fact, Giovanni Amendola, who had emerged as the true leader of the opposition, realizing immediately the value of that 'noble manifestation,' wrote to Croce and praised him for having spoken 'the first free and generous words' in favour of Nitti. Croce's letter, he said, was in stark contrast to 'the silence of others.'[2]

Croce showed his courage on other occasions, too, in February 1923 he issued a public letter in favour of Piero Gobetti when the young publisher and the most intransigent of Mussolini's opponents was illegally arrested for an alleged violation of the press law. Soon afterwards, in the spring of 1923, a Communist paper, Gramsci's *Ordine Nuovo*, was suppressed by the authorities. The police claimed to have found arms and ammunition hidden in the building where the paper was printed. All the editorial staff were arrested and brought before the courts on a charge of sedition. During that trial, Croce went to Turin and appeared as a character witness for Umberto Calosso, an old friend and one of the accused.[3] In November, Amendola himself was assaulted and badly wounded by a Fascist squad. Croce's reaction was immediate. He wrote a letter of solidarity, expressing the hope that general indignation 'would create, as a result, repugnance for deeds of this sort.'[4]

During the first months of 1923, it was natural for Croce, given the close nature of their relationship, to discuss the political situation with Gentile and to express to him his disappointment 'about the news of new violence and insolence perpetrated by Fascist groups.' Their long and close friendship allowed Croce to remind the minister of education, in vivid language, that 'Italy without freedom would be ruined.'[5]

On these occasions, Gentile, 'then still an old and staunch liberal,' reassured Croce that the violence 'was the last spark of a dying fire and that freedom would remain intact.' Croce's reaction to Gentile's explanations confirms Croce's good faith, and perhaps even Gentile's. More important, however, Croce accepted Gentile's assurances because 'I was not able, even for hypothesis and imagination, to represent in my mind an Italy which would resign herself to lose the freedom for which she had fought during a century, and which she had enjoyed for more than sixty years, crowned by a victorious war; that freedom, which was her reason of life and her title of honour.'[6]

Croce not only showed public support to victims of Fascist violence; he also expressed political solidarity with those liberals who tried to remain immune from the allure of fascism and Mussolini, amid an avalanche of turncoats. In Naples he helped to organize a 'club of political studies,' which gathered only Liberals and Democrats, and often met in his own house. Moreover, in 1923 the official Liberal association of Turin became dominated by businessmen who supported fascism without any reservations. In disagreement with this position, Senator Francesco Ruffini, an old conservative liberal but a resolute anti-Fascist, resigned and founded with other like-minded friends a new liberal group. Croce went to Turin and was present when the office of the new association was inaugurated and came into operation. The local Black Shirts resented this manifestation of independence and a few days later assaulted and destroyed the new office.[7]

Gentile's Reform of Education

In 1923 Croce's most important contribution to political life was his public defence of the reform of education undertaken by Gentile during the first months of the year. The Gentile reform offered a coherent and rigourous design to rationalize the Italian education system from elementary school to university. Its aims were to restore a national ethos to education, to lend intellectual rigous to the studies, to strengthen the humanist tradition, to reinforce the powers of the academic authorities, and to assure the control of the central administration. It required students at the end of each cycle, in both public and private schools, to write standard tests and to be examined by external teachers, appointed by the ministry, so that only the best and the brightest students could accede to higher education and university. The creation of a robust ruling class was Gentile's main aspiration. Gentile's education reform has to be regarded as one of the most important pieces of legislation of Italian history, and a great political achievement. The reform was defended or opposed with equal fervour by Fascists and anti-Fascists, by democrats and conservatives alike, and for basically the same reasons. Old positivists and young futurists lamented the pre-eminence given to classical tradition; industrial manufacturers and trade-union leaders demanded a stronger emphasis on scientific and technical education; and, on the other side, many educators, placed great value on the reform, hoping that it would spark a renovation of Italian civic virtues, first in the schools, and then in society as a whole.

In the fall of 1923, the reform of education came under attack not only from the opposition but also from the radical wing of fascism. The criticism was strong, and the defence lukewarm. Gentile became disheartened and feared that Mussolini might abandon the reform program, leaving him no choice but to resign as minister of education. It was then that Gentile asked Croce to intervene in defence of the reform. Croce wrote a personal letter to Mussolini and sent an article to the *Il Giornale d'Italia*. The letter was never delivered by Gentile, but the article appeared as an editorial on 3 November 1923. Croce accused Gentile's critics of preferring the status quo out of personal interest and because of intellectual laziness, and he claimed that the true reason for the opposition was political rather than technical. The reform program was supported by those who were concerned with the future of education, and was opposed by those who hoped to create political difficulties for the present government or for the minister alone.[8]

Despite marginal reservations, Croce did not have any doubts about the merits and the value of the proposed reforms. Instead of the chaos of the old days and the musty smell of the old system, 'thanks to the work of Gentile, we now have a solid system, rational and coherent, directed to the rejuvenation of the thought, character, and culture of Italy.' Since many of the criticisms of the reforms were directed against the person of Gentile, Croce defended the integrity and the personality of his friend. He praised the pedagogical competence, the administrative ability, the passionate zeal, and the dedication to education of Gentile, a man 'who had devoted to the problems of the school the best of his mind and his heart.'[9]

Mussolini must have been impressed by Croce's arguments; the next day, he refused Gentile's resignation, ordered Croce's article reprinted on the front page of his own paper, as the leading editorial, and from then on called the reform of education, realized by Gentile, 'the most fascist of the fascist reforms.' Some historians continue to follow the Duce's lead and to share his judgment. In fact, however, the underlying principles of Gentile's reform program had been proposed and debated during the liberal era, when fascism was not yet born. Some parts of that program had been prepared by Gentile and his friends for Croce himself, when he was minister of Education under Giolitti. Even the national examinations, the cornerstone of the new program, had been first requested by the Popular Party, accepted by Giolitti, and introduced to Parliament by Croce, though without success. In short, the reforms were the fruit of idealist philosophy. Even some of the key men appointed by Gentile to implement the reforms were democrats and known anti-Fascists, like the pedagogist Giuseppe Lombardo Radice, who was put in charge of the elementary schools. The fact that it was accepted and defended by Mussolini, and could be realized by Gentile only under the Fascist regime, shows that fascism and its leader were complex political phenomena indeed.

First Press Interview

Beside the timely intervention in defence of Gentile's educational reforms, Croce's other major public statement about the political situation in Italy took place in October 1923 in an interview given to *Il Giornale d'Italia*. Taking place in the middle of a lively political debate about liberalism and fascism, the interview made evident that, on the nature of politics, Croce had not yet reached a clear conclusion; politics was still dominated by force, as during the war. At this stage, Croce continued to hold that 'all States are always one State, all governments are one government: that is a group of men who dominate and govern the majority; and all governments perform, while they last, a public function.' He reaffirmed his indifference to political forms and attached no importance to the institutions appropriate to liberalism. The distinction between a government promoting freedom and one imposing authority was not made on this occasion, nor was the distinction between the interpretation of the historian and the action of the politician clearly stated. Croce still believed that 'political forms are abstractions of theorists,' and as such they were 'indifferent to the historian, in his interpretation of history and to the man of action, who regards them more or less as respectable prejudices.'[10]

Yet, aside from those theoretical observations, the interview made other elements of Croce's position quite clear. He reiterated his support of the government, but at the same time he began to make a public 'affirmation of the liberal faith,' associated with the defence of the Italian Risorgimento, and denied that fascism had the ability and the necessary ideas 'to found a new regime in Italy.'[11] On the political situation of the moment, however, Croce made some heavy-handed comments, reflecting the animosity of the time, that a modern reader can easily understand if not share completely. Croce showed that he was aware of the many criticisms of the new government, but he added that it would take a while for anybody 'to exceed the sum of mistakes committed in Italy during the first years after the war.'[12]

Despite his support of the present government, Croce left no doubt that he preferred liberalism to fascism and wanted to remain faithful to the liberal ideals of the Risorgimento. He felt liberal, he said to the paper, for the same reasons, 'that I feel as a Neapolitan and a southern gentleman,' because 'personally, I am and could not be but a liberal,' since 'my entire moral and intellectual personality has come out of the liberal tradition of the Risorgimento.' From then on, as he looked back to that tradition and contrasted it with a different present, a constant note of nostalgia began to appear in Croce's writings, together with a celebration of the achievements of that past. 'And how could one not feel liberal,' he continued, 'who has been educated during the first fifty years of the new liberal and united Italy, and has breathed in that air, has taken advantage of those initiatives, of those disagreements, of that rapid growth and modernization of Italian life.'[13]

Given this positive assessment of liberal Italy, the newspaperman asked Croce whether he did not see a contradiction between his liberal faith and his support of Mussolini's government. He replied: 'No contradiction at all. If the liberals did not have the force and the virtue to save Italy from the anarchy in which it was involved, they should blame themselves, should recite the mea culpa, and meanwhile recognize and accept the good from wherever it has come, and prepare themselves for the future.'[14]

The last part of the interview has a polemical tone that reflected the debates both among liberals and inside the Liberal Party itself between the filo-Fascists, charmed by Mussolini and ready to join his cohorts, and the others, who wanted to retain more autonomy for themselves and for the party.

To prepare themselves for the future, the liberals had a duty to overcome their present divisions, to regain the old moral vigour, and to stress their 'devotion to the fatherland,' Croce told the newspaperman, but in reality speaking indirectly to Gentile. He then added: 'I do not believe that they have the other duty to become Fascist, that is to wear the personality of men who have another disposition, have travelled a different path, and belong in the majority to a younger generation.' By remaining 'good liberals' instead, they could avoid much confusion and render 'useful service to Italy in the present and in the future.'[15]

To understand fully Croce's position, one has to remember that on 31 May 1923 Giovanni Gentile had become a member of the Fascist Party. Like Mussolini, but unlike Croce, Gentile had been an interventionist in 1915. Until he joined the Fascist Party, his political orientation had been that of a conservative liberal with an Hegelian and ethical conception of the state. From 1923 until his tragic death in 1944, Gentile put the vigour of his mind, his passionate heart, and his formidable organizational talents at the service of fascism and of Mussolini.[16]

Gentile's decision to join the Fascist Party, together with a flattering letter to Mussolini in which he claimed that now true liberalism was represented by fascism and by his leadership, generated criticism and resentment among liberal leaders. Writing to Salvemini, Fortunato described the 'shameful and foolish,' 'unimaginably hateful' letter of Gentile, 'now gone to fascism.'[17]

Gentile's decision reflected his strong views on Italian history, but it was reached without discussion or consultation with Croce. There is no mention of it in their correspondence or in Croce's diaries. But Croce must have discussed Gentile's action and expressed reservations with some of his liberal friends, as appears evident in the correspondence of Giustino Fortunato and in Croce's later writings.[18]

Croce's true feelings over Gentile's choice in 1923 were clearly revealed in his letters to Sebastiano Timpanaro, an old Hegelian university teacher. Timpanaro was a common friend, in the past closer to Gentile than to Croce but now shocked by Gentile's adherence to fascism. He asked Croce's opinion about 'the relation between fascism and liberalism,' as if he were seeking reassurance. Croce's reply was short and to the point: 'For me fascism is the contrary of liberalism.' With a direct reference to Gentile's decision, Croce then invited Timpanaro 'to use your intelligent interpretation' and to remember that in the history of nations 'a Lucretia violated is worth more than a Messalina prostituted.'[19]

Croce, Gentile, and the Liberal Ideal

Croce and Gentile assumed different positions not only on practical political issues but also on ideological ones. They held contrasting views on the nature and function of the state, the meaning of the last war, the relation between fascism and the Risorgimento, and, even more important, the future direction of the Fascist movement.

During 1923, in the intellectual community and among Fascists themselves, there was a lively cultural debate about the nature of fascism, its origins, and its future. The debate between the moderate and the radical elements of fascism involved the normalization of political life and the continuation of the Fascist revolution or, to put it in the jargon of the time, 'the constitutionalization of fascism' ('the second wave,' to use the ominous words of Roberto Farinacci, general secretary of the Fascist Party). The main contrast, in fact, between the two wings of fascism concerned the nature of the state and the institutions that Fascists wanted to defend, to change, or to create anew.

In this debate, Gentile and his pupils played a leading role and joined forces with the moderate elements of fascism. Their interventions had a special connotation reflecting Gentile's Hegelian heritage, conservative liberalism, and interpretation of the Italian Risorgimento. For Gentile, fascism coincided with idealism; fascism was the realization of the ethical state, providing the synthesis between the individual and the state, and making possible the unity between the rights and the duties of the citizen. Also, fascism was now the true liberalism; in the twentieth century, it represented the revival of the policy of the Destra Storica, purified of all democratic corruptions. Finally, for Gentile, fascism was the heir of the ideals of the Risorgimento, especially the religious aspirations and moral renovation espoused by Vincenzo Gioberti and Giuseppe Mazzini.

Croce's position was, in many respects, completely different from that of Gentile and his pupils. Croce, too, valued moderation and wanted a normalization of political life. But, from the beginning of 1923, he criticized more strongly than in the past the philosophy of Gentile and flatly denied that fascism was the realization of idealism and the continuation of the Italian Risorgimento. Croce's ideas were expressed in short essays which appeared in his periodical *La Critica* from January to December

1923 and were included later in the new edition of his book *Cultura e Vita Morale.*

In March 1923 Croce reminded Gentile and his pupils that idealism was a dialectical philosophy and as such was the foundation of liberalism and the denial of fascism. 'The idealistic theory of reality and of history,' he argued, 'because it is dialectical, is liberal, and recognizes, with the necessity of the struggle, the office and the necessity of all political parties, and of all different men.'[20] While the theoreticians of the ethical state believed that fascism had realized the unity of thought and action – in a famous speech Gentile had even defended the use of the cudgel to achieve political consent – Croce reminded them that life itself was 'a union of opposites' and stressed the value of political disagreements. 'The parties and the individuals are divided, they fight, they struggle against each other.' He then added: 'Woe! if it were otherwise; woe! if to our individual actions would be lacking the counterbalance, even the ballast, of different and contrary actions.'[21]

At a time when leaders of totalitarian movements, in Italy and abroad, claimed special insights, and were given the right, as 'providential men,' to impose their will on their opponents in the name of the nation, the class, or the revolution, Croce stressed the equal dignity of all men and emphasized the moral responsibility of the individual in history and in politics. 'To the conceited presumption of possessing the political truth,' he warned, 'we have to substitute in our mind the humble conscience of playing the part that the internal voice commands us to perform in the drama of history: the part which is not the whole, and knows that it is not the whole, and does not want to be the whole, but at the same time it knows it is indispensable to the whole, and in this knowledge attains its dignity.'[22]

Not only in his periodical but also in private correspondence Croce rejected the attempt made by Gentile and his pupils to identify idealism with fascism. In a letter written in March 1923 to Ugo Spirito, the most gifted of Gentile's pupils, who possessed an uncommon gift for arousing Croce's fighting blood, Croce denied that identification in bitter words: 'When one identifies idealism with fascism, either one comes to a wrong conclusion, or one is dealing with a principle badly conceived because it is evident that the assertion is a stupidity.' In the same letter Croce rejected the philosophical unity as Gentile had elaborated it in his 'actual idealism' or 'actualism.' Croce reminded Spirito that he, too, had posited the unity of life and philosophy, but that he had done so in a different manner and in a dialectical way. 'I refuse to understand it in the foolish way, of which I have seen a recent example in the new and deplorable political periodical.'[23]

The last remark referred to *Nuova Politica Liberale*, a periodical of political studies whose editor was a pupil of Gentile, Carmelo Licitra. The name and the program of the new paper had been devised in 1922, before the March on Rome, and the first issue appeared in January 1923. The original aim was to compare and to contrast the theory of liberalism and the praxis of fascism, and to find a connection, if any, between the ideals of the Risorgimento and the aspirations of fascism. But in the first number Gentile and Licitra identified liberalism with the ethical state, stressed the unity of idealism with fascism, and praised Mussolini as the heir of Risorgimento ideals. Croce had joined Gentile and other figures, even known anti-Fascists, on the periodical's editorial board, but he never wrote anything for the paper and after the first number withdrew from the board with some indignation. Soon afterwards he expressed his disagreement with the ideas of Gentile and Licitra in an essay published in his own periodical, *La Critica*.[24]

There, as on other occasions, Croce poured scorn on those who violated history and philosophy to find the origin of fascism. For him, the origin of fascism was not in idealistic philosophy, or in the liberal tradition of the Risorgimento, but in the futurist movement, both in its artistic aspirations and in political activism. In an essay written in 1924, commenting on a quip by Filippo Marinetti, Croce made his position quite clear, though he displayed a literary verve that may have carried his argument too far: 'Truly, for those who have a sense of historical connection, the ideal origin of "fascism" is to be found in "futurism": in the resolution to go down to the piazza, to impose one's own feelings, to shut the mouths of those who are dissenting, to be unafraid of commotions and riots; in the eagerness of the new, in the desire to break every tradition, in the exaltation of youth, which was proper to futurism, and which spoke to the heart of the veterans, offended by the political skirmishes of the old parties, and by their lack of energy against the antipatriotic and anti-statal violence.' Marinetti, in Croce's opinion, deserved applause for having called Gentile's reform of education 'anti-Fascist and passatista,' and he was correct to describe the reform as mouldy 'old news' from the point of view of futurism. But Croce was not ready to extend similar approval to those who were trying to find a noble pedigree, 'a golden coat of arms,' for fascism, and who, in doing so, were appealing to history and philosophy 'and making use of Gioberti and Mazzini, idealistic philosophy, actual idealism, and similar things and names, which remain surprised when they find themselves in this new company, in which they have been brought by force.'[25]

Croce was among the first to point to futurism, and to syndicalism, as an important component of fascism. But, to use one of his favourite expressions, that was a part and not the whole. The presence beside Marinetti of Gentile and of Mussolini, not to mention the Nationalists Federzoni and Rocco, under the same roof showed the influence and the convergence of other currents and elements in the Fascist movement, where they brewed and coagulated into an explosive cocktail.

Further Reflections on Liberalism and Fascism

Another proof of the complexity of fascism was offered by Croce himself in a book that advanced new arguments against nationalism and that pointed to the pernicious influence that nationalism exerted on Italian society. During late 1922 and early 1923, Croce was writing *The History of the Kingdom of Naples*. This book provided the first example of Croce's ethico-political history, which assigns pre-eminence to the moral and intellectual forces in the life of a people and in the interpretation of their history. The relation between the book and contemporary events was sometimes quite evident; nor was this surprising, given Croce's conception of history, according to which, in the contemplation and narration and evaluation of the past, the historian reveals his personality and his position in the present. Thus history is always contemporary history. By Croce's own confession, this book would not have been 'written without my political passion for the present and for the past.'[26]

The last chapter of this book offered a celebration of 'the great nobility' of the Italian Risorgimento: a political movement without 'fanaticism of religion,' 'pride of race,' and 'narrow nationalism,' but, at the same time, 'animated and moved by moral dignity,' 'inspired by intellectual light,' and 'fraternal towards other peoples.' With a direct reference to the present, Croce wished that the Italians of his day should know better 'the truth' of those ideals and 'the nobility' of that tradition, in order 'to feel again its generous influence.' This was 'a thing especially beneficial,' he said, 'now that the purity of that tradition is threatened, and a bad and pernicious literature is trying to introduce in our feelings a turbid and gloomy and sensual nationalism of foreign origin.'[27]

No wonder Fortunato, who had read and commented on the manuscript, was full of praise when the book finally was published, calling it 'vigorously thought [out] and rendered with a magisterial exposition.' Above all, he said: 'I am infinitely happy for the vindication of liberalism.'[28]

Another vindication of liberalism and Risorgimental patriotism can be found in a 1923 review of a new edition of Gaetano Mosca's famous book, *Elements of Political Science*. There, Croce claimed that, despite the recent experiments, in Italy or elsewhere, 'the liberal state was still the most mature form of European political life,' and 'its inspiring principle was sound.' But he also argued that the ruling classes of the liberal states had to become 'more confident and more courageous'; above all, they needed to acquire a more robust faith. Croce agreed with Mosca that, to maintain political cohesion in the life of a nation, a religious faith was required, and that in modern times, after the decline of traditional religion, only patriotism offered a new civic faith and was able to generate that cohesion. Croce hastened to add, however, repeating concepts that he had used against the nationalists before the war, 'provided that patriotism is understood in an ethical way, and not in a chauvinistic, ethnical, brutal, libidinous and capricious manner, as is common among the different nationalisms.' 'Understood in an ethical manner,' he continued, 'patriotism is the concrete and historical form of the moral idea, the only one now possible, and around which it is given to unite all efforts, which ennoble human life.' For Croce, it was this kind of patriotism that in the nineteenth century made it possible for a Neapolitan to become an Italian, and that in the future could make it possible for an Italian to become a European.[29]

Croce expressed the same ideas in a speech delivered in the city of Muro Lucano, for the inauguration of a public library named after a close friend, who had died in the war.

In that speech there was also a polemical note that needs to be stressed, given the important role that the argument had played in the post-war period and continued to play in Fascist propaganda. While the Fascists and Mussolini pretended to be the only legitimate heirs of the war, Croce reminded his audience that the war had been fought by the entire Italian people, and now families of the veterans and the fallen showed the same pain and shared the same hopes and were entitled to the same dignity, whatever their present political affiliation.[30] Against modern nationalism, with its preaching of expansion abroad and discrimination at home, Croce reasserted the ideals of the Italian Risorgimento, which postulated the union of freedom and fatherland, fostered a patriotism respectful of other peoples, and viewed the nation as an entity embracing all citizens.

The General Elections of 1924

Prior to the elections of April 1924, Mussolini offered an image of moderation, and his government followed a policy of prudent administration, both in domestic and in foreign affairs. The financial problems of the immediate post war years had been brought under control and the national economy continued to grow. Mussolini signed a friendship treaty with Yugoslavia, improved relations with other Balkan states, and finally obtained the return of Fiume to Italy, putting an end, for the time being, to the Adriatic question. As a result of his diplomatic and economic achievements, Mussolini and his government enjoyed considerable popularity. The general population now hoped for lasting political normalization, and the next elections were seen as the first step to achieve that goal.

The undeniable popularity of Mussolini and the continuing expansion of the Fascist Party, plus the fear of personal defeat, persuaded the liberal and moderate political groups to accept Mussolini's invitation to fight the next elections under the same banner and to join the government list as candidates. An electoral alliance among different political forces was made advisable, or even necessary, by the rather unusual and un-democratic mechanism of the new electoral law. The law assigned two-thirds of the seats to the strongest party or list of parties, provided it gained at least 25 per cent of the popular vote, while, the rest of the seats were divided among all the other parties of the opposition on a proportional basis.[31] The approval of the electoral law in 1923 and the formation of the national list in 1924 were part of the perennial and elusive search in Italian politics to achieve a stable majority and lasting consensus among small and diverse parties on questions of national import.

Croce's position during the first half of 1924 did not change; he remained on the sidelines of active politics and continued to maintain the same position towards fascism and Mussolini's government, a mixture of benevolence and criticism. He was not in the Senate when 'the shameful electoral law,' as Fortunato aptly called it, was approved. Croce probably had no undue concern about the peculiar feature of the law, since Giolitti himself had introduced the bill in the House as chairman of the parliamentary electoral committee. He did not participate in the electoral campaign nor did he make any political speech during the period. Croce's only significant political act before the April elections was a press interview at the beginning of March in *Corriere Italiano*, a newspaper with close connections to the leadership of the Fascist Party.

The ideas expressed by Croce on that occasion have to be seen as part of the political debate generated by the upcoming elections and by the electoral alliances; they also reflected the hopes and the aspirations of moderate groups in the run-up to those elections, against the contrary expectations of Farinacci and his friends. Croce's interview in fact followed two different speeches, made in Naples by two prominent Fascist leaders, Francesco Giunta and Michele Bianchi; one promised moderation, power sharing, and a quick return to 'constitutional ways'; the other instead spoke of 'intransigence' and 'renovation,' favourite concepts of Farinacci and of the radical faction of fascism, which wanted a future different from the past and the present.[32]

In the *Corriere Italiano* interview, Croce repeated his position on the Fascist movement. He approved the policies of the government but criticized the ideology of fascism. Croce assured the readers of the paper that he did not fear the effect of the new electoral law. Instead he saw 'the spontaneous beginning, thanks to the political elections, of a return, as it now is called, to legality, that is, to constitutional practices.' With regard to the coming elections, he expressed the wish that 'people would feel the necessity not to compromise the work of political restoration under way,' but give to the government list 'a compact majority.'[33] Behind the reasoning there was wishful thinking, for, like Giolitti, Croce hoped that once the Fascist Party had a parliamentary majority of its own, the emergency would come to an end and a return to normal life without violence would be possible. 'When the dominant party in the new Chamber will have a new majority,' he said, 'it is clear that we will have returned to legality and to the good constitutional system.' The fallacy of the argument and the misplaced expectations aside, the interview made plain Croce's position: 'the hope of a return, through the elections, to the constitutional system.'[34]

In the rest of the interview, Croce was particularly generous to 'the heart of fascism,' as he called it. He conceded that fascism was animated by love of the fatherland and by a feeling for the safety and authority of the state – a sentiment that 'had produced, was producing, and would continue to produce good effects.' However, he had no hesitation in offering a negative verdict on 'the head of fascism.' In the theoretical realm, Croce said, 'I am sceptical about the ideology of fascism.' He denied that fascism had the ideas necessary to create a new political system, or that it could be capable of replacing liberalism with 'the new Fascist state.' Out of intellectual curiosity, Croce had read Fascist publications and analysed the practical acts of fascism, and neither in the writings nor in the facts had he seen signs of 'the new morality,' 'the new thought,' or 'the new philosophy.' On the contrary, he had come to the conclusion that fascism offered no 'new principles.'[35] This rather stark view of 'the head of fascism' would remain unchanged in Croce's future writings, and after the Second World War it would be echoed by others, especially Norberto Bobbio, who affirmed the intellectual and literary sterility of the entire Fascist period.

In the course of the interview, a polemical comparison between fascism and liberalism was set out, even amidst praise for 'the heart of fascism.' Liberalism, too, like fascism, was able to assure the authority of the state. Yet Croce asserted that, unlike fascism, liberalism welcomed political disagreements among different parties and assured the general interest not with violence but by continually maintaining a healthy balance between freedom and authority.

The interview, as was to be expected, was not well received by Fascists; the criticism of the 'head' did not amuse most of them and some of their newspapers replied in kind. A Roman paper with close financial and political ties to government, *Il Tevere*, asked a rhetorical question: 'Is there anybody more idiotic than Bonomi?' The answer: 'Yes, Benedetto Croce.'[36]

Croce's criticism of the Fascist 'head' notwithstanding, the general elections of April 1924 were a success for Mussolini personally, for his government, and even for fascism. Indeed the success was too great and widespread to be attributed only to violence, as the opposition claimed. Despite the many acts of intimidation, participation increased from 58 per cent in the 1921 elections to 63 per cent in 1924; and in northern Italy, the opposition parties together gathered slightly more votes than the government list. The government obtained strong majorities in the central regions, once the stronghold of the Socialist Party. In southern Italy, the support of the old political notables and local dignitaries, more than violence, proved decisive for the Fascist success. But even there a close look at the results showed that a significant shift had taken place; in the last elections, Salandra had obtained more than one hundred thousand votes and come first in his riding of Apulia. In 1924, only ten thousand people voted for him and he placed fourteenth in the government electoral list, well behind the new and younger Fascist leaders, none of whom had a national reputation.[37]

Over all, the Fascist list won 65 per cent of the popular vote, and this figure was reflected in the composition of the new Parliament. When the House reconvened after the elections, the opposition parties had

161 seats combined; the government had 375, of whom 275 were card-carrying members of the Fascist Party. In a chamber of 536, then, Mussolini and the Fascists had a majority of their own, independent of the support of the liberal notables and other allies.[38]

The Matteotti Affair and Its Aftermath

These numbers help to explain the actions and the behaviour of Italian political leaders, inside and outside Parliament, during the next political crisis that suddenly jolted Italy and the Italians into chaos and turmoil, and almost toppled Mussolini from power. The Matteotti affair demonstrated Mussolini's Machiavellian talents and the strength of the Fascist movement; it revealed the weakness and the divisions of the opposition; and, finally, it made manifest that the liberal leaders, unable and unwilling to accept the rules of mass-party politics, had lost power forever.

On 30 May, soon after the opening of the new Parliament, the young leader of the Unitary Socialist Party, Giacomo Matteotti, delivered a bold speech denouncing the violence that had marked the election campaign and, at the end, demanding the nullification of the results. During the speech, there were continuous jeers, and personal threats were heard even from the government benches; then, on 10 June, he was kidnapped and murdered, his body left half-buried in the Roman countryside. Mussolini now entered the most crucial period of his political life, his government and his power in danger of collapsing at any moment for the next few months.

One of the most intransigent anti-Fascists, Matteotti was a political leader of the younger generation and among the first to realize the true nature of fascism. There is no doubt that his murder was the fruit of the atmosphere created by fascism, with its contempt for adversaries, its cult of violence, and its threats against opposition leaders. Historians are still debating the role of Mussolini, with compelling arguments on both sides. However, besides possible criminal participation, there was an evident political responsibility; Mussolini was also minister of the interior and as such responsible for public order and citizens' safety. His failure to protect Matteotti should alone have been enough to compel his resignation.[39]

At that critical moment, opposition politicians made a fatal mistake. Instead of fighting inside the House with determination, calling for Mussolini's resignation in the name of 'ministerial responsibility,' the opposition chose, in typical Italian fashion, to turn a political problem into a 'moral question.' As a result, the train of events unfolded with a different logic than would have been the case in countries with a well-established parliamentary tradition. Soon after the murder of the Socialist leader, the opposition, led by Amendola and Turati, left Parliament, formed the Aventine Secession, and swore never to return while Mussolini stayed in power. At the same time, Giolitti remained in Parliament in a position of watchful independence, and Salandra continued to support the government, still fearful of socialism. Like Giolitti, Croce did not approve of the Aventine Secession and kept urging Amendola to return to Parliament and to organize the opposition inside the House.

In the middle of the crisis, on 13 June, the new speaker, Alfredo Rocco, adjourned Parliament until the next November. It was a master stroke. First the Aventine Secession and then the adjournment deprived the opposition of its best instrument, in a parliamentary democracy, to press its moral advantage to a positive conclusion, exploiting the difficulties of Mussolini and the disintegration of the government majority. The press campaign waged by the opposition parties in the name of the 'moral question' proved not enough, by itself, to compel the government to resign and Mussolini to relinquish power.[40]

With the adjournment of the House, the focus of attention shifted to the Senate, where a motion of confidence was debated between 24 and 25 June. Even that occasion did not create a great deal of difficulty for Mussolini. Despite great speeches by the few senators of the opposition, in the end the government received a vote of confidence, 226 senators voting in favour and 22 against.

That outcome may have disappointed public opinion but probably did not come as a surprise to the political and cultural elites. Since the time of Agostino Depretis in the 1880s, the Senate had lost its parity with the House. It had become the accepted norm that votes in the Senate could not create a political crisis, and that a government was not required to resign after a defeat in the Senate. Senators were then appointed by the crown; most of them were old and deferential to tradition. In the crisis triggered by the Matteotti affair, only the solemn intervention of the king, or his discreet invitation through unofficial channels, could have persuaded the senators to take an unusual initiative. But, for its part, the king would not intervene unless advised, and perhaps urged, by all the senior leaders of the House; he had to be assured that a majority of the House was ready to replace Mussolini with a new leader. However, the old leaders, Giolitti among them, were reluctant to involve the crown in partisan politics, thereby, perhaps, causing irreparable damage to the monarchy, and the king himself was afraid to repeat the mistake of his father in 1898 when political intervention had been fatal to the monarch (leading to his assassination two years later). In the absence both of a royal initiative and of a ready alternative in the House, the Senate could do only what it had done in the past: listen to great speeches and then vote innocuous but well-crafted motions preaching goodwill, inviting all parties to pursue national reconciliation without any reference to ministerial responsibility and personal accountability.[41]

Croce's Position

The murder of Matteotti and the Aventine Secession created 'a great disorientation' in Croce's mind, according to Nicolini, his friend and biographer. Luigi Russo, another close friend, confirms that Croce at that time assumed 'the colours of Caporetto': 'I have never seen Croce so gloomy as after the Matteotti murder.' Yet, despite the horror at the murder and the impression made by the Secession, Croce was not about to vote against the government. For men of his generation, it was not easy to admit that the prime minister of the crown had been somehow involved in a political murder, especially when the murder was also against his political interest and came after an election victory. The murder was clearly in contradiction to the mood set by Mussolini in his first speech to the new Parliament, on 7 June 1924, a week after Matteotti's great speech attacking the regime. On that occasion, Mussolini had been moderate in tone and conciliatory in substance. He defended the role of Parliament, recognized the necessary function of the opposition, and invited the collaboration of all political parties.[42]

According to his memoirs of 1944, Croce believed that Mussolini had nothing to do with the murder. 'I was persuaded that he was not the author of the murder, and that the bad people around him had perpetrated it without his knowledge. And, truly, it seemed folly even against his style that he could have ordered it.' During the debate in the Senate, Croce said that he believed Mussolini, when, 'with grieved and repentant air,' he made 'the solemn pledge' of wanting 'to return to legality and to constitutional rule.' Croce also trusted the promise of Mussolini and of the Senate majority leader when they assured him that the government's aim was not only 'normalization' but also the 're-establishment of freedom.'[43]

In large part, the Senate voted the way it did because of the masterful speech Mussolini delivered in the chamber on 24 June. He deplored the murder of Matteotti with apparent sincerity, condemned all violence, and assured the senators that justice would be done. He hit all the right notes: a change in the direction and composition of government, a reorganization of the militia (placing it under the command of the army), a willingness to work with the opposition. He told the Senators that it was his intention 'to obtain, with every means, and with the respect of the law, political normalization and a national pacification.' He also promised to free fascism of any illegality, expelling violent elements from the party. At the same time, he urged the senators to avoid deepening of the crisis by voting contrary to the electoral results. He put before them the possibility that a new government and a different leader would not be able to control an eventual reaction by an aroused Fascist movement, deprived of its electoral victory and, with more than eight hundred thousand members, still strong.

This was an astute reminder on Mussolini's part. A possible resumption of violence by the Fascist squads and a resurgence of republican sympathies, inside and outside the Fascist ranks, together with the old fear of socialism, blinded the judgment of many senators. The danger of a leap in the dark troubled these men, making it easier for them to accept at face value Mussolini's promises, especially since those promises were repeated the day after to the Fascist parliamentarians in the House and were even published, in point-by-point form, in Mussolini's own paper on 25 June, the day of the Senate's vote.[44]

Yet, despite the solemn promises made by Mussolini, many senators were not completely reassured. For that reason, when the time came to vote, Croce and Alfredo Lusignoli, the former prefect of Milan and a friend of Giolitti, rejected the innocuous original motion of confidence presented by the government side and compelled the majority leader to draft a new one with more binding language and with clear reference to specific policies which the senators wished to see implemented. The new motion urged the government 'to proceed with utmost energy to the restoration of the integral rule of law, to the necessary expulsions from the party, and to the pacification of the nation.'[45]

With that motion, Croce and his friends hoped to control Mussolini and to compel him to keep his promises; they also believed themselves to be in a position to defeat the government at the opportune moment. Croce expressed the same views in a meeting on the day before the Senate's vote with the journalist Giorgio Levi Della Vida, later one of the few university professors who refused to take the loyalty oath of 1931.

According to Levi, Croce said: 'After a long discussion, following the speech of Mussolini, we have decided to vote for the confidence motion. But, mind you, it will be a conditional confidence. In our motion we call upon the government to restore legality and justice, as Mussolini himself has promised in his speech. In this way we are keeping him as a prisoner, ready to deny him confidence, if he does not keep the promises made.'[46]

Mussolini was not a man to quibble about words, or to refuse to make promises in a time of difficulty. In those summer months of 1924, not nice words and well-drafted motions were needed, but political forces ready to do battle and willing to take full advantage of favourable opportunities, in Parliament and in the streets. But no political leader proposed a decisive and appropriate action that would have carried the majority of Parliament and the majority of the population. The general impression, common to all political leaders and expressed even by Amendola to Croce, was that 'The Moral Question' by itself would compel the fall of Mussolini, and soon after, within a few months, fascism would vanish forever, like a bad dream.

Soon after the vote in the Senate, four ministers resigned from the government in order to give Mussolini the chance to form a ministry of national reconciliation. In the reshuffled cabinet, Mussolini included four liberals, as a guarantee of the promises made in the Senate, or so believed Croce and his liberal friends. Croce was invited by Mussolini, through Gentile, to become the next minister of education. He refused the offer without hesitation: 'I told Gentile that I felt an insurmountable reluctance to sit around the same table with Mussolini.' After the first refusal, other friends, Alessandro Casati among them, urged Croce to reconsider. 'But I repeated that I did not want in any way to be a part of that combination.' Instead he and Gentile suggested the name of their common friend, Casati, who was a moderate liberal and had acquired great prestige in the war as an army officer.[47]

Inside the cabinet, Casati and the other three Liberal ministers had the Herculean task of overseeing a policy of moderation and a return to legality, keeping Mussolini faithful to promises made in the Senate.

Turning Point

The crisis created by the Matteotti affair changed Croce's attitude towards Mussolini and his government. In his meeting with Levi Della Vida on 24 June, Croce's new and different political position had become clear. As Levi put it in his rather succinct recollection, forty years after the event, Croce said to him: 'You see, fascism has been a good thing, now has become a bad one, and it must go. But it has to go without shocks.'[48]

His changed frame of mind was again made evident in an interview granted to *Il Giornale d'Italia* on 6 July 1924. In that interview the tone became harder, the criticism harsher, while notes of praise for fascism were fewer and reservations more general. The interview seems to close one period in Croce's life and to open another; it shows disillusionment with the past and new aspirations for the future. Once again Croce defended his vote in the Senate, and this time he used more precise arguments. Again he reiterated that, besides past and recent 'liabilities,' fascism had some positive aspects and had done some good things. For that reason, he said: 'It was not possible to expect nor to desire that fascism should fall at once and suddenly. It has not been an infatuation or a little joke. It has answered serious needs, and it has achieved many good things, as every fair-minded person recognizes. It advanced with the consensus and amid the applause of the nation.'[49] Then, he adopted a new tone, criticizing both the ideology of fascism and its proponents. For him, fascism was 'sterile of new institutions, incapable of shaping ... a new type of state.' Fascism should have been only 'a bridge of passage for the restoration of a more severe liberal regime, in the context of a stronger state,' and should not have had the ambition 'to inaugurate a new historical epoch.' Instead of concentrating their efforts on restoring the vitality of the liberal state, the Fascist intellectuals wasted their time searching 'for the ideal Fascist state' and for 'new and original Fascist institutions.'[50]

In the political field, too, the Fascist leaders had wasted time pursuing wrong policies. 'Giving signs of moderation,' Croce said, they should have returned to the liberal ways long before this choice was 'imposed by an uprising of public indignation,' created by 'this horrible murder, which upsets and wounds our hearts.' The Matteotti affair, besides the human tragedy involved, Croce continued, 'has a specific political meaning, and is indicative of a mistaken policy, which in the extreme brings consequences like this.' For Croce, it was evident now that fascism, unable to find its legitimacy in the liberal state, needed violence to maintain its power. 'Because fascism is not able to create a new constitutional and legal order, which could replace the liberal order, it needs to govern with the same violent means through which it was born, continuing what should have been occasional and transitory.' In this situation, he argued, even the Fascist leaders seemed unable to control, let alone stop, the violence of their movement: 'In the series of these violent proceedings, it is impossible to determine exactly where and when to stop. The insults and the violence belong to the same series, and they pass from one to the other by more or less sensible gradations.'[51]

Croce did not seem to note the evident contradiction between his condemnation of Fascist ideology and Fascist violence and the vote of confidence given to the government in the Senate. He defended that vote and called it 'a prudent and patriotic vote,' 'given not in a rush, but after long pondering,' and 'out of a sense of duty and without enthusiasm.' In choosing a middle road, Croce said, he and his friends had not been alone: 'Even the strongest speeches by the opposition, like those of [Luigi] Albertini and [Mario] Abbiate, seemed to indicate a middle way, to which we have adhered, repressing our personal inclinations.' With their vote, the senators, 'following and interpreting public opinion,' Croce argued, 'wanted to protect the good that fascism had created,' 'to avoid a return to the weakness and the indecision of the past,' and, finally, the vote was intended 'to give time to the process of the transformation of fascism.'[52]

For this evolution of fascism into a moderate party, which would accept liberal and constitutional norms, Croce cited the contribution of leaders like Dino Grandi and Giuseppe Bottai and others of the moderate wing of the Fascist Party, who were then engaged in polemics with the radical faction led by Farinacci. 'This transformation shall depend on the wisdom, the intelligence and the good will of the best elements of fascism. If they will accept the inevitable return to the liberal regime, they will be able to save fascism as a strong and salutary element of the future political competition. They will have destroyed a transient and dictatorial fascism, in order to create a lasting one.'[53]

The last part of the interview was not really connected to the murder of Matteotti and the immediate political situation of the time, and so it has been usually ignored by historians. Yet it did reveal Croce's inner feelings and showed his uneasiness with the prevailing madness. The elections of 1919 and 1921 had seen the defeat of many old politicians, and their departure from the scene that greatly changed the composition of the Italian political class. This trend had continued in the last election, in which many young Fascists, without political experience and often without much ability, had been elected while great parliamentarians and former ministers had been defeated or had not even had a chance to run. This was why Croce now lamented the disappearance from public life of so many politicians of the older generation, 'all of them still young,' 'men with experience,' 'skilled parliamentarians,' 'faithful servants of the state.' Croce confessed to having no sympathy for those who had suddenly replaced the old political class and 'to feel diffidence' towards 'the new and improvised politicians,' 'this other product of the postwar period,' 'like the new rich.'[54]

Mussolini and the Fascist press did not think much of the opinions expressed by Croce in this interview. *Il Popolo d'Italia*, Mussolini's own paper, reacted with acrimony, calling Croce 'a walking ghost' and 'a corpse four days old.' But others offered praise. Luigi Ambrosini, an old friend of Giolitti and a newspaperman with *La Stampa* of Turin, wrote a letter to Croce in which he said: 'I have read your recent interview, and your new orientation gives me pleasure, because, to be frank, your vote in the Senate made me uneasy.'[55]

In his reply to Ambrosini of 14 July 1924, Croce defended again his vote in the Senate, and even denied that his vote was in disagreement with his new position. The vote, he wrote, 'was dictated by love of country.' 'I felt that were I to vote against, I would have pleased my own feelings, I would have achieved my own satisfaction, but I would not have given proof of devotion to my country.' This was a rather dubious argument and showed a residual Machiavellism that later would disappear both from Croce's political theory and from his actions.

But in this same letter Croce made some observations which warrant consideration. He stated: 'To vote against meant to ask for an immediate crisis, to determine a conflict between Parliament and the government; it meant to excite the country: and which were the forces ready for this struggle? Political situations cannot be improvised.'[56] This statement about the political reality in the summer and fall of 1924 has been almost completely ignored by historians, though some have taken the position that the defeat of fascism would have been possible had the Liberal and Democratic leaders of the opposition mustered their courage and made an appeal to the people. Only in recent years have Giorgio Amendola and Giorgio Candeloro expressed agreement with Croce's assessment, though without mentioning its name.[57]

The fact is that in 1924, inside Parliament and in the country as a whole, the opposition was weaker and more divided while fascism was stronger than in 1922. After vacillating in the first weeks that followed Matteotti's murder, Mussolini regained his confidence. In the House, even after the Aventine Secession, some defections, and an attempt at rebellion by some Nationalist members, fascism still controlled a majority of the seats, albeit a slim one. More important, the party had continued to grow in the whole country and become a truly national political movement. The Fascist squads were still in existence, ready and eager for action. Mussolini controlled the levers of the state, was not willing to abandon power without a struggle, and had kept the party in a fighting spirit.

Only the direct intervention of the king could have changed the situation, and only a unified opposition could have compelled the monarch to intervene and to employ the army, if necessary. But the opposition failed to achieve unity and the liberal leaders and the king utterly failed to rise to the occasion.

Croce's hostility to fascism and Mussolini continued to grow during the summer months of 1924, as is evidenced in his letters to Alessandro Casati, the new minister of education in the second cabinet of Mussolini. During the summer and fall of 1924, at regular intervals, Croce criticized several aspects of government policy and urged Casati to remain vigilant about the dangers of new laws and 'to be wary of constitutional reforms, based on syndicalism,' which Gentile and other Fascist leaders were proposing.

Croce, like other Liberals, relied on Casati for the protection of freedom and for a course of moderation in government policy. When Croce heard that Casati might resign from the government, unhappy with Mussolini's policy, he immediately sent a letter of discouragement. 'I have read in the papers the possibility of your and Sarocchi's resignation ... May the gods avert this occurrence.'[58]

Croce's political evolution was in harmony with the position of other Liberals and paralleled the changed attitude of the Italian Liberal Party. At its national congress in October 1924, the majority of the party rejected a motion of unconditional support for the government, reaffirming instead the classical principles of liberalism and inviting the government to return to constitutional ways. Unhappy with this motion, the filo-government minority left the party, formed its own movement, and later joined the Fascist Party.[59]

The Matteotti affair was also a turning point in personal relations, not only for Croce but for other intellectuals. In this period, Croce's relations with those of his liberal friends who were critical of fascism and unhappy with Mussolini became closer; he had more frequent meetings with them, especially with Amendola, Luigi Albertini, and Ruffini, while his friendship with Gentile became increasingly strained. A sign of his new orientation was the support he offered Piero Gobetti, the young and energetic editor of the anti-Fascist periodical *Rivoluzione Liberale*. Gobetti, with a choice of words that were open to a double interpretation, had described as 'moral abortions' the proposals for national pacification associated with Carlo Del Croix, a moderate nationalist member of Parliament who was prone to rhetorical excess, but also a war hero, having lost both his eyes and his arms in action. In the overwrought emotional climate of the time, the Fascist press organized a campaign of denigration against Gobetti, accusing him of having offended a national hero.

In vain Gobetti protested his innocence, and his respect for Del Croix, regretting the misunderstanding. Nor did all his friends, when invited, agree to appear before the special jury that had been convened, or to defend publicly his good name. Some, like Amendola, agreed with his Fascist critics, and urged him to write with more precision and to avoid personal insults when dealing with national politics. Others, Nello Rosselli among them, refused to intervene, not out of personal fear, but because he did not want to increase the damage already done to the opposition and to give the Fascists new pretexts for violence.

Croce's reaction was completely different; asked by Gobetti, he immediately wrote a letter of reference to be used as Gobetti pleased. Not only did Croce offer a favourable interpretation of the text in question, excluding any personal criticisms, but then he put his own personal reputation on the line, claiming that, in a recent meeting in Turin, Gobetti had expressed great respect for Del Croix and his political proposals.

This solidarity with Gobetti was all the more significant when it is remembered that at that time Gobetti, with his usual energy, was using his periodical as a vehicle to organize anti-Fascist groups in the major urban centres. For his political activities and constant criticism, Gobetti had gained Mussolini's hostility, and already had been a victim of fascist violence. The jury accepted Croce's interpretation of the article in question. Soon after that episode, however, Gobetti was again the victim of Fascist aggression, and the severe injuries he suffered further undermined his health.[60]

The Break with Gentile

Then in 1924 came the most important manifestation of Croce's changed political orientation: the break-up of his friendship with Giovanni Gentile. After Gentile heard from Casati that Croce wanted to end their friendship, because he had become unhappy with him 'for moral reasons,' he asked Croce for a note of clarification – for 'two clear words, whatever they are going to be, but which come from the bottom of your heart.'[61]

The next day, 24 October 1924, Croce wrote what was to be his last letter to Gentile. The calm tone of the words hid the gulf now separating the two old friends. 'To be sure,' Croce wrote, 'for many years we have been in a philosophical disagreement, which was not such as to have a bearing on our personal relations. But now to that, has been added another one of a practical and political nature, nay, the first has been converted into the second, and this is more serious. There is nothing we can do. The logic of the situation has to develop through the individuals and despite the individuals.'[62]

So ended, on a sad note, destroyed by fascism, a fraternal friendship and an intellectual collaboration which had lasted for more than twenty-five years and had been beneficial to Italian culture. Together, Croce and Gentile had brought a new vigour to Italian philosophy and given new directions to literary and historical studies. From the beginning, however, they had taken different approaches to history, philosophy, and politics. Yet, until the advent of fascism, philosophical and political differences had never affected their personal relations.

Their friendship had begun to deteriorate in 1923 under the strain of political events. In May of that year, Gentile became a member of the Fascist Party; Croce was surprised by the sudden decision and by the lack of prior consultation 'with a trusted friend about such a grave decision.' Little of these political differences appear in their correspondence, and probably remained confined to private conversations. But by 1924 the disagreements must have become known to and even discussed among their common friends, as is revealed in a letter of Giustino Fortunato in February of that year: 'Croce has not been well disposed toward Gentile lately, and has not been for some time and for various reasons.'[63]

In the crisis generated by the murder of Matteotti, the political differences between Croce and Gentile became more evident and more public. For Croce, the government had to follow a policy of moderation, had to make possible a return to constitutional rule, and had to undertake a restoration of liberal practices. For Gentile, the only moral and political question was 'to save Italy,' and the only duty of a true Liberal was to give his support to Mussolini, to strengthen fascism, to avoid any compromise with subversive forces, and to prevent a return to the confusion and corruption of the past. Committed to this program Gentile refused to change course and rejected all appeals made by some of his closest friends, like Adolfo Omodeo, who urged him to break his ties with Mussolini and with fascism and to resume his independence.[64]

Croce, too, must have given the same advice and made the same appeals. In a letter written in 1925 to an unidentified person. Croce criticized Gentile for making, in these months following the Matteotti murder, 'a profession of Fascist radicalism and extremism,' for becoming 'head of a commission to change the Italian liberal statute in a reactionary way,' and for supporting the radicalism of Farinacci and his stand against moderation.[65]

In his diary of 1944, on hearing of Gentile's death, Croce wrote: 'I broke my relation with him because of his adhesion to fascism, made worse by the contamination of his philosophy with it.' That contamination was particularly offensive to Croce, as he had confessed in a letter to Casati in October 1924: 'Above all it offends me that the white robe, with which in my eyes philosophy goes dressed, love of my youthful years, has become a mop for the kitchen of fascism and for any kind of policy.' In Croce's eyes, Gentile deserved criticism for many things he had done and written, but, as he said in his letter of 1925, nothing was comparable 'to the betrayal of the cause of Italian freedom and the dignity of science.'[66]

The personal and political break between Croce and Gentile was another sign – in many ways, the most significant one – that fascism and Mussolini were now dividing Italian culture as never before; it was then that in Italy the moral divide was created between fascism and antifascism. More or less at the same time as his break with Gentile, Croce refused to become a member of the Academy of Italy, which was formally founded in 1929 but had been set in motion in 1924. The new institution was modelled on the French Academy and was inspired by the same concern with national prestige. Mussolini, through 'a high officer of an heraldic institute,' invited Croce to become a member. But Croce rejected such an honour with an eloquent, if not too elegant, old Neapolitan folk saying, which can be translated as: 'And what now! Do you want to mount me on a pig?'[67]

Others took a different course, however. Bitter with the behaviour of the opposition and critical of democratic ideology, which he blamed for all the troubles of Italy, Luigi Pirandello, the playwright and future winner of a Nobel prize, in the fall of 1924 joined the Fascist Party and expressed admiration for Mussolini. He later became a member of the Academy.

The break with Gentile was the result not only of a different political orientation but also of a deep philosophical conflict. In 1924, as in 1923, there was an evolution in Croce's philosophical system: 'a turning point,' Aldo Garosci has called it. Under the impact of political events, and in response to the challenge of Gentile, Croce felt compelled to offer a clarification of his political ideas and a new formulation of his theory of historiography. He did so in political and historical essays written in 1924 and first published in his periodical *La Critica*. These were reprinted in newspapers the same year and later collected in Croce's books *Elementi di Politica* and *Storia dell'Eta' Barocca in Italia*, which appeared in 1925 and 1929 respectively.[68]

In these essays, Croce reasserted the theory that politics was force and utility, but at the same time he introduced a new relationship, in his system of distinctions, between politics and morality. Before the war he had affirmed the autonomy of political action; now, confronted by new and violent ideologies which gave ethical value to the sanctions of the state, he stressed the superiority of morality, even in the political realm. The first occasion for a clarification came when Federico Chabod published a new edition of *The Prince* by Machiavelli. In a review of the book Croce noted that, even in politics, the force or the virtue of Machiavelli's prince 'represents an aspect necessary and eternal, but only one aspect of the totality and integrity of man.' From then on, 'prudence' and 'morality' went together, one reinforcing the other, as essential elements; but force was dethroned from its former position, and morality became the hegemonic element even in politics, creating the value necessary to achieve consensus and lasting success. For Croce, the ideal politician was no longer 'The Prince,' endowed with virtue, but the 'vir bonus agendi peritus,' the leader who possessed political ability but was also guided by moral energy.[69]

In these new writings Croce continued his old polemics against both the Democrats and the Socialists, arguing that their concepts of justice and equality were abstract and anti-historical. But now the centre of his interest moved towards the authoritarian ideas of the right, and his criticism was directed against this new and more dangerous enemy of the liberal state. For Gentile, the state was the supreme incarnation of morality, and for him the moral life of the citizen coincided with the morality of the state. Croce refused to elevate the state or any other political institution to a moral category, or to a philosophical idea. For him, the state coincided with the governing group and expressed only 'a process of useful actions by a group of individuals,' such actions being indistinguishable from those of other groups. The state was only an elementary and narrow form of political life, which could not contain the full richness of human experience. Beside and sometimes against the activity of the state, for Croce, there was always the life of the 'anti-State,' 'the church,' 'society,' and, above all, 'history,' with its infinite creations. 'This embraces in itself the men of the government and the men of the opposition, the conservatives and the revolutionaries, and these more than the others, because more than the others they open the ways of the future, and cause the progress of human societies.'[70]

Already we have seen that Croce's concept of patriotism contained an ethical connotation which contrasted with the naturalistic elements of the nationalist ideal. Now, as a result of this larger vision of political life, his concept of the ruling class also changed and became less exclusive. For Croce, the ruling class was a moral formation, a confluence of individuals without economic ties but animated by common values; it included the government and the opposition and constituted an ideal 'middle' class, located at the centre of the political spectrum and fighting against both the extremism of the right and the radicalism of the left. Finally, Croce no longer rejected the democratic aspirations of the masses as utopian; instead he regarded them as an essential stimulus to political life and as a force working towards the continuous renovation of the ruling class itself.[71]

In the historical field, Croce's negative assessment of the Counter-Reformation was of particular importance, providing as it did a clear view of his political feelings in 1924. The reactionary nature of the Counter-Reformation 'needed to be stressed again,' Croce argued in a famous and polemical essay, 'especially now when from members of the dominant party are heard frequent invocations to the Counter-Reformation, and instigations and intentions to return Italy to the standards of life which were proper in that age.' For Croce, those who were proposing a return to the ideals of that period showed not only their conservative inclination but also their 'decadentism' and 'muddy aspirations,' typical of 'crude minds' and 'turbid souls' which were 'full of bad literature but empty of sane political concepts.'[72]

In an earlier book review, Croce had expressed the same disapproval of those Italians who, 'for the new greatness of Italy,' 'for an imperial Italy,' were invoking, like Machiavelli, a new prince and asking for 'a return to the discipline and the hierarchy of the Counter-Reformation and the absolute kings.' Croce reminded these Italians longing for the past and proposing a new and undemocratic course for Italy that 'the good and solid policy creates the new, but a new which is richer and more comprehensive, not poorer and more narrow than the pre-existing reality.'[73]

End of Benevolence

All these criticisms of the ideas held by 'members of the dominant party' showed that Croce's political benevolence towards Mussolini and fascism had come to an end. As Gobetti recognized in 1925: 'After the murder of Matteotti one of the most important facts of Italian politics is the passage of Croce to anti-fascism.' Gobetti's opinion found confirmation in Croce's memoirs of 1950. 'In the second half of 1924, he wrote, after a series of fallacious promises and vain hopes in the restoration of freedom, I moved openly to opposition.'[74] The newspaper interview of July 1924, the letters to Casati after that date, and the break with Gentile in October showed that Croce's positive attitude towards Mussolini had lasted for less than two years, with all the limitations that have been noticed.

The best judgment on that period of his life came from Croce himself and can be found in a letter which he wrote to Gioacchino Volpe in 1927. Volpe, one of the best modern Italian historians, had been a friend of Croce and during the Mussolini regime became, with Gentile, one of the most important intellectuals of fascism. 'I have seen,' Croce wrote, 'an article in which you have written that I had flirted with fascism. You know that this is not true, that I never caressed, flattered or in any way ever offered myself to fascism, and always refused the advances made to me. I have for a short time hoped and believed that fascism would not deviate substantially from the liberal way of Italy.'[75]

On other occasions Croce had described what he 'hoped and believed' during that 'short time' as reflecting 'an easy optimism' and 'lack of political wisdom.' One should accept those conclusions and the blame that they imply, but also admire the candour that they reveal.

CHAPTER FOUR

'Continuous and Resolute Opposition,' 1925

On 3 January 1925 the crisis that had begun with the murder of Matteotti ended. With Mussolini's speech to Parliament that day, the illusions of the liberal leaders were shattered forever. Mussolini overcame his previous vacillations, put aside his promises of reconciliation, imposed a radical solution, and achieved complete victory without facing challenge. The coalition government ended and a truly Fascist one took its place. Alfredo Rocco became minister of justice and used his formidable legal talents to destroy the liberal state and fashion a new constitutional fabric for the Fascist regime.

From January 1925, the creation of the authoritarian state began and the establishment of the personal dictatorship of Mussolini was put in place. Then, many gave up the fight and retired from public life in fright or in disillusionment; even more joined the growing crowd and applauded the victorious leader. Benedetto Croce was not one of them. He was perturbed by the new events but not cowed by the new masters. Immediately, he expressed public opposition to fascism, both in the political field and in cultural matters. When 'the true and criminal nature' of fascism became clear, Croce abandoned 'any restraint' and entered 'into a continuous and resolute opposition.'[1]

In 1925 Croce wrote the 'Protest against the Manifesto of Fascist Intellectuals.' He joined the Liberal Party and participated in its executive meetings and national councils. He used the newspapers to express his views and to criticize the policies of the government. In the Senate he voted against all the bills that destroyed the liberal state and created the Fascist regime. He refused any collaboration with the new cultural organizations created by the government, and broke personal relations with old friends who became supporters of the regime. His resistance was not passive but active and not without risk both for him and for his family.

The letters that Croce wrote to Casati in 1925 provide clear evidence of his new fighting spirit and changed attitude. In their correspondence during the second half of 1924, Croce's disillusionment with Gentile and his concerns with government policies were plain. Now, all illusions disappeared, and the criticisms were without equivocation. In a letter of 4 January, after Mussolini's speech, Croce wrote: 'I do not know whether or not you are still a minister, I cannot wish that you stay on in this moment so shameful for Italian life.' After Casati resigned from the government as a protest against the new political course, Croce wrote to him again expressing his approval: 'I am glad that you are out of that company.'[2]

Luigi Russo, who was with Croce in Naples in those days, saw his 'dreadful despair' at the news of Mussolini's new policy. He also noted Croce's transition from 'the previous illusion' to 'bold anti-fascism,' as well as his determination not to accept the new situation with passivity. Russo remembered Croce's words at this time: 'It is impossible to think that from today Italy is without freedom.'[3]

Member of the Liberal Party

In the first months of 1925, Croce's participation in political activity increased. He became a member of a national party for the first time when he joined the Italian Liberal Party, which then was making efforts to overcome the divisions among the old leaders and to provide itself with a more modern organizational structure. Croce's involvement in the party has to be regarded as an exceptional contribution to the political life of the nation, motivated by the same principles that had compelled him to accept Giolitti's invitation to join the cabinet. Aware of the gravity of the situation, Croce tried to assist in the defence of liberal institutions, hoping to stem the ruin of the liberal state. To the president of the party he promised to devote time and effort to the liberal cause: 'My forces are modest ... but whatever they are, I put them at the disposal of the Party.'[4]

After his membership in the Liberal Party was officially formalized in April 1925, Croce sent a letter to *Il Giornale D'Italia* setting out the political reasons for his decision and making explicit reference to the gravity of the current situation. 'In the present moment, I have decided that my duty is to belong to the Liberal Party, even as a modest member.' He reminded the readers of the newspaper that in the past he had defended the liberal idea with books, but now was time to defend it also with action, and he invited kindred spirits to follow his example.[5]

During 1925 Croce made brief speeches and appearances on behalf
of the Liberal Party in various Italian cities, trying to boost its organization and morale. His diaries reflect his increased political activity.
Besides the usual titles of books read and essays written, we find notes
'of political discussions' and of 'visits with political friends' that took
place either in Naples or during his trips to other cities. In the politically
charged atmosphere of the times, even cultural lectures acquired political meaning, and were turned into occasions for expressing support for
the leaders of the opposition and for condemning the program of the
government. In March, during a lecture in Milan, Croce received 'great
applause' and then, after the lecture, 'a train of admirers' followed him
'in Galleria,' where he received more applause from the public. Visits to
Turin and Bari produced the same kind of reaction; after lectures in
these cities, crowds of friends followed Croce to the houses of his hosts
for further discussions. In June, Croce's own residence was used for a
public meeting, when 'politicians and young people' gathered in
Palazzo Filomarino 'for the constitution of the Neapolitan section of the
Italian Liberal Party.' This new initiative had become necessary, since
the old liberal association was 'in the hands of so-called fiancheggiatori'
or Fascist supporters.[6]

During this period Croce participated quite actively in the meetings
of the national council and the executive of the Liberal Party. The
speeches he delivered before these bodies reveal that Croce had
become aware of the new requirements of Italian politics after the introduction of universal male suffrage and the advent of mass parties. In
order to survive, the Liberal Party could no longer rely only on the presence of strong personalities or limit its activity solely to well-sounding
slogans of protest. In a meeting of the executive in May, he urged the
party to embark on a new course, increasing both its organizational
efforts in the country and its opposition in Parliament. 'I have proposed
that, instead of repeating general affirmations, we should think of organizing riding associations, and criticizing the acts of government from
the parliamentary tribune.'[7]

Croce returned to the need for Liberals to possess a stronger organization, a united leadership, and a new program in a letter to Giolitti that
he wrote on behalf of the party's executive. Inviting the former premier
to the next national council, Croce stated: 'We know that the liberal
idea is the only one which gives hope for a civil and progressive life to
our fatherland. We also know that it must be strengthened, made more
efficient and adapted to the times.'[8]

But the efforts of Croce and others to give the Liberal Party a new structure failed; the party remained as divided as before and without an efficient organization. Yet at least it achieved a clarification of its purpose. In February 1925 the executive of the party passed a motion against the government. Immediately, conservative Liberals, but without Salandra, founded a National Liberal Party and transferred their support to Mussolini, while the Italian Liberal Party, under the leadership of Giolitti in the House and of Ruffini in the Senate, played the role of the official opposition in Parliament, carrying on quite a spirited fight, while it remained possible.[9]

At the national council of the Italian Liberal Party in June 1925, Croce delivered one of the best speeches of his political life. The speech revealed both the resolution of the politician and the insight of the historian. His words had the tone of a prophet who knew that a battle had been lost and the time had come to stand firm in opposition, as preparation for the future. 'We do not need to muse on the results of the struggle, and on the probability of the next victory, but we have to maintain our position and fight.' To strengthen the faith of the doubtful and to avoid the wavering of the timid, appeals were made to the great spirits of the past. 'We, like all those who fight for an ideal, need to repeat the words of Luther before the Diet of Worms: Here I stand. I can not do otherwise. God be with me. Amen!'[10]

At the same time, Croce began to look at fascism with the eyes of the historian and tried to understand the deep reasons for 'what has happened and is happening in Italy.' Croce offered ideas and explanations on the nature of fascism, which he later would elaborate in his historical works. The concept of fascism as a moral illness made one of the first appearances in this speech. It was not a vague and empty formulation, as his critics have maintained, but concrete and specific: it made reference to political forces and cultural ideas, did not ignore economic interests, and pointed to the greed that characterized modern capitalism and the new imperialism. Above all, Croce made clear that the concept of moral illness did not indicate a period of time, 'a parenthesis,' but defined a condition of the spirit that was inimical to liberal values.[11]

For Croce, 'the wickedness and the extravagance' which could be blamed on this or that political party 'were not sufficient to explain an historical process.' He attributed the immediate victory of fascism in Italy partly to the composition and the divisions of the Italian Parliament, but also to the errors of judgment made by the Liberals in their dealings with fascism. 'All of us know the conditions, not so much social as parliamentary, which produced in Italy the Fascist movement, and which convinced all, or at least many of us, to accept it as a crisis, which we hoped beneficial, but as all beneficial crises, temporary.'[12]

But, for Croce, fascism was not a peculiar phenomenon of Italy only; it was an historical problem common to all European nations: the expression of a moral illness and the manifestation of a crisis of modern times. 'We have to keep in mind that the illness and the crisis, and the new illness produced by the crisis, is not something particular to Italy, but it belongs to all European life.'[13] The crisis of values and the illness began before the war, when the ideals of liberal societies were challenged by new movements. 'The Liberal regime was, before the war, in great difficulties, because of the enormous growth of anti-liberal forces, which opposed it: above all because of the effect of socialism and of anti-socialism; because of anti-liberal dispositions, which were in the ideals and in the practice of socialism, and because of the new forces of capitalism.'[14] The difficulties of liberal societies were increased by the war and made sharper by the passions unleashed by it. After the war, new facts and new theories further undermined the institutions of the liberal state and weakened the moral energy of society, inducing many people, in all parts of Europe, 'to seek other ways outside the liberal regime' to overcome the crisis and find a solution to the chaos.[15]

Despite the present difficulties of liberal societies and the claims of the new experiments, Croce wished for 'a restoration of a true liberal regime.' The liberal state was still 'the system most open, the structure most solid and at the same time most elastic, which the historical experience had created to moderate social struggles, and to allow a normal development.'[16]

Croce repeated in private what he said in public. He assured a German scholar that in Italy and in other parts of Europe a new form of nationalism, different from the old patriotism, 'with a human and Christian background,' 'was now celebrating its success.' Against this extreme nationalism, which was 'full of Nietzschean and decadent literature' and 'instigated hate among nations,' those with 'a European conscience' had to take their position in the ranks of the opposition, fighting 'with prudence and patience,' without the hope of immediate success but sure that 'the future did not belong to nationalism.'[17]

In May 1925 Croce was named, with Gaetano Mosca and Francesco Ruffini, as an official representative and spokesman of the Italian Liberal Party in the Senate. Already in April, on his own accord, Croce had asked Casati to enlist him in the Liberal group of the Senate. His correspondence with Casati and Ruffini reveal that he agreed with them on the importance of his role in the Senate. Often Croce went to Rome on a quick call from his friends to cast his vote against a government bill. In the new political atmosphere, he had come to dislike the Senate; the empty rhetoric of many made him 'nervous'; he felt 'enervated' by the prevailing servile behaviour. Still, he continued to appear in the Senate out of a sense of duty and to show political solidarity with his friends: 'I have come to make an act of presence, in accordance with the example offered by Giolitti.' In the last years of his long life, the former premier was often in the chamber, sitting gravely among his few remaining friends, fifteen in all, to show that Parliament was vital to the salvation of Italy.[18]

From 1925 to 1929, Croce spoke only twice against government proposals and rose only once on a matter of personal privilege. But he was present at all the crucial moments beside Albertini and Ruffini when, in spite of the criticisms and the jeers of the Fascists, they defended the old constitution and condemned the laws of the new regime. With them and a few others, Croce voted against all 'the laws which suppressed freedom of association and of the press, against the special tribunal and the death penalty, and others similar, and against the so called electoral reform, that destroyed the electorate.' In 1929, when the Senate debated the Lateran Pacts, Croce 'delivered the only critical speech heard in the Italian Parliament against the Reconciliation and the Concordat with the Church of Rome.'[19]

In February 1925, Croce rose in the Senate to rebut a statement made by Gentile and to explain the reasons he had supported the reform of education in 1923. During this brief speech, Croce accused the government of having abandoned the principles that had inspired Gentile's reform and of having introduced changes and adopted practices which, in his opinion, would open academic positions 'to arbitrariness, caprices, and injustices.' By implication, Croce was accusing Gentile of hypocrisy, for preaching a union of thought and action in philosophy, while condoning favouritism and corruption under fascism.[20]

In May 1925 Parliament debated and approved a new law on 'the discipline of associations,' following the anti-liberal and nationalistic principles of Alfredo Rocco, the new minister of justice and a strong believer in the supreme authority of the state. The law forbade civil servants and military personnel from belonging to secret societies. It required all associations to notify the prefects of their statutes and membership list, and to present them to the police on request. The law mortally wounded freedom of association; it offered a powerful tool to police authorities to harass, to curtail, and to destroy the activities of any political organization deemed inimical to the interests of the government in power. Official propaganda, to make the bitter pill more palatable, presented this illiberal law as aimed only against secret associations, and especially against the Masonic Order, always an easy scapegoat in times of difficulty.

During the debate on the bill, Fascist writers used Croce's name, quoting from essays that he had written in the past against what he called 'Masonic mentality.' The aim of the Fascists was clear: they wanted to associate Croce's ideas with the intentions of the law, invoking his authority to justify their policy. With a note to the Neapolitan newspaper *Il Mattino*, Croce clarified his position and stressed the difference between his former intentions and the present aim of the government. He reminded the readers of the paper that he had criticized the Masonic mentality 'in the name of the liberal spirit, which loves the light of the sun, and is repugnant to secret and clandestine sects.' With his writings he had fought for 'a more profound culture,' while the Fascists, with 'the methods of the present struggle,' now wanted only 'to inflict damage on the political opposition of the regime.' The occasion offered Croce the opportunity to criticize the whole intellectual basis of the new regime and to defend liberal ideals. 'The polemic, that I and other men of good will waged, was not aimed at substituting a Masonic order with another Masonic order, the triangle with the fascio, the scratching of the hand with the theatrical Roman salute, but at removing superficial and simplistic conceptions, and at contrasting the powers of the sects and factions, of all the sects and factions, in the social and political life of Italy.'[21]

In November, Tito Zaniboni, despite his military training, utterly botched an attempt to assassinate Mussolini. Betrayed by a police spy, he was arrested before he could even load his gun. With the excuse that Zaniboni was a member of the Masonic Order and a parliamentary deputy of the Unitary Socialist Party, both were summarily dissolved, while acts of vandalism and violence were perpetrated against known anti-Fascists and Freemasons. In this charged atmosphere, the law on the associations came before the Senate for debate and the final vote. Not cowed by threats and violence, the Liberal senators spoke against the law. Croce repeated the arguments he had presented in *Il Mattino*. He again stressed the difference between his earlier views on the Masonic Order and the aims of the government in the present, 'when public liberties were greatly curtailed' and the Fascists were 'proclaiming with ferocious joy the destruction of the Liberal system.' While Fascists hailed the new law, 'its approval by the Senate,' Croce wrote in the diaries, gave him 'great sadness.'[22]

The Anti-Fascist Manifesto

In a meeting in Bologna of all the Fascist cultural organizations, at the beginning of April 1925, Gentile had written a 'Manifesto of Fascist Intellectuals to the Intellectuals of all Nations,' which had then been signed by the major intellectuals of fascism. This prompted Croce's major and most famous activity in the cultural and political field in this period, the publication of the 'Protest against the Manifesto of Fascist Intellectuals.' Later, the two essays became known as 'The Fascist Manifesto' and 'The Anti-Fascist Manifesto'; sometimes they are even referred to as 'Gentile's Manifesto' and 'Croce's Manifesto.'[23]

The request to write a protest against the manifesto of Gentile came to Croce from Amendola, but the immediate dislike felt by Croce against the ideas expressed by Gentile initially found expression in two letters, written to Gioacchino Volpe and Casati, refusing his collaboration in the Italian Encyclopedia, then in the organizational stage under Gentile's direction. In a third letter, written to Giuseppe Lombardo Radice on 1 April 1925, Croce's resentment towards Gentile was even more evident. Lombardo Radice was a common friend, familiar with their philosophies and political differences. Croce reminded him that Gentile's pronouncement in Bologna had left him astonished. 'Have you seen where we have arrived? No more truth, morality, art, culture; but it is fascism that has to create a Fascist truth, a Fascist moral, a Fascist culture.' These criticisms of Gentile's views explain Croce's prompt acceptance of Amendola's proposal, and reveal the animus with which he wrote the protest.[24]

Croce's manifesto represented a rejection of Gentile's philosophy, a criticism of fascism, and a defence of the Risorgimento. Gentile had claimed that fascism had realized the unity of the intellectual and of the citizen. Croce instead drew a clear distinction between the duties of citizens and the responsibilities of intellectuals as men of culture. 'Truly, if intellectuals, that is lovers of science and art, as citizens, exercise their right and fulfill their duty with membership in a political party and faithfully serve it; as intellectuals they have only one duty, with the work of investigation and criticism and with the creation of art, to devote themselves to elevate equally all men and all parties to a higher spiritual sphere, so that these can fight their necessary battles with ever more beneficial effects.'[25]

For Croce, the contamination of these separate spheres already had produced great damage in the life of the nation. For that reason, intellectuals should not confuse their political activities and their intellectual efforts; they had to keep separate their civil passions and their artistic inspirations. 'To cross these limits of the office assigned to them, to contaminate politics and literature, politics and science is an error.' This was especially true in the present circumstances, when such a mistake resulted in support for 'deplorable violence and insolence and the suppression of freedom of the press.'[26]

Gentile claimed that fascism had given Italians a new religion and united them in a common faith. For Croce, however, fascism had created only hatred among Italians, and divisions that created hatred. 'To give the name of religion to hatred and rancour, kindled by a party, which denies to the members of other parties the name of Italian, and regards them as foreigners ... to confer the nobility of religion on the suspicion and to the animosity spread everywhere ... is an assertion that sounds, to say the truth, as a lugubrious jest.'[27]

For Gentile, fascism had created a new unity of thought and action and given coherence to the political life of the nation. Croce showed that the government's very actions negated that claim, creating, as they did, confusion and contradiction. 'On the other hand, the reality, in its mute eloquence, shows to the impartial observer an incoherent and bizarre mixture of appeals to authority and to demagoguery, of professed reverence for the laws and of violation of the laws, of ultra-modern concepts and musty old trash, old regime attitude and bolshevik dispositions, irreverence and courting of the Catholic Church, abhorrence of culture and sterile attempts at producing a new one, languid sentiments and cynicism.'[28]

Against the new religion proposed by Gentile and the motley demagoguery practised by fascism, Croce reaffirmed his faith in the ideals of liberalism and in the tradition of the Italian Risorgimento. 'For this chaotic and unseizable "religion" we do not feel that we can abandon our old faith: the faith that for two centuries and one half has been the spirit of Italy in her resurrection, the faith of modern Italy: that faith which was composed of love and truth, aspiration to justice, generous and human civic sense, intellectual and moral zeal for education, solicitude for freedom: strength and support for every progress.'[29]

Gentile asserted that fascism was the heir of the Risorgimento; Croce denied that fascism had any ties whatsoever with the Risorgimento. 'We turn our eyes towards the images of the men of the Risorgimento, of those who worked, suffered and died, and we seem to see them offended and disturbed by words pronounced and by deeds done by our present adversaries, and gravely warning us, so that we continue to keep their flag strong in our hands.'[30]

Gentile accused the liberal state of agnosticism and called the modern Italian state, as it had emerged after 1875, a degeneration of the ideals of the Destra Storica, governed as it was by a small elite who were almost completely indifferent to the needs and aspirations of the majority of Italian citizens. As he would do later in his *History of Italy*, Croce defended the policies and achievements of liberal Italy, especially the attempt to bridge the gap between the minority and the majority. 'The liberals were not pleased with that situation, and always tried with all their power to involve more Italians in political life.' But, unlike the Fascists, the liberals never tried to deny freedom to Italians and to return political life to the times of the ancien regime. 'It never was in their thoughts to maintain the majority of the nation in passivity and indifference, satisfying only a few material needs, because they knew that in this way they would have betrayed the reasons of the Italian Risorgimento, and would have returned to the bad arts of the old and absolutist regimes.'[31]

At the end of the 'Protest,' the passion of the politician seems to have anticipated the judgment of the future historian, expressing what has to be regarded as the main heritage of anti-fascism: a deeper love of freedom. 'The present political struggle in Italy will be able to revive the value of liberal ideals and institutions, and to make them better understood in a more profound and concrete way and will be able to make them loved with a more conscious devotion.' Croce's belief in the positive and necessary function of that struggle is made explicit at the end. 'Perhaps one day, looking back to the past with serenity, the test which we are now sustaining, hard and painful to ourselves, will be regarded as a stage that Italy had to go through in order to give new vigour to her national life, to complete her political education, to feel in a more severe manner her duties as a civilized people.'[32]

The publication of Croce's manifesto created quite a stir in Italian cultural and political circles. It was first published by Amendola's paper, *Il Mondo*, and then immediately reproduced and discussed by all the major Italian newspapers, Liberal or Fascist. Croce himself helped the publicity with a note to a Neapolitan newspaper, timely placed a few days before the actual public release of the document. To assist readers to reach a better understanding of the nature of the protest, to place that document in the proper cultural context and to assure it a political meaning, Croce used the note to recall his earlier polemics with Gentile and his recent decision to join the Liberal Party.

Croce's manifesto became the occasion to organize a public protest against the incipient regime. In each major city, literary personalities, alone or in groups, organized the collection of signatures in support of the document. Luigi Albertini in Milan, Salvemini in Florence, and Amendola in Rome worked to assure the success of the campaign. Ultimately, Croce's manifesto was signed by the most distinguished writers of the country, representing most parties; some were friends of Croce, others were adversaries. The manifesto had become a rallying cry of anti-Fascist intellectuals.[33]

The success of Croce's manifesto greatly annoyed Mussolini and was deeply resented by Gentile. Those who signed were harassed or discriminated against in their careers. Their signatures were never forgotten, even when, in some cases, they repudiated their earlier support of the document. The manifesto of Gentile was completely overshadowed by the protest of Croce. The product of a committee, Gentile's manifesto lacked the coherence, the literary finesse, and the pathos of Croce's. Written to prove that fascism cared about culture, and to rebut the accusation that fascism was a barbarian movement, it failed in its intent, leaving historians still debating whether fascism produced a culture or remained only a political movement based on violence.

With the writing of the protest, Croce, in Gaetano Salvemini's words, *si mise allo sbaraglio*, or put himself in jeopardy. Attacks on him by Fascist newspapers increased in frequency and in virulence. They criticized his politics and ridiculed his statements, while some even blamed him for the misfortunes of Italy, past or present. The futurists and intransigent followers of Farinacci were the harshest critics and would remain in the future ever suspicious of and hostile towards those who had signed the manifesto. For his part, Gentile deeply resented Croce's 'Protest.' In public and especially in private, he mentioned it always with disdain and scorn. Even in the late 1930s he referred to it in a tone of anger, revealing in the process a personal wound, deep and still bleeding.[34]

Annoyed by the success of Croce's manifesto, and by the resonance of his public positions, Mussolini, joined the crowd of Croce's detractors. At the national congress of the Fascist Party, in June 1925, Mussolini distanced himself from the moderate wing of fascism by declaring, to thunderous applause, that he had 'never read a single page of Croce's publications.' It was a sally typical of the man, but Mussolini unwittingly offered Croce the opportunity to send to the *Il Giornale D'Italia* an amusing letter which soon made the rounds throughout Italy and provided momentary relief to the hard-pressed adversaries of fascism.

Croce reminded Mussolini that it was always better to know the opinions of adversaries, otherwise curious accidents could befall a person.

With tongue in cheek, Croce stated that 'the professed and complete abstinence from the effects of my works ... could not keep even Mussolini immune from my judgments on literary things.' He then clinched the argument and closed his trap. 'Here I have in front of me a beautiful edition of *The Betrothed*, published by the Fascist Father Pistelli, and I read on the front page of the volume three epigraphs on Manzoni: one by Goethe, another by Verdi, and the third by the Honourable Mussolini. But that of Mussolini has been taken literally from one of my own writings on Manzoni.' Immediately, the case became a popular news item, and other writers joined the fray, mostly in defence of Mussolini.[35]

One should not read too much into this incident, and certainly one should not come to the conclusion that Mussolini was a man of little culture, as it has often been claimed. Mussolini was not reluctant to use exaggeration when it fitted his purpose. Later, to a professor of the University of Naples, he claimed the exact opposite to what he had said at the congress, emphasizing that Croce had been one of his favourite authors and one of the most important in his intellectual formation. As for the quotation used by Father Pistelli, Mussolini was only an innocent victim; he put his signature, probably without reading it, to a piece of paper prepared by a secretary in his office who was unable to conceal a blatant plagiarism, as Croce, himself, in a letter to Fr. Pistelli, had previously indicated.

But the incident revealed that Croce had the courage to poke fun at Mussolini and was not afraid to incur the resentment of his followers, in a time when people were beaten or punished for much less and after Mussolini himself, during the congress, had promised a new policy towards the opposition that would be 'more ferocious' than that in the past. One has also to remember that Croce was calling attention to Mussolini's personal frailty, when many intellectuals, Gentile among them, were eager to sing paeans to the genius of the Duce and had begun to call the leader of fascism 'the providential man,' 'the man of massive faith,' or simply 'the Man of Providence' (the last being a title to which Pope Pius XI would later lend his pontifical imprimatur).

Ciarlantini and Amendola

Soon after this episode, and for more serious reasons, Croce entered into a polemical contest with another Fascist leader in a position of power, Franco Ciarlantini, who was a member of Parliament and responsible for the promotion of Italian culture abroad. Because he was in a position to dispense favours, he was greatly courted by many writers. Ciarlantini had been one of the organizers of the Fascist cultural gathering in Bologna; now, in his capacity as promoter of Italian culture among foreign nations, he wrote a piece in a Bologna newspaper outlining his ideas and proposals for the creation of a new 'Italian spiritual empire,' as he put it. Unfortunately for him, his enthusiasm for the job was not equal to his knowledge of Italian history. While he was immediately applauded by the many sycophants in the cultural business, his literary blunders and historical confusion offered Croce another occasion to ridicule a nationalist zealot and to condemn the oppressive atmosphere created by the policies of the government.

In an article published by *Il Giornale d'Italia*, Croce showed that the new 'exporters' of Italian culture 'were ignorant of Italian traditions,' and often so befuddled so to make 'foreigners laugh,' confusing 'the Renaissance with the Risorgimento' and the Counter-Reformation with the Enlightenment. Passing from the personal to the general, Croce also criticized the atmosphere being created by the fascist regime. If the Fascists cared about works of art and poetry, Croce wrote, they should stop celebrating 'violence' and organizing 'parades' every day; they should also realize that 'bad words' and 'noisy events' and 'sport activities' were hardly significant contributions to culture.[36]

Meanwhile during 1925, the correspondence between Croce and Amendola, the leader of the Aventine, increased, and their relationship became closer than before, reaching the level of a warm friendship that rested on mutual respect and led to political collaboration. In February, Amendola proposed to Croce the creation of 'a great committee of opposition made of Senators,' inviting him to be 'the leader of such an initiative together with other senator friends of ours.' The aim of such a senatorial committee would be to help the leaders of the Aventine to fight fascism with more efficiency in Parliament and in the country. As was to be expected, Croce promised his cooperation with such a committee but refused to become its leader. 'It is superfluous to say that I would be happy to take part in a committee such as you are proposing, and give to it my contribution. But I do not live in Rome, and moreover I do not have enough familiarity with the present politicians, so I could not take the initiative or the leadership of it.' There is no reason to doubt Croce's sincerity on this occasion. His reluctance to assume positions of political leadership was then well known, and it would reappear again in later years.[37]

In July, Amendola asked Croce to be a character witness on behalf of

Emilio Scaglione, a reporter for *Il Mondo*, in a sensational trial involving powerful political and financial interests. In the early months of 1925, the textile industry of Naples was the subject of a bitter dispute as the biggest owner tried to reorganize his business and reduce the workforce. The Fascist leaders of the local trade-union movement appealed for help to the Fascist Party in Rome. Roberto Farinacci, the general secretary of the party, sent Giovanni Preziosi, then a member of the national executive, to Naples with instructions to reach or impose a settlement. A settlement was, indeed, achieved as a result of Preziosi's efforts: wages were reduced, workers were laid off, and the industrialist was able to report a profit at the end of the year. Soon afterwords, however, Preziosi became editor of the second most important paper in Naples, *Il Mezzogiorno*, owned by the same textile industrialist, and immediately fired all the anti-Fascist reporters. By this strange coincidence of events, the anti-Fascist cause lost important support and Farinacci and his friends gained another ally for their radical policies.

Scaglione, with the help of a rival Fascist faction, turned the labour settlement into a political scandal of the first magnitude, accusing Preziosi of having used the dispute in order to gain control of a major Neapolitan newspaper. Charges and counter-charges flew back and forth until the matter ended before the courts. Unafraid to walk into this nest of wasps, or to step on the toes of a vitriolic and anti-Semititic former priest, Croce accepted Amendola's invitation and appeared before the tribunal to give his support to a courageous reporter harassed by powerful interests. Unable to say anything specific about the case, Croce, in his brief statement, praised instead Scaglione's good reputation, pointing out to the jury that Scaglione was 'an idealist' and 'a young man of burning faith' who enjoyed 'the esteem' of all those who knew and worked with him. In an indirect way, and not too subtly, Croce was telling the jury that Preziosi could not claim the same reputation and deserved a different consideration from them than the idealistic Scaglione.[38]

When Amendola, in July, during his vacation in Tuscany, was the victim of a treacherous ambush in which he was severely beaten by a Fascist squad, Croce immediately sent him a letter of solidarity. In September, from France, where he was recovering, Amendola expressed his resentment of the insults and abuses that the Fascist press, instructed from above, was daily hurling against Croce, especially after his criticism of Ciarlantini's initiatives: 'As an Italian,' Amendola wrote, 'I am humiliated, when I read so many vulgarities and such gross banalities against you and your work.'[39]

In September 1925, Croce wrote his last letter to Amendola. It showed the political strategy that Croce preferred and the political forces he now counted on for the regaining of Italian freedom. Croce advised Amendola, as he and Giolitti had done before, to return to Parliament and to carry on the fight from inside the House. 'I understand the sacrifice of pride which this decision requires; but not all battles are won, and this has been lost; in order to regain strength, we have to accept the accomplished fact. This strong people do when they lose a battle or even a war; you should do the same. We should not abandon ourselves to feelings of disdain, annoyance, or renunciation.' Croce indicated the political forces that he regarded as necessary for a possible future victory. 'In my opinion, there is now the elementary question of freedom, and this should unite in a block all the constitutional parties, from the moderates to the democrats and the reformist socialists.'[40] This statement demonstrated the evolution of Croce's political position. Liberals were no longer the only guardians of freedom; Democrats and Filippo's Turati's Socialists had become their natural allies, essential to the promotion and restoration of freedom. These were going to be the groups with whom Croce maintained close relations during the Fascist regime, sharing hopes of a better and different future.

Amendola refused Croce's suggestion, as he had refused Giolitti's urging before. At the time of this letter, Amendola no longer had the physical strength to undertake any new political initiative. A few months later he died in France as a direct result of the beating suffered in July. Croce and Amendola had different personalities, and so it was natural that they proposed and followed different ways to oppose Mussolini and to fight fascism. At this time, Croce seemed more realistic and Amendola more intransigent. Yet, from their letters and other writings, one also senses a common pessimism as well as a realization that, with the fight for freedom now lost, a different duty was incumbent upon them: the duty to testify to their faith, as the only way to prepare the ground for a future revival of liberal Italy.

In this same letter, Croce confessed to Amendola: 'I can do little, and perhaps nobody can do very much at the present, but that little I shall not stop doing.' In conversation with Giolitti, and in letters to Turati, Amendola kept repeating more or less the same thing with insistence: 'We have chosen this road now and we shall travel it to the end.' Even a year before, in the middle of the Matteotti crisis, the same sense of duty was well expressed in a conversation with Levi Della Vida: 'The only thing that we can do, that we have to do, that we will do is to give witness to our faith.'[41]

The Italian Encyclopedia

In the changed political climate Croce became closer to leaders of the opposition and often supported their activities. In 1925 he made a large monetary contribution to the Giacomo Matteotti Institute, which had been organized in December 1924 to honour the martyr and to publish biographies of Socialist leaders and trade-union activists. At the same time, from the beginning of 1925, Croce refused to have anything to do with the new organizations created by the regime or with the institutions directly under the authority of the government. In October 1925 Croce resigned from the board of governors of the University of Naples and from the Belle Arti, the committee that looked after the museums and art galleries of the city. The government authorities, for their part, dissolved the administrative council of the libraries and the archives of Naples, solely to remove Croce as president. But the most important development was Croce's refusal to collaborate in the Italian Encyclopedia.[42]

The Liberal governments had been rather indifferent to cultural activities and preferred to leave them to private initiative or to the enthusiasm of strong individuals. In contrast, Mussolini and his government showed from the start a special sensibility towards cultural organizations. In 1925 Italy saw the foundation of several academic institutes, some of which became quite important later and still exist. But the Italian Encyclopedia was and remained the most significant example of these new creations.

Mussolini envisaged the encyclopedia as part of the creation of the new totalitarian state, a Fascist instrument to achieve consensus among the cultural elite and to keep intellectuals within the party's orbit. But the encyclopedia responded also to an old aspiration of the Italian cultural elite. After the war, many desired the creation of a collective work capable of standing beside or even surpassing the Britannica, to show the new maturity of Italian culture and to shed the country's old inferiority complex. In this connection, collaboration on the encyclopedia created a moral problem for some anti-Fascist intellectuals.

The encyclopedia was prepared between 1925 and 1929 and was realized between 1929 and 1937. The driving force behind this monumental task was Giovanni Gentile. From the beginning, Gentile proclaimed the apolitical character of the Italian Encyclopedia, and he stressed his willingness to call on the best scholars in each field without regard to their political affiliations. The encyclopedia had to be 'the faithful and complete mirror of the scientific culture of Italy.'[43]

Gentile wanted Croce to become a member of the encyclopedia's board of directors and to contribute essays to the work. Unable to invite him directly, after the rupture of their friendship in 1924, Gentile used the offices of their common friend, Alessandro Casati, for the purpose. After Croce responded negatively to Casati's offer, Gioacchino Volpe, one of Gentile's right-hand men on the encyclopedia project was asked to try. Once again, on 7 April, Croce refused without hesitation, stating the political reason this time. He could not 'work under a director, who had dared to proclaim in Bologna, during the meeting of the Fascist cultural organizations, that culture had to be Fascist.' Under the circumstances, Croce's collaboration was impossible: 'There is no need even to talk about it.'[44]

Croce's unwillingness to collaborate on the project, and his scepticism about Gentile's assurances, would appear again in his correspondence with Casati, when events vindicated his concerns. But the personal and political reasons for his refusal were even better explained in a long letter that Croce wrote in late April 1925 to Giuseppe Lombardo Radice, Gentile's main collaborator during the reform of education. Their long friendship gives the letter added importance and special meaning. Croce stated flatly: 'I refused, for the single reason that Gentile was head of the enterprise.' He did not trust Gentile's 'assurance of impartiality,' 'based on the experience of the recent past.' Croce was sure that 'at a certain point, the Encyclopedia would become the cultural monument of fascism and we would appear as the caryatids of this monument. That is what he did for the reform of education.'[45]

The encyclopedia would suffer the same fate as the reform of education. Despite a few refusals, Gentile was able to recruit major representatives of Italian culture. Many known anti-Fascists worked on the project – Liberals, Democrats, and even Socialists – and in fact these scholars did enjoy freedom of expression. Gentile, however, had to defend repeatedly the integrity of the project from clerical and political interference. He was often subjected to criticism and personal attack from the radical wing of fascism, which did not want the collaboration of anti-Fascists in a Fascist enterprise, especially those who had signed Croce's manifesto. But, in the end, despite his best intentions, Gentile had to accept a compromise and to pay a political price. Gentile protected the anti-Fascist scholars that he had enlisted, but he was compelled to proclaim the Fascist spirit animating the work and its realization.[46]

Gentile's admirers have claimed that he directed the encyclopedia with a 'liberal spirit.' Many Democratic collaborators on the project offered a similar judgment and attested to the generosity of Gentile towards anti-

Fascist scholars. But others thought differently. After the Lateran Pacts, at the end of 1929, Adolfo Omodeo was compelled to end his collaboration in the encyclopedia in the name of scientific freedom. He found the clerical interference in the section on religion unacceptable. In his last letter to Gentile, he confessed that the 'painful experience' of the encyclopedia persuaded him that he did not have 'the gift of adaptation.' Even Giorgio Levi Della Vida, as a scholar of Semitic literatures, engaged by Gentile despite his anti-fascism and retained by him after his refusal to take the loyalty oath to the regime in 1931, had to confess that 'I would feel better with my conscience if I had persisted in my original refusal.'[47]

Despite his non-involvement, Croce had an influence on the final product. His refusal encouraged other scholars, like Casati, Luigi Einaudi, Lombardo Radice, and Ruffini, to reject Gentile's invitation. At the same time, Croce's example forced those who did become contributors to maintain academic standards and not to compromise their scholarship if they wanted to retain his admiration and, in many cases, his friendship. They knew that their literary weakness would be noted and exposed in *La Critica*. The joke then among scholars engaged in the Encyclopedia's work was that, in the dialectical scheme of things, Croce provided the spirit and Gentile gave the bread. It was because the best scholars defended their integrity and refused academic compromise in their fields that the Italian Encyclopedia became a great collective work under Gentile's political leadership.

Literary Activity as Political Opposition

In the midst of his political activities, Croce's literary work continued with accustomed regularity. In his writings, Croce often made Gentile the object of his criticism, accusing him of misusing philosophy in defence of fascism. As in the past, the aim of these new essays was to clarify the nature of liberalism, to defend the heritage of the Risorgimento, and to deny that the Fascist regime was superior to the liberal state. The importance of these essays was increased by the role they played. Croce first published them in his periodical *La Critica*; later, they were adapted and revised as editorials for *Il Giornale d'Italia*, reaching a wider audience and becoming part of the general political debate; and finally they were included in the new edition of his book *Cultura e Vita Morale*.[48]

One of the most interesting essays was that on 'Liberalism.' In it, Croce rejected the claim of fascism that, in the present time, after the Russian Revolution, the fight was only between fascism and communism and that those who rejected communism and cared about Western civilization had no choice but to join the Fascist movement and to support the government of Mussolini. Croce argued instead that the choice was always between freedom and authority imposed from above. Faithful to a dialectical conception of life, Croce recognized that both socialism and conservatism were expressions 'of eternal needs of human societies' and represented, on the one hand, the natural aspirations to social justice, and, on the other, the equally powerful necessity of law and order. But only liberalism provided a philosophical doctrine and a political conception that 'looks to the life of society as a whole.' As such, it was the only system of ideas able 'to make conflicts beneficial,' not only to particular groups but to the entire community. Among political movements, only liberalism was not afraid of freedom; indeed, it welcomed the open interplay of individual aspirations as the necessary condition to assure both progress and stability.[49]

Croce identified liberalism with the 'party of culture,' requiring 'historical sense' and 'moral and mental finesse.' For this reason, liberalism was the natural party of the centre, able to promote progress and to preserve tradition, open to requests for social justice and, at the same time, able to maintain social discipline in the midst of political differences. From now on it becomes clear that, whenever Croce spoke of liberalism, he was no longer referring to a particular historical party with a definite program but rather to a philosophical conception of life, a meta-political view of practical action. Freedom began to assume in his thought the character of an immanent religion.[50]

As he had done in his manifesto, Croce defended the achievements of liberal Italy and denied that fascism was creating a better form of the state than the liberal one that it was destroying. 'It is fashionable now to vituperate Italian life in the years that preceded the war, talking of it as a period of laxity and cowardice. But those like me, who have shaped themselves in those years in free competition, and have shaped others with the energy of thought and with the practice of discussion and persuasion, will not share that slight judgment, that easy condemnation, that unworthy insult.'[51] At the end of the essay, Croce tried to give encouragement to the faithful, to dispel their doubts, and to bring new hope to the hard-pressed opposition. Quoting a refrain that Francesco De Sanctis used to sing to himself while in jail under the Bourbons, Croce concluded the essay by reminding the sceptics that freedom always achieves victory even though it suffers momentary defeats. This faith in the immanent success of freedom will return later as the dominant theme in his *History of Europe*, while defence of liberal Italy will also inspire his *History of Italy*.

In this essay, a different tone becomes evident when Croce expresses his views on socialism and nationalism. Criticism of socialism is sharp but respectful, historically motivated and based on philosophical premises; the movement's positive contributions to western European societies are always recognized. Criticism of nationalism has a harsh dimension, however, denoting a personal antipathy. He accused the Nationalists of being foreign to Italian tradition, borrowers of foreign ideas from Maurice Barrès and Charles Maurras. He argued that the Italian Nationalists were all decadent literati, had a superficial culture, were ignorant of history, and were even unaware that social oppression imposed by authoritarian regimes always generates 'more terrible explosions.'[52]

In other essays, Croce poured scorn on the cultural efforts of Gentile and indeed all Fascist intellectuals. He practically accused fascism of being indifferent to culture, hostile to its requirements, even fearful of its results. Croce offered an almost Marxist interpretation of fascism on one occasion: 'Fascism has been a movement in defence of the social order, supported first of all by industrialists and by agrarians, and, as such is not only indifferent to culture, but intimately hostile to it, feeling that from culture and thought have come the dangers ... to the social order, but unable to realize that from culture has also come the strength, progress and honour.' The article was also an indictment of Fascist intellectuals; Croce accused them of having become servants of the party, of having promised 'docility and submission ... to the iron discipline of the party,' and of having abandoned 'the independence and the dignity of men of study and thought.'[53]

Croce's harsh feelings towards Nationalist intellectuals remained constant during the regime and were also present in the literary and historical essays. These were mostly written in 1925 and published in *La Critica*, and were later included in the book *History of the Baroque Age*.

In those essays Croce, unlike most other historians of the time, offered a negative judgment on the Baroque period. For Croce, 'the concept of the Baroque' did not designate 'a new and original moment of thought, art or social life.' The book certainly does not fail to indicate the positive aspects of the age, especially in social and natural sciences, but as a whole it claims that the Baroque era, unlike the Renaissance and the Reformation, lacked creative energies. With evident reference to the present time, the book, Croce said, has to be regarded as 'a protest against flirting with the Counter-Reformation, the Absolutism, the rule from above, and the sensual art and decadent literature' that was 'flourishing' in the 1920s, especially among intellectuals and writers favourably disposed towards fascism and nationalism.[54]

New and Old Friends

Croce's increased political activity, his continuous criticism of Gentile, and his open opposition to fascism gained him many insults from the Fascist press, but also many favourable appraisals from other quarters. In March 1925, Adolfo Omodeo wrote his first letter expressing solidarity with Croce and condemning the insults hurled by the nationalists against him. 'No greatness of Italy can be expected from those who forget the duties towards men which have honoured Italy before the world. This too is a sad fruit of that very nationalism, that ignores the history of Italy, and that you are scourging with good reason.'[55]

In July, Gaetano Salvemini, writing a letter to the wife of Luigi Albertini, the editor of *Il Corriere della Sera*, had high praise for Croce and for his political stand. Salvemini was in trouble with the regime for his anti-Fascist activities in Florence, had been in jail for a few weeks, and was followed in his movements by two policemen. During the summer he went to Naples to see his old mentor, Giustino Fortunato. While there, Salvemini also saw Croce and the three men discussed the political situation created by the new policies of Mussolini. In a letter to Piera Albertini, Salvemini made perceptive comments on the present situation of Italy, and the future that likely awaited it under fascism. In the difficulties and uncertainties of the time, Salvemini had one idea clear in his mind: 'Never come to terms with the Communists or with the Fascists, and be ready to pay personally in order to acquire the confidence of honest people.' This was necessary so that, when the collapse of fascism came, Democrats could rightfully claim the political succession. For Salvemini, the only hope for the safety of Italy, in the present and in the future, was 'the emergence of a group of men of strong character, ready to stand fast against fascism, willing to pay any price for their ideals, even to go to jail or to face a worse fate.' Salvemini discussed these ideas with Croce, and the two men reached the same conclusion on how to oppose fascism. Salvemini concluded the letter to Albertini: 'Croce was in agreement; and I believe that, should he be called on to stand the test, he would sustain it with strength and dignity.' It is clear that, by 'the test,' Salvemini meant jail and the danger of death.[56]

In September 1925 Piero Gobetti wrote one of the most insightful articles on Croce, one that characterized well Croce's personality and his position as a public man. Gobetti recognized the value of Croce's anti-fascism and the importance of his participation in the struggle against Mussolini. He also added that, in the present political crisis, 'the constant preoccupation of Croce is to offer a concrete example of personal behavior' as a man and as a citizen rather than as a philosopher and as a politician. When Gobetti considered the anti-fascism of Croce, he made useful distinctions between his political and cultural opposition. In his political opposition, Croce showed preference for moderation. 'In his adhesion to the Liberal Party, in his discipline as a member of this party, Croce is practising a sort of ideal Giolittism,' faithful to parliamentary institutions and to the traditions of the liberal state. But, for Gobetti, there was another aspect of Croce's anti-fascism. Alongside the rational behaviour of a man of good taste, there was 'the rebellion of the European and of the man of culture.' This demanded a different posture. 'In a time in which we are witnessing one of the most radical attempts to break the Italian connection with the European intelligentsia, the cultural position of Croce had to become one of political intransigence.' In this context, 'his impartial and even-handed mind had to put itself on one side only, totally and rigorously.' For Gobetti, Croce was fighting not only for the present but also for the future. 'His preoccupations are geared towards the future: with trepidation and commotion he realizes that in today's battle are involved great destinies; he feels acutely these dangers to civilization.' Gobetti had frequent talks with Croce. Familiar with his ideas and feelings, he not surprisingly concluded that, 'in the security of his own intransigence and in the belief of his own faith,' 'Croce has found the just tone of the rebellion to the present' and the 'ability to stand fast.'[57]

Gobetti's intuitions and judgments found an echo in Croce's own 'Autobiographical Notes' of 1934. There he confessed that his political and cultural activities in opposition were undertaken 'without any hope of practical and immediate effect,' but with the desire to defend the ideals and the heritage of liberal Italy.[58]

Unlike Gobetti, Croce's ties to the ideals of the Risorgimento were strong, and his determination to defend them was well expressed in a long letter that Croce wrote in October 1925 to Vittorio Enzo Alfieri, then only a student but already in political trouble for his anti-fascism. Croce's comments on this occasion have more significance since they were made to a young man of nineteen, not yet a friend of his, and in response to a private letter. 'My liberalism is something which I have in

my blood, as a moral son of the men who made the Italian Risorgimento.' As an heir of that tradition, he felt that he had a duty to fulfil and ideals to defend. 'History will put me among the victors or will throw me among the vanquished. This is not my concern. I feel that I have a place to defend, and for the good of Italy this place has to be defended by somebody, and among these I am called to take my stand.'[59]

The Croce's Diaries

With the advent of the dictatorship, the nature of Croce's diaries changed. Until then, the diaries had offered an intellectual account of his readings and writings; exceptions to this rule were rare. From 1925 on, comments on political events and revelations of personal feelings appear more frequently, and sometimes completely replace other kinds of entries. In October and December 1925, Croce confided to the diaries his sense of oppression, created by the political climate of the time, but he also expressed his determination to remain resolute in his opposition to fascism.[60]

In October 1925, during a trip to Turin and a meeting with Senator Alfredo Frassati, Croce learned of FIAT's effort to acquire control of *La Stampa* and of Mussolini's manoeuvres to change the political orientation of that faithful Giolittian paper. The discussions of that meeting kept Croce awake for a full night and generated one of the most sorrowful meditations in the entire diary. 'The trip to Turin and the meeting with Frassati kept me awake until the morning in sad meditation: painful sense of suffocation at the suppression of freedom of the press, rebellion of the mind at this injustice, violent and hypocritical at the same time.' But then Croce offered a further thought. 'I have examined again,' he wrote,

> the present situation in all its aspects; this examination would have left me in sadness and depression, if I had not remembered something about which I have reasoned as a philosopher: of the mistake, that is, to pose the political question in the extrinsic term, looking to Italy, and fearing or hoping for Her: while the only way to pose those problems is the personal and the moral one, which seeks and finds the solution in the determination of the individual quid agendum, of one's personal duty. And it has not been difficult to be strengthened in the resolution, that it is my duty to continue to do that which I can do, whatever may happen ...

Having solved that problem, Croce had to confront another one.

Croce was concerned that in the future he would no longer be allowed to publish his books in Italy, which would deprive him of the opportunity for 'conversation with contemporaries and fellow countrymen.' He was upset, even nauseated, 'to see around so many transactions and so many treasons,' for momentary and personal advantages. But, despite the fear of a painful future, he also felt comforted by the thought that, in the midst of so much corruption, he was not alone: 'I know other Italians, who feel and think and do like myself.' From this knowledge came the strength to continue the good fight: 'Let us, then, go on with courage and with faith.'[61]

With the gradual consolidation of the authoritarian regime, Croce's meditations in the diaries became more gloomy and even more dramatic, especially in December 1925. In three days that month, the Senate debated and passed the law that destroyed freedom of the press. Croce went to Rome to vote against the measures; he was disgusted by the show of servility offered by the Senate and was tempted to return immediately to Naples; instead, however, he remained 'in order not to leave alone the few friends that are speaking against the law.' In the middle of that debate, he made another sad entry in his diaries after spending 'the evening and part of the night in painful thought, usual by now. The struggle of the opposition is no longer possible, because of the suppression of the newspapers. In the Senate I will vote against the laws before us; and that will be all.' He then underlined the painful dilemma that he and other opponents of the regime faced: 'But it is also impossible to accept the situation; and one cannot choose to die, for the duties that bound us to family, to studies, to society.' Croce found a solution out of this dilemma in the strategy of 'honest dissimulation,' as the moralists of the eighteenth century called this expedient, which was sometimes useful 'in order to bear the difficulties of life.' In this way, Croce found his resolution: 'We have to live, then: to live as if the world went or were starting to go according to our ideals.' In practical terms, his position emphasized the need to keep true 'to our inner life' and not to be unduly concerned about 'the dangers of external life,' because 'these are things that we do not control and for which it is convenient not to worry but rather to trust in providence.'[62]

By ignoring external dangers and trusting instead in Providence, Croce remained faithful to his ideals and maintained the integrity of a free man. This appeal to personal responsibility, this faith in self-reliance, gives a special charm and pathos to Croce's writings during the Fascist era. It also explains his appeal and moral influence in those years, when people often had to face dramatic choices alone.

CHAPTER FIVE

New Forms of Opposition, 1926

Once put into motion, the march of oppression continued inexorably. Under the newspaper law passed in December 1925, editors had to be recognized by the courts before they could assume their positions, while journalists were required to belong to a professional organization, controlled by the state and run by Fascists. Within a few months, the most important papers came under Fascist control, one by one. Some owners were compelled to sell under economic or political pressure. All the liberal editors had to resign and were replaced by more accommodating men.

This affected *La Critica* in a small way and later caused some nuisances. Croce was not a newspaperman, technically speaking, and had no intention now of becoming one under the new conditions. As a result of the stringent press regulations of 1925, Francesco Flora, a literary critic and a trusted friend, acted as 'legal editor' of the periodical from 1926 until 1943. Croce's name continued to be present on the front cover but disappeared from the last page and was replaced by 'Francesco Flora, redattore responsabile.' But *La Critica* never observed the order, imposed on all publications, to mark the years of 'the Fascist Era.'

As a result of the new conformism, Italian papers neither published nor sought Croce's opinions from 1926 on; they tried to avoid even mentioning his name. When that was impossible, literary euphemisms were used. From a subject, Croce became an adjective, as he jokingly put it.

On two occasions at the beginning of 1926, the suppression of freedom of the press involved Croce personally, and both times he took a position against the policies of government and in favour of its political opponents. Late the previous year, under pressure from the government, Luigi Albertini was forced to sell his shares in the *Corriere della Sera* to his partners and to resign as editor of the paper. In 1926 Ugo Ojetti, a well-known writer but a more pliant man and a friend of Mussolini, became the new editor of the paper. During a luncheon in Casati's house, in March 1926, Ojetti invited Croce to write literary essays for the new *Corriere*. Croce's answer was immediate and unequivocal. 'I refused for reasons of political coherence, for respect towards the Albertinis, the former editors, and also, to avoid future difficulties for Ojetti himself, sure that after a while he would have been compelled to stop publishing my essays.'[1]

The other case involved *La Stampa* of Turin, whose editor Alfredo Frassati, was an old and faithful friend of Giolitti. In this case, alluded to in the previous chapter, the government was directly involved; the prefect had closed the paper with the excuse that one of its leading writers had violated military secrets, reporting on army manoeuvres in Piedmont. As a condition of reopening the paper, the government demanded a change in its policy and the ousting of Senator Frassati and the editor-in-chief, Luigi Salvatorelli. In his battle to retain control of the paper, and to refute the accusations against him, Frassati asked Croce and Ruffini to appear before the court as experts and offer to the judges their historical and legal opinions on the matter. But the assistance of Croce as an historian and of Ruffini as a professor of law was not enough to turn the tide against other, more powerful interests. Frassati lost the case, Salvatorelli lost his job, and FIAT acquired full control of the paper.[2]

La Critica

From then on, Croce relied exclusively on his own periodical, *La Critica*, to express his political ideas and to continue his opposition to fascism. Between the end of 1925 and the beginning of 1926, he wrote two essays on Spaventa and De Sanctis, using the opportunity to make those authors his allies against the policies of the government.

In the spring of 1926 a monument to Francesco De Sanctis was erected in Rome. Croce suggested in an essay that a better way to honour De Sanctis was to read and to meditate on his political writings, published in newspapers between 1876 and 1878. Like the present times, Croce wrote, the years that followed the fall of the Destra Storica were ones of general delusion and personal confusion, lack of faith in Parliament, disdain for political parties, moral scepticism, and fatalism. The words of De Sanctis were used by Croce as a warning against the dangers of these feelings, which made possible 'the rule of illiterate and violent persons, with all the consequences that history teaches.' On the origins of such sentiments and the policies that they encourage, and hence on the origins of fascism in Italy, Croce, on this occasion, accepted the theory of fascism as 'a revelation': the victory of fascism had revealed the traditional weakness of the Italian nation. 'It has to do with the old Italy ... with Italy of the decadence that we are still carrying with us ... it has to do with a superficial and vitiated culture.'[3]

During De Sanctis's times there had been a failed attempt against the king. Frightened by that event, the conservatives of the day had clamoured for drastic measures against freedom of expression, demanding its curtailment in the press and even in parliamentary debate. In the spring of 1926 even stronger measures were proposed and enacted with the approval of the nationalists and the conservatives after another failed assassination attempt against Mussolini. Quotations from De Sanctis were employed by Croce to criticize in a direct way those measures and the nationalist writers, who had proclaimed that the original sin from whence all the troubles began was freedom of thought, 'which was attained many centuries ago and was favoured by our greatest writers' as a superb achievement of modern Italy.[4]

During De Sanctis's time and in Croce's period as well, the reactionary intellectuals were busy criticizing Parliament and demanding its abolition on the ground that it was responsible for all the scandals and corruption afflicting society. Croce and De Sanctis offered a different opinion, praising instead the value of debate and political differences: 'On the contrary, I have the firm conviction that these institutions, if they cannot produce all the miracles that we expect of them, are creators of morality, when they are served with sincerity and in the proper spirit. Parliamentary struggles create character; they induce courage and initiative.'

At the end of his essay one also finds a note of self-criticism. Croce confessed that reading the old writings of De Sanctis 'was bound to give us a sense of mortification and of regret, showing us that we have not been prudent, and have not heeded the warnings of those men who were conscious of the dangers fermenting in Italian society.' Croce offered a clear definition of the nature of his anti-fascism. Like De Sanctis, he urged not violent reaction but constant opposition to the regime. 'I want resistance day by day, which is difficult, but also necessary.'[5]

On another occasion soon afterwards, Croce used the letters of Silvio Spaventa to criticize Gentile's historical interpretations and his defence of fascism. In 1926 Giovanni Castellano published a collection of Spaventa's letters, and Croce wrote an introduction to the book that appeared first as an article in the last number of *La Critica* in 1925. Croce intended the essay as 'a protest, because recently we have seen Silvio Spaventa presented as the man and the thinker whose doctrine inspires the theory and the practice of the party that now is dominant in Italy.' Against that assertion, Croce stressed that Spaventa 'in words and deeds was not, and never wanted to be, and never thought to be, anything but a member of the moderate party, founded by Cavour. Moreover, he was a loyal believer in parliamentary democracy ... and in the alternation of the parties in government responsibility.' Croce also reminded the supporters of a one-party state that Spaventa, faithful to liberal ideas, recognized the constitutional role of the opposition and did not call his adversaries anti-national; when he criticized parties or opposed the government, he never asked for the end of freedom, or the abolition of the parties, or persecution of fellow citizens.[6]

To appreciate fully Croce's criticism, one has to remember the legislative activities of the government at this time. In 1925, under Alfredo Rocco's leadership and with Gentile's enthusiastic approval, the powers of the state were immensely increased and the government was given new tools to intervene in the functions of the courts and the civil service. Croce reminded Gentile and Rocco that the constant aim of Spaventa, as a politician and a magistrate, had been 'to assure equal justice to all citizens, and to avoid, or to restrain, the arbitrary acts of the party in power.' Had Spaventa been alive, Croce continued, 'he would have been an opponent, as he had been in his time, of what has been happening in Italy in the last few years, and of the dangers and threats that are being prepared against the independence of the courts and the dignity of civil servants.' Finally, Croce reminded his readers that Spaventa had a different conception of the state than Gentile and Rocco; he did not view 'the State' as an idol, or a new divinity, but as an instrument for the public good, and 'he never subscribed to the conception that those governing are the expression of morality, and he was always respectful of the rights of the individual.'[7]

New Means of Opposition

Even in 1926, with freedom of the press abolished and political debate greatly curtailed, it was still possible to play an opposition role – if one had courage. Croce employed several novel methods of expressing his political opinion and of making known his opposition to government policy.

In February 1926 the Liberal Association of Turin organized a public ceremony in honour of Francesco Ruffini, 'to express the gratitude of all members for the defence of liberal ideas made in the Senate of the Kingdom.' Croce was invited and, unable to travel to Turin, sent the organizers a message, which was then read during the ceremony. 'Please, consider me spiritually present at the ceremony on the 20th in honour of my friend and colleague, Ruffini, to whom we all owe a deep gratitude for the nobility and firmness with which he has defended our common ideals in the Senate and outside the Senate.'[8]

In the spring, Croce read an historical essay at a well-attended session of the congress of the Italian Philosophical Society, held at the University of Milan. Those who gathered in the university's auditorium to hear him speak came more for political reasons than out of any interest in the culture of the sixteenth century, the topic of his essay. That evening, the Liberal Association of Milan organized a reception in Croce's honour, and several speeches were made by Croce and others, despite 'the great array of policemen and carabinieri.' Unhappy with the free discussion taking place at the congress, the Fascist participants created disturbances, and the prefect and the minister of education abruptly suspended and dissolved the congress. That same night, another dinner at which Croce was feted turned into a protest against the arbitrary measures of the authorities.[9]

In 1926 the Academy of Italy was formally established, though it did not begin full operation until 1929. Once again Croce was invited to be a member and again he refused; he advised his friends not to succumb to the 'allurements of that academy' and to resist the appeal to 'our vanity.' Others proved more susceptible to flattery, attracted by the perks and privileges that a position in the Academy conferred.

In Naples, Croce helped to maintain the independence of the Pontanian Academy. At the annual election for the renewal of the executive, in February 1926, despite the efforts of the Fascist faction, the sudden presence 'of members never seen,' and 'a great deployment of political forces,' the Fascist candidate was soundly defeated and 'our candidate,' a Liberal, became president.[10]

The violence and persecution of the Fascist regime caused a political exodus from Italy. Many Italians were compelled to seek freedom and safe refuge in other European nations, especially France. Once there, they created political parties, founded newspapers, and went on to criticize the Italian government, to Mussolini's annoyance. After the assassination attempt against the Duce by Gino Lucetti, who had just returned

from France, Mussolini raised the question of the political activities of
Italian immigrants with the French ambassador, demanding repressive
measures against them. In Italy, Fascist newspapers organized a campaign of insults against former political leaders who were now in exile, *I
fuoriusciti*, as they were called with contempt.

One newspaper in Rome even sent a letter to all known members of
the opposition, asking them, in no uncertain terms, to express their
opinion on the activities of the *fuoriusciti*. The instructions were also precise; the letter had to be returned duly signed. Croce refused to answer
the letter 'out of a question of decency,' and immediately advised his
friends to follow his example. He regarded the request of the newspaper,
as he said in his letters to Gaetano Mosca and Alberto Bergamini, 'gratuitous and offensive' and 'unworthy to be answered, precisely because it
contained ... an imposition and a menace.' While some followed his
advice, others, cowed by past violence, sent the letter back with derogatory remarks about the exiles. The paper published with some relish the
politically correct answers received and in a separate column printed the
names of all those who had refused to answer the unusual survey. The list
of the reprobates was followed at the end by the old battle cry: 'Thou
shalt see me at Philippi.' That promise was kept shortly.[11]

Sometimes even the refusal to express personal views could be a
rather eloquent expression of one's opposition to the regime. In June
1926 Croce was asked by the American periodical *Survey Graphic* to collaborate on a special issue on fascism. Croce replied with a short note. 'I
would like to satisfy your request, but in Italy now the manifestation of
free discussion on the arguments you mention is forbidden; I cannot
decide to take this discussion before a foreign audience. It is necessary
that everyone of us resists and fights as he can, for what little he can, but
here in Italy.' In that simple way and with that short reply, American
readers were informed about the political situation in Italy, and of the
price for making the trains run on time.[12]

Correspondence and Resistance

In 1926 militant politics were no longer possible, nor were newspapers
available for political debate or cultural polemics. Besides his periodical,
Croce used private letters to make his views known, despite the fact that
censorship was already in effect and letters routinely opened. Both
Croce and Fortunato, and some of their friends, were aware that their
private correspondence was tampered with by police authorities. Yet

they continued to write freely and to express their opinions without hesitation. Often Croce used personal letters as an instrument to support, encourage, and reassure friends in need or to condemn a weakness and to deplore sudden changes of position.

In the new and difficult political conditions, many who had at first joined the opposition became discouraged, went to the other side, and then tried to offer excuses and justifications for their conduct. Mario Missiroli was among the first to cross that bridge, announcing his conversion in a famous essay that immediately became infamous.[13] A brilliant newspaperman and a successful editor, Missiroli had been a friend of Croce and Georges Sorel and had published some of their essays. In his better days he had turned *Il Resto del Carlino*, the leading daily of Bologna, into one of the most lively papers in Italy, giving it a liberal flavour. It was in its pages that he had characterized fascism as 'agrarian slavery.' That was in 1921. Now, in 1926, discouraged by the turn of events and unable to endure isolation, he announced, with his usual pyrotechnical elegance, that it was time to accept the victory of Mussolini and the legitimacy of fascism, to recognize that fascism was 'a popular movement' and that Mussolini had remained a socialist. When the article, *Fascism and Monarchy*, was published, Croce made known his negative views on the sudden conversion, writing to Missiroli: 'I would not be sincere, if I were to tell you that your famous article gave me pleasure. There are moments, dear Missiroli, in which there is no need to rationalize, but to accept and to sustain the positions that one has taken; to change them quickly is not useful under any regard.' The trouble with Missiroli, Croce had said on another occasion, was his inability, unlike monuments, to stand still.[14]

Sometimes Croce had to write to trusted friends to reassure them, trying, with his authority, to overcome their sense of solitude and feelings of depression. Roberto Bracco, a well-known playwright of this period and an anti-Fascist member of Parliament, complained to Croce that, among the literate elite of Naples, only Croce and Bracco had been excluded from the committee established to organize the centennial celebration of the Neapolitan painter Domenico Morelli. Croce replied half jokingly, citing an historical anecdote and advising Bracco not to worry; during the meeting of the committee and even during the public celebrations, both of them 'would shine for their absence,' and then everybody would enquire about their whereabouts and know the reasons for their exclusion.[15]

On another occasion, the tone had to be more solemn and the advice more austere. In a gloomy moment of his life, made gloomier by a conversation with Giustino Fortunato, Bracco received from his friend the right words to restore and to fortify his faith. With his usual and prophetic pessimism, Fortunato had assured Bracco that fascism would last for another twenty years. The prediction had plunged Bracco into a state of sadness and created a feeling of 'profound solitude.' With his usual common sense, Croce reassured Bracco that the future lies always on the knees of Jupiter, and that nobody, not even Fortunato, knew how long fascism would last. But long or short, during that period they had to keep faith with their ideals and to continue in their opposition, for in no other way could a different and better society come about. The letter has a religious tone, sounding almost like a confession. 'The opposition is now apparently weakened or even nullified, but only apparently. The Fascists are doing their share to keep it alive and to increase its size by offending the most sacred feelings of man's dignity.' Croce urged Bracco to remain strong, trusting in the virtue of moral forces. 'The men of our generation and of our faith have to continue in what we are doing: give the example and stand firm.' 'We shall or we shall not see better times, this is of secondary importance: for the moment, we have them in our heart, and this is enough to comfort us and to reassure us.'[16]

During the spring of 1926, Salvemini, as a result of the continuous harassment suffered for his political activities against fascism, decided to emigrate to London, before it was too late. Croce and Salvemini were very different men, and agreement between them was not always possible. In their relationship, cordiality had often been followed by bursts of acerbity, sometimes unjustified on both sides. Even in this period, Croce was, perhaps, a little too supercilious when he refused to sign a petition in favour of Salvemini with the excuse that it was an exaggeration to call Salvemini, as his colleagues in Florence did, 'one of the greatest historians in Europe.' Despite this, when Fortunato, on behalf of Salvemini, asked Croce for a letter of reference to a British university, Croce agreed to the request without hesitation, producing, as Fortunato informed Salvemini in June, 'a very sincere' and 'efficacious ... piece, which is a critical appraisal of your abilities as an historian and teacher of history.'[17]

Not only was the testimonial sincere, it was also a model of its kind; the praises were concrete and not vague, and reflected Salvemini's personal qualities. Croce wrote that 'Gaetano Salvemini holds one of the foremost places in the most recent phase of Italian historiography.' He reminded the British authorities that he had written an essay on Salvemini in 1915, lauding his achievements. 'Salvemini brings to his work a happy union of philological discipline with political, economic and social experience, and a constant effort to discover the reality concealed under the usual formulas and generalizations, in a spirit of great impartiality and open mindedness.' Croce did not hide their different philosophical ideas. But their differences, Croce said, only enhanced his opinion of Salvemini. 'I shall only add that he brings to his historical studies a deep feeling of humanity and enthusiasm for morality and justice, which can be truly called Mazzinian.' Croce did not fail to mention either Salvemini's qualities as a teacher or the reason for his political troubles. 'All his students consider him as the best of teachers; and as to the causes of his leaving Italy, these are to be found in the conditions of the present political struggle, in which he has kept faith with his old liberal and democratic ideals.' Not surprisingly, in thanking Croce, Salvemini expressed his satisfaction: 'You have said in it everything that I could have wished.'[18]

Sometimes it was Croce who expressed sadness and depression in his letters and needed the comfort of his friends. In March 1926 Gobetti died in Paris, and the following month Amendola died in Cannes, both victims of political persecution and Fascist violence. In April, Croce confessed to Casati, now a close friend, 'I am very sad at the news about the health of Amendola,' adding: 'It is a great sadness: it seems there is little hope.' But, though he was expecting it, when he received the news of Amendola's death, he was overwhelmed by grief and, as usual at such times in his life, he remained unable to write or even to concentrate for a few days. In this depressed condition, Croce needed to express his sorrow to a kindred soul. 'And now I have gone back to my routine: that routine which is my salvation, now. But in the depth of my soul I have the image, as a reproach, of poor Amendola. Why to live, when others die like this? When our friends are thus sacrificed? I will overcome even this pang; but it is a pang.'[19]

After the death of Amendola, a group of Liberal friends, under the leadership of Nitti and Albertini, organized a trust fund to provide financial assistance to his family and a good education to his three sons. Croce and Fortunato gave a generous contribution to the fund, and when the sons moved into the house of an uncle in Naples, they offered the three young men their friendship and intellectual support and welcomed them into their homes.

The affection and support of family and friends became a necessity in the struggle against the Fascist regime. This kind of solidarity was vital

especially among Liberals, Democrats, and Socialists, who could not rely
on the resources of a well-organized party, or the support of a foreign
country, or the assistance of the Catholic Church. Material assistance
was certainly important, but it was not enough to assure the continuation of the struggle. Anti-fascism was more than organized political
opposition. The resistance to the Fascist regime demanded a daily fight
within each person, the acceptance of years of solitude, social ostracism,
and even persecution. To continue the struggle, to remain faithful to
the ideals, to have hope in a different future, required personal commitment and moral energy. The letters of anti-Fascists to their families or to
their friends reveal that strength of character and a religious devotion to
the cause was essential to philosophers, to workers, and to simple people. In Croce's case, to maintain his sanity and keep up his spirits,
Croce, besides the affection of his family and the support of his friends,
relied on work and daily routine, which allowed him to overcome bouts
of depression, sadness, and personal suffering.

The Zamboni Incident and the Fascist Response

In 1926, at the end of October, in Bologna, the fourth attempt against
Mussolini's life occurred. During a parade to celebrate the anniversary
of the March on Rome, Anteo Zamboni, a young man of sixteen, fired
on Mussolini, missing the target. The attempt was regarded with suspicion then and has remained mysterious. The police preferred to blame
Zamboni and, it seems, with good reason. More important for the
future of Italy, however, was the reaction of the government and of Mussolini himself. The government used the case, and the emotions it created, to abolish the few remaining fundamental liberties.[20]

That same night, writing on a piece of paper and in pencil, Mussolini
issued Draconian orders to the police for the protection of the Fascist
regime, thus contributing to an overwrought atmosphere and almost
inviting and sanctioning violence against the leaders of the opposition.
Within days, the government approved, and Parliament ratified, almost
without discussion, a series of resolutions that destroyed the liberal state
and created a dictatorial government. As a result of these new laws, all
political parties of the opposition, their papers and organizations, were
dissolved and banned; members of the Aventine Secession were formally expelled from the House of Deputies and lost their parliamentary
immunity; the police were given the power to deny new passports, to fire
on those crossing borders, and to banish opponents of the regime to

small towns (in the jargon of the time, to *confino*); the death penalty was reintroduced for crimes against the state and for attempts against the person of the king and the prime minister; a Special Tribunal for the Defence of the State was created outside the normal courts, empowered to deal with 'anti-national activities' and to apply martial law.[21]

When the news of the Bologna incident became known in the rest of Italy, the Fascist Party organized 'retaliations' against the leaders and the parties of the opposition. Catholic organizations and even a few bishops suffered the same treatment, prompting the pope to condemn 'the tempest of violence and devastation against people, property and institutions.' That night and the days following, Fascist squads invaded and destroyed the offices and newspapers of the opposition parties. People were assaulted and beaten in the streets or inside their own houses, and often compelled to leave their residences. The city of Naples was not spared and had its own share of violence. During the night of 31 October and the morning of 1 November, the houses or the apartments of Amadeo Bordiga, Roberto Bracco, Benedetto Croce, and Arturo Labriola were invaded and ransacked; papers were burned and books damaged. The initiative came from the Fascist Party. The public authorities allowed it to happen, though they, it seems, did not encourage it.[22]

Once again the events proved that a citizen had no legal protection against violence organized or sponsored by the Fascist Party or even by one of its factions. On many occasions the aim of the violence was not to kill an opponent but to generate fear among the population, to humiliate the victims, to destroy their will for resistance and cow them into submission. Like their comrades in other Italian cities, the Neapolitan Fascists wanted to give Croce 'a lesson,' as it was then fashionable to call such actions against opponents of the regime.

The Invasion of Croce's House

Croce's house was invaded at four in the morning by more than a dozen individuals, arriving in a truck, while Croce and his household of eight women (wife, four daugthers, and three servants) were deep in sleep. The invaders deceived the doorkeeper, and then terrorized with guns the other servants, compelling them to open the doors. Once inside the house, they broke doors and windows, smashed glasses and vases, and damaged paintings and a piano. No one was hurt, nor was the main collection of books touched. When Croce and his wife appeared, those in command shouted Fascist slogans and hurled insults and threats against them. By all accounts, Croce remained calm and the women did not show fear. Indeed, Adelina Croce, Benedetto's wife, behaved bravely. She rebuked the intruders, who, believing they had accomplished their task, or feeling ashamed and afraid to be recognized, turned off the main light switch and fled in the confusion, leaving the family to contemplate the ruins.[23]

The police were immediately called by neighbours, but did not arrive until five hours later. Soon afterwards, the danger passed, soldiers appeared and were put on duty to protect the house against a repetition of the violence. During the day, the prefect, who was on cordial terms with Croce, visited the residence and offered the government's excuses, at the same time promising a full investigation and severe punishment of the culprits, once arrested. As it turned out, however, the majority of these thugs, some of them belonging to middle-class families, were already known to the police but were left undisturbed throughout the Fascist regime; only after the war did the state prosecutor lay charges against them, and then Croce and his wife refused to pursue the matter. The damage to the house was estimated at twenty thousand lire. More important than material damage was the offence given to Croce and his family, and to Italian culture.[24]

At the time of the incident, the government ordered a press ban, but the news travelled fast. The shock was especially great among the cultural elite and among Croce's friends, old and new. No one was more shocked and saddened than Giustino Fortunato. Though he was then almost blind and enfeebled by illness, he was among the first to arrive at Croce's house once the incident became known. He visited Croce during the following days to show support and to offer his affection. He wrote to several correspondents; to all, he praised Croce's 'great serenity,' condemned the 'despicable case,' and lamented 'the offence received.' In his letters Fortunato contrasted the nobility of Croce with 'the foolishness' spoken in those days by Fascist leaders against Croce and the other intellectuals who had signed his manifesto the year before. The possibility of a visit to the king was discussed but soon discarded. On his own, Fortunato sent a letter of protest to Tommaso Tittoni, the president of the Senate, pointing out the injury done to the institution itself besides the personal offence to Croce. Prodded by Fortunato, Tittoni spoke to Mussolini and then wrote to Fortunato a hypocritical letter: Mussolini deplored the incident and had assured the president of the Senate that the case was the work of unknown elements, which the police had been unable to identify yet. No wonder the old politician lamented to all 'the terrible nature of these interminable times.'[25]

The incident offers another instance of Croce's iron discipline. In his diaries, at the end of the description of the night's events, we find this revealing passage: 'In the morning I resumed historical readings, and took notes from books previously read; but there was such a throng of friends, who came to ask news about the facts of last night, that I could barely continue the work, from which I had resolved not to be distracted.' These historical readings led to Croce's *History of Italy*. The notations in the diaries for the following days also show that Croce, despite the turmoil caused by the invasion, tried to carry on with his normal routine, but without much success, until, unable to endure any longer the well-intentioned interruptions, he shut himself in his library and left to his wife the task of dealing with the visitors and their questions.[26]

Despite continuous distractions, Croce wrote letters to his closest friends, informing them of the incident and also reassuring them of his safety and that of his family. Giolitti was among the first to be informed. The letter is important because it shows how close the friendship between the two men had become, but also because it provides a better understanding of the feelings and ideas, which motivated Croce's opposition to fascism and underlay his next book, the *History of Italy*. 'While I inform you of this incident, it is sweet to turn my thoughts to you, representative of the old, honest and liberal Piedmont, and to renew in my mind the sentiment of Italian brotherhood, which united the patriots and the liberals of Piedmont with those of Naples, to whom I feel united not only by historical memories but also by family ties. It seems that now in our turn we are called to sustain the same trials, that they suffered at the time of the "Holy Faith"!'[27]

As was to be expected, the letter to Casati had a different tone and even contained some light-hearted remarks. Croce gave him all the details without exaggeration of any sort. He even noted the restraint shown by the intruders. 'They could have beaten me; I was in pajamas and barefoot; they did not do it; therefore this was not part of their orders.' He could not resist, however, a polemical joke about the philosophy of Gentile, as the theoretician of the ethical state. 'I console myself with the happy idea that finally I had the honour of receiving a visit from the ethical state.'[28]

In his letter to Casati and on a few other occasions at this time, Croce wrote in a more intimate tone, revealing his deep feelings for his wife and family. 'Adelina and the girls,' he told Casati, 'rose to the occasion.'

Similarly, to V.E. Alfieri, a much younger friend than Casati, Croce wrote: 'The house has suffered significant damage: but luckily my wife and my first little daughter, who saw the havoc, behaved bravely and did not allow themselves to be cowed by the scene.' Months later, when Croce was recounting the events to Luigi Russo mentioning the quick wit of his wife that night, Russo was surprised to hear him say: 'I really love Adelina'.[29]

The political struggle against the Fascist regime destroyed close friendships and other relationships of long standing. It hardened feelings. At the same time, however, it brought kindred people closer. Ties to trusted friends acquired new meaning and became deeper. For those in jail or on the run, the love of a woman was the greatest gift, a shield against the blows of fortune. In the sadness of the times, Croce, like others, was heartened by the affection of his family, the constant support of his wife giving him new strength to continue his fight.

The invasion of Croce's house was widely regarded not only as a violation of a private residence but as an offence to the most outstanding representative of Italian culture. It was a sign of the return of barbarian times, a warning to all that, in the new Italy under Mussolini, there were no sanctuaries and no individual was safe or protected by special immunity. After the incident, many wrote to Croce, expressing solidarity, enquiring about the safety of his family, deploring the event, condemning the violence, and openly blaming the government. For Croce, the incident became a moral and political victory.

Casati travelled to Naples as soon as he received the news of the invasion. He went not only as an old friend but also as the official representative of the Liberal Party. With Casati, Croce discussed the possibility of his leaving Naples and going to live in Turin, his wife's home city. But his wife opposed the move with the argument that Naples, despite everything else, offered Croce a more congenial atmosphere than Turin. The presence of his friend must have bolstered Croce's spirits. A few days later he wrote to Casati to assure him that he had regained his customary equanimity. 'The usual disposition of the spirit has come back, as it is expressed in the old saying: do what you ought to, come what may.'[30]

The incursion into Croce's house had international repercussions, as we can gather from the letters between Croce and his German friend Karl Vossler. Vossler expressed his astonishment at what had happened to Croce and to other Neapolitan intellectuals, some of whom were also his friends. He informed Croce about the reaction of scholars in Germany and other nations, and told him that liberal intellectuals in Europe and in America wanted to organize a public protest and an international show of support. 'I have had with [Joel Elias] Springarn an exchange of telegrams. From America they would like to send a protest against this violence.' On a more personal note, Vossler informed Croce that his old friend Springarn, the American educator and social crusader, for many years professor of comparative literature at Columbia and later president of the National Association for the Advancement of Colored People, had phoned his wife, who was vacationing in Paris, and had asked her to go to Naples and to offer the Croce family whatever assistance was needed.[31]

To understand Croce's reactions during those days and also to gauge the views of other people, Vito Galati's memoirs are an important source. Galati was an old friend of Croce and a literary critic of some repute; he was also a member of Parliament for the Italian Popular Party. As soon as he heard the news of the incursion, he went to Naples. When he arrived at the railway station, a common friend advised him to avoid Croce's house, for the simple reason that, at the door, 'there are policemen, who monitor those who enter and those who leave.' Undeterred, Galati went to the house; he found Croce saddened by the experience, showing in his face the signs of 'the insult done to the inviolability of his domicile.'

During the discussion, several alternatives were discussed. Croce expressed the desire to resign from the Senate. Galati was quick to dissuade him, pointing out the inopportuneness of the gesture. 'I believe you should not do it. The position of Senator offers a little personal guarantee against future violence, still possible; also, we need somebody who can speak for the opposition in the Senate.' Croce agreed that future violence was a real possibility, and he never resigned from the Senate. Galati, for his part, suggested the possibility of expatriation at a later date, something he had been contemplating for himself. To that, Croce's response was immediate. 'No, it is not possible. We need to remain here, in our country. We need to fight where the struggle is most difficult.' But there was also another reason. 'I cannot tear my family from its normal environment. My daughters need to be educated in an Italian climate, with its tradition, its customs, and its sensibilities. It is necessary to remain here.' Galati, too, never emigrated; after that discussion, the thought disappeared from his mind.[32]

The ravaging of Croce's house also shocked those Fascists who had retained a measure of humanity or remembered the friendly relations of the old days. The news created a stir in Gentile's mind; after learning of the event, he asked for more precise information from Fausto

Nicolini, a close personal friend. Gentile also wrote immediately to Croce's publisher Giovanni Laterza and mentioned again 'the very disturbing facts.'[33] It must have been a sad moment for Gentile. In the past, he would have been the first to be informed of such an event, and the first to show support in person or by letter. Now, political disagreement compelled him to ask a third party about his old friend, whom he once regarded almost as a brother.

Political events had separated Croce from Gentile, and no personal feelings would be able to reduce the gulf between them. It was different with other people. Resistance to fascism was able to cement new solidarity, to overcome old rivalries, even among those who in the past had fought bitter battles. Croce received many expressions of support from his old adversaries; none was as significant as the letter he received from the historian and Socialist Guglielmo Ferrero. It revealed the feelings now uniting all those who opposed the policies of Mussolini, as well as the ideals sustaining the anti-Fascist struggle 'among the few who could and wanted to resist.' In the past, Croce and Ferrero had belonged to different schools: One was a liberal and a Hegelian, the other a socialist and a positivist. Once they had disagreed, and with some bitterness, on questions of history and philosophy. But 'now,' Ferrero wrote, 'we have to forget our old little disputes with which we tormented ourselves in the happy years,' because, as members of the opposition, another task was upon them: 'to fulfill in solidarity the common and dangerous duty towards our unhappy country.' In full agreement with Ferrero's feelings, Croce replied that it was no longer the time to indulge in scholastic debates. Instead, it was urgent to defend 'the most basic principles of the spiritual life' and 'to protect our dignity as free men,' forsaking 'peace and honour ... come what may.'[34]

If the aim of the Neapolitan Fascists was to cow Croce and to put a stop to his political activity against the regime, they failed. On the afternoon of the assault on his house, while demonstrations were still taking place in the streets of Naples, Croce went for a long walk and visited an old friend; he did so on his own to show in a public manner his 'undisturbed tranquility.' Some of his younger friends were not as calm, and, worried about possible incidents, followed him at a distance, armed with walking sticks.

When later in the day Giorgio Amendola, the eldest son of Giovanni, went to visit Croce and his family, the time was spent not in lamentation but in discussing his own future. During the conversation, Amendola expressed his desire to become acquainted with the writings of his father and the works of Marx. On his part, Croce encouraged him to visit again and to make use of the library, if he wished.[35]

When, three weeks later, the Senate debated the 'Law for the Protection of the State,' Croce went to Rome, sat beside Ruffini, and applauded his speech in defence of the old Albertine Statuto; together, they then voted against the government bill. The vote of the Senate provided the occasion for another protest. When the official record of that sitting was published, by mistake Croce's name did not appear under the list of those who had voted against the bill, but among those who had abstained. Immediately, Croce sent a letter to the president of the Senate, pointing out the mistake, asking for rectification, and demanding a written reply. With the vote coming so close after the invasion of his house, Croce wrote, he did not want to leave the impression that he had abstained from voting out of fear.[36]

In his memoirs of 1944, Croce recognized that the invasion of his house had produced an unintended result: 'That deed was beneficial to me, because foreign newspapers discussed it, and even exaggerated it; from abroad I received telegrams, letters and even visitors.' Croce had known that Mussolini was advised by his political informers in foreign countries that such acts were not helpful to the regime and to his personal reputation. As a result, while Croce was to suffer further harassment of various kinds, he 'was no longer threatened physically' – even though that same month, in 1926, the threat of another incursion into his house compelled him to move some papers to a safer place for the time being.[37]

Croce's social life now changed a great deal. Two policemen were put near his house; they were there to protect his safety, the regime said, but in fact their purpose was 'to monitor visitors to his house and to follow him when he went out.' Croce took their presence in stride, even reacting with humour. After a while he approached them, told them his usual itinerary, and even advised them about how to follow him, or how to find him again should they happen to lose sight of him, as happened every time he took a taxi. But, as a result of the police presence, from then on the cheerful group that accompanied Croce in his nightly walks in the old city streets began to dwindle, until only a few close friends remained to keep him company.[38]

Another sign of the changed times was the gradual end of the social gatherings that took place every Sunday, like a cultural institution, in Croce's house. In the old days, these informal meetings had been open to all; it was an opportunity for young writers to meet famous scholars and to exchange views with them. Foreign visitors had a chance to establish connections with Italian colleagues. For Croce, these guests were a part of his extended intellectual family. After the invasion of his house and the arrival of the policemen, some habitual visitors began to avoid the Sunday gatherings, and soon these gatherings came to an end. Yet, at the same time, Croce acquired new friends and welcomed different visitors during the week. The old scholars were replaced by intellectuals of the new generation, critical of fascism and not afraid of persecution. Croce's young daughter observed the arrival of these different and younger people. 'Often there arrived mysterious visitors, who gathered in father's study for talks that we imagined dramatic and passionate.'[39]

The same phenomenom occurred in other Italian cities. Many who once had been on cordial terms with Croce, and would have regarded it as a great honour to be seen and to speak with him, began to avoid him, showing 'fear to be seen in my company' though they were ready to offer him 'friendly and warm greetings in deserted streets and in solitary corridors.' Such sudden changes in personal behaviour and public mores, which are the usual fruits of dictatorial regimes, would be described by Croce in great detail in his *History of Europe*, written in 1931. For example, in Croce's description of French society under Louis Napoleon, particularly its observations on the turncoats, servility, and corruption of the second empire, a reader senses a reference to Italian society under Mussolini. This was another example of history as contemporary history, of the present illuminating the past.[40]

The invasion of his house and the consolidation of Mussolini's power also had a profound effect on Croce's frame of mind. Among the general public, Croce has always been regarded as a man of Olympian serenity. In fact, however, his diaries and personal correspondence at this time, as throughout his life, reveal an individual of deep passion, subject to periods of emotional torment for personal and especially political reasons. In his 'Autobiographical Notes' of 1934, he wrote that 'during fascism my life was full of anguish, a feeling of insecurity, an incubus of destruction and ruin, and I lost since then that trust in awakening in the morning, that turning of the eyes towards the world and seeking the things beloved, that re-entering among them with joy.'[41]

Yet the Fascist regime had no less significant impact on Croce's intellectual development and political evolution. On the same page of the 'Notes,' we find this statement: 'But, despite all this, my mental vivacity was rather increased than diminished.' Fascism gave Croce almost a second youth. The necessity of opposition spurred him with new vigour;

the sense of duty increased his determination. As he confessed to Luigi Russo in those years: 'You see: I had reached an age in which a man can grow childish from too much applause. Providence now has brought us this fascism that opposes me, that torments me, and persecutes me; but at the same time it rejuvenates me, and gives me a renewed vigour to fight.' Eugenio Garin made the same observation and noted the outstanding results: 'In the fire of the struggle against fascism Croce found himself again'; 'to fascism Croce owed a second youth, but also a splendid maturity of thought.'[42]

Close to the end of his life, in an address to the students of his Historical Institute, Croce stated that fascism had changed his life in fundamental ways. 'Even I owe some gratitude to fascism because it infused me with a new youth, filling me with increased activity and with fighting spirit; it compelled me to reconsider political problems, which otherwise I would not have studied with a similar anxiety and so in depth; it made me feel that the work of the thinker and of the writer ought to be one with that of the citizen and of the man.'[43]

Indeed, for a minority of Italians, a heightened sense of personal responsibility was one of the unintended results of fascism. It was this new-found moral energy that sustained the resistance of opponents of the regime, whether they were in Italy, in exile, or in jail. Not only Croce but also other political leaders, after the triumph of fascism and the defeat of the opposition, felt compelled to recognize the mistakes made and, more important, to rethink their political ideas and goals, in the process giving a new value to the concepts of freedom and democracy.

CHAPTER SIX

Towards a New Definition of Liberalism, 1927–1928

By the end of 1926, liberal Italy had died. Mussolini had consolidated his power and created the legal instruments for the continuation of his dictatorship. Political parties had been outlawed, and freedom of the press destroyed. The opposition had been disarmed and Parliament reduced to impotence. In 1927 it became almost impossible to undertake any open political action; it was also dangerous to express critical opinions in personal letters or in public places. Civil employees could lose their jobs if they expressed views contrary to government policy. Besides a powerful and revitalized police division in the Ministry of the Interior, under the direct responsibility of the chief of police, a new and efficient secret police organization, ominously and mysteriously called OVRA, was created with the aim of repressing any sign of anti-fascism and controlling any expression of dissent. In a short while, it collected files on more than one hundred thousand people, including Fascist leaders, and built an impressive web of special agents, spies, and informers whose reach extended throughout the country and even abroad.[1]

Police Surveillance

In the new political situation, even a peaceful man like Croce was under police surveillance. Not only did two agents stationed in front of his house, follow his movements and take note of his visitors, but police began to monitor Croce's private correspondence after 1926, creating files on him and his correspondents. To this end, they recruited spies among his acquaintances and those who frequented his library. In similar conditions, other people felt intimidated and became frightened. Croce responded differently: he went to the prefect and told him that he was aware of the government's special attention but was not afraid of it and had no intention of changing his way of life. 'I went to the High Commissioner, Castelli, to discuss various things, and in particular to tell him that it is ridiculous that the authorities trouble to monitor my house and my person for fear that I may escape abroad.'[2]

Michelangelo Castelli, a senator, had been and still was on cordial terms with Croce. By a simple visit Croce shifted the burden and put Castelli in an awkward personal and social position; it turned the prefect from a representative of the state into a symbol of persecution. Castelli's position, however, was more awkward than Croce suspected at the time. The authorities' fear was real and originated in higher places. The chief of police had been misinformed by spies that Croce was planning not a normal trip abroad but rather 'a clandestine expatriation' and 'participation in an anti-fascist meeting to be held in Paris in January 1927.' To block these plans, Chief of Police Arturo Bocchini, on behalf of the minister of the interior – in this case, Mussolini himself – recommended 'utmost sagacious vigilance' of Croce's movements to all prefects, including all border police stations, on land and sea. He also sent a special telegram to the prefect of Naples, ordering him 'to arrange immediate measures of vigilance to avoid absolutely that [Croce's] planned trip could take place.'[3]

Despite the government harassment, Croce did not take refuge in an ivory tower, nor was he unwilling to take personal risks. He kept in touch with kindred people through gathering at his home, personal correspondence, and frequent trips. Writing about his anti-Fascist experience in Naples, from 1926 to 1930, Eugenio Reale, a prominent Communist after the war but then still a democrat, revealed that during those years he and his university friends, Marxists and liberal alike, regarded Croce as a teacher, treated him 'with respect and admiration, and visited his house often with one excuse or another,' finding him 'always liberal with encouragement and help.' Giorgio Amendola, too, has confirmed that Croce in that period 'was always willing and pleased to receive my anti-Fascist friends,' whether from Naples or out of town, like Nello Rosselli. From northern Italy, Eugenio Colorni and Aldo Garosci, who were then still students but who later played prominent roles in the Resistance, one in the Socialist Party and the other in Giustizia e Libertà, made trips to Naples and visits to Croce's house.[4]

Travels

In the changed political conditions, Croce's increased number of trips in Italy and his forays abroad were a form of political activity, a way to demonstrate the continued existence of the opposition. At the same time, in the absence of a free press and with government control over his correspondence, Croce's visits to his friends in other cities were a means to keep in touch, to share news, and to offer support. Starting in 1927, month by month Croce's diaries register his trips to Rome, Florence, Milan, and Turin. Unfortunately but understandably, few names are mentioned, and often details are not given, but the presence of words like 'lively conversations' 'large gathering of friends' are enough to reveal the nature and purpose of the meetings. Police records, for their part, show that Croce's movements were closely monitored from one city to the next.[5]

Throughout the Fascist regime, the political value of Croce's presence in these and other cities was enhanced by social activities during his visits. He did not go incognito, and he certainly did not remain closed in his room once there. People knew that he was in town and came to see him even from the surrounding areas. Often his guests organized social gatherings for him, turning lunch and dinner or country excursions into occasions for political discussion. A great walker by nature, he strolled along the streets, went to libraries, and visited bookstores, always in the company of old friends or university students. His presence was noticed by the authorities and naturally became a topic of conversation in newsrooms, academic halls, and private houses. The opponents of the regime who saw him or heard him may have taken heart from his presence; others may have been encouraged to read his books or to discuss his ideas.

In 1928, besides making trips to various northern Italian cities, Croce travelled to the province of Basilicata, the land of Nitti and Fortunato, ostensibly to do research for a biography of Isabella Morra, a poet of the Renaissance involved in a tragic love story. The political importance of the trip rests with the warm reception that the local people offered Croce wherever he went. He visited numerous towns and everywhere was received with respect and cordiality. When he stopped at the town where the Morra castle was located, he was 'greeted by many gentle people of the place,' and these were joined by others who had 'arrived from the surrounding area.' After the visit to the castle, Croce and his friends spent the evening in the house of the local doctor, among 'many guests and in lively and varied conversation.' Many of these guests had been personal friends and political supporters of Nitti and Fortunato; the lively conversations were not confined to poetry of the Renaissance and romantic tragedies.[6]

But the most important foray in 1928 was Croce's trip in September to

Paris in the company of his daughter and the publisher Giovanni Laterza. That trip took place despite some unpleasant and unnerving incidents that were connected with his passport. Given the report received from spies the year before, the police likely feared that Croce would take advantage of a visit abroad to go into permanent exile.

In April two young men, probably secret agents, entered the house of Croce's brother-in-law in Turin and tried to ascertain the date of Croce's planned trip to that city and the names of those who usually visited him there. In July, while the Croce family was enjoying their vacation in Piedmont, a police officer arrived and asked for Croce's passport, which he had obtained in Naples seemingly without difficulty. The event prompted Croce to send a letter of protest to the prefect of Turin, demanding 'to know the reason for this trick.' Two days later a captain of the Royal Carabinieri appeared, assuring Croce 'that the withdrawal of the passport was the result of a misunderstanding on the part of Turin's police officials' and promising quick restitution. Despite the evident provocation and intimidation, the trip to Paris took place as planned. In fact, as we now know from police reports, the renewal of Croce's passport had been granted not as a matter of course but only after the prefect of Naples asked and received authorization from Bocchini, the chief of police. As a result, Croce's departure from Naples and his arrivals in Milan, Turin, and Paris were noted by police, following Bocchini's instructions that Croce 'be followed with discretion.'[7]

Once in Paris, Croce did historical research at the Bibliothéque Nationale, saw French scholars, and shopped in bookstores; he and his daughter also visited all the places usually included in a well-planned tourist trip. But they also did something unusual for tourists; on the day of their arrival, they went 'to Le Père Lachaise to visit the tomb of poor Gobetti,' as a sign of respect for a fallen comrade but also as an expression of friendship for his wife, Ada, now one of their most intimate friends. The next day, they made another visit of political significance: 'With Elena I went to see the Nitti family.' After an initial stay in Switzerland, Nitti had moved to Paris, where he spent most of his exile years. Croce had visited Nitti the year before in Switzerland on his way to Germany, and he continued to see him every time he went to Paris. During their conversations, with his usual certainty, Nitti showed Croce financial statistics and economic calculations which proved beyond a doubt 'that fascism could not last, and would soon be buried under a financial crush.'[8]

That evening, in his hotel, Croce received a visit from another political friend: 'Sforza came from Brussels, and I spent the evening with him.' Croce and Sforza had been colleagues in the last cabinet of Giolitti, and they would be together again in the government of Badoglio in 1944. Croce also was visited by Luigi Sturzo, the former leader of the Popular Party whom Mussolini and the Vatican, joined in an unholy alliance, had compelled to emigrate. The notation in the *Taccuini* is brief and terse but eloquent: 'I received Don Sturzo, who spoke with great nobility.' Croce's admiration for 'that little Sicilian priest,' for whom Giolitti had no sympathy, is obvious and shows the solidarity among former adversaries created by fascism.[9]

Those are the only names mentioned on that occasion in the rather concise prose of the *Taccuini*. But we can be sure that Croce met other people, as we can judge from a tantalizing entry: 'In the morning I received many visits.' From other sources we know that he also met the Socialist leaders Filippo Turati and Claudio Treves. In those Parisian meetings, besides the usual cultural discussions, various accounts show that the main topics of interest were the political situation in Italy and the personal condition of the exiles and their families in Italy.[10]

Helping Anti-Fascists

In the absence of political parties and in the presence of an oppressive police apparatus, even personal relations could become an expression of anti-fascism. Indeed, in helping friends in need for political reasons, Croce was at his best, for in such cases solidarity had to be direct and immediate, requiring personal intervention. This was best illustrated in 1927 in his relations with Giustino Fortunato and Ada Gobetti.

Not cowed by the returned 'Bourbonic times,' Giustino Fortunato continued to write letters to Nello Rosselli and to Giovanni Ansaldo even after these two young scholars and publicists were arrested and sent to jail. Despite having 'the honour of some police surveillance,' he kept in touch with his political friends, freely expressing his opinions, to old and young alike, and always lamenting 'the new follies of those in power.' When Nello Rosselli was arrested Fortunato thought that he had been the cause of this misfortune, having sent him a parcel with the new introduction to his old book, *Pagine e Ricordi*, whose publication had been censored by police authorities. Full of apprehension and remorse for the anguish caused to the Rosselli family, Fortunato asked Croce for advice. Croce was prompt to help his old friend; he visited his house frequently, reassured and calmed him, and finally advised him to write to the prefect explaining the innocence of Rosselli and assuming full responsibility in the case.

When it became evident that Rosselli had been arrested not because of Fortunato but as a reprisal for the activities of his brother, Carlo, who had organized the escape of Turati to France the year before, Fortunato, in several letters, expressed gratitude to Croce for the 'fraternal advice received and for the support,' adding in one: 'You have saved me literally from folly, and worse from ridicule.' Fortunato also mentioned the case, and the help received from Croce, in his correspondence with other people, which must have increased Croce's reputation. In a letter to Giovanni Ansaldo, a newspaperman with a wide circle of friends, Fortunato's praise for Croce was explicit: 'He was my special benefactor in the first two weeks of June, among the most terrible of my life.'[11]

If Fortunato called Croce a benefactor, for Ada Gobetti, the young widow of Piero, Croce became 'the only steady and reliable point' in those uncertain and tormented times. Croce had met the Gobettis before, but only in 1927, and after the death of her husband in France, did they begin a friendship which also involved all the members of their families. Besides the championing of a political cause, their correspondence reveals a domestic Croce, always solicitous and deeply concerned, in small and large matters, with the health and welfare of those he loved and respected. After the death of her husband in 1926 and the birth of their son, Ada Gobetti lived like 'a wounded beast'; she closed herself 'in a painful seclusion' and felt 'without support and without a guide.' At that moment Croce offered Ada his support and the friendship of his family.

That friendship played no small part, she recalled years later, in giving her new strength and making it possible to overcome her pain. The constant affection of Croce and his family helped her to return to cultural and political activities, to a new marriage and to a happy family life. During that time, Croce encouraged her to write and to translate, read her manuscripts, and found publishers for her books. He 'followed my work with paternal satisfaction,' she said, not only during the Fascist regime but even after the war, despite their disagreement about the policy of the Party of Action to which Ada belonged. It was Croce who first encouraged and then persuaded her to write and to publish her war diary of 1943 to 1945, so other Italians could learn what had happened in Piedmont in those years and could appreciate 'all the efforts, the devices and the intricacies the actions of the partisans required and the difficulties that they had to overcome.' Finally published in 1956, Gobetti's *Diario Partigiano* was praised by the writer Italo Calvino, who noted that the diary 'had been written at the urging of Benedetto Croce.'[12]

In translating books from English into Italian, Gobetti tended to follow her literary inclinations, but the projects suggested by Croce were directed to a political purpose and were published by Laterza. Under Croce's supervision, Gobetti translated in the mid-1930s the three-volume *History of Europe* by Herbert Fisher. The books appeared after some difficulty with the censorship authorities, who found 'the work conceived with a spirit and an intonation which are contrary to the principles of the regime ...'[13]

The censors of Bari were not the only ones who kept a close eye on the cultural activities of Croce and Gobetti. The publication of their correspondence has revealed that all the letters of Ada, and probably those of Croce, were opened and copied by the police in Turin, thus, unintentionally, assuring their survival. Despite police surveillance, the homes of Croce and Gobetti in Turin and especially in the Piedmont countryside became a favourite meeting place of anti-Fascist intellectuals, who went there as a sort of political pilgrimage, attracted not only by the beauty of the Alps and the refreshing breeze from the mountains but by the intellectual inspiration they found there.

Even in 1928 there were many occasions to support morally or to help financially old friends and new followers, though, for lack of evidence and because of Croce's natural discretion in these matters, it is hard to distinguish one activity from the other. During 1928 and in the following year, Croce helped Ivanoe Bonomi and Meuccio Ruini with the publication of their books, using his close relationships with the publishing houses of Ricciardi in Naples and Laterza in Bari. Excluded from political activity, some of former politicians became historians, or returned to the law and other professions. This work provided them with income but also allowed them to continue their political battles by different means. Bonomi published biographies of Mazzini and Leonida Bissolati while Ruini wrote a history of Switzerland and an essay on Madame de Staël – books that made a contribution to keeping alive liberal and democratic ideals.[14]

Croce was also quite solicitous about the needs of young people, especially when he met promising scholars whose future was clouded by political difficulties. During 1927–8, at various intervals, he received in his houses in Naples and in Turin some of the students who had been arrested and then released in April 1928, no doubt to offer them reassurance or assistance. In one of these cases he offered more than the usual moral support. With gratitude and evident pride, almost as a badge of honour, V.E. Alfieri has revealed that Croce advanced loans to him whenever he found himself in dire straits for political reasons. This happened quite often in those years, and every time he was made to understand that he need not worry about repayment.[15]

During the Fascist regime, for political reasons and as a part of the opposition strategy, Croce advised Laterza to publish works by anti-Fascist writers and to translate books useful to the struggle against fascism. Alfieri has indicated that during that time as well, Croce asked Laterza to pay more than the standard rate to needy anti-Fascist writers and translators and to charge the difference to his own account. This practice remained a secret; it was known only to a select few and kept hidden even from those directly affected. But it was well known to the police authorities, including Mussolini and Bocchini, as the records in the personal file of Laterza at the National Archives show. The police read and copied the letters sent by Laterza to Croce, in which were indicated the agreement reached and the payments made.[16]

Not only did Croce help individual writers in economic difficulty, he also directly or indirectly supported the literary activities of the few who tried to remain independent of Fascist influence. Domenico Petrini was one of these. A young man of liberal ideas, and a promising scholar, he lived in Rieti, a provincial city of Latium, where he had a small publishing house. Croce allowed Petrini to publish some of his political and philosophical essays, and when it was time to be paid he simply advised the publisher 'to employ the money for the continuation of the collection.' After the young man died in 1931, Croce continued to advise his young widow and offered support so she could continue her husband's activities.[17]

Political Activity

In 1927 and 1928, Croce's political activity went beyond the writing of books and essays. He continued to participate occasionally in the meetings of the Senate; he did not take part in the debates but sat beside Albertini and Ruffini during their opposition speeches, and voted against the bills that further destroyed the old Statuto. In May 1928 Croce cast his vote against the law that abolished free elections in Italy and compelled the electors to vote for a single list, whose candidates had been suggested by the Fascist organizations, approved by the Grand Council of Fascism, and in many cases chosen by Mussolini alone. 'I took part in the sitting and the vote, casting my ballot against the so-called electoral reform, that is the abolition of the representative regime in Italy.'[18]

In November 1928 Croce voted against the law that turned the Grand Council of Fascism from a party organization into an organ of the constitution, infringing on royal prerogatives. Not even the generals came to the defence of the king's ancient rights, seemingly unaware of the danger. No wonder that on this occasion the *Taccuini* have another sad entry: 'We were only nineteen to say no.'[19] It pained Croce to witness so many sudden conversions in the Senate, where 'old liberals and once fierce democrats turned fascist' showed 'a false cordiality' or displayed 'the badges of the new faith' but avoided political questions, 'fearful ... and suspicious of any free discussion.'[20]

During his visits to Rome, Croce never failed to visit Giolitti, admiring his tenacious liberal faith and his constant presence in Parliament, where he spoke with calm eloquence against the electoral law, despite his venerable age. In July 1928 Giolitti died, and even the funeral held in Piedmont acquired a political significance. To no one's surprise, Mussolini did not go, but the absence of the king and the crown prince, in gross violation of protocol, was regarded as a disgraceful act of cowardice by the entire political establishment. Croce attended the funeral with a few friends, 'those faithful,' he described them, with evident reproach to those absent.[21]

Croce's writings reveal that the king's servile attitude towards Mussolini and his acquiescence to the Fascist regime created dismay and resentment among the old Liberal leaders. The same resentment is found in the memoirs of Marcello Soleri, Giolitti's lieutenant. As for Croce, in his capacity as a senator and especially as a minister, he had met Vittorio Emanuele in Rome and in Naples during official visits and public ceremonies, where he was always entertained with cordiality. However, Croce stopped attending royal functions in 1927, after the king visited Naples, where he was received with great enthusiasm by the people but showed a great deal of deference toward the Fascist authorities, as if he were seeking their approval. In his last meeting Croce found the monarch 'older and ill at ease.' He avoided serious conversation, preferring to indulge in innocuous pleasantries, at the same time giving the impression that he was almost in fear of the minister of education, Pietro Fedele, a man for whom Croce had no respect.

The year 1927 was also the last time that Croce joined the other Neapolitan senators at the Royal Palace, 'for their annual visit to the Crown Prince, Umberto.' During the years of the prince's residence in Naples, Croce's absence from official ceremonies was noted, and the prince made known his regret. He even expressed the desire to see Croce, wanting to ask him for 'some historical information.' But an invitation never came, nor was one ever sought. Prior to 1944, Umberto and Croce met only once, during a patriotic ceremony in Piedmont. the encounter was accidental, brief, and without political significance, but it did not lack comic aspects. Before the arrival of the prince, the authorities asked Croce to leave; he refused. After the friendly salutations with the prince, the same persons invited Croce to join the dignitaries; Croce left, shaking his head.

However, during the Fascist regime, through common friends, Croce maintained some contacts with Maria José, the liberal-minded Belgian wife of Umberto. At her initiative, early one morning in 1931, soon after her arrival in Italy, Croce and the royal princess had a clandestine meeting in Pompeii, with the complicity of the director of excavations. On that occasion the princess asked Croce 'about the conditions in Italy and the dispositions of the Italian people.' At her request Croce also autographed a French translation of his *History of Italy*, given to the princess by her father, the King of Belgium, perhaps as a guidebook to her new land.[22]

At critical moments, attempts were made in private meetings to impress upon the old monarch the need to take a royal initiative in defence of the Statuto, to protect not only Italy but also the destiny of his royal house. All attempts were in vain. Croce, too, at various times, was urged to meet the king, but he always refused, in the belief that any such meeting would be useless and possibly dangerous. The king made it known that it was his duty, as a constitutional monarch, to refer to the prime minister any political conversation, even a private one. Perhaps there was no need for Croce to have a special meeting in the Royal Palace to make his political views known to the monarch or to Mussolini. From the report of a political informer to his masters in 1930, we learn that Croce openly and without restraint criticized the conduct of the king in conversations with his friends and even with his acquaintances, accusing him of having betrayed his oath of office and allowed the destruction of the Statuto.[23]

Armando Gavagnin, one of the most active and brave young men in the democratic underground organizations, has given, in his memoirs, an account of a meeting in Croce's house, without providing, unfortunately, many details. In 1927 a new secret movement was organized in northern Italy, repeating the name and the ideals of Mazzini's Young Italy. The new organization gathered elements from the various democratic parties. Its aims were to publish a weekly bulletin and to maintain ties among opposition groups in Italy and France. The organization was active mostly in Turin, Milan, and Bologna. When it was decided to expand its reach to southern Italy, Mario Neri, a magistrate from Turin, went to Naples, carrying a letter of introduction from Senator Ruffini, and met with Croce. The result of his mission exceeded expectations. As Gavagnin put it: 'There were some doubts, and perhaps they remained, about Croce's disposition to action; but the fact is that he gave his adherence without reservation.'[24]

Gavagnin's assertions are confirmed by police reports, which in several places, directly or indirectly, associate Croce's name with Young Italy. In 1927, with a short telegram devoid of explanations, Mussolini ordered the prefect of Naples to stop police surveillance of Croce's house. Soon afterwards, however, as a justification for past and present actions, making clever distinctions between 'surveillance,' 'vigilance,' and 'information,' a note from the political branch of the police informed the minister of the interior that information on Croce was collected and his movements followed, 'since Senator Benedetto Croce has not appeared completely unrelated to the anti-Fascist movement called Young Italy.' The files in the National Archives prove that surveillance and the collection of information on Croce continued until the end of the regime, in one form or another.[25]

Cultural Activity

While some political groups and a few energetic young people went underground and carried out direct action against the government, Croce, after the consolidation of the Fascist regime, decided to follow a path more congenial to his personality. In his 'Autobiographical Notes' of 1934 and 1941 he confessed that he did not have the personal ability or the moral inclination to undertake conspiratorial actions, nor did he have much faith in the efficacy of those actions. On the other hand, he did not discourage them. He wrote that he did not 'close my ears entirely to those in Italy and among the exiles, who longed for more promptly resolute actions and conspired.'

Croce decided to devote most of his energy to cultural activities, and in particular to promote the philosophical ideas underlying a liberal society, because this was 'my best opposition, the one more suitable to my nature and in which I could produce the best results.' Croce thought that this theoretical activity had become more necessary and acquired a new urgency because, during the liberal age, the concept of freedom

had not received an adequate philosophical justification, and in fact
'had been disarmed.' With his cultural activity, then, Croce wanted to
offer to political action the support of philosophical theory, inviting, at
the same time, the politicians involved in the struggle against dictatorship and especially the new generation 'to rethink the problems of freedom.' He also hoped to 'light anew in their minds and in their souls the
central fire of the Risorgimento.'[26]

In 1946, speaking as president of the Liberal Party to its first national
congress after the war, Croce expressed with more precision the purpose
of his resistance to the Fascist regime and the aims he had hoped to
achieve with his cultural activities. First of all, with his historical essays he
tried to defend the liberal ideals of the Risorgimento and 'to keep
immaculate for the future the most precious heritage of our fathers.'
Similarly, with his philosophical and political writings, Croce endeav-
oured to give a better expression to the concept of political freedom,
because this concept 'had not received an adequate elaboration in the
thought of the nineteenth century,' 'had been treated empirically by the
English theorists,' and 'had been sacrificed to the state by the Germans'
while the positivists had stressed the utilitarian aspects but neglected its
spiritual dimensions. As a result of the new elaboration the concept of
political freedom was 'fully identified with conscience and with moral
life in all its comprehension and extension.' One of the consequences,
in Croce's view, was the separation of political freedom from economic
organization, which made it possible to break the ties that had been
established in the nineteenth century between political liberalism and
liberismo, meaning economic liberalism or laissez-faire.[27]

In carrying out his cultural program, Croce was not alone – he had
the support of many friends, scattered throughout Italy, all joined in a
common purpose. This solidarity made it possible for his writings to
reach a wide audience. Croce was lucky to have in Giovanni Laterza a
faithful and courageous publisher who was unafraid of political and economic harassment. With the collaboration of Laterza, Croce was able to
mobilize Italian literature and European culture in defence of the liberal tradition, especially through three collections in which his influence was paramount: *Scrittori D'Italia*, *Classici della Filosofia*, and *Biblioteca
di Cultura Moderna*. The *Biblioteca* in particular brought together different authors, and their different ideas all converged to create a common
front of cultural resistance. Nor was Laterza the only resource on which
Croce could rely for carrying out his program. In other publishing
houses a few people, in key positions, were willing to accept Croce's rec-

ommendations for a book or an author. In Guido De Ruggiero and Adolfo Omodeo, Croce acquired congenial collaborators who gave to *La Critica* a wider appeal and an extra zest. In the universities and high schools, in the libraries and bookstores, teachers and librarians used, discussed, selected, displayed, and recommended Croce's books and other Laterza publications. In every Italian city a network of friends, or sympathizers and supporters, young and old, men and women, stood ready to help, to protect, to support, and to take a risk. All of them constituted what Croce liked to call 'the Italian family.' Without doubt, Croce's intellectual output was impressive both for quantity and quality in those years, but his achievements in the production and distribution of books were no less remarkable. He was a great impresario.

Croce's cultural program and opposition to fascism encompassed not only the publication of new writings but also the reprinting of old ones. The new editions offered a link between generations and made possible a continuation of old debates. Ideas that were now ostracized by the regime but that had once inspired many, were put back into circulation. When necessary, the connection between these ideas and the current political situation was made explicit by a new introduction, which often was an occasion to rectify a misconception or to invite readers to reflect on the book from a different perspective.

In 1927 Croce published a new edition of his essays on Marxism. In the previous edition, he had used rather heavy and inappropriate sarcasm against the ideals preached by humanitarian Socialists and Democrats. The new introduction remedied the bad impression created by that sarcasm and offered Croce the occasion to clarify his political ideas. In 1917, in the middle of the war, Croce had expressed gratitude to Marx for the realism of his ideas and especially for the emphasis he had given to force, which had helped the young Croce, as he claimed, to resist and to reject the charms and the 'seductions of the Goddess Humanity and the Goddess Justice.' Those words, after the war, had been interpreted by some commentators as an indication of Croce's 'adhesion to the party or to one of the parties that are called authoritarian,' a conclusion that, Croce wrote, 'is contrary to my feeling and to my thought.' In 1927 Croce clarified his position, stressing that force is a neutral element in politics, to be used when the situation requires it by all politicians, with the difference that the liberals employ force to protect or to promote a liberal society while reactionaries use it to impose their authoritarian solutions or to defend their own interests.[28]

The same ideas were expressed in the new edition of his book *Italy*

from 1914 to 1918. Once again the introduction was used by Croce to criticize the ideas of the Fascist regime and to condemn the writers serving
it. Croce reminded his contemporaries that his intention in 1927, as
during the war, was to defend the common European heritage against
all the various nationalisms. But the introduction contains also a self-
criticism. The book's essays continually stressed the concept of politics
as power and force. Now Croce recognized that force cannot be materi-
alistically understood, and that politics cannot be separated from ethics.
In the name of this new conception, he criticized 'the idolatry of the
State,' and, with direct reference to Gentile, rejected with scorn the idea
'that the State is Duty and it is God.' At the same time, he invited Italians
to return to Christian precepts, 'giving to Caesar what only belongs to
Caesar,' and to follow 'the moral and religious conscience' in the determination of practical action, without waiting for the orders or the
approval of government. Personal responsibility now had completely
replaced considerations of realpolitik.[29]

The new introductions and the other historical essays written in 1927
were signs of Croce's political and philosophical evolution. By now he
had abandoned the strident polemic against the Democrats; his liberalism was more inclusive and more progressive and embraced democratic
ideas, so much so that he could be regarded as a liberal democrat.
Under the impact of fascism, he was offering a new view of politics, one
more in accord with his inner feelings, better attuned to the needs of
the time, and in fuller harmony with his philosophical system. Facing a
different adversary, Croce changed his ideological instance; force was
no longer emphasized, and the accent was put on freedom and morality. In politics, the dialectic between force and consensus remained, but
freedom had to be the result of the struggle, giving value to political
action.

Redefining Liberalism and the 'Bourgeoisie'

Croce's evolution was evident in three essays that were first published in
La Critica in 1927 and were included later in the book *Etica e Politica.* In
these essays, Croce made an effort to redefine the nature of his liberalism, providing it with new attributes and a different connotation than in
the past. The essays made it clear that, for Croce, liberalism was more
than a political program; instead it 'coincided with a total conception of
life and reality': 'It has its foundation in immanent philosophy,' and 'it
is centred on the idea of dialectic and becoming, that, through diversity

and opposition of spiritual forces increases and continually ennobles life, and gives to it its full and true meaning.'[30]

Liberalism rejects dogmatism and definitive solutions; it favours diversity and required opposition, and regards both as beneficial to society and necessary to life; it also demands participation on the part of citizens and the free interplay of social forces. For this reason, liberalism is rejected by philosophies based on transcendence and authority that condemn struggle and diversity and that fear contrast; it is rejected by institutions and regimes that prefer to impose solutions from above, accept only passivity from its citizens, and demand continual obedience. In its perfect form, liberalism finds its antithesis in the Catholic Church. But the liberal ideal has an adversary also in communism because this doctrine, too, has eschatological elements, presents a total conception of life based on authority, and believes in a final and perfect society where conflict disappears and history comes to an end.[31]

For most of his life, Croce, in the name of liberty and free choice of the individual, opposed both fascism and communism as expressions of the authoritarian tendencies in modern society. During the Fascist regime, he fought a continuous battle against fascism and communism. This had to be done to counteract the appeal of Marxism and the allure of the Russian Revolution, but also to refute Fascist propaganda, which always presented fascism to the fearful middle class as the only alternative to communism and the only bulwark against the triumph of bolshevism: Rome or Moscow was a popular Fascist slogan in those days.[32]

While Croce criticized the theoretical aspects of Marxism and communism, in its Leninist interpretation, he recognized the positive historical role played by the Socialist parties in Italy and western Europe and the beneficial results produced by these organizations for the working classes but and society as a whole. He stressed that socialism was a component of the modern age and a product of immanent philosophy. For that reason, Croce invited modern Socialists to develop their ideals further in terms of a dialectical conception of reality, accepting freedom as essential to life and avoiding dictatorial solutions. In contrast, Croce's criticism of reactionary elements was always harsh. He rejected with sarcasm their continual harping back to a feudal past and their longing for a theocratic and authoritarian future. Finally, Croce admitted that liberalism and democracy are based on the same ideals and can be regarded as similar, under certain conditions – that is, when they oppose authority, favour moral equality, and try to ameliorate the conditions of the working classes.[33]

In these essays, Croce not only gave a dialectical foundation to his liberalism, but he also introduced a distinction between liberalism and capitalism. For Croce, liberalism did not coincide with the market economy, or *liberismo*, as he called it. Capitalism was only an economic organization born to satisfy certain economic needs of society, and it could be changed, modified, or replaced as needs change or when different solutions are found to produce more wealth and better address economic problems.[34]

Croce elaborated a further distinction between liberalism and laissez-faire, reiterating that liberalism is an ethical and political principle while *liberismo* is only a way to produce and to exchange goods. Liberalism in practical life, Croce argued, dislikes the regulations that limit the freedom of individuals, but it also recognizes the need to impose limitations on economic activities in order to achieve a greater good for the community. Laissez-faire, on the other hand, is only an economic rule, concerned with the production of material goods produced in an efficient manner as a result of private initiative. Liberalism, on the contrary, cannot be concerned only with the economic results of production; it has to be preoccupied with its total effect on man and society. And it does not accept as 'goods' only those produced to satisfy economic necessities; instead, it regards as 'goods' all the creations of the human spirit. If one is concerned with the production of economic wealth, the other has 'the value of a supreme rule and law of social life' and is guided 'by the promotion of spiritual life in its totality.'[35]

In practical terms, liberalism approves of many measures proposed by laissez-faire, but it can also reject them when they do not promote freedom or when economic factors clash with higher values. At the same time, and for the same reasons, liberalism can even welcome socialist proposals when these improve the protection and promotion of freedom. The difference and the opposition between liberalism and socialism rests not so much on economic principles as on an ethical and political ideal, one based on individual freedom and the other on authority.[36]

Croce's separation of liberalism from capitalism and his distinction between philosophical liberalism and economic laissez-faire gave rise to a long polemic with Luigi Einaudi, who defended a more traditional view of liberalism, inspired by the ideas of classical political economy. But in the political situation of the time, Croce's ideas created also the condition for a possible synthesis between liberalism and socialism. As the historian Nicola Tranfaglia has recognized: 'In this essay [by Croce]

Rosselli found the theoretical arguments ... for his formulation of liberal socialism.'[37]

The political consequences of Croce's distinction between liberalism and laissez-faire were far-reaching. The distinction made possible, in the present and in the future, an alliance or at least cooperation between Liberals and Democrats and Social Democrats; it allowed the new generation of Socialists, not only Carlo Rosselli but also Giuseppe Saragat, Aldo Garosci, and Leo Valiani, to introduce elements of liberalism into their revisions of socialism. At the same time, it compelled some young liberals to look towards socialism with more sympathy. But Croce's assertion was also directed at those liberals of his time who identified liberalism with the capitalist economy and applauded the free-market policies of fascism. Croce reminded them that the litmus test for true liberals was always political freedom, not economic policy, and one could not be bartered for the other.

In his last essay of the year, Croce discussed the use and abuse of the terms 'bourgeoisie' and 'bourgeois' and rejected the political equivocations and historical confusion that these words tended to generate.

The essay analysed and debated the theories and books of Werner Sombart and Bernhard Groethuisen, but the political necessities of the times were also quite evident. Supporters of the authoritarian movements of the right and of the left often proclaimed that they were fighting not against true freedom but only against bourgeois ideals and capitalist society. Responding to the sophistry of these claims, Croce argued that at stake in the struggles of modern times were not bourgeois ideals but the dignity of man as a free agent. Many progressive intellectuals criticized and even rejected liberal ideals because they did not like elements of capitalist society or found questionable the morals of the bourgeois class. Also, Fascist politicians often contrasted the materialism and the egoism of the bourgeoisie with the spiritualism and the heroism of fascism. Croce made the argument that there are no bourgeois or proletarian ideals but only human ideals, produced by the human spirit in its struggle against forces denying its free expression.[38]

In the age of dictators and authoritarian movements, Croce tried to bring the concept of freedom to its pristine purity, devoid of contaminations. It was a reminder to all that the fight in modern times was between freedom and authority, between political systems that promote liberty, and are based on free participation, and those that proclaim dogmas and dictate solutions by force, imposed on all by a single party, by a small elite, or, more often, by a single man.

CHAPTER SEVEN

The Defence of Liberal Italy, 1926–1928

Besides all his other activities, from the middle of 1926 to the end of 1927, Croce was occupied in writing his *History of Italy from 1871 to 1915*. The research had begun in June 1926, and by July 1927 the writing was under way. In the first days of December, Croce went to Bari and gave the manuscript personally to Laterza; in January 1928 the first edition was published and immediately became a best-seller. The book's publication was an extraordinary event then and has remained the subject of a lively debate ever since, praised and blamed with equal force, always with political motivation clearly evident. In 1928, the *History of Italy* fully achieved Croce's aim, which was the defence of liberal Italy from the denigrations of fascism.[1]

But, despite the linearity of the argument and the clarity of the prose, this work remains a difficult and complex book, as Professor Gennaro Sasso has shown. The *History of Italy* is not only a book of history, it is also a work of philosophy; its pages are full of philosophical statements reflecting Croce's vision of life. The historical judgments presuppose a dialectical conception of reality and Croce's particular insistence on the unity and distinctions of the categories, especially between morality and politics. One also has to keep in mind the changing nature and function of that troubled and troubling category of vitality, which originally, in Croce's writings, indicated the useful but now took on the meaning of the sources of life.[2]

The History of Italy in Summary

As a work of history, the *History of Italy* offered a positive evaluation of the liberal period from 1870 to 1915. But the book never became a hagiography. It was contrary to Croce's nature 'to invent or exaggerate facts,' as one critic rashly claimed. It was also contrary to his philosophy to write a 'splendid eulogy' when dealing with issues of historical interpretation. Croce knew the historical weakness and political difficulties of the young Italian state; he did not hide the mistakes made in foreign affairs and national policy. He recognized that agriculture was sacrificed to industrial development, that the few southern industries disappeared under the competition of northern companies, and that the disparity between north and south was not reduced but grew. He did not ignore the social and public backwardness of Italian society when compared with the more progressive nations of Europe. Yet, despite these reservations Croce praised the ruling classes for the progress Italy achieved in this period, marked as it was by a significant improvement in the standard of living and greater participation by citizens in European life. Above all, he celebrated the beneficial effect of freedom, which gave new direction and vigour to all aspects of Italian society.

This positive assessment reflected Croce's political evolution after the war and the influence of Giolitti on his ideas. The democratic nature of his liberalism had made possible a better understanding and appreciation both of Giolitti's policies and of his personality. At the same time, Croce's new perspective allowed him to give a more balanced evaluation of Agostino Depretis and his so-called transformism; his judgment on the historical left after 1876 was much different from the negative and corrosive comments he had heard in the house of Silvio Spaventa.

The events that followed the Great War in Italy and the rest of Europe compelled Croce to revise many of his earlier ideas. As he was to write in his 'Autobiographical Notes' of 1934: 'Since then [1918] my philosophical and historical works, without ceasing to be severely scientific, and without acquiring political contamination, expressed with greater and quicker correspondence than before the new demands that the moral conscience posed, and provided the light that it demanded.' This new attitude can be seen in all his writings, 'but especially in the political essays and in the historical books which I have been writing, that, devised before the war, by the new events acquired an accent that they would not have had before, and also an awareness of certain processes, that before would not have been as clear.'[3]

Alongside this intellectual evolution was a changed personal attitude to politics. Until the war, Croce had left political affairs to professional politicians. After the advent of fascism, he became personally involved and deeply concerned with political events. From then on, with his cultural activities Croce tried to influence political events in a more direct way.[4]

For all these reasons, the *History of Italy*, besides its philosophical and historical value, has to be regarded as a political statement. Given the times in which it was written, and the ideas animating it, the book rightly came to be regarded as a political protest against the ruling party and Mussolini.

Mussolini and Rocco, with the acquiescence of Vittorio Emanuele and with the support of Gentile, were destroying the liberal state and building an authoritarian regime using violence and persecution. In the midst of the oppressive atmosphere created by the dictatorship, Croce defended free debate and political parties as instruments to assure social progress and to avoid political disasters. He described Parliament, a free press, and political opposition as vital and essential elements in maintaining the authority of the state and in creating the moral unity of the nation.[5]

Fascist intellectuals were creating the myth of the Duce, the chief who is always right, the leader who dares where others vacillate, and looked to Francesco Crispi as an earlier example of a bold leader overcoming a reluctant Parliament and an indifferent population. Croce offered a critical judgment of Crispi and, by implication, of Mussolini, condemning the former's methods and policies and showing his shortcomings, particularly his constant vacillations and tendency to blame Parliament for his own personal failures. He stressed the dangers of that leadership style by recalling that many of Crispi's mistakes had their origin in his disregard of Parliament, and that his foreign policy, unrestrained by Parliament, ended in national disaster.[6]

Against the failures of Crispi, Croce contrasted the success of Giolitti, who throughout his career remained faithful to the Statuto, respectful of Parliament, and always willing to accept the cooperation of the opposition. The result was a period of peace, economic development, and social progress. Without ignoring the difficulties of this period, Croce praised the Giolitti system for following the liberal approach to politics: an approach able to maintain law and order while assuring individual freedom, and to achieve a synthesis of progress and conservation that avoided the pitfalls of reaction and revolution.[7]

Given that the Giolitti period was also the time of King Vittorio Emanuele, it is surprising to find in Croce's work little praise for the king and much indirect criticism. Throughout the book there is an evident contrast between the cordiality and humanity of King Umberto and the known aridity and scepticism of King Vittorio Emanuele, between the ability of the first to share the joys and sorrows of the Italian people and the cold indifference of the second. In his narration of the upheavals of 1898, Croce underlines the similarities to and differences from the developments of 1922. In a rather direct way, he reminds the present king, using his own words at his accession to the throne, that oaths have to be kept and that 'the protection of freedom' and 'the defence of the monarchy' go together, both being 'tied to the supreme destinies of the Fatherland in bonds indissoluble.'[8]

Besides Giolitti and his liberalism, another man and movement received high praise in Croce's book. When Croce was writing the *History of Italy*, the organizations created by socialism had already been destroyed and their leaders persecuted. Turati, despite old age and illness, had been compelled to escape to France to avoid the continuous harassment of the government. Croce recognized the historical role played by the Socialist Party and its necessary presence in the political life of a nation; he praised the achievements of its organizations and the positive contribution they had made to the social progress of Italian society. At the same time, Croce paid tribute to the personal honesty, natural moderation, democratic faith, patriotic spirit, and common sense of Turati. In 1926 Ferruccio Parri, Carlo Rosselli, and Sandro Pertini had rescued Turati from Fascist harassment in Milan and arranged his expatriation to France, where political activity gave a new life and purpose to his broken heart after the death of his beloved Anna Kuliscioff. In 1928 Croce's book restored the old Socialist leader to his deserved place in the history of modern Italy and defended his reputation to younger generations who often read only criticisms of him, from the right and also from the left.[9]

Turati and, to an even greater degree, Giolitti are the real heroes of Croce's *History*, and he points to their leadership and policies as examples worthy to be followed by present-day Liberals and Socialists.

The Origins of Fascism

But Croce did not simply want to compare and contrast the fruits of the liberal state with the oppression of the Fascist regime; he also sought to understand the reasons for the collapse of the liberal forces and the victory of Mussolini and fascism. This was in accordance with his theory of history: historical questions about the past arise from practical needs and demand clarification if we are to understand the present and prepare for future action. In the historical debate about liberal Italy and the nature of fascism, many critics have complained that the *History of Italy* does not explain the origins of fascism and leaves a chasm between what preceded and what followed Italy's entrance into the First World War in 1915. But a candid reader of Croce's book, reflecting especially on the content of chapter 10, has to agree with Gennaro Sasso and recognize that the nature of fascism and its origins are clearly indicated in *History of Italy*.[10] Unlike other historians, then or later, Croce saw the origins of fascism in the ideas, moral attitudes, and political aspirations that began to transform Europe in the second half of the nineteenth century, a process that accelerated especially after the defeat of France and the triumph of Germany in 1870, and that came to maturity in the years just before and after the First World War. The rise and fall of liberalism would be the central theme of Croce's next book, the *History of Europe in the Nineteenth Century*. In that work he would analyse in detail the forces of irrationalism and nihilism that undermined liberal institutions and prepared the ground for the authoritarian movements and dictatorial regimes of modern times. But in the *History of Italy* too, Croce discretely called attention to the elements of irrationalism, activism, and sensualism that were brewing in Italian society, poisoning the heritage of the Risorgimento.[11]

In the Italy of Giolitti, there was 'something unsafe and a little unhealthy' amid the bloom of cultural and economic progress. Those unhealthy elements were the germs that, once nourished by the war, produced fascism. Before 1914, the younger generation was increasingly attracted by new theories, all expressing 'a rapacious spirit of conquest and adventure, attitudes of cynicism and violence,' as well as 'an expectation of the superman.' The new forms of belief weakened the sense of distinction 'between morality and utility,' 'duty and pleasure,' 'truth and falsehood.' The traditional ideal of patriotism was replaced by the passions of nationalism and the will to power of imperialism, often accompanied by 'a religion of the race' and by 'a cupidity of conquest' that ignored human rights and placed the state above morality. As the new theories gained currency, liberal ideals became unfashionable: 'Liberalism was then reduced to a practice and was no longer a living faith'; the old ideal was no more 'an object of love, something held sacred, to be defended with passion at the first sign of danger.' The gap between modern culture and Giolitti's politics did not bode well for the future, especially for a young nation without a robust tradition of free institutions. 'In Italy liberalism already lacked the religious support of the church, ...

now because of irrationalism it was losing also the critical support of the intellectuals, necessary to face with confidence an eventual crisis.'[12]

These elements of irrationalism and anti-liberal reaction found new inspiration in the Libyan War and were further cultivated by the Great War. Croce characterized the latter conflict as 'a cataclysm of worldly interests,' 'the war of historical materialism,' and 'the war of philosophical irrationalism,' 'devoid of ideal motivations' but 'full of commercial and industrial considerations,' 'nourished by immoderate desires and morbid fantasies.' To this mix the Italians contributed something of their own. The nationalists wanted to destroy the Giolittian system and to replace it with an authoritarian government; D'Annunzio promoted the war less for patriotic reasons than for personal ones, seeking exotic and violent adventure for its own sake. Even the Democratic interventionists accepted violence and inflicted a wound on the parliamentary system. They organized rowdy demonstrations and appealed to the piazza against Parliament, thus forcing the hand of government, violating the rights of the neutralist majority, and establishing a dangerous precedent.[13]

Once we remember that, for Croce, fascism had its origins in the irrationalism and activism of the Giolittian era, then we are able to appreciate his characterization of Mussolini, offered in Chapter 11. There, Croce stressed Mussolini's intellectual modernity. Unlike the old leaders of socialism, still embracing the ideas of positivism and a determinist interpretation of reality, Mussolini tried to rejuvenate the socialist ideology by 'using Sorel's theory of violence, Bergson's intuitionism, the pragmatism, the mysticism of action, all the voluntarism that was in the air, and that seemed idealism to many.' Mixing all those elements together, Mussolini was able to give a new vigour to the Socialist Party and a new importance to its newspaper. Preaching 'utopias and wonders,' he became popular not only among Socialists but also among the Italian cultural elite.[14]

The implication is clear. Before the war, Mussolini had been the best political expression of all the irrational forces that were undermining liberal and democratic ideals; after the war, he became the leader who was able to organize and to lead those same forces to the destruction of the liberal state and the suppression of democracy.

In *The History of Italy* there was a good dose of self-criticism; Croce recognized the importance of his own work and his contribution to Italian culture. But he also admitted that neo-idealism, which he and others had promoted at the turn of the century, had elements of irrationalism in its less guarded formulations. These had deleterious consequences in political life, as evidenced especially in the position of Gentile, who was described, to his great resentment, as: 'a non limpid political adviser,' while his actualism was labelled 'a mixture of old theological speculation and decadentism.' For several reasons, then, the new philosophy had not been able to overcome the appeal of irrationalism and influence the praxis, let alone acquire hegemony.[15]

Even Croce's theory of art as lyrical intuition and pure expression, devised to define the nature of poetry in its relation to the other philosophical categories, had been used to justify the new forms of literature and art fashioned by the avant-garde movements, none of which appealed to Croce. There was also his admission that in those years he was not unduly worried about political problems, and as a result had devoted his effort to philosophy and literary criticism, paying less attention to political theory and political history. Above all, we learn that, at the time, he did not yet possess a full theory of liberalism, which could have supported Giolitti's politics and offered justification for his method.

Writing *The History of Italy*

The origins and function of the *History of Italy* were indicated. by Croce himself. Since 1920 he had decided 'to write a moral and political history of Italy in the last two centuries, alone or as part of a history of modern Europe.' Shelved for a long time, the project never materialized in the form originally planned. In finally writing the book in 1927, Croce was moved by several new considerations, all of which had their origins in the political conditions of Italy after the triumph as fascism. As he said in his 'Autobiographical Notes' of 1934:

> The break with tradition, caused by the World War and by the political perturbations that followed; the ignorance of the new generations about the life of Italy after the achievement of unification; the slanders and the ridicule that for calculated partisan reasons were thrown against the honest and solid work of our fathers, through which Italy had taken up again her place in modern culture and in international affairs; all of this inflamed my spirit to write *History of Italy from 1871 to 1915*.'[16]

In 1946 Croce gave a more precise explanation of how the *History of Italy* came about. His aim had been to write a political and moral protest against those Fascist intellectuals who 'for partisan reasons considered it useful to promote calumny and scorn towards the previous generations of Italy,' and began 'to ridicule and to make a mockery of what they called the Little Italy or the Umbertine Italy.' In writing his book Croce had in mind particularly the younger generation, and his intent was to offer a book 'that told them briefly and honestly what had been, with its lights and its shadows, the modest and laborious country of their fathers and grandfathers.'[17]

Because that was the time in which he 'had been educated and could give witness,' Croce approached the history of this period with reverence. Its major events and great accomplishments moved his mind and heart less than the moral qualities animating 'the feelings and the thoughts of those three industrious generations.' 'I have loved and love the air of the Risorgimento, that respect for recognized truths, that coherence and honesty, that feeling of humanity, that gentility of customs, that rebellion ... against lies.'[18]

This nostalgia for a lost world gives a particular pathos to many parts of the *History*. In its pages there is a constant contrast between 'the memory of the happy time' and the spectacle of 'the sad present,' between 'the comfort and the pride' in the contemplation of 'the free fatherland among free nations' and 'the shame and the reproach' for the old 'ideals and customs now lost, despised and derided.'[19]

This sadness is also expressed in private letters and in the *Taccuini*. At the beginning of July 1927, Croce made a revealing entry in his diary:

> I have finished reading the notes ... and thought a great deal about the order of the work. But the ties of this history with the present situation have led me to meditate with anguish on the present and on the future. It cost me a painful effort to devote myself to this history that I have undertaken to write as a duty towards my fellow citizens. Old wounds are opened again which would not occur if I could occupy my mind in other studies, not so close to the present political life.'[20]

By following closely Croce's diaries and correspondence with his friends during the preparation of the *History of Italy* and before its publication, we can understand the political nature of this book and the particular role it played in the fight against the Fascist regime.[21]

The political aspect of the *History* was clear to Fortunato, who read several chapters in manuscript 'with a mountain of emotion' and 'with joy, wonder and gratitude,' 'in this hour so dark for Italy, of such obscurity, and such offence to truth.' He confessed that he 'was grateful' and his mind 'was fired ... for the justification of Italian resurrection ... achieved under the aegis of freedom' and '... for the exaltation of the fifty years of our Italian national life, so much ridiculed and scorned in the present hour.'[22]

Besides Fortunato, Croce also asked some of his closest friends to read chapters, still in manuscript, and to share with him their views on the work before its publication. These friends no doubt mentioned the upcoming book in their correspondence and also in their meetings with other friends, increasing interest in it and appreciation of its political value.[23]

In 1927 Gioacchino Volpe published *L'Italia in Cammino*. It covers roughly the same period as Croce's book but does so from the vantage point of a nationalist who was more concerned about the power of the state and the growth of the nation and yet who was also able to recognize the positive achievements of liberal Italy and even the contribution of socialism. Since then, many have assumed that Croce's book in 1928 was the liberal answer to Volpe's history. In fact, however, the two works have no direct causal relationship.[24]

But the publication of Volpe's book did heighten the excitement surrounding Croce's work-in-progress, as we learn from a letter of Guido De Ruggiero, who also had been asked to read the first six chapters of the manuscript. From Bologna, in October 1927, De Ruggiero wrote to Croce: 'Here the presentiment of your book is in the air; I did not mention it to anybody, but fame flies. I have learned that G. Volpe has received the news with disappointment, because he is afraid to be pushed from his nest.'[25]

The Publication of the *History of Italy*, 1928

The *History of Italy* was not published in the same manner as Croce's other books. In the past, Croce published chapters of his books first in his periodical. This time, he followed a different procedure, which was made advisable by the changed political conditions and especially by the extent of censorship. The *History* was published at once, without a single chapter appearing elsewhere.

On the advice of his closest friends, who were afraid that the police might seize the book before publication, Croce took other precautions as well. A copy of the manuscript was sent to London, and the possibility of an English edition was discreetly raised so the message could reach the right ears. For reasons of safety, instead of using the Post Office,

Croce delivered the manuscript personally to Laterza, 'travelling to Bari in the company of Laterza's young daughter,' a stratagem intended to disguise the true nature of the trip.[26]

History of Italy was finally published in January 1928 and immediately became a best-seller despite its high price of twenty-five lire. The first edition of five thousand copies was sold out within days – 'like a novel,' a bookseller remarked. A second edition of five thousand copies was printed in March, followed within the same month by a third. The book was reprinted in 1929, and it appeared four more times during the Fascist regime, with the last reprint appearing in 1943 just before the fall of Mussolini; in total, about 40,000 copies of the book were printed. A comparison with Gioacchino Volpe's book highlights Croce's commercial success. For the first edition of Volpe's book in 1927, two thousand copies were printed, followed by a second edition of one thousand in 1928 and a third of two thousand in 1928. A fourth edition of two thousand copies appeared in 1932, and this was followed by a fifth of similar scale sometime later.[27]

Croce's book, then, was printed more times and sold more copies than Volpe's despite the boycott of the cultural establishment and the hostility of the government. Given the size of the literary market and the conditions of the publishing industry in those times, even Volpe's book has to be considered a commercial success; however, Croce's achievement is more significant when we consider that Volpe's work had the support of official propaganda and benefited from the financial resources of the Treves publishing house, then the leading publisher in Italy, with a commercial and marketing organization far superior to Laterza. The explanation for the remarkable success of Croce's book lies in the work's political importance and in the reputation of Croce among the Italian people. Its success also demonstrates that, during the Fascist regime, news and information could travel outside the normal channels of communication, using both old and new trails.

Once the book was published, its success attracted the attention of the police. In March 1928 Arturo Bocchini, the able and efficient chief of police, asked the prefect of Bari 'discreetly to ascertain how many copies have been sold of the last book by Benedetto Croce.' With promptness, the prefect replied that 'The publishing house Laterza has until now printed and sold five thousand copies of B. Croce's last book, *History of Italy*.' Then the prefect added, 'Another five thousand are in the process of being printed.' Even the Fascist press took notice. In April, Rome's newspaper, *Il Tevere*, reluctantly conceded that 'the book

... has enjoyed a colossal success. In a few days two editions of five thousand copies each have been sold out. And it cost the good sum of twenty five lire.'[28]

After the publication, Mussolini was asked to ban and to seize the book. But he refused, and instead ordered the press to ignore it. When the book became a best-seller despite the boycott, and could no longer be ignored, the orders were changed and the press was asked to scorn the book and to ridicule the author, which it immediately did with relish.

The book of 'the stubborn senator' was denounced 'as an evident libel against fascism,' 'an obscene thing,' 'a mystification of history,' 'a bad and bitter book,' 'a poor thing' by 'a poor man,' and 'a case of spiritual exile.' The last suggests that, for many Fascists, Croce had become, like the political exiles, a foreigner in his own country.[29]

Naturally, these personal insults increased interest in the book but also generated reactions which were not anticipated by their authors. Many Italians not only bought the book but debated the issues it raised. If it was not possible to discuss the work at length publicly in scholarly reviews, as in the past, it was still possible to discuss it in private letters. In the political situation of the time, private correspondence, in this case at least, replaced discussion in periodicals. And, beyond letters, one has to imagine, to appreciate fully the book's influence, the conversations among friends, the debates carried on in the privacy of homes, and even the discussions in clubs and restaurants.

Old friends and political leaders of liberal Italy received the book from Croce or from Laterza, and all of them wrote back to the author, expressing their admiration and offering comments. All recognized the book's political value, regarding it as 'a true hymn to freedom,' as Giolitti put it. 'The book will have an incalculable influence on Italian contemporary life,' Guido De Ruggiero wrote from Bologna. Salandra, for his part, agreed with Croce's assessment of Crispi's personality. Giustino Fortunato, from his sick bed in Naples, became Croce's best publicity agent, writing letters praising the book and inviting his friends to buy or to ask Croce or Laterza for a free copy.[30]

Croce also received letters from university students and teachers. Some of these raised knotty theoretical questions, about, for example, the relationship between historical judgment and political action, and between the positive past and the negative present born of that past; others revealed that they had discussed the book with friends, inside and outside classrooms. All of them read the book 'with great interest' and 'with feelings of gratitude.' All appreciated its 'defence of liberty' and recognized the implicit critique of 'the novus ordo.' 'I had the feeling mainly that the narration is connected without effort with our present experience,' De Ruggiero again reassured Croce.

Writing from jail, Carlo Rosselli asked Croce to send him the three essays on liberalism written in 1927 and mentioned in the *History* notes, assuring him that, given the discussions about the book *History* that he had heard among his fellow prisoners, 'I would not be the only one to read them.' For his part, Salvemini read the book in London and wrote, with his usual polemical verve, a favourable review for *Time and Tide* noting the *History*'s attack on fascism and approving of its defence of liberal Italy.[31]

Volpe's Reactions

Croce's polemic against the regime was noted by Fascist intellectuals; they had no trouble in establishing a relationship between Croce's defence of liberal Italy and his evident condemnation of Fascist Italy, between his criticism of Crispi and his implicit attack upon Mussolini. Three months after Croce's book was published, Gioacchino Volpe wrote a review in *Corriere della Sera* in which he rejected the general thesis of the book but expressed respect for Croce personally and even offered some praise for the work itself.[32]

Besides the reservations expected from a nationalist historian, Volpe's review of 1928 contains a great truth. He recognized that, in writing his book, Croce had two purposes: to defend liberal Italy and to criticize the present political order. 'Croce not only wanted to vindicate to the Italians of yesterday their just part, but he also intended to fight a battle: for liberalism and for the liberal method, and for the so called liberal government, and even more for Giolitti, and his so called liberalism.'[33]

Despite the sarcasm of the last sentence, Volpe's review did not meet with the approval of the Fascist authorities. Augusto Turati, the national secretary of the Fascist Party, wrote a letter to Volpe complaining about the 'weak tones' used in his review. He even threatened Volpe with the denial of the party membership that Volpe was then asking for. 'I have read and read again your article on the *History of Italy* by Benedetto Croce,' Turati wrote. 'Should I decide your admission to the Party on the basis of that article, I can not hide that I would have to give a contrary opinion.' Taking issue with Volpe's respectful tone, Turati insisted that 'it was dutiful to fight resolutely Croce's premises and conclusions,' for the simple reason that 'the book is the exaltation of all that we have fought against and transformed: it is the affirmation of a spirit and a conception antithetical to ours.'[34]

Turati's letter to Volpe reveals that Croce's book was discussed at the highest level and had become a matter of delicate politics which demanded an official response. Whether under political pressure or on his own volition, Volpe in 1931 wrote a lengthy introduction to a new edition of his book, *L'Italia in Cammino* which was critical of Croce and of his *History*. Its substance was not much different from the previous review, but the tone was acerbic and hostile, without any of the earlier reverence. The difference did not escape Fortunato's attention. He called the new introduction 'an aggression against Croce.'[35]

More than anything else, what really irked Volpe was Croce's open polemic against the policies of the Fascist regime. 'This book, by the agreement of all, those who like it, and those who do not like it, is wholly polemical, implicitly or explicitly, by rapid allusions or by demonstrations, in the text and even more in the notes.' In agreement with Augusto Turati, Volpe made a point that often has been forgotten. 'The truth is that Croce is fighting desperately against the Italy of today; and every judgment of his on the past, from 1871 to 1915, assumes the colours of this fight.' For this reason, Volpe recognized that the book was part of the anti-Fascist struggle. 'This *History of Italy* ... will remain more as an historical document of the years in which it appeared than as an historical reconstruction, with objective value, of the times to which it refers.'[36]

In recent years, Denis Mack Smith has come dangerously close to sharing Volpe's assessment; others, however, notably the historians Federico Chabod, Walter Maturi, and Rosario Romeo, three former pupils of Volpe, have advanced solid arguments in defence of their view that Croce's book was both a courageous political statement and a magisterial historical reconstruction of liberal Italy.

Alfieri and *Pietre*

This certainly appears to have been the view in Pisa and in Milan, where, among young students and other intellectuals, Croce's book provided the stimulus to undertake a politico-cultural initiative. After the publication of Croce's book, V.E. Alfieri bought and donated to his friends twelve extra copies, and then this group decided to initiate the publication of a new cultural periodical: 'The idea was to publish a small historical revue of the Risorgimento: this idea was the fruit of the enthusiasm generated then in young people by Croce's *History of Italy.*' According to Alfieri, the aim of the periodical was not only to study the history of the Risorgimento but also 'to raise political issues' and defend liberal ideas.[37]

Unable to fund their own journal, the group tried to join forces with *Pietre*, then a small literary bi-monthly periodical published in Milan under the editorship of Lelio Basso, the future Socialist leader. Basso, for his part, welcomed the initiative, for he was already in the process of changing the format of *Pietre*. With the help of the new recruits, he hoped to give the periodical a more political orientation and to turn it into a vehicle for connecting like-minded people throughout Italy. To that end, in 1928 he travelled to Rome and Naples in an attempt to establish contacts with other members of the opposition and to solicit material for *Pietre*. In Naples he met, among others, Croce and his friend Mario Vinciguerra, who was already involved in anti-Fascist activities as a member of Young Italy.

But the effort came to naught and *Pietre* was soon suppressed. In April 1928, during the king's visit, a mysterious bomb exploded at the Milan Fair, killing twenty men and wounding forty more. Soon afterwards, under various pretexts, in Milan and in Naples, the police arrested many anti-Fascists, especially students and teachers. Among those arrested were all the writers of the periodical and some other friends. In both cities the young intellectuals were apprehended by the police 'under the charge of conspiracy and participation in the founding of a new Young Italy.'[38]

In his report, the prefect of Milan wrote that Basso and Vinciguerra wanted to increase the circulation of the periodical and had agreed to turn *Pietre* into 'the organ of spiritual connection among those affiliated with Young Italy.' On the same occasion, the police of Naples stated that no evidence was found against Vinciguerra 'except his frequent visits to the notorious Senatore Benedetto Croce,' and the only accusation against Alfieri was: 'He is a friend of Croce.'[39]

The Value of the *History of Italy*

From 1928 to 1943, Croce's *History of Italy* was read by all those who counted in the republic of letters; it was passed from hand to hand among friends and relatives, as was then the custom. It could be found in public and school libraries; it was discussed at the universities and in high schools; it became a part of the culture of the time. For its commercial success, for the discussions it generated, for the reactions it sparked among the Italian cultural elite, in the government and in the opposition, Croce's *History of Italy* has to be regarded as one of the most important acts of resistance to fascism and probably the most successful.

This fact was recognized at the time by friends and foes alike. One of Croce's correspondents compared the *History* to Silvio Pellico's *My Prisons* – the book that during the Italian Risorgimento was regarded as having damaged Austria more than a lost battle. Two police informers reported to their master the unusual success of the book, adding also that in Rome 'diplomatic and cultural circles say that this success has a much greater value than a political demonstration, nay that it is the biggest and most recent silent demonstration in Italy.'[40]

At the same time, the commercial success of Croce's book and the correspondence it generated among his friends revealed that Croce was at the centre of a vast but loose network without rules but kept together by moral ties. In the political situation of these years, the publication of the *History of Italy*, and the fact that so many bought and read it, represented a clear and public expression of anti-fascism.

CHAPTER EIGHT

The Lateran Pacts, 1929

With the publication of his *History of Italy* and after the death of Giolitti, Croce became the symbol of liberal Italy. And so it was natural that, when the Senate was called to approve the Lateran Pacts, the role of the leader of the opposition should fall upon Croce rather than upon a more experienced parliamentarian. Parliament had become a rubber stamp of the government's decisions. Speeches of the few remaining members of the opposition were ignored, or more often shouted down by jeers from the floor and from the public galleries. The only task left to the opposition inside Parliament was to defend the democratic tradition and to give witness to its ideals. Giolitti had done that in the House until the approval of the new electoral law, just a few months before his death. In 1929 Croce performed the same function when he spoke for the last time in the Senate against the new concordat and the repeal of the Law of Guarantees, which had unilaterally regulated the relations between church and state in liberal Italy.

The Lateran Pacts

The official negotiations between Italy and the Vatican began in secret in 1926, after both sides had made suggestions and presented proposals for a possible agreement the year before. The final accord was divided into three parts: a treaty, a financial convention, and a concordat. Despite minor reservations, the financial convention and the treaty were approved by all: Liberals, Fascists, and Catholics were in agreement on this point. A painful wound in the Italian nation was finally healed. For the first time since unification, Catholic citizens felt completely at home in Italy.

It was different with the concordat, the true bone of contention. The concordat changed in some important aspects the lay character of the state, introducing elements of clericalism in its administration and in its schools and limiting its jurisdiction in some fields. The church increased its influence in civil society; the state renounced some powers and controls and allowed the church to influence public education and marriage legislation.[1]

But the most important feature of the condordat was the political nature of the agreement underlying it. Instead of a unilateral solution, there was a bilateral accord; the separation between state and church ended, and it was replaced by a regime of mutual concessions. Among leading Italian politicians, Mussolini was the only one willing to seek a solution to the 'Roman Question' outside the Law of Guarantees. He did not have the 'preconceptions of the liberal school,' nor was he hampered by what Pope Pius XI liked to call 'liberal fetishes.' He viewed religion as an *instrumentum regni*. Since his first speech in Parliament, he had sought a rapprochement, even an alliance, with the Catholic Church in the interest of the country's unity and prestige. The concordat was the culmination of this policy.

Long before the Lateran Pacts were presented to Parliament for ratification, Croce had made known his opposition to the reconciliation between church and state. While some of his closest friends, like Casati, were willing to vote in favour, or suggested abstention in the Senate, Croce decided immediately to oppose the Lateran Pacts, a decision reached 'out of great moral rebellion,' as Adolfo Omodeo put it.[2]

This feeling of outrage was directed as much against Mussolini as against the pope, and was created by their alliance against liberal ideals. The heir of the Destra Storica could not countenance the abrogation of the Law of the Guarantees, which he had praised in the *History of Italy* as a 'monument of wisdom and moderation'; nor could he approve the abandonment of one of liberalism's fundamental tenets, the separation of church and state. Not surprisingly, notes of sadness appear frequently in the *Taccuini* during the first months of 1929. The day the reconciliation between the Catholic Church and the Kingdom of Italy was announced to the Italian people, and received with general jubilation, the nephew of Silvio Spaventa expressed different feelings in his diary: 'Great sadness for the announced conciliation and the concordat with the pope and similar delights.'[3]

On 11 February 1929, the Lateran Pacts were signed by Mussolini and Cardinal Pietro Gasparri, after long and tortuous negotiations. The pacts brought to an end the 'Roman Question,' closing the enmity between the pope and the king, which had lasted since 1870. The solution of a problem that had eluded Liberal leaders was a personal triumph for Mussolini: his prestige increased at home and abroad. The reconciliation gave fascism a truly national character; besides the middle classes, now the regime acquired the support of the traditional, conservative sectors of the Italian nation, the rural masses and the Catholic hierarchy. It was now recognized that the Fascist regime would last for many years; hopes for Mussolini's fall or for the disintegration of his government disappeared. The testimony of Giorgio Amendola is eloquent on this point: 'Fascism became stronger than ever. The reconciliation, and then the plebiscite, showed that year that there was a great deal of consent around the Fascist regime, more or less conscious.'[4]

The Plebiscite of 1929

To exploit the enthusiasm among the Italian people, Musssolini called a general election for 29 March, in the hope of obtaining popular approval of his personal rule and a consecration of the Fascist revolution. More important, he hoped to put an end, once and for all, to the 'moral question' and the Aventine Secession. He was successful and obtained all his aims. For the first time in Italian history, the clergy instructed the faithful to vote for the party in power, urging them to show their appreciation for the man and the party that had given Italy back to the church, and the church back to Italy, as the clever slogan then stated. Despite the moral pressures and the open harassments, the elections of 1929 were a victory for Mussolini, if not a vote of complete approval for fascism.

The elections took place under the new electoral law, against which Giolitti had made his last speech in Parliament and which really marks the end of the Statuto. Four hundred candidates ran for Parliament; all had been previously approved and selected by the Grand Council of Fascism from lists proposed by various national associations controlled by the Fascist Party. No opposition candidates were allowed. The electors had to vote for the entire list by marking yes or no on the ballot.

The elections not only were not free, they also were not secret. Electors were handed two ballots, one for yes and another for no; the ballots were folded in different ways. With these subterfuges, those who abstained and those who voted against the list could be easily identified, and in fact the police reports not only indicated the number of those not voting yes but also their names.[5]

Before the elections took place, the Democrats and the Socialists advised their followers to abstain, while the Communists ordered their adherents to vote against the national list. Despite increased police controls before and during the electoral campaign, in Naples and in Turin, and probably in other Italian cities, flyers were posted and distributed in the streets, inviting people to abstain from voting. There is good reason to believe that Croce and his wife abstained from voting in the elections of 1929. In the *Taccuini* the act of voting in national or municipal elections is always mentioned and acknowledged until 1924; there is no mention of ever going to vote during the Fascist regime. During the election campaign of 1929, the *Taccuini* register the arrival of Senator Casati in Naples on 21 March and then a trip by Croce and his wife to Bari from 25 to 26 of March, the voting days. The evidence suggests that the trip to Bari and the visit to Laterza was just an excuse devised by Croce to avoid voting. Thus, Croce and his wife have to be counted among those Italians who abstained, a little more than 10 per cent of the electors (the nays were less than 2 per cent, and the government obtained the rest).[6]

The elections of 1929 encouraged naive expectations. Many believed, or dreamed, that fascism would evolve towards a moderate regime. Mussolini had several meetings with Emilio Caldara, the former Socialist mayor of Milan, and with other old Socialist friends. These meetings created the impression of something new in the air, even of a national reconciliation. Some dared to hope for a political amnesty and the abolition of the Exceptional Laws approved at the end of 1926. For his part, Mussolini never entertained the idea of any substantial political changes. Among the few initiatives undertaken, Bruno Buozzi, the former trade-union leader, was asked to return to Italy from France and to assume unspecified responsibility in the labour movement; Croce and Bracco were invited, again, to become members of the Academy of Italy. All refused the advances made by the emissaries.[7]

Ratification of the Lateran Pacts

The new Parliament was called to ratify the Lateran Pacts soon after the elections in May 1929. The House approved the pacts with barely a hint of opposition, 357 members voting in favour and only 2 against. Nobody spoke in defence of the Law of Guarantees. But during the 'debate' Mussolini's old anti-clericalism came to the surface. Some Fascists, Gentile included, were not too happy about the reconciliation and the concessions made to the church. Mussolini tried to placate them and also to dampen the enthusiasm of the Catholic hierarchy. Some of his statements could have been made by the old anti-clericals: 'In the state the church is not sovereign, and it is not even free.' No liberal leader had ever dared to say that. Mussolini bluntly stated, too, that the Fascist state had 'a moral character' of its own, independent of any religion: 'The Fascist state proclaims in full its ethical character; it is Catholic, but it is Fascist, it is above all, exclusively, essentially Fascist.' Mussolini also limited the role of religion in the education of Italian youth. In the Fascist regime, he said, the teachers and the schools had to give to the pupils 'the sense of virility, of power, of conquest.' The task of Catholicism was to further this aim. The pope was not pleased by Mussolini's speech, and he made known his displeasure. Before the parliamentary discussions were over, Mussolini was compelled to offer reassurances, and in his speech before the Senate he toned down or corrected some of the most contentious assertions, and instead vented his resentment against Croce.[8]

When the Lateran Pacts reached the Senate, on 24 May 1929, among the Fascist senators only Vittorio Scialoja, whose father had been a colleague of Cavour and a member of the Destra Storica, defended with eloquence the liberal tradition, reminding the assembly that 'the political spirit of those who proposed and voted the Law of Guarantees was admirable.' But Croce alone spoke for the opposition and merely 6 senators voted against the Lateran Pacts, while 316 voted in favour. The decision to oppose the pacts had been discussed earlier by Croce and his friends. Albertini, Bergamini, Ruffini, and Croce had meetings in Naples and in Rome during the months of April and May. During those discussions they agreed to designate Croce as the speaker of the opposition. When the debate began in the Senate, Croce went to Rome, met his friends, read to them his speech, and all gave 'their full adherence.' But all also expressed fear and were concerned that Croce would be interrupted and shouted down, making it impossible for him to deliver the full text of the speech.[9]

During Croce's speech, a few senators, helped by members of the press gallery, tried to shout him down, but they did not succeed. Croce proved more tenacious than expected, and he was able to deliver the full speech despite continuous noise and heckles. In the *Taccuini*, Croce wrote a short account of that session in the Senate and the reactions his speech generated among Fascist senators. He revealed a modest sense of satisfaction. 'I took part in the meeting of the Senate and spoke against the bill. Noises were made and an attempt was undertaken to interrupt the speech from a group of senators ... and from the press gallery. But I repeated the words which had been covered by the heckles, raised my voice till I could read my speech fully, and in an audible way to the end.'[10]

Unwittingly, the hecklers created sympathy for Croce and gave his speech greater impact than it might have had otherwise. That evening in Rome, and two days later when he returned to Naples, a number of friends went to see Croce and had long conversations with him. Evidently, news of the speech had circulated despite the press blackout, and many people agreed with Croce's position.

Croce's Speech

Croce told the Senate that he spoke for himself and the small group of friends sitting around him. Since 1925, these Liberals had agreed to designate one of their member as a spokesman. On this day the natural speaker should have been Senator Ruffini. As a professor of canon law, he had the legal training and historical background to analyse the nature and the implications of the new concordat. But the occasion required the political defence of an historical tradition more than a legal analysis. For that task, Croce was better qualified; the *History of Italy* had given him special authority. He rose to defend the heritage of liberal Italy and the ideals of the Risorgimento against the policies of the Fascist regime and the clericalism of the Catholic Church. Croce declared that he and his friends had nothing against the treaty and the financial convention, nor were they against 'the idea of a reconciliation between the Italian state and the Holy See.' He reminded the Senate that the Law of Guarantees would have achieved such an aim, if only it had been accepted by the church. 'The repeated attempts, made in the course of many decades, from either party, prove the desire to put an end to a disagreement that created damage and inconvenience to both sides.'[11]

Croce defended the ideals of the Risorgimento and the inspiration of the men who had proposed the Law of Guarantees, as the heritage of modern thought and as a rejection of the secular pretenses of the Catholic Church that had become a burden for the church itself. The result had been 'the mitigation and the virtual disappearance of jusnaturalism, and the freedom recognized to the church inside the Italian state.' The separation between church and state had been beneficial not only to the state but also to the church. 'It is certain that the church, thanks to the new order, not only was able to carry out its work and its propaganda, but gained a consideration of respect, and even of reverence, which she had lost for centuries in Italy among the best minds.' Croce and his friends opposed the Lateran Pacts not because they objected to the idea of a reconciliation between church and state, 'but solely for the way it has been gained, and for the particular conventions that accompany it.' The concordat was a painful break with a great tradition – the abandonment of the separation between church and state negated the policy followed by Italy for the last sixty years. 'Conscious of the past, solicitous of the future, we contemplate with pain the break in the equilibrium that had been realized.'[12]

Croce was not afraid 'of the resurrection of a confessional state in Italy,' but he predicted, and was soon proved right, that the new concordat would create disagreements and different interpretations. For Croce, the disagreements in interpretation while the treaties were still being debated in Parliament proved that the 'equilibrium had been broken' and that soon would start again the traditional conflicts that 'the so-called concordats always produce,' followed by 'painful and sterile struggles on irrevocable facts, and pressures and menaces and fears, and the poisons poured on the souls by the pressures, the menaces and the fears.'[13]

Croce answered those, inside and outside the Senate, who regarded the reconciliation between Italy and the Vatican as a brilliant achievement, worthy to be supported despite the shortcomings of the concordat, in accordance with the old dictum that 'Paris is worth a Mass.' Croce reminded the senators, and also the pope, who had made disparaging remarks about Liberals and liberalism recently, that 'beside and against the men, who regard Paris worthy of a Mass, there are others for whom to listen or not to listen to a Mass is a fact infinitely more important than Paris, because it is an affair of conscience. Woe to society! to human history! if men who feel so differently had not been there in the past or were not here now'![14] Those sentences became immensely popular and were then and later repeated throughout Italy, as a concise powerful expression of opposition to fascism and to the opportunism of the Catholic Church.

The abandonment of a Machiavellian conception of politics is also evident in the speech's conclusion. There, Croce turned his attention to those who had reservations about the concordat but nevertheless were going to vote in favour of the pacts 'because they regard them as fruitful of unexpected good effects in the future, according to the other trite saying that from bad is born good, and from error truth.' Croce invited these people to leave aside hypothetical speculation on the future and 'to seek and simply do one's duty, in the present.' It was an obvious reference to Gentile, who disliked the concordat but had decided to vote in favour of the treaties, putting all his faith in Mussolini. Croce ended his speech by touching again a raw nerve in his old friend and others in the same predicament, when he reminded them that his vote and that of his friends was 'dictated by our conscience, to which we cannot refuse the obedience that it commands from us.'[15]

Reactions

Mussolini did not like Croce's speech, and during the debate he showed signs of annoyance. Afterwards, he instructed the newspapers to downplay Croce's intervention by giving a short summary followed by derogatory remarks. But, despite the incomplete accounts provided by a few newspapers, Croce's speech became known and generated discussion and approval among Liberals and Democrats.[16]

Croce himself was instrumental in achieving this result. He sent copies of the speech to all his friends and to those who requested a copy. Moreover, a week after the speech, evidently to satisfy the increasing demand for copies, Croce craftily took advantage of a privilege still open to members of the opposition: he asked the printing office of the Senate for 300 extra copies of his speech, which was then produced in a booklet format. In Naples, either under his direction or certainly with his knowledge, 400 more copies were printed in the same format and still additional copies were typed in loose sheets, to the concern and annoyance of the police who were unable to discover the printing press and to locate the typewriter that had done the clandestine job. Croce mailed the speech to his acquaintances, in many cases personally writing the address on the envelopes and using not only the Senate booklet but also the clandestine materials of Naples. Often he sent more than one copy with the evident intention of encouraging further diffusion. Sometime later the speech was also published in *La Critica*.[17]

As a result of Croce's speech in the Senate and the interest it generated in the country, police surveillance of his movements and control of his mail were increased, officially reversing an order of Mussolini in 1927, which had in any case never been fully observed. The chief of police, Bocchini, was soon informed of Croce's request to the Senate's printing office, and he immediately ordered the prefect of Naples to adopt against Croce 'careful and direct measures of surveillance,' to make 'discreet inquiries' about Croce's correspondents, to find out their names and their addresses, and finally to seize all the speeches sent out by mail. This was no longer possible, but the prefect of Naples took the order seriously and began to stop and control all Croce's mail, informing Rome every time a politically sensitive letter was found, and forwarding the compromising piece to Croce only after the approval of Bocchini had been received, but not before it had been copied and filed. As a result, two of Croce's close friends were questioned by the police, Pietro Pancrazi in Florence and Barbara Allason in Rome. Moreover, at regular intervals, the prefect sent reports to the minister of the interior, that is, to Mussolini, making a faithful summary of letters seized: 'in which are written phrases of support for the speech recently spoken in the Senate by Senator Croce, and also expressions less than respectful to the head of government.'[18]

The archives now contain, owing to the zeal of the prefect, many of those letters, which reflect the anti-Fascist faith of Croce's correspondents and even the honesty of police reports. The letters came from all over Italy but also from Europe and even from the United States. Sforza, from Paris, sent international press clippings, mostly in English. The writers included former members of Parliament and academics but also ordinary citizens. A Roman poet even sent six sonnets praising Croce while commenting on the Lateran Pacts, as the police noted, 'with ironical and anti-national feeling.' The letters seized by the police expressed admiration of Croce's stand. All shared his criticism of the Lateran Pacts. Some blamed Mussolini for the accord, others condemned the pope, while Bonomi questioned the king's conduct and his changed attitude, from opposition to support of a concordat. Many of those who wrote to Croce claimed to express not only their personal views but also the feelings of others, 'and there are many, more than we sometimes think,' as one of them said.[19]

The number of letters in the police file alone and the statements they contain prove that Croce's speech had touched a popular chord and was widely discussed. This evidence also demonstrates that, despite the press boycott and police harassment, opposition groups were still alive in the country and able to communicate among themselves.

News of Croce's stand and copies of his speech also reached the various places where anti-Fascist militants were jailed or confined. As Leo Valiani later wrote: 'When, on the 24th of May, 1929, Croce spoke against the Lateran Pacts, negotiated in the name of an enslaved Italy, by the man who had enslaved her ... we felt that he was also speaking for us, who were crowding the fascist jails and the islands of deportation.'[20]

Political Initiatives

In his own city, Croce's speech had repercussions not only among his traditional friends but also among the students at the university. Despite police controls, as Giorgio Amendola recalled in his memoirs and as Eugenio Reale confirmed in his, 'by now the Sunday afternoons in Croce's house had become the only existing meeting place among anti-Fascists.'[21] Similarly, in the *Taccuini*, Croce noted that, two days after his speech in the Senate, 'many people came to the house for the usual Sunday conversations.' It is easy to imagine that the conversation that day was mainly about the Lateran Pacts and the implications for the future. But the university students did not limit their interest to philosophical discussions; they also did something more concrete and more alarming for the police.

In their regular quarterly reports to the minister of the interior and to the chief of police on the political situation and public order, several prefects in 1929 commented on the Lateran Pacts. The majority assured Rome that the reconciliation had been well received throughout Italy, especially by the Catholic clergy. But the prefect of Naples also had to report 'an attempt at anti-Fascist propaganda,' telling Bocchini and Mussolini that students of the university tried to distribute on the streets of Naples 'copies of the speech made by Croce in the Senate on the concordat between the state and the church.' The police had also found that the students had mailed Croce's speech to other universities and to friends in other cities. The prefect hastened to add that he had no worries about the activities of these young people. Yet he also wrote that their actions were closely followed by the police and the police informers. The prefect's report confirms in a direct way what Amendola and Reale have said in their memoirs, namely, that, inspired by Croce, in Naples there was a group of liberal and democratic young men willing to take risks and able to make their presence felt. In fact, at that time they also published at regular intervals a clandestine periodical, called *L'Anti-fascista*, which often printed or reprinted articles by Croce, Salvemini, and others.[22]

The most interesting and certainly the best-known reaction to Croce's speech and to debates on the reconciliation happened in Turin. During the discussion in the Senate, an angry Mussolini had replied directly to

Croce's criticism, calling him *imboscato della storia,* or a shirker of history, the real meaning of which left Croce and others bewildered. Later, to make amends or to correct the bad impression, Mussolini explained that he was referring less to Croce's speech than to his decision to end the *History of Italy* at 1915, without including and discussing the war and the advent of fascism. If the literal meaning of the expression, when it was uttered, was not clear, the moral slur was plain, considering the bitter attacks on the *imboscati* during and after the war.

The moral and political implication of that expression aroused the indignation of a group of university students in Turin who circulated on campus a letter of solidarity with Croce. The letter was signed by some students who, during the resistance and after the war, became famous in Italian cultural and political life in the Party of Action and the Communist movement. 'Unable to protest in public and through the press, we want to express, in private and among ourselves, our affection and our devotion.' Offended by Mussolini's accusation, they now wished to protest 'against the insult hurled at you by the Prime Minister,' and also they rejected the accusation of shirker 'because all your work as an historian is inspired by an intense love of Italy.' The students expressed their faith in Croce's moral leadership and their gratitude for his political stand, describing him 'as the only one who has raised his voice in the name of moral conscience.' Having written the letter, the students asked their professor to sign it. Umberto Cosmo, one of Gramsci's teachers and the man Croce had defended during the war, not only signed willingly but also added a note of his own: 'to express to the illustrious friend his admiration and his devotion,' and to assure him that '… a higher honour could not have come to the work of the free philosopher and proud character than from the insult of the powerful against him.'[23]

Tipped off by spies, the police intercepted the letter and Croce never received the students' message. However, he was immediately informed about those events by Augusto Monti, another anti-Fascist teacher, politically closer to Salvemini but always respectful of Croce. Monti had in mind two reasons for writing to Croce. One was to inform Croce that his speech had become known in Italy despite the official boycott: 'Anyway I wanted to inform you soon, so you could see what kind of an echo a speech not reported by the papers has had in Italy.' The other reason was even more political. 'I believe that it would be useful and also of comfort to know that some university students on their own initiative were writing to you a letter of thanks and approbation before they were arrested by the police.'[24]

Those students and their teacher were immediately arrested and put in jail; however, on the whole, they received mild sentences and were able to regain their freedom in a few weeks. But, even after their release, Bocchini ordered further inquiries into the case and the students' background in order to ascertain their political connections. In fact, the police authorities always regarded them with suspicion and kept a watchful eye on their activities. Nevertheless, despite the police surveillance, Croce met those students soon after their release from jail and every time he went to Turin or during his summer vacation in the Piedmont countryside. In some cases he read their university dissertations and found publishers for their books. In Turin he had long walks with Umberto Segre, who had taken the initiative for writing the letter and then for collecting the signatures. From the letter of Monti and entries in the diaries, there is good reason to believe that Croce, as he had done the previous year, intervened in favour of those students, using his personal connections. Others in positions of influence did the same, with good results.[25]

During the Fascist regime, old friendships, family relations, and business connections often were used to lighten the burden of oppression or the asperity of the law for the young. These interventions were possible and sometimes successful when members of the middle classes were involved, not only because they had the necessary connections with the party in power and the old establishment that was still influential in the civil service, but, more important, because their requests did not conflict with government policy. For ideological and political reasons, the regime preferred to be tough with the Communists and to be lenient with the sons of the bourgeoisie. This allowed the government to point to the Communists as the only enemies of Fascist Italy, and to present fascism as the true defender of Italian civilization. Official propaganda, then, used the granting of clemency to foster the image of Mussolini as a generous and benevolent dictator.

Treves, Vinciguerra, and Russo

One of the students from Turin was not as fortunate as the others: Paolo Treves, contrary to regulations, was separated from his friends, kept in isolation, and detained for a few months longer. Paolo was the second son of Claudio Treves, the exiled former Socialist Party leader, who had always been hated by Mussolini since his socialist days, when both had worked for the party newspaper, *Avanti!* Always under close police surveillance, for political and family reasons, Paolo Treves had met Croce for the first time in 1928, while he was attending university in Turin. In the typical fashion of the time, the Liberal senator and the son of a Socialist leader met 'in the back room of a Turin bookstore,' since 'it was not advisable to be seen together in the streets.'[26]

After that first meeting, Croce took an interest in Treves's studies, wrote letters to him, encouraged him to turn his thesis into a book, and then persuaded Laterza to publish the volume. After Treves was released from jail and graduated from university in 1929, his family moved to Rome, where they had great difficulty in finding jobs and apartments. But, at the first opportunity, Treves took a trip to Naples, where he was warmly received by Croce and his family and engaged in a conversation that 'lasted the whole afternoon' and later was continued while Croce and the young man warlked along the streets of Naples, 'although there were two guards following us.' Afterwards, Croce and Paolo Treves, and his brother Pietro, met again on various occasions and in other cities; they discussed political questions but also private matters and, eventually, the possibility of escaping to France because of the 1938 racial laws against Jews. But no other occasion matched that meeting in Naples at the end of 1929, when Paolo was only twenty-one years old. His memoirs, published in England in 1939, expressed his gratitude for 'Croce's benevolence and affection' and 'for sharing ideas in history and politics' 'during those years of loneliness,' 'after father in 1926 was compelled to leave the country.'[27]

In 1929, Treves was not the only man who visited Croce and came away with words of encouragement or more concrete help. That same year, Mario Vinciguerra, Lauro De Bosis, and others tried to organize a new underground movement, which they called the National Alliance, making direct reference to the moderate tradition of the Risorgimento. The group directed its appeals to the traditional forces of Italian society. The ultimate aim of the National Alliance was to convince the king to employ the army to oust Mussolini from power – that is, to do voluntarily in 1930 what he would be compelled to do in 1943. Croce encouraged Vinciguerra and gave his support to the new organization, looking 'with sympathy at the attempt of the National Alliance,' as Salvemini wrote in 1954. In Croce's diaries, during 1929 and 1930, there are reported visits to Naples and meetings in Rome with Vinciguerra and Irene di Robilant, who was one of the most active members of that small group.[28]

The memoirs of Eugenio Reale in the National Archives provide more details about Croce's support of the Alliance. When in 1930 Vinciguerra was arrested under the accusation 'of having organized an anti-Fascist movement and wanting to procure the fall of the regime,' Croce tried to help his unfortunate friend, devising a little subterfuge. Hurriedly he wrote and had printed another flyer in the name of the National Alliance. He then asked Reale and his young anti-Fascist friends to mail and distribute the flyer in a clandestine manner, to lead the police into believing that Vinciguerra had no connection with the organization. The stratagem did not work, however; Vinciguerra was sentenced to fifteen years in jail.[29]

After Vinciguerra's imprisonment, Croce's support and friendship for him and his little daughter increased. His involvement in the political and family troubles of Vinciguerra was reported to the police but also became known in Paris among the anti-Fascist exiles. In 1931 the organ of the Democratic anti-Fascist groups in France, *La Libertà*, carried a news item on the front page under the title, 'The most beautiful work of Benedetto Croce.' The piece was probably written by Claudio Treves or by Carlo Rosselli. 'Mario Vinciguerra, sentenced to fifteen years in jail by the Special Tribunal, has left behind two things: a great book on *Romanticism* and a little girl of seven ... But we have just received the beautiful news that a man has taken care of the two things left behind by Vinciguerra. This is Benedetto Croce ... In fact, under Croce's sponsorship, Vinciguerra's book on the romantics has just been published. Moreover, Benedetto Croce has taken under his charge Vinciguerra's daughter, and has placed her in a private school, providing for her future needs even in case of his death. The mind of Croce is great but his heart is even greater.'[30]

Remembering these events in 1973, Livia Tilgher, Vinciguerra's sister-in-law, reported that after his arrest many friends abandoned Vinciguerra, but she found Croce 'moving in his support and generosity toward his unfortunate friend and toward his daughter.'[31]

In 1929 Croce used his wealth for another political purpose. That year, Gentile, displeased with the political contents and irreverent polemical style of the periodical *Leonardo*, ousted Russo from the editorship. Immediately, Croce, in agreement with Albertini, Casati, and Fortunato, decided to help Russo, providing the funds necessary to start a new periodical, which appeared in 1930 as *La Nuova Italia* and lasted for a few years. With his intervention, Croce kept alive in Florence a centre of cultural independence. Russo was not only an old friend, he was also a good polemicist and an independent spirit, faithful to the ideals of the Risorgimento. *La Nuova Italia* could now supplement the work of *La*

Critica, devoting less space to high culture but paying more attention to current literary events. In its short existence, the new periodical fulfilled these expectations, defending the liberal tradition against radical Fascists and, with no less pugnacity, against the new spirit of clericalism created by the reconciliation, which was rather strong in Florence.[32]

Croce was closely involved with the editorial content of this periodical; he gave advice; made suggestions; sent newspaper clippings; and finally, invited by Russo, wrote short and polemical notes that appeared under the name of Russo, who changed or deleted and then added a few words, here and there, to reflect his personal style and to make the camouflage more believable. Or so Russo and Croce liked to believe: the stratagem in all probaility did not fool the police; it certainly did not fool Gramsci, then in jail, who noticed the strange presence in Russo's writing of words and turn of phrases peculiar to Croce's prose. Croce's collaboration in *La Nuova Italia*, like the collaboration of Omodeo and Ruggiero in *La Critica*, shows that there was unity among Croce and his friends and that they did not fight their battles alone but rather acted with 'the spirit of a religious community.'[33]

'To Serve God with Joy'

After the reconciliation between church and state, the police increased their surveillance of Croce's movements and their control over his correspondence. Croce noticed this and complained to the prefect, more to embarrass him than anything else. In June 1929 Croce wrote, 'I went to speak with the high commissioner, Castelli, for the renewal of my passport, and I showed him that I have become aware of the special attention that the police are giving to my person, and to my correspondence that is all opened and then glued again, and often delivered incomplete. But I only made the statement, and told him that I will not write a complaint, as something useless.'[34]

Croce invariably recognized the agents following him or watching his house. He spoke to them, wished them well, and even told them when he was leaving town. This kind of unexpected friendliness created some embarrassment, and prompted the usual excuses. But, despite the smiles and the salutations, every time Croce left Naples, the agents did their duty, and the police in Rome or in Turin were notified, as recorded in the archives.[35]

Police surveillance continued even when political reasons were absent. In June 1929 the authorities saw fit to send special agents and spies to a small town near Naples, where Croce and his wife had been invited to attend a baptismal ceremony by the family of an old friend. The prefect was even required to file a report to Rome for that occasion. From this report, and the other four written by local spies, it is possible to understand the efforts made and the devices used to create fear and suspicion among opponents of the regime. In the old southern Italian tradition, the Fusco family, Croce's host, had made preparations for a great feast and, as the prefect wrote, 'had invited the best people of the place, but all these, knowing the political views of Croce, refused the invitation. Only relatives and the closest friends took part in the festivities.'[36]

Incidents like this, and the political atmosphere that they reveal, explain the moments of sadness experienced by Croce during the Fascist regime, especially in 1929, when often we find such revealing entries in the diaries as this: 'Suddenly the usual crisis of sadness came over me.'[37]

After the Lateran Pacts, in personal correspondence or private conversation, other friends confessed to Croce the same feelings of frustration and impotence. On these occasions, he told them, or repeated to himself, that whether sailing with favourable winds or rowing against the currents, one has to do his best, because the fulfilling of duty provides the only hope for a better future. In a letter written during this time to console his old friend Giuseppe Lombardo Radice, Croce wrote: 'The world unfolds as it should; we cannot make it go according to our desire. What is important is that ... we behave well, trying to serve God with joy' and 'carrying on our work as best we can, despite the present adversities.'[38]

CHAPTER NINE

'Faith in the Future and Courage in the Present,' 1930–1940

The elections of 1929 and the Lateran Pacts marked the end of one era and the beginning of another in the history of fascism and in the fortunes of Mussolini. The elections were a vote of confidence for the government, and turned into a plebiscite for Mussolini, showing that the regime had consolidated its original success and now rested on solid foundations. For fascism, those were years of consensus, but for the opposition, or what remained of it, the period was one of despair and isolation. Many lost hope for a different future, became disillusioned, and abandoned the struggle as a useless and quixotic undertaking. Yet, amidst the general consensus in favour of the regime, political opposition to fascism never disappeared completely in Italy; instead, it continued in different and precarious ways, and was carried out, more or less, by all parties, according to their own traditions and expectations. More important, in all walks of life, there were men and women who remained faithful to liberal and democratic ideas. By their example, they were able to preserve the memory of the past and to offer a set of values to the younger generation different from the one preached by the regime.[1]

The political work of the anti-Fascist opposition now assumed new forms and employed different means. When the normal avenues and activities became impossible, the Communists tried to build an underground organization and some Socialist and Democratic groups did the same. For the other movements of the opposition, one can say what Croce claimed after the war about the Liberal Party. 'The party, that did not have legal existence any longer, and for that reason had neither an office nor the possibility of holding meetings, nevertheless continued to live from one end of Italy to the other in the personal relations, in the reciprocal visits, in the hospitality of friendly houses, in the agreements

that we reached and in the comfort that we gained from those young
men that remained immune from Fascist seductions and did not care
about intimidation.' In these conditions, political continuity with the
country's liberal past was assured and a new generation of leaders was
created. The political and moral function of those 'friendly houses' was
recognized a few years ago even by the Communist leader Giorgio Amendola in one of his last books: 'During fascism in every Italian city around
liberal personalities were formed centres of contacts, meetings, information and orientation. Some of these centres assumed a national and
international function, and became required stops for foreign observers
and academics.'[2]

Under the Fascist regime, the Liberal opposition was centred around
old political leaders, university teachers, lawyers, and intellectuals.
Moreover, in their contacts and actions, these personalities tended to
act less as members of a political party and more as the point of reference of a wider movement. In this manner their influence went beyond
party ties and assumed the form of moral leadership, at least for some of
them. Most of them were well connected with the old establishment and
the civil service, and they could count often on their national and international contacts. Some did more than others and assumed functions of
leadership. Luigi Albertini, who had organized a special fund for the
education of Giovanni Amendola's sons during the Fascist regime, continued to send money to anti-Fascist leaders in exile and to help promising young people in Italy. Luigi Einaudi, on behalf of the Rockefeller
Foundation, offered scholarships to needy anti-Fascist students so they
could continue their education abroad. With his advice and financial
support, he was *magna pars* of his son Giulio's publishing house. Also, as
editor of prestigious economic periodicals, Einaudi published essays by
anti-Fascist scholars, even when they were in jail, as was the case with
Ernesto Rossi, one of the first leaders in Italy of Guistizia e Libertà.
Mario Ferrara, a criminal lawyer, gave free legal assistance to young men
in political trouble, and even defended Communists before the Special
Tribunal. Raffaele Mattioli, as general manager of Milan's Banca Commerciale, sheltered in the research department of that bank many who
later played leading roles in the Party of Action. He also had regular
meetings with a wide circle of friends critical of fascism. Among these
there was Piero Sraffa, the Cambridge economist friend of J.M. Keynes,
who was also in close contact with the imprisoned Gramsci. It was to
Mattioli that Sraffa entrusted the safety of Gramsci's *Quaderni* (Notebooks) after his death. Alessandro Casati was an indefatigable travelling

salesman for the liberal cause, in the process making a police informer 'greatly suspicious of his frequent visits to Naples.' Another great traveller who also visited Naples quite often was Umberto Zanotti Bianco. Living in Rome, he had access to the capital's influential circles and, according to police, had 'relations with a great number of persons, contrary to the regime' and carried out 'a great deal of activity against the regime, but in a quiet way.' But Croce was the most influential leader of the new liberal forces and was at the centre of the new opposition, and already had become the symbol of liberal and democratic anti-fascism. As Gramsci recognized in one of his jail *Notebooks*, Croce had acquired that position and enjoyed that 'relative popularity' not only for his literary style and the nature of his writings but also for 'an ethical reason,' especially 'for the steadiness of character demonstrated by Croce on several occasions of national and European life,' and 'for his behaviour maintained during the war and after.' Gramsci chose these words carefully, no doubt to avoid censorship, to indicate the years of Mussolini's dictatorship.[3]

Croce's Life under Fascism

The police reports and the comments of the prefects make it possible to understand the peculiar conditions under which Croce exercised his position of moral leadership. During the Fascist regime, Croce was never openly persecuted, but he was constantly harassed. Police reports always described him as *noto oppositore*, or notorious adversary, in full agreement, this time, with the international press, which during the same period, referred to Croce as 'the well known anti-Fascist.' Against him the police could not employ the tough measures used against the *sovversivi*, as the communists, anarchists, and members of Giustizia e Libertà were called. As a senator, Croce could neither be arrested nor jailed without the consent and advice of the Senate, but the political authorities tried to isolate him from his friends by keeping his life and his activities under close police scrutiny. As we have seen, Croce's house in Naples and his summer residence in Piedmont were under police surveillance. Visits to his homes became a political liability and a matter for police suspicion. The policemen on duty made lists of Croce's visitors, and then the prefects ordered inquiries into their affairs. Often, 'frequent visits to Benedetto Croce' is the only accusation against a given person found in the police reports.[4]

Croce was allowed to travel in Italy and in Europe, and no legal restric-

tions were ever put on his movements, but often some annoying obstacles were placed in his way. His departures from Naples and his arrivals
in other cities were communicated by the police authorities or by the
prefects to their counterparts elsewhere. His passport was not renewed
as a matter of course and certainly not as a citizen's basic right, but always
after some delay and never before the prefect of Naples had asked and
received the approval from the chief of police in Rome. Croce's trips
abroad were always followed by special agents acting 'with judicious discretion,' to quote Bocchini's favourite advice.[5]

Not only were Croce's movements followed and his residences monitored by regular police agents, but the political branch of the police, as
was customary at the time, also employed informers to try to understand
Croce's inner motivations and goals. These were highly cultured people, recruited from Croce's own entourage and thus able to gain his
confidence and that of his collaborators by discussing cultural matters
and even initiating political conversation. Their reports contain astute
observations and prove that the confidence of the police in their work
was well placed. The chief of police read the reports and then passed
them to Mussolini himself, who signed his famous 'M,' in red or blue
pencil, and sometimes scribbled grammatical corrections, short instructions, or even sarcastic comments, as when one informer tried to report
something out of nothing on second- and third-hand hearsay.[6]

Croce never stopped writing and publishing his books and his periodical, *La Critica*, during the Fascist regime. But at regular intervals, especially after 1934, his editor, Laterza, was confronted with unexpected
difficulties which caused moral distress and financial loss. Under the
censorship law of the time, revised with more severity in 1934, the censors in Bari had to read Croce's books before they could be printed and
published. These censors made known their dislike of Croce's works,
and often delayed or denied their approval and the printing permit with
one excuse or another, depending on their mood or their superior's
orders. Sometimes the sale of a book was banned after permission for its
printing had been granted. Once the books were finally published and
sent to the bookstores, often the police took note of those who were
seen buying the books or reading the periodical in the libraries.[7]

Moreover, the newspapers were ordered to ignore Croce's works – no
reviews of them were permitted – and to ridicule the man himself. In
1933 Mussolini complained that a certain periodical had mentioned
Croce's name too often and greatly exaggerated his importance. Also in
1933, with a short note to the minister of education, he expressed sur-

prise, 'as something incredible,' that many public and school libraries still had subscriptions to *La Critica*. Francesco Ercole, the minister, acted with speed; however, instead of issuing a direct order, he merely expressed the view that 'directors of the scholastic institutions' should 'cut any association with the periodical.' Some institutions followed the minister's advice, while others simply moved the periodical from the open shelves to the stacks. But, soon afterwards, this time without any equivocation, the same minister ordered the high schools to remove one of Croce's books on aesthetic theory from the list of adopted textbooks, and his intervention also resulted in the dismissal of Giuseppe Lombardo Radice from the editorship of the periodical *L'Educazione Nazionale*. One of the charges against Lombardo Radice was that in a recent essay he had defended some of Croce's literary judgments.

During this period, at the University of Naples, Adolfo Omodeo was not allowed to display a large collection of historical books that Croce had donated to his department. In 1937 the catalogue of the Laterza publishing house, which had been reprinted for more than twenty years without changes in its format, was seized by police and ordered out of circulation, because it had been published without prior authorization and, above all, 'because it contains an apology for Croce's thought.' Finally, in 1940, with a rather chilling expression revealing the mentality and atmosphere of the times, the minister of propaganda informed Laterza that the prior order of suspension had been revoked and *La Critica* could continue its publication 'because Mussolini does not want to give any hemlock cup to the philosopher.'[8]

At the same time, the censorship of Croce's private correspondence intensified in the 1930s. In Naples, all incoming letters to Croce were stopped, and most of them were read, copied, and filed, including letters from his wife and from his daughters. In other cities, letters sent by Croce to his friends were also opened before being forwarded, usually after long delays. Many of his letters were sent to the chief of police and even to Mussolini, and forwarded after approval had been received. In some cases, letters considered politically sensitive, especially those supporting Croce's position, never reached their destination. As we have already noted, owing to the work and the zeal of the police and the censors, a great amount of material has been collected in the National Archives of Rome. Judging by the correspondence between Croce and Ada Gobetti found in Turin, similar documents in all probability are also located in the prefectures of Bari, Florence, Milan, and other cities.

Materials in the National Archives

In the collection of personal files at National Archives, the Croce file contains twenty boxes, or *buste;* in these boxes there are 1,368 folders, or *fascicoli,* one for each of Croce's correspondents. In the collection of the Prime Minister's Office, or Segreteria Particolare del Duce, there are two heavy folders, containing documents collected from 1926 to 1943 for the special attention of Mussolini. There are also other files on Croce in other sections and collections of the archives. Letters of Croce to his friends or documents mentioning his name can be found in the Central Political Files, or Casellario Politico Centrale, where the police authorities kept the files of all Mussolini's political opponents during the Fascist regime. A close but far from complete study of these records has revealed that the police authorities were in possession of the full subscription list of *La Critica,* and that informers had supplied the names of Croce's most trusted friends in major Italian cities. Between the work of the regular agents and the reports of the informers, the prefect of Naples, the chief of police, and Mussolini knew the most important aspects of Croce's life and activity, public and private, at all times.[9]

The evidence suggests that Croce was one of the main targets of the secret police. The information in their possession left them without any doubt about the political opinions of the regime's '*noto oppositore,* senatore Benedetto Croce.' Because it knew Croce's tenacious liberal faith, his unchanging opposition to fascism, and his critical view of Mussolini, the regime never entertained the hope of one day winning Croce's support for its causes and never seriously tried to lure him into the fold of fascism, as it had done successfully with many others. When one informer suggested a sort of peace treaty between Croce and fascism, with concessions coming only from the regime, the chief of police rejected the proposal 'as too complicated,' knowing from other sources that it was a waste of time for both parties.[10]

Faced with police surveillance, the reading of his mail, and subtle harassments, Croce adopted some elementary precautions but in general continued his usual way of life, receiving and visiting friends and writing and publishing books. Without violating any law, he put into practice with shrewdness and tenacity what has been called, quite appropriately, an open conspiracy, *una cospirazione alla luce del sole.* While fascism celebrated its triumphs and the new leaders strutted about in special uniforms, flaunting their power, Croce stood his ground and even increased his efforts against the authoritarian regime, defending the ideals of liberalism and 'the traditions of studies, the way of life and the moral concepts, that belonged to the men to whom we owe the resurrection of Italy.'[11]

In a time when the new regime was destroying venerable institutions and creating new myths, Croce remained faithful to the ideals of the Risorgimento, inspiring others to share his faith and to join the anti-Fascist resistance. In 1932, writing from jail to his sister-in-law, Gramsci expressed well, and better than anybody else, Croce's magisterial role during those years: 'While many people lose their heads, and grope among apocalyptic feelings of intellectual panic, Croce becomes a point of reference and is able to give inner strength by his unshakeable faith that evil cannot metaphysically prevail and that history is rationality.' Beyond the philosophical jargon, necessary to avoid censorship, Gramsci is saying that there is no need to despair or to abandon the struggle, because political victories are always temporary and freedom is the spring of life, destined to prevail again after momentary defeat.[12]

La Famiglia Italiana

Because of his intellectual prestige, Croce became, in Italy and abroad, the moral leader of the anti-Fascist opposition and the symbol of Italian resistance to Mussolini's dictatorship. He found himself at the centre of a political movement which was loosely organized but united by moral commitment and common aspirations, pre-eminent among them a love of freedom and a desire for the return of political liberty. This *Famiglia Italiana*, as Croce called it, was made up of members of the cultural elite, who in the past had been Liberals, Democrats, or moderate Socialists. These men had once been engaged in bitter debates, had even disagreed on fundamental issues, but now they had been brought together by the loss of freedom and by the need to regain it. Even more important for the future, the requirements of the struggle and the nature of the adversary compelled all of them to reassess their differences, spurring them to rethink old conclusions, to seek new solutions, and to reflect on the reasons for their common defeat. Members of this 'family' were present in all major urban centres and were able to maintain regular contacts among themselves and the surrounding areas, not without some degree of danger.[13]

In this unstructured movement, an important role was played by women, as wives, sisters, friends, or militants. Under the guise of innocent gatherings, the residences of Barbara Allason, Giuliana Benzoni,

Bianca Ceva, Maria Cittadella, Irene Di Robilant, Ada Gobetti, Nina Ruffini, and Elena Croce became discreet centres of opposition. Especially in Capri, Rome, Turin, Milan, and Veneto, these women provided the venue for cultural and political meetings, away from police interference. In their elegant living rooms, kindred people met with some security, exchanged news, and discussed political events and future actions.

On one of these women, Maria Cittadella, 'an ardent friend of liberty,' we have a brief but moving tribute written by a great historian, Gaetano De Sanctis, like her a liberal and a Catholic. De Sanctis writes: 'In Rome she kept a salotto in which we talked mainly of freedom and expressed without fear the most absolute hatred and contempt for tyranny.' In her house, 'often trying to cover their tracks before entering, gathered the most eminent men of the opposition against fascism.' On these occasions, 'there one could meet Benedetto Croce, Alessandro Casati, the duke Colonna di Cesarò, the count Umberto Zanotti Bianco,' and sometimes even a famous friar, Father Giovanni Semeria. During the meetings and the conversations, 'we reaffirmed our unshaken faith in freedom and our firmest hope in its triumph, which unfortunately,' De Sanctis concludes, 'the noble woman, who died before her time, could not see.' Cittadella belonged to the upper classes; she had residences also in Milan and Venice, where she maintained the same hospitality. The other women, more or less, enjoyed a similar social status. Giovanna Benzoni was the niece of Ferdinando Martini, a former minister and colonial governor; she divided her time between Rome and Florence and had a villa in Capri, where she often entertained, besides her many Italian friends, the Czecho-Slovak leaders, Tomas Masaryk and Edvard Benes. The meetings that took place in Ada Gobetti's house in Turin are the best known, but the gatherings in other cities – if not as well documented – were as frequent.

In this long chain of concentric circles, covering all Italy, Croce was the strong link, providing inspiration and solidarity through his writings, his frequent trips, and his constant correspondence. 'During those gloomy years,' wrote Barbara Allason in her memoirs, 'Benedetto Croce was truly the beacon and the guide.'[14]

Even the police informers and the political authorities recognized, at various times, the existence of this unorthodox political movement and the role played by Croce. In 1934 a promising young historian-turned police informer, with the name of Cesare, provided the prefect of Naples with a list of Croce's friends who frequently went to his house, making astute, if unflattering, comments on their personal qualities and political ideas. The same year, prodded by his masters, he sent to the prefect 'a partial list, which could be useful for further investigation.' In this second list were 'the names of persons in various Italian cities who have relations of a political nature with Benedetto Croce.' The cities mentioned were Genoa, Turin, Milan, Florence, Rome, and Messina in Sicily. Among the people listed were old politicians, university teachers, a businessman, and recent university graduates. 'Almost all of them,' to use the informer's own words, 'are university teachers and personalities of great influence in the fields of politics and culture, and they have a great many connections.'[15]

In 1935 even the chief of police, Bocchini, in a departmental note, recognized the political implications of Croce's cultural activities and personal relationships. He had to admit that a group of university teachers, living in different cities, 'under the pretense of literary and philosophical discussions are increasing their correspondence and personal relations, which have their centre in Benedetto Croce, whose unchanged feelings of hostility against the regime are well known.' Finally, in a report to the prefect of Naples, the learned Neapolitan informer, using some vivid expressions, concluded that Croce did not belong to 'a proper structured organization' but 'is the head of a *centro di affari*,' adding that this 'business centre' was 'a small coterie of university teachers and dreamers, made up of friends with great social connections, scattered in various Italian cities.'[16] Because Bocchini was a learned man himself and knew the power of culture, he never eased police surveillance of Croce's circle.

Croce's Houses as Centres of Opposition

For Croce, political activity and opposition to fascism really began at home. During the entire Fascist regime, his house remained open to all those who wanted to see him for personal or cultural reasons. In particular, the opponents of fascism knew that they would always be received by Croce and his wife 'with a friendly smile,' to use the words of Mario Vinciguerra, who had personally experienced such a welcome more than once. Croce was even willing to break his work routine, as he told Giorgio Amendola, 'to meet my anti-Fascist friends.'[17]

At one time or another, in fact, some of the most important leaders of the anti-Fascist movement in Italy made trips to Naples, seeking Croce's support or his advice. Inside his library, Croce and Omodeo wrote some of their major essays and prepared the publication of *La Critica*. Senator

Casati made frequent visits to Naples, not only to see an old friend but also to bring news from northern Italy and sometimes from Europe, and then to carry back information to common friends in other parts of Italy. Guido De Ruggiero and Luigi Russo brought information from their universities in Rome and Florence. When Croce's eldest daughter married, she and her husband, Raimondo Craveri, became roving ambassadors and helped to maintain the close ties between Croce and his friends in Rome, Milan, and Turin.[18]

Besides old friends, there were also frequent visits to Croce's house by members of the younger generation, not only from Naples but also from Rome and other Italian cities. In the early 1930s, the informer regularly assigned to the Croce case noted that 'every evening there are meetings of young students in Croce's house.' In 1937 other young scholars from Bologna in central Italy went to Naples to seek Croce's inspiration and support. After they returned home, one of them, Carlo Ludovico Ragghianti, wrote a note of appreciation to Croce: 'My friends and I wish to thank you for your cordial hospitality given to us on our visit to Naples.' In Croce's diaries and in Amendola's autobiography, one finds the names of young persons who visited Croce and later played prominent roles in politics and culture, bringing to their activity a special 'Crocean' flavour, admired by some and disliked by others.[19]

With all these friends coming and going, Croce's residence in Naples became one of the best places to gather free information about Italy and Europe. Croce corresponded with writers, journalists, and academics from France, England, Germany, and the United States, and they visited Naples when they went on holiday to Italy or passed through the country on route to Greece or Egypt. Walter Lippmann always stopped in Naples on his European tours to gather fresh information about the continent's political situation. Often, ambassadors of European nations paid a visit to Croce with one excuse or another. The British Council, which offered classes and lectures on English language and literature, even rented two rooms on the second floor of Croce's building, providing, no doubt, the occasion for discreet visits. When national or international conferences of a cultural nature took place in Naples, some delegates made a point of visiting Croce, or he invited to his home those of them he found intellectually congenial.

Mussolini and his movement tried in subtle ways to keep Croce in isolation, but the outside world kept in touch with him, and he kept in touch with it. After returning from Russia and after a meeting with Maxim Gorky in Capri, Stefan Zweig went to Naples and paid tribute to

Croce's anti-fascism. 'I could not but admire the freshness and the mental elasticity which the old man preserved in the daily struggle.' He also noted that 'this hermetic isolation of a single man in a city of millions, in a nation of millions was at once weird and magnificent.'[20]

Piedmont and Turin

Visitors also descended upon Croce's summer residence in Piedmont, which was conveniently located near the vacation residences of Albertini, Franco Antonicelli, Frassati, Gobetti, and Ruffini. Friends from Turin and other parts of northern Italy went there as well. During his vacations, Croce saw not only university professors but also other senators and former ministers of the Giolitti cabinets; a few times he had meetings with Enrico Caviglia, among the few generals critical of fascism. Because of its location, friends going to or returning from France stopped at Croce's Piedmont house for a day or two, to discuss French politics and in general to share information. And, as at his Naples home, Croce's summer residence also welcomed young men still attending university or recently graduated but already active in the underground and in contact with the exiles in Paris.

The political importance of Croce's summer residence, and his connection with members of the underground movement of Giustizia e Libertà was recognized in 1934 by a police informer, who felt that Croce carried out most of his political activity during the summer months and in Piedmont. He was among the first to note, too, the importance of Leone Ginzburg, husband of the Italian writer Natalia Ginzburg and father of the historian Carlo Ginzburg, in Croce's entourage: 'Until last summer the Russian was one of the most frequent visitors in Croce's summer residence, together with Signora Ada Gobetti, widow of the notorious Piero.' The informer also reported that among Croce's frequent guests were Barbara Allason and Umberto Cosmo 'and all the others that the recent police arrests and investigation have shown were involved in criminal activities against the regime.' The informer referred to the arrest of a group of young people belonging to Giustizia e Libertà, 'a bunch of anti-fascist Jews on the exiles' payroll.'

The city of Turin was equally important in Croce's political activities. In 1937 Croce's daughter, writing from Turin, told her mother in Naples that there were 'many friends who wanted to see father.' During his frequent visits to Turin, in the house of his brother-in-law or in other friendly places, Croce met not only famous university teachers, like Giole Solari,

Luigi Einaudi, and Francesco Ruffini, but also younger leaders of the Liberal Party. Among these, Franco Antonicelli later became president of Piedmont's Committee of National Liberation, while Manlio Brosio, then a lawyer, became a minister in Ferruccio Parri's cabinet and later an ambassador, ending his career as NATO's secretary-general. In Turin, too, Croce also kept in close contact with younger people who were critical of fascism, associated with Giustizia e Libertà, and grouped around Leone Ginsburg and Carlo Levi and their many friends, working in Giulio Einaudi's fledgling publishing house and writing in La Cultura.[21]

Among the Italian cities, Turin had a special place in Croce's mind and heart, not only because it was the city of his wife but also because of its historical role as the centre of the Risorgimento. Since his marriage, his presence in the streets and porticoes of the city had been a familiar sight, while his intellectual influence at the university had been constant for years and deeply touched generations of students who later became Liberals, Socialists, Communists, and members of the Actionist Diaspora following the Party of Action's collapse in 1946. Rather than 'the city of Gramsci and Gobetti,' as the city is often described, Turin more properly deserves to be called – without detracting anything from the historical merit of those two men – the city of Croce. Certainly, his intellectual influence among teachers and students was far greater there than in his own city of Naples; in Turin between the wars, Croce's political presence was more evident and remained more fruitful. As the literary critic Natalino Sapegno has recognized, 'Croce's example was always present' not only among the friends of Gobetti but also among the members of other movements. In 1934 the well-informed historian-spy came to the same conclusion. He recognized that Turin was the city where Croce 'does most of his political activity' and 'where are living many who belong to Crocean anti-fascism.' For their part, after the war, in historical essays or autobiographical notes, several intellectual personalities of Turin acknowledged the influence of Croce in shaping their political and cultural ideas in their formative years despite 'the interferences and oppressions of the state' during the Fascist period.[22]

Italian Travel

To relieve his isolation, Croce travelled to various Italian cities throughout the 1930s. The frequency of these excursions was dictated by his recognition of the insecurity of the mail and by need to communicate freely with trusted friends. His trips in this period bear a striking similarity to the underground activities of the Communists and of Giustizia e Libertà; the only difference was that they were carried out in the open and accomplished their aim without breaking existing laws. From 1930 to 1940, month by month, the diaries of Croce register his trips to Bari, Rome, Florence, Milan, and Turin to meet kindred people, young and old. To quote V.E. Alfieri, a young teacher often in jail and out of work for his opposition activities, who was visited several times by Croce in different cities of northern Italy: 'During the Fascist regime the main scope of Croce's trips was to keep contact with those he used to call "the Italian family", to see trusted friends, to give and to receive news, to encourage the afflicted, to strengthen the doubtful,' and, young Alfieri adds, 'to teach some logic and common sense to hot heads.'[23]

Police records and the reports of the prefects make clear that, at one time or another, directly or indirectly, Croce became acquainted with people who played a leading role in the Resistance or assumed positions of command in the liberation struggle after 1943. In Rome, Croce maintained close ties with Guido De Ruggiero and Gaetano De Sanctis, leading university teachers and well known then for their opposition to fascism. In the capital Croce also had meetings and conversations with a group of young men who later became leaders of the Liberal Party during and after the war, like Leone Cattani and Nicolò Carandini. Also in Rome, Croce had contact with Umberto Zanotti Bianco, 'a dangerous person,' according to police reports, who maintained connections with many people in high places 'notoriously contrary to the regime.' In Florence, Croce was usually the guest of Luigi Russo, who gathered in his house students and teachers from the universities of Florence and Pisa. Among the attendees was the jurist Piero Calamandrei, one of the fathers of the Italian constitution, and the philosopher Guido Calogero, the founder of the clandestine movement *Liberalsocialismo*, which had two of its most active centres in the universities of Florence and Pisa. In Florence, Croce was often invited to the house of Nello Rosselli, the younger brother of Carlo, and to that of Alessandro Levi, the brother-in-law of Claudio Treves, the old Socialist reformist leader and friend of Turati. As well, in Florence, and probably in other cities, Croce also expressed his views in enemy territory, so to speak. Once in a while he visited Ugo Ojetti, an old friend who was now a member of the Academy of Italy and on good terms with Mussolini. 'During fascism,' Croce wrote in his diary, 'Ojetti always showed great deference towards me, and even some courage; in fact he invited me to his house, where I spoke my mind freely before him and his other guests.'[24]

In the hospitable house of Casati in Lombardy, Croce was greeted not only by his traditional friends Alfieri, Francesco Flora, and Paolo and Pietro Treves but also by other Socialists, a group of influential liberal Catholics, and 'similar elements of the Masonic Order,' as the police informer described them. The same informer added that Tommaso Gallarati Scotti and Stefano Jacini, like Casati, had strong ties with the industrial world and connections with the great publishing houses of the city, Rizzoli and Mondadori, 'still full of the wreckage of anti-fascism.' In reality, the general managers of these firms were friends of Casati and Croce and often, with or without the knowledge of the owners, provided jobs to anti-Fascist scholars in trouble. More important for the future, when Croce was in Milan he also met Adolfo Tino and Ugo La Malfa, who later were instrumental in the creation of the Party of Action and were then working in the Banca Commerciale, under the tutelage of Raffaele Mattioli, a steadfast friend of Croce at all times whose 'feeling of loyalty toward fascism' left something to be desired, according to police reports. Sometimes, Croce was the guest speaker at a meeting of a 'philosophical society' that Casati had organized in his house to avoid police suspicion. But the political nature of those meetings did not fool police authorities. In 1934 an informer reported to the chief of police that Croce had held a large meeting with anti-Fascist personalities and in the course of it had urged his friends 'not to lose faith in their ideals,' and to remain optimistic 'about the fall of fascism in the near future.' Perhaps those were not Croce's precise words, but his faith in the future, or in the *intreccio storico*, is a constant in his thought and can be found in many of his historical and political essays.[25]

When Croce went to Bari to discuss editorial matters, Laterza gathered in his villa or in his bookstore a group of bright intellectuals, including Tommaso Fiore and the much younger Michele Cifarelli, later active in the Socialist and Action parties, where they brought a new awareness of the problems connected with the 'Southern Question.' And, when the occasion required it, Croce used a trip away from Naples to express a silent protest or to avoid unwanted meetings. In 1938 Croce borrowed a leaf from the pope, who left Rome for Castel Gandolfo during Hitler's visit to Italy. Out of the same repugnance, Croce, together with Omodeo, went to Bari, 'not wishing to breath air polluted by the incoming guests.'[26] As in earlier years, Croce on his travels did not remain inside an hotel or a house but rather went about town in the company of his friends, becoming a topic of conversation in the process. His presence in any town was an event, and often created a stir. Luigi

Russo has recounted one such occasion, when he and Croce went to the University of Florence to pay a courtesy visit on Ernesto Codignola, a professor of pedagogy there but also owner of an important publishing house and editor of several periodicals. While Croce was waiting outside in the hall, the students recognized him, pressed around him, and spontaneously burst into applause, which moved Croce and Russo to tears, and then the philosopher had to improvise a little speech.[27]

Croce himself has given a charming account of a trip to the city of Campobasso, in the province of Molise, which showed that his moral influence remained as great as ever among the cultural elites of Italian provincial towns. For a few days, Croce's visit kept civic life buzzing. He was received with cordiality by the mayor and other dignitaries, and was then invited for lunch at the hotel. In his research on that visit, local experts helped Croce enthusiastically and accompanied him from place to place. When he went to the bishop's palace to consult old parchments, the bishop came out of his living quarters, greeted him warmly, and proudly showed him a copy of his last book, *History of Europe*, recently published and quickly placed by the church in the *Index Librorum Prohibitorum*. Even the report of the local prefect to the chief of police shows signs of respect for Croce and his reputation.[28]

Croce as Letter-Writer

A few years ago, Toni Iermano of the University of Naples brought to light 'a small but intense correspondence' between Croce and Gaetano Perugini, a doctor who lived in Avellino, a city not far from Naples. Those letters show the deep relationship between Croce and Perugini, though they never met in person. The two friends did not write much about private matters but, in a relaxed fashion, discussed literary currents, debated historical subjects, and lamented the general condition of Italian society. In addition, on his own initiative or at the discreet request of the doctor, Croce sent to Avellino some of his books and political essays.

The Croce–Perugini correspondence opens a window onto the cultural and political life of an Italian provincial town during the Fascist regime. As a doctor, Perugini was in touch with the bourgeois elite of the city, and, as a man critical of the regime, he had close ties with other anti-Fascist intellectuals and especially with the social critic and historian Guido Dorso, 'who during the Fascist regime,' Croce wrote in his diary, 'came often to see me.' These congenial friends often met in their favourite café facing the public square, and there they discussed political events and shared cultural news. The letters they wrote to Croce, and the replies they received from him, no doubt became part of their general conversation, making Croce's ideas a familiar presence in their gatherings. When one of them bought a book by Croce, or received by mail his periodical, the book and *La Critica* surely were shared and then discussed and commented on with excitement in their meetings at the café or in the more secure setting of their homes. When Perugini suddenly died, it was Dorso who informed Croce of the sad news, and Dorso's and Croce's notes of condolence to eath other attest not only to their grief over the sudden loss of a friend but the strong intellectual intimacy and deep mutual respect among them all.[29]

When Croce's complete correspondence is published, the presence of similar circles will be shown in other Italian cities. Already, in the National Archives, it is possible to find, in unexpected places, letters revealing the use Croce made of his correspondence. In 1933, from Florence, Nello Rosselli informed Croce of his desire to publish a new historical review. Croce must have replied, offering encouragements and also advice, for what he said was then discussed with the other scholars involved in the project. Similarly, writing from Rome in 1937, Antonio Amendola, the younger brother of the Communist leader Giorgio, expressed to Croce his gratitude 'for past benevolence' and also reported 'the deep admiration' of his university friends 'for everything you do and say' – and this, he added, was in spite of Croce's anti-communism and their Marxist inclinations. One more example: on the eve of the war, Carlo Ludovico Ragghianti, an art historian by profession but also an underground organizer, assured Croce from Bologna that his work and his thought supported 'me and many others in daily life,' encouraging them 'to seek and do better things' – in plain language, to continue the fight against fascism.[30]

Croces, the Exiles, and Foreign Travel

As noted earlier, when political parties were banned in Italy, Croce rejected the idea of emigration but many others did not. In other European countries, they continued their political activity, trying to maintain contact with Italian comrades and to influence public opinion about the nature of fascism. From the beginning to the end, the exiles remained a thorn in Mussolini's side, and the regime subjected them to a relentless campaign of moral denigration, continually organizing dirty tricks against them or even worse in the case of Carlo Rosselli. *Fuoriuscito*, in the propaganda of the regime, became a term of political opprobrium and a symbol of anti-patriotism.

None of this intimidated Croce. Undeterred by the official propaganda and by personal danger, Croce, in private conversations, praised the exiles for their personal courage, stressed their international reputation, and blamed Mussolini for turning political adversaries into personal enemies. He also remained in correspondence with his exiled friends and maintained personal relations with Liberal and Democratic leaders in exile, visiting them in London and Paris, Geneva and Grenoble, Berlin and Brussels, and probably also in Budapest and Vienna. He also read their publications, given to him during his trips abroad or sent or brought clandestinely to Naples and Turin by common friends. In the National Archives there is some evidence to suggest that Croce and Sforza at least used members of their families to send and receive personal letters and political news in the form of newspaper clippings and articles.[31]

The experiences of the exile – the separation from their families, and the hard choices that they had to make in order to remain faithful to their ideas – affected Croce profoundly. His feelings found expression in one of his best historical writings, a short biography of Galeazzo Caracciolo, whom the emperor Charles V had made Marquis of Vico as a reward for his services. After his conversion to Calvinism, Vico decided to emigrate to Geneva and to abandon his family, preferring to renounce all his Italian possessions in order to live in conformity with his new faith. When Croce describes Vico's plight, *le amarissime rinuncie*, one senses that he is talking about the exiles of his times.[32]

For their part, the exiles were aware of Croce's sympathy towards them. In 1936 the periodical of Giustizia e Libertà in Paris lamented the official silence maintained by the Italian authorities on the occasion of Croce's seventieth birthday. Rosselli's paper went on to stress Croce's contribution to European culture and his influence on the education of several generations of young Italians. It also praised Croce's past resistance to fascism, concluding with a revealing observation: 'Today he understands and shares our passions.'[33]

This community of feeling was the result also of private conversations held in foreign lands. From 1930 to 1938, Croce made several trips to France, England, Belgium, Germany, Austria, Hungary, and Switzerland. The main reason, or excuse, was to do historical research, or to offer his young daughters occasions to broaden their education. On these trips, however, he was not only accompanied by family members, but also followed by agents of the Italian police, acting under Bocchini's instructions. But, despite the presence of a police escort, Croce never failed to meet the exiles and to be a guest in their houses. In 1930 and again in 1933, first in Paris and then in London, Croce had meetings and long conversations with Don Luigi Sturzo, the former head of the Popular Party. Besides politics, Croce and Don Sturzo discussed, with the usual gusto, their literary and philosophical works, already published or still in progress. Croce gently dissuaded Sturzo from publishing an opera libretto in which Lucifer and his rebel angels, in their rebellion against God, acted and talked like Mussolini and his Fascists.[34]

Whenever in Paris, in this period, as he had done before, Croce never failed to visit his old friend Francesco Saverio Nitti, the former Italian premier. Their last meeting took place in 1937. Then, the two friends not only discussed 'the present political situation'; they also talked, with poignant nostalgia, about Naples and common friends, lamenting or praising 'the tenacity of some and the changes of others.' In the early 1930s, in Nitti's house, which was a meeting place of Italian anti-Fascists, Croce also met the old Socialist leaders Filippo Turati and Claudio Treves. Relations between Croce and Turati had always been rather cordial, but in the past he had had sharp polemics with Treves; now those quarrels were almost forgotten and superseded by a new respect and a new solidarity, in the name of which Croce was helping Treves's two sons, still living in Italy with their mother. Among the exiles, Croce had the longest conversations with Carlo Sforza, the minister of foreign affairs under Giolitti. As a former ambassador, Sforza had close ties with the diplomatic circles of European capitals, and probably was able to apprise Croce of the latest developments in those quarters when they met in Paris or in Brussels, where Sforza lived. They came to agree on many points then, and that agreement reappeared after the war, when both of them worked together to demand the abdication of the king and later, accepting a compromise, served under Badoglio.[35]

Croce's most important political meetings in Paris were held with Carlo Rosselli and took place in the house of Lionello Venturi, a famous art historian and father of Franco Venturi, the historian of the Italian Enlightenment and Russian populism. There, Croce met all the leaders of Giustizia e Libertà and other 'dangerous subversives,' as the police reports called them. Among these was the much younger Aldo Garosci, who had escaped from Italy in 1930, avoiding arrest after his group's clandestine activity in Turin had been discovered by police. Over the years, Garosci remained warmly disposed towards Croce for moral and intellectual reasons and respected him even when questioning Croce's political choices. Not worried to be dealing with a man wanted by the Italian police on a charge of sedition, Croce played the role of emissary between Garosci and his mother in Turin, and carried their letters back and forth. Once he even stopped for half a day in Grenoble, so that, via him and his famous old suitcase (likely containing all manner of incriminating material), a son could send a reassuring letter to a worried mother. On that occasion, Croce assured Garosci that the police did not dare to open the luggage of a senator.[36]

The conversations between Croce and Rosselli touched on political questions, both practical and theoretical. Those discussions were always cordial, according to Gaetano Salvemini, who was present at most of the meetings. A report written in 1934 by the usual police informer confirmed that 'Croce has a great consideration for Carlo Rosselli.' In a letter sent to his wife in 1931, Rosselli wrote that Croce's visit had been 'very interesting, as always.' In another brief note of the same year, he told her, without giving more details, that 'his visit at this moment is valuable for the launching of Les Cahiers.' Probably, Rosselli wanted to discuss with Croce the essays that had been prepared for the publications of Giustizia e Libertà, or even, perhaps, other business connected with that organization, especially the distribution in Italy of its materials.

From Croce's memoirs, written in 1944, and from his review of Garosci's biography of Rosselli, we can gather both Croce's admiration for Rosselli and their political disagreements. Croce paid tribute to the personal generosity, political courage, and determination of Rosselli in the struggle against fascism and Mussolini. At the same time, he expressed reservations about Rosselli's philosophical ideas and political program. For Croce, Rosselli's attempt to reconcile liberalism and socialism was unsuccessful, marred by eclecticism, contradictions, and lack of coherence; more important, his social program demanding 'a complete economic revolution,' in Croce's opinion, was devoid of political realism and showed dangerous signs of authoritarian tendencies, with traits common to communism.

In all his references to the deaths of Carlo and Nello Rosselli, Croce remained certain that the order for their assassination originated with Mussolini himself, and with his desire to get rid of indomitable adversaries. After the two brothers were murdered in France by members of the Cagoule, acting on the orders of the Italian regime, Croce wrote a letter to Nello's wife in Florence, which can be found now in the Nationale Archives. On his last trip to France in 1937, Croce paid a visit of respect to the mother and the wife of Carlo, then still living in Paris.[37]

Croce's relations with Guistizia e Libertà and his friendship with its leaders were rather remarkable, since he differed with the ideas and program of the movement on key points. Yet, despite his disagreement about the abolition of the monarchy, a federal organization of the state, and the socialization of key economic industries, Croce admired in Rosselli and his associates their moral energy and passionate commitment to the cause of freedom and to the struggle against fascism. This admiration probably explains Croce's lack of animosity when debating Rosselli's theory of liberal socialism. It is also true that Rosselli's liberal socialism, unlike similar theories elaborated later in Italy, retained several elements of Croce's political philosophy. As we saw earlier, Rosselli had been influenced by Croce's essays on liberalism, written in 1927, and especially by the distinction Croce drew between liberalism and capitalism.

On his trips abroad, Croce also met prominent European intellectuals and was cordially welcomed in their circles. He established lasting relationships in Germany especially with Thomas Mann, Friedrich Meinecke, and Albert Einstein, in France with Daniel Halevy, and in England with Robert Collingwood. In 1933, during his trip to Paris and London, he used his international reputation and tried to organize a petition, signed by prominent personalities, to Mussolini, asking for the release of Mario Vinciguerra, who had been sentenced to a harsh penalty three years earlier for anti-Fascist activity. The letter did not materialize because George Bernard Shaw, the author chosen for the job, wanted to include in the letter ideas that Croce and others judged to be demeaning of Vinciguerra's dignity. Later, another letter, written by Aldous Huxley and signed by Sidney Webb and Paul Valery, was sent to Mussolini without producing any concrete result.[38]

During this period, Croce participated in two international cultural and philosophical congresses. At Oxford in 1930, he read one of his most important essays, which was later printed in *La Critica* and soon afterwards also published by the German *Historische Zeitschrift* (the congress's proceedings and Croce's speech were also reported with a favourable comment by the French paper *Le Provencal*). On that occasion, Croce compared the authoritarian forces of modern times to the barbaric invasions that had destroyed the Roman Empire, and he invited intellectuals and men of culture to perform the same functions and to assume the same role as the medieval popes and the Catholic Church had performed in the preservation of classical civilization. For his part, he much preferred the example of a Boethius to the behaviour of those who had welcomed a Totila and an Attila and the invading hordes, supporting and praising their destruction, vandalism, and oppression. *Le Provencal* commented that 'the meaning of the speech was obvious to all who were present.' As for those who read Croce's speech in *La Critica*, Gentile personally resented Croce's remarks and wrote a bitter rebuttal of the historical comparison. But a few months later, from the University of Padua, Concetto Marchesi, the classical scholar and militant Communist, wrote a significant letter to Croce: 'I have read with profound satisfaction your pages, even where my immovable Marxist spirit could find it hard to consent. Among so much intellectual ruin and moral poverty there always is one light: yours, which has illuminated before and enlightens even more, now.'

In 1931 the Italian government invested great effort to avoid Croce's election to the presidency of a cultural congress in Budapest. The annoyance of the participants at the political interference was expressed at the final session. The official head of the Italian delegation, the historian Gioacchino Volpe, received the polite applause that usually concludes these occasions. However, when Croce rose and made an unscheduled short speech, he received a standing ovation. The moment was especially memorable because Croce's speech mentioned the close ties between the Hungarian and Italian patriots during the Risorgimento and the comparison to the present conditions of the two countries was clear.[39]

Croce's last trip abroad came in 1938 when he and Casati met in Geneva with Joyce Lussu, the sister of the historian Max Salvadori. Croce had appreciated her poetry in the past and had met her in Naples, before she and her family were forced into exile. The official reason was to receive a new poetry collection and to agree on its publication. But the poet was also the wife of Emilio Lussu, a fine writer himself and one of the leaders of Giustizia e Libertà. In this movement and in the underground organization, before and during the war, both of them played active and dangerous roles. That day she and Croce spent several hours together 'in long walks and conversations, strolling along Geneva's old streets,' Croce says in his diaries, and 'talking about everything,' as Lussu wrote in her autobiography. Joyce Lussu's book was finally published in 1939, but not without some bureaucratic snags and a confrontation with the censorship board of Naples.[40]

Croce and the Underground

In the fight against fascism, Croce did not join any underground movement, recognizing that he did not possess the intellectual and personal qualities required for such an undertaking. At the same time, it is also true that he did not have much faith in the efficacy of the methods of conspiracy, nor did he have great hope that those methods would achieve lasting results. Apart from personal inclinations, however, there was a more profound reason for Croce's non-involvement in the underground resistance. For Croce, fascism was a moral illness, a crisis of European civilization, a rejection of liberal values in favour of irrationality and blind activism. To achieve a lasting recovery, to restore a love of freedom, other means had to be employed, and a different cure had to be administered. When young anti-Fascists asked him what to do, Croce, always reluctant to give personal advice, replied that they had to find their own way, follow the dictates of their consciences, and be prepared to face the consequences. For his part, he recommended that young people devote time and energy to study and to acquiring a solid intellectual preparation for the future. In these cases, Croce also advised young people to have faith in providence, and hope in the *intreccio storico*, trusting in historical development that continually creates new realities, unforeseen conditions, and unexpected opportunities that one has to be ready and prepared to exploit.[41]

Some energetic young men among the Democrats or even among the Liberals found Croce's advice too passive. To them, the possibility of doing something concrete, in the here and now, the elation that came with participation in a large movement with national and international ramifications was bound to have more appeal than the prospect of spending long hours in lonely rooms, hoping for an uncertain future. But, if Croce did not encourage people to go underground, at the same time he never discouraged those who 'dreamed more resolute action' and undertook conspiratorial activity to express their anti-fascism. Once they had made that dangerous choice, he always respected their decision, continued to befriend them, and even tried to help them when they inevitably were caught by the police and ended in Fascist jails or were sent to *confino*. Once in these places, the young men often read and discussed Croce's books, alone or together, as we have learned from the memoirs and letters of Vittorio Foa, Giancarlo Pajetta, Ernesto Rossi, Leo Valiani, and others.

From 1926 to 1943, Croce maintained personal contact with all the underground movements and helped some of their most important leaders. He received in his house members of Young Italy and helped them after they were arrested. When Giorgio Amendola abandoned the liberalism of his father and joined the Communist Party, Croce remained on good terms with him. After his arrest, he sent books and periodicals to him in jail and continued to receive his brothers in

Naples. He maintained close relations with them and their friends at the University of Rome even after they had joined the clandestine Communist organization and their activities were known to the police. After the failure of the National Alliance, Croce followed the peregrinations of Mario Vinciguerra in the Italian jails. With the help of Casati, he tried to improve the conditions of his friend and to have him transferred to a jail with a less authoritarian director, where he would be allowed at least to read and write.[42]

In the early 1930s, a group of young Socialists in Milan, under the leadership of Eugenio Colorni and Rodolfo Morandi, created a *centro interno* and tried to give a new impulse to the clandestine organization of the old party and to establish closer contacts with the exiles in Paris. Croce helped Colorni and Morandi to publish their books, and for this reason had several meetings with them in Milan and in Naples. It is significant that Morandi's book, a history of Italian industry which offered a Marxist analysis of the Risorgimento in many ways different from Croce's interpretation, was published by Laterza in *The Library of Modern Culture* – a collection that was under Croce's direct supervision.[43]

Above all, from 1930 to 1936, Croce was in close contact with Rosselli's movement, Giustizia e Libertà. Many members of this movement were good friends of Croce and greatly influenced by his ideas. In 1934 the historian – turned – informer was convinced that Croce was aware of Rosselli's activity in Italy; he also suspected that Croce was somehow deeply involved in the movement. 'The fact that many of those arrested of Giustizia e Libertà (Bauer, Rossi) were his friends, the friendship and political relations between Ginzburg and Nello Rosselli and other facts similar give me the sensation that he has more than knowledge of the events that, directed by Rosselli in Paris, have taken place in Italy.' When, in May 1930, the Milan group was discovered and its members sent to jail, Croce remained in correspondence with Riccardo Bauer, through the good offices of Bianca Ceva, a common friend. When, Umberto Ceva, brother of Bianca and a member of the same group, committed suicide in jail, Croce paid a special visit to the widow and, with Arturo Toscanini, was among the few to whom the family showed the letter that Ceva had written to them as a last testament. Moved by this experience, Croce, in a letter to Salvemini, called Ceva 'the best hero of Italian anti-fascism' and likened him to the martyrs of the Risorgimento, for his great courage. Croce often compared the struggle against Mussolini to the events of the Risorgimento. Ceva was another example of the 'new Italian Risorgimento,' which was Croce's term for the Resistance to Fascism.[44]

On two occasions, Leone Ginzburg, the head of the Turin group, took verbatim notes of Croce's opinions and passed them to the periodical of Giustizia e Libertà in Paris; to Ginzburg's chagrin, one of the pieces was thrown into the wastebasket by 'the Parisians,' who judged its tone too moderate (the periodical however, did publish another piece, in which Croce made disparaging remarks about the minister of education). When, in 1934, Ginzburg was arrested and then confined to a village in Abruzzi, Croce took the initiative to find his new address so he could send him books, periodicals, and translation work.[45]

One of the primary aims of the underground organization was to collect money to help the victims of persecution and their families. Unlike other movements, the democratic underground groups did not receive any help from foreign nations or from private Italian corporations. Instead, they had to rely on the private wealth of Carlo Rosselli and the individual contributions of wealthy sympathizers. Concrete details are scant, owing to the personal and political discretion of those involved, but there is enough anecdotal evidence to suggest that Albertini, Casati, and Croce made financial contributions to the cause alone or together. They also helped a particular friend in difficulty, with whom they happened to have ties of affection. It has been revealed recently by close friends that Croce sent his monthly Senate salary of two thousand lire to 'the exiles in Paris.' Similarly, Luigi Albertini, who had become a successful rancher in the Roman countryside, sent his son Leonardo regularly to France to bring money to needy exiled friends.[46]

The assassination of Rosselli was a great blow to Italian democratic antifascism from which Giustizia e Libertà never recovered. From 1937 to 1939, however, especially in the universities of Pisa, Florence, and Rome, a new movement, called Liberalsocialism, attracted followers among students and teachers. The new movement, the child of Aldo Capitini and Guido Calogero, tried to achieve a synthesis between liberalism and socialism, hoping to avoid in the future the divisions among the old parties that had weakened liberal Italy and opened the door to fascism. Croce read their clandestine publications, was critical of their ideas, rejected their political conclusions, mainly for philosophical reasons, but remained on cordial terms with Calogero. He also published Captini's book *Elementi di una Esperienza Religiosa*, in his Laterza collection.[47]

Despite political difficulties and the scarcity of economic resources, a loose democratic underground movement continued to exist throughout Italy from 1936 to 1943, sometimes referred to as *movimento di rinnovamento politico e sociale italiano*. Not formally affiliated with any party, and without a recognized leader, it included Liberals, Democrats, and Socialists. All of them had been, more or less, greatly influenced by Croce's ideas. Later, in the great majority of cases, the members of this organization went on to organize the Party of Action and played important roles in the military organizations of the Resistance. One of the most active organizers of this movement, continually in and out of jail for his efforts, was the already mentioned Carlo Ludovico Ragghianti, Croce's close friend since 1933 and after 1943 head of Tuscany's Committee of National Liberation. This man, who was deeply immersed in the underground organization and who had frequent contacts with Croce, gave unambiguous testimony on Croce's relationship to the antifascist underground. 'After 1933, when my relations with him became regular, and until the first months of 1943, Croce was always informed about the underground movement and the conspiracy, and often he participated with his advice and criticism in the clandestine political writings ...' 'It needs to be made known that ... Croce did not confine himself to advice and observation, remaining 'au dessus de la mélée ... but he also took an active part in the conspiracy, despite his friends' invitations to prudence.'[48]

CHAPTER TEN

Cultural Activity as Political Opposition, 1930–1940

In the struggle against fascism, Croce's most important contribution was his intellectual activity. In this respect he assumed a position of leadership, and his influence was unmatched, affecting in different ways the old and new generations and the cultural and political movements of the time. His books were Croce's way of defending liberal and democratic ideals, and their wide readership gave him the moral leadership of the anti-Fascist resistance, as well as assuring his personal security against the dictatorship. It is now evident that, given the nature of fascism, Croce's refusal to go into exile or to join the underground was an inspired and fruitful choice. He chose the field and assumed the position in which he could be most effective and where his contribution could be most productive and influential. That choice allowed him to continue his mission in Italy and to remain part of the cultural discourse. It compelled the political powers to tolerate his activity and to accept the presence of his books and the influence of his ideas in the country, and even inside the schools.[1]

From 1925 to 1943, under the pressure of political events, Croce shifted his cultural interests, devoting much of his intellectual energy to works of an historical and political nature. The critical aim was still to defend the concept of freedom, to oppose dogmatism, and to show the fruits of a democratic society, animated by liberal ideals. Whereas the regime employed the mass media and the education system to promote the cult of Mussolini and to inculcate submission to authority, demanding from the new generations, in mystical union with the Duce, without asking questions, 'to believe, to obey, to fight,' Croce instead offered a set of liberal values, preached freedom, defended the dignity of man, as a free agent, and urged individual decision and personal responsibility.

In the end, Croce's works constituted a block of ideas opposed to fascism and other authoritarian regimes and have to be regarded as one of the most important contributions to the Italian anti-Fascist Resistance. Those works usually had a wide readership among the general public, often were discussed at university classes, and sometimes were even used as course manuals. The readers debated their contents and were compelled to compare and to contrast different positions, assuring circulation of Croce's ideas. Croce's writings were popular also in the jails among Democratic and Communist militants, greatly influencing their future intellectual development. A few of the books generated political enthusiasm and inspired action against tyranny, creating or reviving opposition to the regime. All in all, Croce's historical essays were effective tools in preserving the heritage of the Risorgimento and in undermining the moral authority and the national claims of the Fascist regime. And, similarly, his philosophical and political writings offered to young people the essential elements of a critical education and provided them with an alternative to Fascist ideology, thus breaking the corrupting influence of the rhetoric and propaganda of the Fascist Party.[2]

Even Salvemini, despite political differences, had to recognize that from 1925 to 1943 'the teaching and the example of Croce' 'had a powerful effect,' created 'invincible opposition,' and 'encouraged ... many young people to believe in freedom' and to join the resistance to fascism. More recently, in a stringent analysis, Renzo De Felice has come to the conclusion that, among the opposition movements, Croce's resistance was 'the most important and the most fruitful.' With his personal example and his cultural activities, Croce achieved two fundamental aims. First, he protected the cultural and moral life of Italy from the mortal danger of 'paralysis and corruption,' which by necessity would follow 'the isolation, the conformity and the politicizing imposed by fascism.' Secondly, Croce offered to Italian culture and especially to the young generation 'a critical alternative to the official position,' providing 'the essential elements for an autonomous education to moral and intellectual freedom and to the spiritual values of a true culture.' De Felice's judgment is confirmed by the testimonies of several intellectuals who belonged to different political movements at the time, and is also shared by other historians, belonging to different schools. In an essay marking Laterza's hundred years of publishing activity, Alessandro Galante Garrone, a well-known magistrate and historian in Turin, in his youth a member of Giustizia e Libertà and the Party of Action, stressed the formative importance for his generation 'of those books that arrived in Piedmont from Bari in the stagnant atmosphere of the Twenties and Thirties.' He then added that he could never forget the effect on him of reading '*History of Italy*, when I was in high school and then afterwards *History of Europe*, at the time of my university graduation.' He concluded with a touching tribute: 'If at the end of my long journey of work, I can look back to my past without too much shame, I owe much to those passionate pages of Croce, to his optimism, to his faith in history, to the religion of liberty, that in the end always wins and finds nourishment even in its own defeats.' Another Actionist, Norberto Bobbio, who graduated and began his university career in the 1930s, states that in those years 'Croce's books and Laterza's editions were read and reread, discussed among friends, used for our exams and our university lectures and seminars.' A similar tribute to Croce's influence is offered by the Marxist historian Armando Saitta, then a university student at Pisa.

And consider one other example. In the late 1930s, Croce's writings influenced a remarkable group of students at the Uniersity of Rome who, after the war, played important roles in the Communist and Socialist parties and in the publishing house of Einaudi. One of them, Antonio Giolitti, a nephew of the former prime minister and a leading politician and intellectual of the left between 1950 and 1990 in his own right, has stressed that Croce's ideas had more impact on the group's thinking than their university teachers. Remembering his youth, Giolitti writes in his memoirs: 'In the context of criticism against fascism, the voice of Croce sounded clear, familiar and persuasive ... I read him avidly, and not only his books of history and philosophy but also *La Critica* ... He provided the element and the stimulus to passionate discussions among friends ...' Giolitti also tells of another effect that the writings of Croce had on his university friends: 'The books of Croce revealed to us the existence of a movement still unknown and mysterious to us; Marxism, in its two incarnations called Socialism and Communism.'[3]

Croce's writings, even those of a more literary nature, were aimed, directly or indirectly, against the ideas and the practices of the Fascist regime. But, at the same time, these writings also defended the ideas of freedom and individual responsibility against the other totalitarian movements of the modern age. In this period, as in others, before and after, Croce waged a constant battle not only against fascism but also against the clericalism of the Catholic Church and especially against Marxism and communism, in their new Leninist and Stalinist incarnation. Unlike many European intellectuals, Croce never succumbed to the allure of Russian communism, nor did he have any illusions about the authoritarian and dictatorial nature of the new Soviet society. While his early anti-democratic attitudes softened and almost disappeared, Croce's hostility to Soviet communism never relented, then or later. In his *History of Europe*, written in 1931, Croce recognized the magnitude of the experiment of Lenin and Stalin, but he was among the first to predict the internal implosion of the Soviet system and 'the collapse of the structure,' which would occur when the Communist Party would not be able to satisfy the revived demands for freedom from the Russian people.

Some critics have regarded Croce's anti-Marxism as a sign of his conservative philosophy, or, more damnable, as a political expression of his agrarian interests. In the historical context of the times, however, Croce's anti-Communist polemics should rather be seen as a necessary part of the struggle against fascism. During this period the Communists and the Fascists liked to present their own movements as the only true alternative to the other. The Communists rejoiced, before the adoption of the Popular Front, in calling every movement to their right, including the Socialist parties, social-fascism. On the other side, exploiting the old fear of communism, the Mussolini regime presented fascism as the only bulwark of Western civilization against the new Mongolian hordes. 'Rome or Moscow' was a popular and effective slogan of the time, and, strangely enough, it also represented the choice that the Communists posed to the Italian public. Croce's position was different. He proposed a more fundamental choice. As he had done in the 1920s, Croce offered arguments for a liberal alternative to both movements, showing that the real struggle was between freedom and oppression, between the rights of the individual and the dictates of a modern Moloch, whether acting in the name of a class or a nation. Croce's message was clear and so was understood in those times: those who loved freedom had to fight fascism in the present and had to remain wary of communism in the future.[4]

The History of Europe

Among Croce's books, *The History of Europe in the Nineteenth Century* has a special place and fulfilled an important function in the struggle against fascism. It helped to give a new appeal to the ideal of freedom as well as to invigorate the opposition to totalitarian regimes. The book describes the rise and fall of European liberalism after the Napoleonic Wars; it narrates the victories and the defeats of the national movements, contrasting the different aspirations of the Italian Risorgimento and German unification, 'Cavour's faith in parliament' and 'Bismarck's iron fist'; and finally it stresses the great changes brought to European society by the Prussian wars and especially by the First World War. Here, more than in any other previous book, even more than in his *History of Italy*, Croce tried to explain the conditions of present times, offering a cogent analysis of cultural trends, social forces, and political movements that had weakened and undermined the democratic institutions and shaken the liberal foundations of European civilization, preparing the ground for the spread of nihilism, activism, imperialism, and totalitarianism.

The book's political inspiration was evident to all readers. Croce's analysis of past cultural trends and political movements, with their beneficial or deleterious influence, makes reference to contemporary society and sometimes points to 'turbid adventurers of the spirit' who were still living and easily recognizable. The *ruere in servitium* of the French nation during the Second Empire resembles Italy's falling into slavery under Mussolini. The generous patriotism of the Italian Risorgimento evokes condemnation of the violence of fascism and the crude aspirations of an aggressive nationalism. The beneficial influence of liberal ideals is continually contrasted with the depressing and corrupting effects of authoritarian interventions. In his analysis of European progress, Croce shows that political freedom is necessary to assure economic welfare and to satisfy the social needs of man. The concept of freedom is presented as a tool to interpret the past but also as an ideal aspiration for the present, worth the sacrifice of one's own life. Readers are invited 'to contemplate' the liberal age and see the fruits of freedom, but they are urged as well 'to take part in our historical age' and to participate in the political arena 'with actions according to the role that is incumbent upon each of us and which conscience assigns and duty demands.' In the face of totalitarian ideologies, freedom acquires the connotations of a modern religion, a new civic faith.

In the *History of Europe*, the narration of historical events has an eloquent pathos, almost a hieratic tone in some parts, as the literary critic Gianfranco Contini has pointed out; indeed, some of the sentences became famous and were and still are repeated in conversation. Especially the epilogue of the book, pointing to the future success of freedom against present adversaries, had a special appeal to those who were involved in the opposition or imprisoned in Fascist jails. 'It was natural that those pages spoke to the hearts and minds of those who were engaged in the struggle,' Natalino Sapegno said, talking about those years and the emotions created by the book. For his part, Eugenio Garin bought and read the book in 1932 in Palermo where he was a high school teacher. He read some chapters to his class, and saw that the reading 'had an effect, and that the students were impressed and deeply touched.' The emotions must have been even stronger in the jails when the political inmates read, or someone read aloud to them, the famous epilogue, in which Croce urged or reassured his readers not to despair of the present because even in defeat freedom knows but victory, and 'not only the future but eternity belongs to liberty.' Writing to his mother from jail in 1931, Ernesto Rossi told her that Riccardo Bauer 'used to read us a few chapters of history,' which afterwards 'we discussed and commented about.' Among these had been chapters of Croce's *History of Europe*, presumably those that had appeared in *La Critica* or in a separate pamphlet before the book's publication. In 1934 Rossi assured his mother that, on the superiority of liberalism to other movements, he was 'in complete agreement with the thought of Croce, whose *History of Europe* I am reading again with renewed interest.' Finally, in a letter of 1937, perhaps in a difficult period of their lives, Rossi told his wife that he agreed with the ideas expressed by Croce in the conclusion of his book, and invited her 'to read again those words ... they are so beautiful and resonate so much passion.' Massimo Mila, who was in jail at the time and was part of Rossi's group, years later still remembered the importance of Croce's book and the strong emotions that its reading created among them.

Mila was not alone. Recently, in a television interview, Carlo Azeglio Ciampi, the respected president of Italy, stated that Croce's *History of Europe* has been one of the two most important books of his life, and 'the one that has left a deep mark on my intellectual development.' Ciampi read the book for the first time in the late 1930s, when he was a student at the University of Pisa, under the guidance of Guido Calogero. In those years 'the book was bought ... and exchanged among those interested in the subject with much circumspection.' Like many young men who later joined the Party of Action, Ciampi was especially impressed by the first chapter, 'the one with the evocative title: The Religion of Freedom,' in which Croce defined 'the ethic of liberalism' and offered 'a particular definition of freedom and personal behaviour.' In reading that chapter, Ciampi felt a special affinity with 'the anxieties, aspirations and hopes of the European peoples after the Napoleonic period.' Like Rossi in jail, during those gloomy years, Ciampi at university 'found memorable also the conclusion, which contains a warning inspired by the liberal thought.' In the last pages of his book, Croce urged those who shared a liberal conception of life to work for those ideals 'with all your heart, every day, in every act' and to trust in 'divine providence, which knows more than each of us, and lives within us and with us.' Repeating verbatim Croce's words, Ciampi told the television audience that those ideals and the warning are still valid and relevant today, 'as a universal imperative.'[5]

The *History of Europe* was written in 1931 and published in 1932. It immediately became a best-seller, enjoying a commercial success almost equal to that of the *History of Italy*. The first edition of three thousand copies, costing thirty lire, was sold out within a week. A second edition of the same size was printed the same month. Four more editions appeared during the Fascist regime. The book's success attracted the attention of the authorities and became the subject of report to the chief of police, Arturo Bocchini. One informer, writing from Switzerland, claimed that the commercial success of the *History of Europe* 'could be blamed,' as he put it, on 'Masonic organizations.' As was traditional for Croce, several chapters were first published in *La Critica*, whetting appetites for the rest, as is evident in Gramsci's letters. By deliberate choice, parts of the book were known and discussed in large circles in manuscript, long before they even appeared in the periodical.

This time, too, several precautions were taken to thwart the censors, and to avoid the danger of confiscation. As soon as chapters were ready, Croce sent copies to friends and trusted scholars, soliciting their views and comments. The full manuscript was brought to Nitti in Paris and to Gaetano De Sanctis in Rome, where it was seen and read by visiting friends; for example, Paolo Traves read it on a visit to De Sanctis's house. At the right moment, news was leaked to appropriate ears, and Laterza and others spread the word that the book was already in the hands of foreign publishing houses and was ready to be translated in all major European languages. Above all, before publication, Croce himself read all the chapters of the book in weekly gatherings of five trusted fellow members of the Royal Society of Naples, whose proceedings, by law, had to be published in the acts of the Academy of Arts and Sciences of Naples and could not be seized by the police under any circumstances.[6]

Perhaps Croce's resistance to fascism was only cultural, as his critics have claimed, but he certainly knew how to protect his rights as a citizen, and he was definitly not afraid to exploit existing laws to his advantage. Not all the traditions of liberal Italy, and certainly not all the old academic freedoms, disappeared under the Fascist regime; often what was lacking was the moral courage to use the protection that they offered. This could never be said of Croce.

Other Writings

Besides the *History of Europe*, other books of Croce enjoyed great success and fulfilled the same political function, though in a different and smaller way. In 1938 *History as Thought and as Action,* despite the rather high price of thirty-five lire, had a second edition of fifteen hundred copies within a short time of the first. No Italian newspaper mentioned the book, but Croce's new work, for the ideas it discussed and the intellectual power it showed, generated much interest, as is attested by personal letters and also by the reports of police informers. Roberto Bracco from Naples and Luigi Russo from Florence assured Croce that his book was selling well, and stated their view that the second edition was a minor miracle under the prevailing circumstances. At the University of Pisa, Guido Calogero used manuscript proofs of the book in one of his philosophy seminars, to the great annoyance of Gentile. From Turin, both his wife and daughter informed Croce that people had been waiting with impatience for his new publication, and then had received or bought the book with joy. Writing from France to his parents in Turin, Garosci expressed a similar feeling, marvelling at Croce's vitality in his old age. A letter of Elena Croce provides us with another example of the devices employed by Croce to assure the circulation of his ideas and the success of his books. She told her father that in her house their friends had snatched and copied, as soon as they were ready, the chapters of the manuscript sent to her for typing. As for the informer Cesare, he had the honesty and the intelligence to report both the commercial success and the political value of the book, recognizing that Croce, 'with great ability and erudition,' had produced a work of 'exceptional theoretical importance' and, 'as usual in his recent writings, not free from clever and critical references to the present regime.' In agreement with the informer, himself an historian, Armando Saitta, who was in Calogero's seminar at Pisa as a student, regards *History as Thought and as Action* as 'the most anti-Fascist of Croce's books.'[7]

Another book, *Il Carattere della Filosofia Moderna,* was published in 1940. Its immediate success seems to have caught the attention of Mussolini himself, since the minister of popular culture was required to send a written note to his office on that very subject. Alessandro Pavolini, the author of that report, or as it appears in the archives, 'Appunti per il Duce', readily acknowledged 'the commercial success of the book, as shown by two printings in short succession,' but he chose to dwell on the political aspect of the matter, stressing that Croce's new work had a clear political thesis and that in the book the author 'defended the principle of freedom and condemned authoritarian politics.' In particular, the minister called Mussolini's attention to chapter six, titled 'On the Philosophical Theory of Freedom,' which was a new edition of an essay previously published by an American periodical in English. Pavolini found it rather worrisome that on every page Croce indulged in 'the exaltation of freedom' and tried to prove 'its identification with modern thought and its superiority over authoritarian principle.'[8]

There is another book that needs to be mentioned and that instead usually is forgotten, perhaps because it was not published by Laterza. In 1934, at the request of his anti-Fascist young friends from Milan, Croce published a small collection of short political essays: *Orientamenti: Piccoli Saggi di Filosofia Politica*. The essays are in the form of answers to particular questions and deal with aspects of political philosophy, and especially with the changing idea of the state. The criticism of fascism and the rejection of authoritarian ideas is present in every essay and is made evident by reference to similar historical periods and to the Soviet Union and Nazi Germany. The essays make an eloquent defence of freedom, presented as an essential element to assure the vitality of the state itself. Throughout the book, there is an invitation to writers and to intellectuals to avoid political servility and to reject materialistic ideals, and instead to celebrate human values and to cultivate the love of freedom. One also notes a constant appeal to kindred people of the opposition to keep faith and to maintain hope in the liberal spirit and not to be discouraged by the present success of authoritarian ideals. Writing from jail in 1934, Ernesto Rossi told his mother, referring to the chapter in which this argument was evident: 'There are five pages under the title: The World Goes Towards ..., which I find very clear and that correspond completely to my feelings.' This little jewel was published in Milan by a small publishing house, Gilardi e Noto. The size and the modest price allowed the book to reach a different and larger audience than the massive tomes published by Laterza. The first edition, probably of five thousand copies, was sold out in a few days. Incensed by its success, the authorities denied permission for a second printing. But the publishers protested, and Croce wrote a letter of support pointing out that the essays had already appeared somewhere else in the past. Within the same year, two more editions of the book were issued, which sold 'very well, like the first one,' Laterza wrote in a letter to Croce.[9]

La Critica and Continuing Resistance

Perhaps the most effective weapon in Croce's arsenal was not any single book but his periodical, *La Critica*. During Fascist regime, its circulation increased from seventeen hundred to three thousand copies. *La Critica* appeared regularly every two months and could be bought at major bookstores, and then loaned from friend to friend, as was then the fashion with periodicals of that nature. Without much difficulty, the periodical could also be found in many public and university libraries. In the conditions of the times, La Critica became almost the organ of democratic opposition, providing a secret tie among anti-Fascists, who often used it as an identification card and thus unwittingly facilitated the work of spies. In the absence of freedom of the press, the periodical filled a vacuum and played a crucial political role. Because it appeared regularly, La Critica kept its readers in touch with each other, offered a constant point of reference, and provided vital information on intellectual life in Italy and in Europe, often in contrast with the academic conformity of the time. Massimo Mila, speaking for a different audience, has recalled the interest and the emotion created among political inmates in Rome's jail by 'the arrival every two months inside the walls of Regina Coeli of La Critica, avidly read, exchanged and discussed with Riccardo Bauer, Vittorio Foa and Ernesto Rossi,' the fascinating and lively quartet of Italian anti-fascism, noted for both their different personalities and their unity of purpose.[10]

Opposition to the Fascist regime and criticism of authoritarian ideals appeared indirectly in all the major historical and even literary essays, and in a more direct way in the book reviews, especially in a polemical section called 'Postille e Varietà,' which can be roughly translated as 'views and news.' It became the most popular section of the periodical, and also the most dreaded and the first to be read by friends or foes of Croce. In the long critical essays, Croce celebrated the beneficial power of freedom or lamented the deleterious effects of 'activism' and nationalism, which had replaced the patriotism and the ideals of the Risorgimento. Omodeo offered a Mazzinian interpretation of the First World War to criticize the imperialistic views of the nationalistic historians, and debunked the Savoyard celebration of the Risorgimento in favour of a more dialectical and European view of Italian unification. The book reviews were used adroitly to score political points. A notorious speech by Martin Heidegger and his sympathy for Hitler provided the occasion to criticize Gentile once again and to point out the practical effects of his philosophy, or any other philosophy based on irrationalism. A book by Karl Barth was used to defend the separation of church and state and to praise personal responsibility and religious freedom against dictatorial authority. In other essays, the democratic dreams of Marx were compared with the authoritarian practices of Stalin; or the young Marx inflamed by the ideals of 1848, and willing to unite socialism and democracy, was contrasted with the absolutist tradition of Russia and the autocratic mentality of Lenin. In his special column, with short notes and biting words, Croce debunked the servility and the peccadilloes of Italian writers, who in many cases abandoned their old ideas in favour of more fashionable ones and praised the new masters, often to obtain personal favours. These rebukes, or *Strigliate* as Ernesto Rossi called them, immediately ran along the grapevines of the literary public, increasing the effect and the resentment.[11]

The authorities understood the periodical's great impact and at regular intervals attempted to impede its circulation, but they never dared to stop its publication. Despite the minister's 'advice' of 1933 to schools and libraries to cancel their subscription, *La Critica* remained available in many public and university libraries to students and teachers, who were not afraid to be seen reading it or to ask the librarian for a copy from the stacks.

In the National Archives there is ample evidence that the periodical was read and its fortunes followed closely by government leaders and by Mussolini himself. In 1933 the chief of police asked for and obtained from the prefect of Bari the full subscription list, which contained 1,294 names and addresses, located in Italy or in other countries. It was after reading this report that Mussolini complained to the minister of education about the schools and public libraries found on that list as subscribers. During the following years, the reports of the informers, in Bari and in Naples, kept Bocchini abreast of the affairs of *La Critica*; he was made aware of Croce's special device 'to talk of Germany' when he really intended 'to speak of Italy'; the informers never failed to underline Croce's frequent polemics against those intellectuals 'who belong to fascism' and his 'rather transparent allusions to the regime.' Mussolini, too, notwithstanding his earlier outburst, found the time to read *La Critica* with attention, finding of special interest its most polemical sections. When necessary he also brought to the attention of the appropriate minister the news and views found there, expecting a reply. In 1940 Giuseppe Bottai, the minister of education, had to write a defence of an anthology of modern poetry whose adoption by high schools he had recommended and Croce instead had condemned in *La Critica*. And this took place while Europe was already engulfed in war.[12]

Laterza's Publishing House

In the publication of *La Critica*, Croce continued to be helped by the contributions of his friends, Adolfo Omodeo and Guido De Ruggiero, but also by the steady solidarity of the publisher, Giovanni Laterza. Without the support of Laterza, Croce's opposition would have been more difficult and probably taken a different form. Laterza not only published all his books, it also published books recommended by him. It was a real collaboration between two strong personalities, the man of culture with a mission and the liberal businessman proud of his profession, both willing to take risks and even to suffer economic loss in the name of a higher interest. Laterza offered his business expertise and the resources of his company for the marketing of Croce's books. With his assistance, Croce was able to create a wider front of cultural resistance, and during the Fascist regime the *Edizioni Laterza* became a point of reference for the opposition. In his editorial choices, as Eugenio Garin and others have noted, Croce followed a clear political line, but he also accepted writers who had ideas, even political aspirations, different from his own. This was especially evident in the collection for which Croce was personally responsible, *The Library of Modern Culture*. In this collection appeared the classics of European liberalism but also books written by modern Italian and European democratic thinkers. The collection also included works of young Italian scholars at the beginning of their academic careers or just out of university but already in trouble with official authorities for their unorthodox views. Often these young writers had a different point of view from Croce's but nonetheless made important contributions to the critical debates of the time. At the request of Giorgio Amendola and his Communist friends, Croce also republished in that collection Antonio Labriola's old essays on Marxism, followed, however, by a long essay of his own with a rather eloquent title: 'The Birth and Death of Theoretical Marxism in Italy.' Intellectual variety of the collection was appreciated inside Fascist jails, as is attested by Manlio Rossi Doria, a young Neapolitan agrarian economist who was then a member of the Communist Party and would later become a leader of the Party of Action. 'From 1930 to 1935, in my case,' he says, 'with other friends inside the prisons, we kept ourselves awake and informed really by reading Laterza's editions. Very few of the two hundred volumes of *Biblioteca di Cultura Moderna*, published until then, were not present in the cells, or on the shelves of the prison's common room. Many of those books generated ideas, debates, doubts, never to be forgotten.' Not only was Croce liberal in his editorial choices, he proved to be generous in his monetary remuneration. Whenever possible, the translation of foreign books was entrusted to anti-Fascist intellectuals. When personal circumstances so required, as had happened in the

1920s, some writers were paid a higher fee than normal, and the difference, without their knowledge but not without that of the chief of police, was put on Croce's account and sometimes probably absorbed by Laterza himself. For his friendship and collaboration with Croce, Laterza paid a price and lost economic opportunities. Yet he remained faithful to Croce and true to his liberal ideals even when the authorities of the regime harassed his firm. 'During the whole duration of fascism,' to quote the art historian Giulio Carlo Argan, 'Laterza was an impregnable fortress,' and the editorial activity of his publishing house has to be regarded as 'a miracle of skill, prudence and courage.'[13]

Reasons for Croce's Relative Freedom

The freedom of expression that Croce enjoyed during the Fascist regime has raised some questions. In 1944 Palmiro Togliatti, followed after the war by other Communist leaders and some Marxist historians, even claimed that Croce had been guilty of a secret agreement and a hidden connivance with fascism: continuous anti-Marxism polemic in return for 'timid arrows' against the regime. For his part, Denis Mack Smith argued that Croce's opposition was for many reasons even useful to fascism, first of all as an advertisement abroad of Mussolini's tolerance, and also because Croce himself, on account of the foreign royalties earned by his books, was, in Smith's amusing but empty expression, 'a considerable dollar asset.' Yet this issue deserves a better explanation. Croce's position under fascism was not only unusual but sets him apart from virtually all other writers under modern dictatorships. A close look at Croce's life in the Fascist era provides a more accurate picture both of Mussolini's dictatorship and of Croce's personality.

The reason why Mussolini allowed Croce to publish his books and his periodical generated some 'wonder' even during the regime, as we learn from Croce himself in his 'Autobiographical Notes.' In 1934 Croce confessed that he was not in a position to explain 'the reasons for this sort of immunity,' nor could he foresee its duration. He listed four possible reasons to explain the policy of the authorities: his literary fame abroad, and the scandal that had been caused by the invasion of his house in 1926, with consequent damage to the prestige of Mussolini in Europe; the desire of Fascists to show that freedom of expression was alive and well in Italy, and to use Croce's situation to prove the point; the traditional respect and social prestige, usually transcending partisan politics, accorded in Italy to great men of letters; and, finally, Croce's own age, which probably led the authorities to take the view that it would be better to allow nature to do its work than to take a political decision that would be bound to have messy results. In June 1940, when the minister of education suppressed *La Critica* with a hypocritical excuse – 'to limit in the present circumstances the number of periodicals' – Croce used another argument, which must have carried some weight since he won the case and the decision was rescinded. In the protest that he wrote, Croce told the minister that, though his periodical belonged to 'a man who had remained faithful to the ideals of his youth, and which are not those that are prominent in the new times of Italian history,' *La Critica* was not a political publication but rather dealt only with ideas. On other occasions, from 1930 to 1940, when he had to protest against the suspension of his books, Croce also stated that his books had not violated existing laws and he was not guilty of any 'common crime.'[14]

Both claims were certainly true. Even the political and historical essays of Croce never criticized the policies of the government directly and hardly mentioned fascism by name. When reference had to be made to fascism, it was done with synonyms like 'authoritarian movements,' 'anti-historicism,' and, more often, 'activism' or 'irrationalism.' In his writings Croce expressed ideas contrary to the ideology of fascism which undermined the position of the regime, but those ideas did not amount to liability under the law and could not be regarded as a threat to the security of the state. The government could harass Croce, even remove him from official positions, and it did so with impunity, but it could not mount a legal case against his activities. The courts retained a certain degree of independence, as the trial of Parri and Rosselli showed in 1927. Defence lawyers were in general free to speak their minds and to argue their cases as they pleased, which is exactly what Mario Ferrara did in defence of Communist militants, quoting with eloquence from Plato's *Apology of Socrates*. In 1934 Croce himself was involved in a legal case which could have turned ugly. But, in this case, he won a civil suit against one of his tenants even though that tenant was defended by a powerful party boss in Apulia, Giuseppe Caradonna. The special laws of Rocco protected the security of the state rather than the ideology of fascism, and they did not cover ideas. And furthermore, as a senator, Croce could neither be arrested nor jailed; instead, he had to be tried first by the Senate, and inside the Senate, acting as the High Court of Justice. In such a trial only those senators who had been present at all the sittings from the first to the last could vote on the final verdict. A prosecution or persecution of Croce had to be based on a political decision and had to employ measures outside the existing legal system. The authorities never resorted to such an expedient, unwilling to create a complicated situation that might spark unforeseen reactions even among Fascist supporters, not to mention the bad publicity that would be the result in international public opinion.

In reality, the reason for Croce's relative freedom has to be found in the nature of fascism and in the personality of Mussolini. Croce was not the only one to publish a periodical outside the control of the regime that challenged cultural orthodoxy. Apart from the Catholic press, there were other liberal personalities who enjoyed the same precarious privilege as Croce and, like him, were relatively immune from censorship. Luigi Einaudi, Gaetano De Sanctis, Cesare De Lollis, Ernesto Codignola, Piero Martinetti, and Luigi Russo published periodicals in their fields of interest, for short or long periods, free from political control. Nor was Laterza the only publishing house faithful to liberal ideals. Under the advice of his father and the leadership of Leone Ginzburg, Giulio Einaudi in Turin followed a similar policy, publishing modern authors useful to a democratic education. Italian Fascism created an authoritarian regime, ever increasing its reach, but it did not have the time, perhaps did not even possess the strength, to build a totalitarian society. The movement was not based on a single philosophy, and it did not have a well-defined theoretical system to guide all its actions according to a coherent program. Within the movement, philosophical and artistic currents co-existed in changing alliances, and people were free to embrace different beliefs and even different religions. Even after the racial laws, the government and the party never tried to impose an official line on artistic and literary matters, though it did introduce new restrictions. The press could still debate cultural events and promote ideas, or artistic trends, old   and new, without too much fear. The rivalries among Fascist leaders increased this relative freedom, and sometimes, under the protection of powerful party bosses, ambitious people could sponsor unorthodox ideas and even criticize single ministers and their policies, though never question the leadership of Mussolini himself. In this situation, the position of Mussolini acquired paramount importance, and his personality, and the contradictions of that personality, assumed a central role in explaining the policies of the regime.

One of the reasons for Croce's relative freedom can be found in Mussolini's attitude towards culture and cultural leaders. Mussolini had an instrumental approach to culture; for him, cultural activities and cultural organizations were to be used to increase the prestige of the regime at home and especially abroad, and also to assure the Fascist education of new generations. A blatant persecution of top cultural leaders would be an impediment to achieving those aims. For this reason, he was rather indifferent to higher education and instead concentrated his efforts on controlling the mass media and creating organizations able to influence the opinions of the masses. Cultural activities that involved small elites could be left undisturbed.

Mussolini also had a contradictory attitude towards cultural leaders. He could be brutal, as in the case of Gobetti; he could be tolerant with others, even accommodating when it fitted his political needs; but he was authoritarian when the education of young people was involved or his authority was challenged. His long conversations with Ivon De Begnac in the 1930s reveal that Mussolini regarded the collaboration of cultural leaders as necessary to achieve national consensus and essential to ensure the regime's success among the people. He also seemed to realize that great writers enjoy a sort of natural immunity that provides them with a shield against the pressure of political powers. There are revealing statements in those conversations showing that Mussolini was willing to respect some limits in the area of culture. He wanted cooperation without seeking recourse to terror, and was not ready to use extreme measures because 'revolutions that send poets to their deaths are destined to fall.'[15]

During the course of those conversations, Mussolini talked a great deal about Croce: he expressed gratitude for Croce's early support, regretted his subsequent opposition, and lamented his refusal to join the Academy of Italy, but he never uttered threats against Croce or even used angry words; on the contrary, he always maintained a rather respectful tone. In the past, to be sure, Mussolini had sometimes hurled insulting expressions at Croce, but even then he had made sure that an emissary would later offer Croce, if not excuses, at least reasonable explanations. There is reason to believe that Mussolini read Croce's most important writings, and he sometimes liked to show surprised Italian and foreign visitors Croce's latest book or the last issue of *La Critica* sitting on his desk and to praise the author. In his memoirs, Bottai has revealed that, even during the war, Mussolini liked to engage in discussions about Croce and to debate some of his controversial essays. It is, therefore, not far-fetched to say that Mussolini admired Croce's intellectual achievements and regarded his prestige as a national asset not to be tampered with lightly, especially given the negative publicity both at home and abroad that had followed the invasion of Croce's house in 1926.

One can also speculate that Mussolini had his own peculiar reasons to like and to appreciate what Croce wrote. In private conversations and in his books, Croce always had harsh words for nationalism and especially for the Nationalist leaders, but Mussolini did not have too much sympathy for them either, regarding them, except for Rocco and perhaps a few others, with suspicion. After the reconciliation with the church in 1929, Croce increased his criticism of the Catholic Church, giving an anti-clerical tone to his attacks that must have been music to the ears of Mussolini – an old anti-clerical and notorious blasphemer from Romagna – while also providing him with ammunition against the ever-increasing demands of the pope in the field of education. Similarly, Croce's constant criticism of Gentile could be used by Mussolini to curtail the dynamism of that strong personality, or to undermine the influence of other intellectuals, or even to promote his own cultural policies. Finally, the conversations with De Begnac and other documents show that Mussolini strongly believed that the future belonged to fascism and that the regime was creating a new culture, giving the young Fascist education and relegating Croce and his traditional culture to the past. In the last analysis, it is fair to conclude that Mussolini did not engage in direct and extreme persecution of Croce primarily out of political considerations but also, perhaps, because he regarded the great man with a certain respect.

Whatever the reasons for the attitude of Mussolini and fascism towards Croce, one has to accept the conclusion of Ernesto Ragionieri, a Marxist historian often not kindly disposed to Croce, that during the Fascist regime 'Benedetto Croce was able to utilize with extraordinary ability the margins of freedom that fascism had to concede to him, because of his fame and his reputation in Italy and in Europe.' But it is still better to leave the last words to Croce himself: 'Whatever one wants to think about all this, I have used this personal and relative freedom not as a concession and as a donation, for which I owed gratitude to somebody, but as one of my rights, using, though, moderation and observing the austerity that good taste advises in such conditions, so grave and at the same time so delicate.'[16]

To the ever-present question of why Croce was allowed to publish his books and his periodical during the dictatorship of Mussolini, the answer now has become rather simple. Croce enjoyed relative freedom under the 'Axe of Fascism,' to borrow the title of a famous book published by Salvemini in 1936, because he felt free, had the courage to act as a free man, and expressed his ideas with sobriety but without fear. The prestige thus gained further increased his safety, and fascism was compelled to tolerate his activity because it was unable or unwilling to challenge public opinion and to risk moral and political discredit.

CHAPTER ELEVEN

Difficult Choices, 1930–1940

During Mussolini's dictatorship, prudence and courage were required not only in literary affairs but also in other aspects of life, public and private. After 1930, the regime became more demanding and made it more difficult to remain faithful to liberal values. Sometimes it was even hard to maintain professional dignity. Government policy often put personal convictions to the test, and the appropriate answers were not easy to come by nor the choices easy to endure. In those troubled waters, the navigation became perilous for members of the opposition. In order to have a better appreciation of Croce's position under the Fascist regime, it is necessary to explore his reaction to some of the important events of that period, and to consider the difficult choices that they imposed.

Oath of Loyalty

In 1931, in order to increase political control in higher education, Mussolini forced university teachers to take a loyalty oath to the Fascist regime. Until that year, the oath of office required the teachers to observe loyally the Statuto; now, however, they also had to swear 'to be faithful to the king and his successors and to the Fascist regime.' It was no longer enough to turn students into good citizens: the aim of university education was henceforth to produce graduates 'devoted to the country' and to the government. This humiliating law had been first suggested and inspired by Gentile, who had various concerns but deep down was motivated by a desire for vengeance against those intellectuals who had signed Croce's anti-Fascist manifesto in 1925. Mussolini accepted Gentile's request for his own political reasons; the new law offered him an easy opportunity to give small satisfaction to the radical wing of the party and at the same time to reaffirm the authority of the state against the increasing demands of the Catholic Church in matters of education. Of about twelve hundred university teachers, only nineteen did not take the loyalty oath. Twelve simply refused, while others resigned or took early retirement before the law came into effect. None of them turned the occasion into a public protest, and no attempt was made to mount a political response. As a police informer astutely remarked, decisions remained individual ones and did not produce a united movement with effective leadership, as had happened in 1925 at the time of Croce's anti-Fascist manifesto. Such a response would have required freedom of the press, which was still available in 1925 but had disappeared by 1931.[1]

The overall reaction of the academic community left much to be desired: 'a shameful result for Italian high culture,' in Gaetano De Sanctis's judgment. The number of resignations was small, even if one has to admit that in the economic conditions of the 1930s few teachers were in a position to take a different road or could afford the loss of employment. As it turned out, the oath proved less onerous in practice than it first seemed in theory. During the official ceremony that accompanied the oath, the chancellor of the university read the formula of loyalty, and afterwards the professors signed a piece of paper without having to say a word. After the oath and the ceremony, life in the universities returned to the normal routine. The professors were able to resume their lessons as before, free to teach what and how they wanted. At academic functions, the anti-Fascist teachers could make a statement by choosing to wear business suits instead of party uniforms, as became fashionable. But this is how things turned out in the long run; at the time the oath was first introduced, individual teachers sincerely believed that their very future were at stake.

Croce was not a university professor, so he was not personally affected by the new law. But the law did affect some of his closest friends, and he became deeply concerned that the oath placed them in a difficult position, requiring a dramatic choice that would either affect their economic welfare or their moral status. In the last months of 1931, Croce was writing the *History of Europe*, the prose of which has a pathos not present in his other writings; no doubt, the tone reflects the pain he was experiencing with his friends. Entries in the diaries for 1931 also reveal Croce's concern for his friends and their families, as well as resentment of the law and those who had sponsored it, especially Gentile. As an immediate consequence, Croce's antipathy to his old friend increased and soon found concrete expression. Croce refused with a quick response, *con perentoria secchezza*, Guido Calogero's innocent invitation to contribute an essay to a Festschrift in honour of Ernst Cassirer which was being prepared at the time by Raymond Kliblansky and which included Gentile among its authors. The book was published in 1936 at Oxford under the title *Philosophy and History.*[2]

At that time of painful choices, Croce played the role of father confessor. When the law was announced, the police soon noted an increase of mail and personal visits to Croce's house; the informers, too, noticed several meetings in Rome and in Naples between Croce and other leading intellectuals. Croce's diaries report frequent meetings and conversations, especially with De Sanctis and Ruffini. Many wrote or went to Naples to seek Croce's advice or to find comfort in his understanding. Friends asked for guidance, to be strengthened in their resolve or to be forgiven for their capitulation. Before taking a definite decision, Luigi Einaudi travelled to Naples and spent a day in long conversation in Croce's studio. After he returned to Turin, Croce sent him, as a gift, a rare old edition of an economic classic which Einaudi received with emotion as 'a sign of unchanged benevolence' and then placed in a special place in his library, recording on the title page the donor and the occasion of the gift. Ultimately, three of Croce's best friends refused to take the oath: Francesco Ruffini, a Liberal; Lionello Venturi, a Democrat; and Gaetano De Sanctis, a Catholic; another friend, Luigi Einaudi, and three of Croce's closest collaborators, Adolfo Omodeo, Guido De Ruggiero, and Luigi Russo, complied with the government's request. As in other similar situations, Croce did not try to impose his personal views but accepted and respected individual decisions, showing a sympathy that was treasured and long remembered.[3]

Croce did not advise absolute intransigence for a rather simple reason, as reported by De Sanctis: 'With pain and sadness he told us, "I feel I cannot urge you to refuse the oath, because you are in danger and I am not, because I am not a teacher, and am protected by senatorial immunity."' On the other hand, Croce, unlike De Sanctis, did not regard the oath as one of those insurmountable cases of conscience, demanding a flat refusal. The university teachers faced an evident case of necessity, which for some could justify a political choice. A personal sacrifice could be made in the name of a higher responsibility, in this case to protect the welfare of the universities. With other anti-Fascists, Croce shared the view that university education should not be abandoned to the complete control of Fascist teachers. For the sake of a different future, the hateful measure could be accepted, and the bitter pill swallowed, in order to remain inside the classrooms and so preserve a tradition and offer to new generations ideas different from those preached by the regime.[4]

In the name of political realism, the Communist Party advised its members or sympathizers to obey the law, and Concetto Marchesi at the University of Padua took the oath and continued to teach classical literature, creating future scholars and Communist partisans. Even Ernesto Rossi, a pupil of Salvemini and an indomitable anti-Fascist, member of Giustizia e Libertà, who was in jail at the time, shared that view. In a letter to his mother, he praised the economist Antonio De Viti De Marco for his resignation while also expressing solidarity with Luigi Einaudi, who had chosen a different road; in the following months and years, he continued to correspond with Einaudi and to treat him with deference. More than the formal ceremonies of the oath, for Rossi, the fate of university education remained of paramount importance. Inside the universities, the students themselves appreciated the choice made by their anti-Fascist teachers. When Leone Ginzburg's father-in-law, Giuseppe Levi, an old Socialist friend of Turati, entered the classroom for the first time after taking the oath, shaken and with a sad face, the class gave him a standing ovation, anti-Fascist and Fascist students joining together. Years later, in their memoirs, three Nobel prize winners – Salvatore Luria, Renato Dulbecco, and Rita Levi Montalcini – expressed gratitude for Levi's teaching abilities and personal qualities.[5]

Party Membership

University teachers were not the only ones in those years subjected to political pressure and compelled to accept official rules imposed by a dictatorial government. During Mussolini's regime, membership in the Fascist Party always increased career opportunities, and in the late 1930s it became a condition of employment in the civil service. But even before then, there were regular rumours, spread by party officials, that soon a new law would make it mandatory for all public employees to join the party. Civil servants felt pressured by friends, families, and superiors, all urging conformity and acceptance of the inevitable. In 1933 one of these civil servants, a friend of Croce, wrote to him asking for advice. This time Croce's advice was more explicit but also consistent with his previous position: one should avoid 'acts of insincere spontaneity,' but 'if something is imposed by law or by violence, and in the present they are synonymous,' then one had to decide whether to 'submit to the absolute necessity' or to face the consequences of the refusal. In either case, a personal decision was required; an individual had to draw his own conclusion and accept the responsibility for the choice.[6]

During the same period, and for the same reasons, Adolfo Omodeo faced a similar experience and was urged to ask for Fascist Party membership. Strangely enough, the strongest pressure came from well-meaning friends, afraid that he was in danger of losing his university position for his political views and friendship with Croce. Omodeo had a large family, and teaching was his only source of income. In this period of trial, Croce stood by his friend, suggesting that he stay calm and avoid a rushed decision. He pointed out that this time 'the evident necessity' did not exist and that rumours of pending legislation were not yet the law itself. When Omodeo took courage and refused to join the Fascist Party, Croce immediately wrote him a letter of praise, lauding his choice and his determination. On reading this letter, one can almost feel Croce's sense of relief at the decision made by his friend.[7]

In these two episodes one notes Croce's sadness over the isolation that began to be the lot of those who refused to join official organizations. The closeness experienced in those years by opponents of the regime and the difficulties they faced together probably explain the strong value that Croce always attached to his friendship with Omodeo, among many others. It also explains the paternal benevolence that Croce felt for Leone Ginzburg, who, with bold letters to his superiors, refused in 1934 to take the loyalty oath and lost his teaching positions in high school and university.

Expulsion from Academies

In 1933 the government compelled the members of the old learned societies and the national academies to take a loyalty oath, similar to the one imposed on university teachers. This time Croce was directly affected, being a member of long standing of a few of those institutions. Again there were meetings with Gaetano De Sanctis and conversations with other friends. Not surprisingly, both Croce and De Sanctis refused 'the capitulation,' 'to avoid the scandal,' as De Sanctis said, quoting Saint Paul. When Croce was officially notified of the new requirement and invited to appear at 'the solemn ceremony' called for taking the loyalty oath, he refused the invitation with letters that were short and to the point but that were sent by registered mail to assure their delivery and official receipt. To the presidents of the Reale Accademia of Naples and the Accademia dei Lincei of Rome, Croce wrote that an oath of loyalty to a political party was 'in contrast with the nature and dignity of the academic office,' whose only function was 'the free search for truth.'[8]

After Croce refused to take the oath, he was no longer invited to the meetings of the Reale Accademia of Naples. Again he protested against the illegality of such conduct. He sent a letter to the president, reminding him that he had been made a member of that society 'by a Royal decree' 'and that 'until a new decree, from the same source' revoked his nomination, he had to be regarded as a member in good standing and entitled to receive all the communications and invitations sent to the membership. The letter, needlessly to say, never received a reply, nor did Croce expect one.[9]

After the introduction of the oath of loyalty, and later as a result of the racial laws against Jews, all the Italian academies lost members and reputation. While Croce was still an effective member of those organizations and in a position of influence, he tried, not without some success, to protect their integrity. The most memorable incident occurred in Naples and involved the minister of education, Pietro Fedele. In 1930 Croce publicly opposed the nomination of the minister as a member of the Accademia Pontaniana. During the general meeting, he reminded the audience that, in its long history under the Bourbon kings, in order to preserve its political independence, the academy had never elected as one of its members a minister of education while he was still in office. Amidst the general silence and embarrassment, Croce invited the assembly to reject the nomination not only because it was politically incorrect, and violated a long tradition, but also because of the simple fact that the present minister of education did not 'possess the required scientific qualifications.'[10]

The Ethiopian War

In October 1935 Italy invaded Ethiopia, and in May 1936 General Badoglio brought the war to a victorious conclusion. The same month, speaking in Rome to an enormous crowd, *una folla oceanica*, as the Italian papers reported, Mussolini proclaimed the new Roman Empire amid thundering applause. The Ethiopian war was immensely popular among the Italian people, and the proclamation of the empire marked the zenith of Mussolini's prestige. The regime was able to mobilize public opinion against the League of Nations, appealing to old aspirations and to ancient resentments against the Western powers.

Unlike some other former Liberal leaders and even some Democratic anti-Fascist exiles, Croce did not share the general enthusiasm for this new incarnation of Crispi's imperial aspirations. His private correspondence of the time did not contain any praise or approval for the event, and the diaries instead reveal the same sadness that Croce always expressed when faced with troubling political news. During those months, when it was fashionable to attack 'perfidious Albion,' Croce had several meetings with British newspapermen, especially with his friend Cecil Sprigge of the Manchester Guardian, to whom he relayed his disappointment over the vacillations and obsession with appeasement that then marked British foreign policy. Finally, in private conversations with a police informer, Croce expressed worries about the consequences of 'a nefarious policy.'[11]

Three months after the beginning of the war, the Italian government, to mobilize public opinion but also to boost the gold reserve bled dry by the African campaign, asked Italian married women 'to donate' their wedding rings to the cause of the Fascist revolution. As part of this well-orchestrated publicity campaign, the president of the Senate, Luigi Federzoni, invited the senators to give back to the state the gold medal that they had received when appointed to the assembly. At first, Croce decided to ignore the request. But, in a series of meetings in Naples and in Rome, the other few remaining anti-Fascist senators, including Albertini, Bergamini, and Casati, pressed for compliance. All of them wanted to avoid the accusation of anti-patriotism; they were also concerned that a gesture of defiance could provoke a political backlash, involving more harassment and perhaps even new forms of persecution of a more personal nature. After a night of discussion, Croce reluctantly accepted their arguments, against the advice of his wife. In the end he 'returned' his medal to the secretary of the Senate but also sent a brief letter to Federzoni which, in a cold tone, reaffirmed his political opposition to fascism and stated the reason for his decision. 'Excellency, though I do not approve the policy of the government, I have accepted, in the name of the fatherland, the invitation of Your Excellency, and I have returned to the offices of the Senate my medal, that has the date of 1910.'[12]

The decision of Croce and the other anti-Fascist senators on this occasion has to be seen both as an act of political expediency and as an expression of traditional patriotism, still strong in men of that generation, all of them with personal and emotional ties to the Risorgimento. But that decision left the door wide open to political speculation – the very speculation that it was meant to avoid and that has continued ever since. The government, or at least the chief of police, was aware of Croce's negative feeling about the war and the regime's foreign policy, but the mass media, controlled by the regime, reported the event in a light favourable to the official line; no mention was made of the letter, as was to be expected, and 'the return of my medal' was altered to become 'the donation of the gold medal' made by Senator Benedetto Croce.

Future historians and newspapermen, even recently, have preferred to ignore the documents and instead accept and repeat the propaganda of the Fascist regime. More important, in the conditions of 1935, Croce's gesture created confusion among his friends and provoked deep consternation among anti-Fascists in jail or in exile, who, ignoring the letter and reading the newspapers, felt abandoned by Croce and came to believe that now even he was approving the policy of Mussolini. Croce was made aware of their reaction in Milan during a dramatic meeting with Bianca Ceva, who has left a touching account of their discussion in which Croce mentioned his original doubts, explained the reasons for his decision, and asked her to convey his unchanged feelings to their friends in jail, and in particular to Riccardo Bauer. Ceva's respect, like that of Bauer, for Croce never wavered, then or later, and indeed her affection for him even increased after that meeting. Nevertheless in retrospect, it would have been much better and politically more opportune if Croce had followed his first instincts and had chosen the advice of his wife, instead of accepting Casati's arguments.[13]

More documents that make possible a better assessment of Croce's position during Mussolini's African adventure are now available. In 1935 four hundred senators endorsed a resolution expressing approval of the Ethiopian war and praising Mussolini's leadership. When asked, however, Croce and his few remaining friends, less than a dozen, refused to sign that document, thus denying it the unanimous consent of the assembly. In May 1936, when the Senate voted the proclamation of the new Italian empire, Croce made a point of being absent from the chamber. From 1929 on, in fact, Croce's absences from special occasions assumed the function of a vote of non-confidence and were duly reported to the proper authorities by those senators who were in the employ of the secret police and whose names were not unknown to Croce. Finally, in 1936, after Badoglio conquered Addis Adaba, Croce broke his relations and correspondence with an old friend, Giovanni Castellano, who had acted almost as his private secretary until the advent of fascism, when their political paths separated. Full of imperial enthusiasm, Castellano had invited

Croce to renounce his anti-fascism and 'to make public amends' for his political mistake. Not only did Croce not follow the clumsy advice of Castellano, but in the very midst of the imperial euphoria that prevailed in the Italian press, at the end of 1936, he published the little book of Aldo Capitini, *Elementi di una Esperienza Religiosa*, that was inspired by the ideas of Gandhi and his commitment to non-violence and also preached brotherhood among nations according to Mazzini's teachings.[14]

On the international stage, Croce's views were consistent with his anti-fascism and anti-imperialism. In December 1935, while the Italian mass media were foolishly singing the praises of Nazi Germany, Croce, at the request of German political refugees, joined Thomas Mann in urging the Nobel Committee to assign its peace prize that year to Carl von Ossietzhy, the German journalist who had campaigned for peace among nations, opposed German rearmament, and been jailed for the last three years for his political ideas. When the Spanish Civil War began, in private correspondence and in personal conversations, Croce expressed sympathy for the republic. Also in 1936, when the traditional Italian alliance with the Western powers was in pieces, and Fascist propaganda stressed the differences between Italy and the Western 'plutocratic powers,' Croce wrote a political essay for the American periodical *The New Republic* which was then republished in *La Critica*. In that essay, Croce reaffirmed his faith in the future triumph of freedom and condemned all forms of authoritarian regimes, then rather fashionable among many Italian and European intellectuals. He also urged 'all men of good will to work every day, in every condition, with all means available, using appropriate ways ... to protect and to promote the liberal spirit.'[15]

The Racial Laws

The Ethiopian adventure had great consequences for Italian society; it changed the ideology of fascism and affected the personality of Mussolini, pushing the government towards more authoritarian policies. The traditional friendship with Great Britain came to an end and was replaced by a more cordial collaboration with Germany. The ties between fascism and nazism assumed a novel intimacy. Slowly the regime acquired a more totalitarian character; fascist doctrine became prevalent in the schools, and the government increased control over social relations and personal morals. In the Italian colonies, racial separation was preached and applied with a new vigour. Mussolini embarked on ideological propaganda against 'the bourgeois spirit' and began a relentless campaign against the traditional 'pietism' of the Italian people, preaching instead 'heroism' and martial virtues as the necessary attributes for the creation of the new fascist man. At the end, all these changes affected the nature of Italian society and, unfortunately, dramatically altered the legal status of the Jewish community inside the Italian nation. Suddenly Italian citizens, belonging to the Jewish faith, were deprived of their rights and made foreign in their own land, persecuted without having violated any laws.

Until 1938 there had not been a Jewish question in Italy, apart from the rather innocuous but annoying prejudices of old. The Jewish community was small and well integrated in Italian social life, participating fully in national affairs and sharing the same aspirations as other Italians. Even under the Fascist regime, the Jewish people had equal opportunity and enjoyed the same freedom, or lack of freedom, as the rest of the Italian population. Some had positions of influence in the schools, the civil service, the government, and the armed forces. Mussolini himself, in his conversations with Emil Ludwig, recently had denied the existence in Italy of a Jewish problem. More than other people, he could claim with good reason that some of his best friends, male or female, were Jews. For many years he carried on a public relationship with a Jewish woman, Margherita Sarfatti, whose fashionable salon in Milan was well attended by Fascist personalities in positions of influence in politics and in the arts.

This natural harmony was abruptly shattered by the introduction of the racial laws. With those laws a definition of Jew came into existence in Italian legislation, and Italian citizens were divided into two categories and put into two different races, one of them subject to discrimination and persecution and after 1943 to deportation and death. As a result, Jews were forbidden to marry outside their religion, were not allowed to attend public schools, and could not hold public office. They were immediately expelled from the civil service, the armed forces, and professional organizations. Finally, underlining the regime's hypocrisy, Jews were no longer allowed to be members of the Fascist Party, and those who already were members were expelled or compelled to resign, while the families of Jews who had died 'martyrs of the Fascist cause' were exempt from the law.

When the racial laws were introduced in Italy, Italo Balbo was almost alone among politicians in his opposition and in the Grand Council of Fascism he spoke and voted against the measures, showing his usual bravado. As a result of that opposition, a few categories of Jews were exempt from the laws, in particular those who had earned, in peace or war, special patriotic merits! To their shame, many Italian writers supported the racial laws and participated in the anti-Semitic campaign with articles, essays, and books. To be anti-Semitic became fashionable, especially among young intellectuals in the making. To write against Jews and to pose as anti-bourgeois was also profitable. Among well-known Fascist intellectuals, only Giovanni Gentile and Filippo Marinetti on occasion expressed their disagreement, and then tried to help some of their friends who were victims of the new persecution. But most of the ninety-seven university positions that Jewish professors had held until then with great prestige and were now compelled to vacate were grabbed with shameful haste by Italian scholars, often possessing academic credentials much inferior to those of the former occupants.[16]

Croce's position on racial theories and against the persecution of Jews was well known long before the German and Italian racial laws came into effect. Already in 1928, in his book, the *History of Italy*, he had praised the liberal policies of Italian governments, stressing at the same time the contribution of the Jewish community to the Risorgimento and to Italian public life in general. And even before the publication of that book, on many occasions, with sarcasm or irony, he had rejected or ridiculed the extravagant claims that nationalist historians employed to extol the primacy of certain races or the mythological accomplishments of their own people. When the new racial persecution began, first in Germany and later in Italy, Croce remained a courageous defender of the Jews and a tenacious opponent of racism, expressing his solidarity with the Jewish people in the name of a common humanity that 'through them,' as he wrote 'was offended in all men.'

From 1933, in his periodical, Croce engaged in frequent battle against racial ideas. From time to time in *La Critica*, when news items or the publication of a book provided the occasion, small, trenchant notes attacked arguments of racial superiority. In those notes and in other essays, Croce lamented the decline of German culture and the steady march from the idealism of Kant to the materialism of Rosenberg. With sardonic irony, he pointed out that the Nazis were destroying German science and at the same time, unintentionally, had succeeded in showing to the world how great had been the contribution of the Jews to German cultural and social life. When Mussolini saw fit to imitate Germany, and Italian writers borrowed freely from German racial theories, Croce pointed out how those arguments were offensive to Italy and to Italians. He reminded those naive writers that often German scholars blamed the Latin heritage for its corrupting influence on the German spirit, downgraded Roman civilization, and praised the achievements of classical Greece instead, stressing at the same time the inferiority of the Latin race and the affinity of Germans to old Greeks.[17]

Besides his periodical, Croce used other means to express his anti-racism and to make public statements against the persecution of the Jews. In 1933 he protested against the new German racial theories in a letter that Croce sent to Charles Beard, as president of the American Historical Association. The letter made observations about the nature of historiography, but it also included reflections on the political problems of the times. Croce urged American historians to reject racial and ethnic principles that reduce history almost to a fight of cats and dogs, of beasts hunting beasts. He warned that those principles, with their emphasis on the satisfaction of biological needs and materialistic aspirations, not only make impossible a proper interpretation of human history but also weaken the moral forces of society and increase prejudices among people and rivalries among nations.[18]

In 1934 Croce wrote an article for *The American Hebrew and Jewish Tribune* in which he reaffirmed his rejection of 'the stupid concept of race' and 'the various forms of oppression against minority groups.' The article was later republished in his own periodical, and so the Italians, like the Americans, could read that 'the persecutions against the Jews have never brought benefits to any nation' and that the new persecution would give 'no benefit to the life and culture of Germany' but instead hasten its moral and political decline. With a clear reference to the Italian experience under the Fascist regime, the American and Italian readers were told that in Germany 'the men of science and culture, who were serving the oppressors and persecutors of freedom had renounced their mission and were betraying their office.'[19]

In 1936 Croce sent a long essay to the Swiss paper *Die Nation* with the expressive title, 'The Germany That We Have Loved.' In this essay he lamented that the Germany that he and the men of his generation had admired for its great culture was no longer, destroyed by the oppression and the racial policy of the Nazi regime. With sadness, he also observed that German universities and scholars had abandoned the great philosophical principles of the past and replaced them with zoological concepts of race, leaving their cultural life arid and materialistic. Croce pointed out that, quite appropriately, the University of Heidelberg had recently changed its motto from 'To the Spirit of the World' to 'To the German Spirit,' pleasing Rosenberg if not Hegel.[20]

In August 1938, while persecution of Jews and Italian anti-Semitic propaganda were increasing, Croce wrote a letter to the president of Stockholm University expressing his support for an international appeal launched by the Swedish press in favour of German Jews. In his letter, 'as a man and as a liberal,' he expressed his 'horror at today's dreadful persecutions against the Jews in Germany and Austria.' He also confessed that what was happening in many parts of the world 'before our astonished eyes' was contrary to his generation's most basic principles. He made a keen observation, too, when he noted that the increasing mass accumulation of political crimes, and the impossibility of opposing them in any adequate manner, was generating among the people a sort of dull indifference and moral torpor. Unfortunately, Croce proved right on another point: in his letter he lamented the increased agitation against Italian Jews and expressed fears for their future safety. The letter was published by the Swedish papers and soon became known in Italy and brought the usual outburst of insults and threats against the author; Croce was accused of anti-patriotic activity, soiling abroad the good name of Italy. Finally, in 1938 Croce published the already mentioned *History as Thought and as Action*, where the concept of freedom is presented both as 'an explanatory principle' for the interpretation of the past and as 'a moral ideal' for conduct in the present. The references to contemporary events, noted by the police informer soon after the book's publication, became even more evident in the third edition of March 1939. In that edition, which appeared only a few months after the introduction of racial laws in Italy and in the middle of a press campaign against the Jews, Croce added five more chapters. One of these repudiated racial theories and political discrimination based on race, arguing that the very concept was full of 'passions and fantasies' but devoid of historical reality and scientific merit. Croce condemned the demagogic appeal to traditional prejudices then under way, and he urged 'the moral man, the religious man ... to fight incessantly the preconceptions of race and to reassert instead ... the common and universal humanity of all men.'[21]

Croce not only wrote polemical notes and historical essays against racial discrimination; he also tried to help those of his Jewish friends who were deprived of their academic positions and compelled to emigrate from Germany, hoping to find employment in more hospitable countries. Among many acts of solidarity, in 1933 Croce wrote to Nicholas M. Butler, president of Columbia University, urging him to find a position for Leo Spitzer, a professor of Romance literature recently expelled from the University of Koln. Croce hardly needed to explain that the employment of Spitzer would be a definite gain for American universities, and, at the same time, 'an act of human brotherhood.' Croce also approached Bernard Berenson, the famous art historian, living in Florence but with strong ties to Harvard University, to interest him in the case. Croce urged Berenson to use his American connections to help the victims of 'what was happening in Germany against humanity and science.' By giving employment to people like Spitzer, American institutions would acquire distinguished scholars and simultaneously give 'a lesson in humanity to Germany, now no longer the fatherland of Lessing.'[22]

The Senate's Silence

In the late 1990s, the former Christian Democrat prime minister, Giulio Andreotti, launched a rather gratuitous attack against Croce and Einaudi, remarking that the Liberal senators remained silent and did not speak against the racial laws when they were debated in the Senate. This was unfair. When the racial laws were introduced in Italy, the members of the Senate were no longer in a position to voice their concern, let alone their opposition. The Senate had changed in a fundamental way after 1936, when Giacomo Suardo replaced Luigi Federzoni as president. Its sittings lost their old dignity, the atmosphere became more partisan than in the past, and the great majority of senators wore Fascist black shirts or even appeared in full party uniform. More often than not, the president began and closed the sessions with party slogans and with the Roman salute. Not only were the anti-Fascist senators made uncomfortable inside the assembly by the behaviour of the government members, they were also plainly discriminated against; frequently, they did not receive the reports of Senate committees or even the agendas. Above all, the Senate changed its method of work and, as a result, for all practical purposes, the senators lost their legislative functions and were deprived of their power to influence national policy. With the exception of the budget, international treaties, and the judiciary, legislative powers were transferred from the Senate to standing committees, *comitati legislativi*, where no political opposition was allowed and only technical changes to new legislative measures were accepted. Once government proposals were approved by a committee, the chairman reported the result to the Senate, the president asked the assembly for the vote, and no further debate was permitted.

To avoid any surprises, the selection of the committee was also altered. Unlike the old commissions, chosen at random and renewed every year, the members of the new committees and their chairmen were appointed by the president of the Senate and served at his pleasure. In the new organization of the Senate, Croce, Albertini, Casati, Einaudi, and their few remaining Liberal friends were left out with cold deliberation. From then on, no anti-Fascist senator became a member of a commission or participated in its work even as a technical expert. In this way they were deprived of their legislative rights and remained senators in name only, and in fact they no longer took part in the activity of the Senate, and rarely even visited the building. On one of the few times Luigi Einaudi was there, he was invited by a new and younger senator to sit in his old place without fear 'because the occupant never comes.'[23]

In 1938 the racial laws were debated and approved by the Grand Council of Fascism, and afterwards they were dealt with in a cursory way in the standing committees and finally acclaimed by Parliament and by the Senate without further debate. When the bill reached the floor of the Senate, Croce and his Liberal friends did not take part in the sitting, as the only way left to them to express their opposition and to make a protest. In 1938 Croce was unable to repeat what he had done in 1929 during the debate on the Lateran Pacts, standing before the Senate and defending the traditions of liberal Italy. For the same reason, the few Jewish senators still present in the chamber were compelled to remain silent in the face of persecution against their community. Had a senator tried to speak against the racial laws, the president of the Senate would not have recognized him, and the majority of senators would have shouted him down immediately. The new rules of the Senate did not allow any debate and denied freedom of expression.

Solidarity with Jews

In these conditions, deprived of their rights, without the possibility of a public tribune, the only thing left for anti-Fascist senators was to act alone and to offer help and moral support to their friends, to the extent of their means. When racial laws became a reality in Italy and Jewish scholars were deprived of their university positions, and in many instances compelled to seek new opportunities abroad, Croce wrote letters of reference for several friends, and, as he had done for the German scholars before, used his international reputation in their favour. In the National Archives, owing to the zeal of Fascist censorship, one can read many letters written to Croce by those he had helped. All these letters contain warm expression of gratitude.[24]

After the war, Croce, as part of a larger essay, published the letter that he had sent in 1938 to the British philosopher Robert Collingwood, asking him to help Arnaldo Momigliano, who hoped to find a teaching position at Oxford. The censors of Naples, however, were the first to read the rather sad letter that Momigliano wrote to Croce on that occasion: 'I thank you for your letter of reference, that you kindly sent to me. I regard it as an inspiration and an encouragement. It should have some effect on others, but unfortunately the world is tired.' Despite his pessimism and that of Collingwood, after some difficulties, Momigliano, like a number of German classical scholars, found a university position at Oxford, where he became a renowned scholar in classical historiography, writing his many books no longer in Italian but in English.[25] Similarly, in December 1938, Antonello Gerbi, a keen historian by vocation but at that time working in Peru as branch manager for the Italian Banca Commerciale, wrote a letter to Croce asking: 'If I could have from you a certificate, even of a few lines, to be included in my curriculum vitae, which I am afraid soon I will have to write for "professional reasons."' Croce complied promptly and Gerbi wrote back: 'Your certificate made me blush ... It represents a prize that I hardly hoped to receive for those small old works of mine.'

From England in 1939, Enzo Tagliacozzo expressed his appreciation for the letter of reference that Croce had sent to an American college and 'for your cordial and warm hospitality during these last years.' The same year, from Florence, a well-established scholar but no longer in the prime of his life, Alessandro Levi had to ask Croce for a letter of reference 'just in case I should decide to emigrate.' For the same reason, another professor, Attilio Momigliano, abruptly removed from university even though he was one of the most important scholars of Italian literature, went to Naples in person instead. Once Jewish friends had emigrated abroad, Croce tried to maintain contact with them until the war made it impossible. Before the outbreak of hostilities, Paolo Treves sent a typed letter to Croce from London, 'to facilitate the job of the censors in Naples,' giving his news but also asking Croce's help for the publication in Italy of a book written by one of his new English colleagues.[26]

Separated suddenly from their university friends, living and teaching in a new environment, often in a precarious condition, these Jewish scholars treasured Croce's letters to them. Renato Treves probably spoke for many, when he wrote to Croce from Montevideo, after receiving one of his letters: 'Every sign that reassures me that my teachers have not forgotten me is of great comfort to me.' From such letters we also learn that the arrival of *La Critica* generated much excitement among expatriate Jewish scholars, helping them to maintain intellectual ties with Italy. In 1939, from Lima, Gerbi wrote: '*La Critica* is the only Italian paper that I receive from Italy. Thus the distant fatherland and the beloved studies have the same voice. A familiar voice and an unmistakable one. What a pity it rings once every two months.' Some of the Jewish scholars who received *La Critica* from Italy shared it with friends who were teaching at the same university or living in cities nearby. This was the case in Argentina with Treves and Rodolfo Mondolfo, the Marxist scholar associated with Turati. It is quite evident that the presence of the Italian Jewish diaspora in England, the United States, and in South America increased the popularity of Croce's ideas and enhanced his political reputation. In 1939, writing from Argentina, Mondolfo informed Croce that a group of students and university teachers wanted to translate some of his books and had asked for his help.[27]

Croce also employed his Italian connections to help those Jewish scholars who could not emigrate or had decided to remain in Italy. In this case he made appeals to friendly publishing houses, and as a result the historians Giorgio Falco, Paolo Alatri, and some others could publish their books or do translations, after they had assumed an innocent Aryan name. As Falco wrote after the war in a new introduction to *La Santa Romana Repubblica*: 'This book was published in 1942, under a false name in difficult times, through the kind interest of Benedetto Croce and the thaumaturgic virtues of Raffaele Mattioli.' Paolo Alatri brought his manuscript to Naples and spent a full day in the city, talking, dining, and walking with Croce. His biography of Silvio Spaventa was published in 1941 by Laterza in Croce's *Library of Modern Culture* and performed an anti-Fascist function. The last two chapters of the book offered a liberal interpretation of Spaventa's political actions and ideas in direct contrast with Gentile's authoritarian view of the Risorgimento. Alatri adroitly stressed Spaventa's preference for a liberal constitution of the state that protected freedom of expression, assured the rights of citizens, and recognized the useful role of the opposition in curbing government abuse of power.[28]

Not only did Croce help scholars in their hour of need, but, during the *bonifica* or 'ethnic cleansing' of Italian books, he also protested against the confiscation of the published works of Jewish authors, pointing out the illegality of the measure and also the damage done to Italian studies once those books were no longer available. The letters that

Croce wrote, and that Laterza sent to national and local authorities as part of his lobbying campaign to retrieve confiscated books or simply to register a protest against an arbitrary measure, are admirable for the arguments employed and not the least for their pointed barbs. Once, Croce asked the censors why they were still allowing the sale and republication of the Bible, certainly the most Jewish book ever written by authors with Jewish blood.[29]

The most admirable quality of those letters was the plain courage they showed in a time when this was becoming a scarce commodity, not only in scientific matters but also in social relations. In a period when relations with Jewish families were avoided, when old acquaintances were shunned and sometimes even taken advantage of, Croce maintained steadfast relations with all his Jewish friends, receiving them with his usual liberality in his house where they continued to go in search of support or consolation. Of particular significance was Croce's constant benevolence towards Leone Ginzburg and his young family, and towards the Treves brothers and their mother, who probably consulted him before they decided to escape from Italy to seek refuge first in France and then in England. In Turin, Croce paid several visits to Mrs Michele Giua, whose husband was in jail for anti-Fascist activity and whose young son had been killed in the Spanish Civil War, fighting with Rosselli's volunteers.[30]

After the war, remembering these tragic events and the persecution suffered by the Jews, Arnaldo Momigliano paid a tribute to Croce: 'Few eminent men have been like Croce so closely sympathetic to the Jews, Italians or Germans, victims of racial persecutions.'[31] Momigliano spoke from personal experience; he had witnessed Croce's kindness in good and in bad times, when he was still a student and when he had been discriminated against as a Jew.

Croce's diaries of 1938 and 1939 reveal his emotional participation in the tragedy of the Jewish people. In their pages we come across the names of the Italian Jews whom Croce saw or visited and tried to help when Italian society was almost submerged by 'lies, wickedness and stupidity.' There, too, the persecution is described for what it really was: 'a cruel crime ... and a cold spoliation' against 'our fellow-citizens ... and our friends ... who loved Italy no more and no less than we did.' We glimpse as well the emotions that the political events and the persecutions were stirring in Croce's mind and then found expression in three of his best books: *History as Thought and Action*, *Poetry*, and *Il Carattere della Filosofia Moderna*. We come to know the books and the authors that

Croce read to overcome his anguish and to restore his faith in the human spirit: the Bible, Goethe, Don Quixote helped him to maintain his mental equilibrium and to keep in check the desire for death, and even suicide. In the diary of 1939 are some of the saddest pages ever written by Croce, a lament worthy really of a Jewish prophet in captivity, contemplating the ruin and folly of his own people.[32]

Croce's diaries clearly reveal that the racial laws not only created havoc in the Jewish community, they also inflicted a moral wound on the whole society. Yet they had another effect, too, one that the regime had not anticipated: they compelled many Italians to question anew the nature of fascism and the leadership of Mussolini. As had happened during the Spanish Civil War, it was then that new elements joined the ranks of the opposition and more cracks began to appear in the structures of the regime. The racial laws and the imitation of German policies weakened the popularity and the authority of Mussolini. Two years later, the fortunes of war completed the rout.

The Second World War

Mussolini's declaration of war against France and England in June 1940 put Croce and other Italians who shared democratic ideals in an awkward position, forcing them to make a dramatic choice. Men of Croce's generation had been shaped by the heritage of the Risorgimento and regarded the fatherland and the unity of the nation as one of the supreme political ideals. In time of war, this tradition demanded that partisan divisions come to an end, with all forces joining together to achieve victory and avoid defeat. But the Fascist war against the Western democracies created a contrast between fatherland and freedom, and Croce and men like him were torn between, patriotism and liberty. Slowly and painfully, however, Croce came to the conclusion that true patriots and those who loved freedom had to wish for the defeat of Italy and Germany and the victory of the Western democracies to avoid the enslavement of Europe to nazism, and to make possible the return of freedom in Italy. In reaching that painful conclusion, Croce was helped by the contacts and the discussions that in those months he had with friends of the younger generation, men who had achieved maturity in a different environment and who had been shaped by the aftermath of the First World War. For these younger men, the new conflict was not a traditional war, fought to defend borders or to complete unification; it was instead a clash of ideas, of civilizations. At the end, and in accordance with the inner logic and moral dictates of his philosophy, Croce came to regard the war as a war of religion, and a true patriot had to accept even the defeat of his own country in the name of the religion of freedom.[33]

As the historian Rosario Romeo has argued, the choice imposed by the war and by fascism, and the decision taken by Croce, really marks the end of the Risorgimental tradition in Italian political life: 'The union of the fatherland and freedom, of monarchy and parliament, of national feeling and liberal institutions that was the main feature of the Risorgimento was broken by fascism' and did not survive the war. It is not without some irony that in 1940 Croce came to accept the conclusion reached by the 'naive democrats' in 1915: modern wars are conflicts of different ideals, and international alliances involve choices of civilization. However, unlike his younger friends who could not remember Adua, Croce foresaw the political and moral damage that a military defeat, even a welcome one, would inflict on the Italian nation. For that reason, patriotism, or civic nationalism as we call it now, remained a strong ideal for Croce, necessary for the political cohesion of a people and for the moral authority of national institutions. After the war, even when he became an advocate of European unity, he lamented the disappearance of the old Risorgimental patriotism among the new generations and especially among the new mass parties.

CHAPTER TWELVE

The Fall of Mussolini and the Kingdom of the South, 1940–1944

In 1940 Mussolini had entered the war sure of a quick victory, hoping to enjoy the spoils of the defeat of France and England. But his hopes soon turned into ashes. In 1942 the Germans were halted before Stalingrad, the Italians and the Afrika Korps were defeated at El Alamein, and the Americans landed in North Africa. Then, many Italians realized that the nature of the war, and the fortunes of fascism, had changed. By the end of that year, political parties had been reorganized and were active again, publishing and distributing clandestine papers and pamphlets. At the beginning of 1943, the regime began to crumble.

When the invasion of Italy turned into a probability, the overthrow of fascism and the replacement of Mussolini became a necessity to avoid further destruction and to assure the very survival of the Italian nation. The most responsible elements of Italian society began a desperate search for a way out of the tragedy. In the end, despite the strikes and the economic difficulties, Mussolini and the Fascist regime were brought down not by a popular insurrection but by an old-fashioned royal intervention, precipitated by military defeats and moral collapse. Croce's *intreccio storico* had proved more realistic than the contradictions of capitalism postulated by the Marxists.[1]

The Fall of Mussolini

The role of Pietro Badoglio and Dino Grandi in Mussolini's fall in July 1943 is well known, but the part played by the old Liberal leaders has remained less evident. In fact, this group performed a decisive role in persuading the king to act, allaying his fears and reassuring him that his action would have the support of democratic forces. The Liberal leaders also had meetings with Badoglio, and these contacts and the agreements reached allowed the old marshal to speak on behalf of public opinion in his dealings with the king, the generals, and the British agents, and not just to express his personal views.

The leader of this Liberal group was Ivanoe Bonomi. During the regime, the former premier had retained the trust of the king. In 1942 and 1943 he helped to revive the opposition and to create a loose organization made up of old politicians and young recruits belonging to the liberal and democratic traditions. The centre of action was, for obvious reasons, Rome, but the diaries of Croce and the memoirs of Bonomi and Soleri make it clear that the liberal and democratic opposition was active also in other Italian cities.[2]

Croce played an important role in this movement; he participated in its major decisions and was promptly informed about new initiatives or new developments. In all the future governments envisaged, after Mussolini's fall, Croce's name was always mentioned. No one had comparable prestige in Italy or was more respected abroad. All agreed that he would have to play an important role in the immediate future. Indeed, even the Fascists recognized Croce's moral authority and tried to use it for their own ends, without success. In the spring of 1943, the leaders of the Fascist Party organized a propaganda campaign to boost the morale of the nation. Hoping to regain the political initiative, they invited leading figures of Italian culture to make public speeches in favour of the war effort. Gentile accepted; Croce refused. The new secretary of the party, Carlo Scorza, through an intermediary, approached Croce and asked him 'to make a patriotic speech, inviting Italians to resistance against the Anglo-Americans.' Needless to say, Croce rejected the invitation and rebuked the messenger.[3]

This episode demonstrates how the nature of war had acquired a new dimension since the last one. During the days of Caporetto, Turati spoke in Parliament like a patriot of the Risorgimento, Giolitti returned to Rome from Piedmont to show support, and Croce wrote a stirring appeal against the invading enemy. Now for many Italians, Mussolini was the enemy and the British and Americans had become the liberators. Such were the fruits of fascism.

Croce's Involvement

During the war Croce continued to travel to central and northern Italy, visiting Rome, Florence, Milan, and Turin. In each city he had meetings with friends that lasted well into the night, as they no doubt discussed military developments and made plans for the future. Besides the familiar names of university teachers and academic scholars, one notes the more marked presence of old politicians and younger conspirators in those meetings. The contacts with Bonomi and other politicians in Rome became more frequent than before. In Turin, Croce had long discussions with Marcello Soleri, the old lieutenant of Giolitti, who was in touch with Piedmont's anti-Fascists but also had maintained cordial relations with the king.

In 1942 and 1943, Croce had several meetings in Milan, Turin, and Naples with Raffaele Mattioli and Ugo La Malfa. Mattioli, as president of the Banca Commerciale, was at the centre of the Italian economic system and thus in a good position to know the precarious condition of Italian industry and the fears of businessmen. La Malfa was an employee of the bank, but above all he was one of the most energetic and intelligent young leaders of anti-Fascism, in close touch with the underground organizations of northern Italy and with Ferruccio Parri, the recognized leader of the democratic groups that coalesced in the Party of Action. In those meetings, Croce received fresh news of national and international developments, but during the long conversations, which lasted hours, he was also urged to use his prestige to put pressure on the king, and even to be prepared to succeed Mussolini as head of the government.[4]

From the second half of 1942 to the first months of 1943, as is attested by his diaries, Croce was actively involved in political activities, mostly of a conspiratorial nature. In Naples he helped to reorganize the Liberal Party and encouraged Adolfo Omodeo and other friends to join the more progressive Party of Action. He wrote political tracts for the clandestine newspapers that were circulated among friends in order to initiate political debate and to clarify personal positions. In the fall of 1942, Croce was advised, for reasons of personal safety, to move from Naples to Sorrento, on the Amalfi coast. There, living in the villa of the Albertinis, he continued to receive a steady stream of visitors from all over Italy who kept him abreast of the situation and then carried his opinions to friends in other cities.

The most important meetings of the Liberal and Democratic conspiracy took place in Rome, where Croce had several meetings with Bonomi, Casati, Alcide de Gasperi, Ruini, and other politicians. The anti-Fascist senators of this group attempted to call the Senate into a special session to debate the gravity of the situation and to offer the constitutional case for the king's intervention. Without success, they also tried to organize a meeting with the king of all the members of Italy's highest royal order (Collare dell'Annunziata), hoping that a collegial gathering of such people could encourage the king to take a political initiative. Both times, the meetings did not materialize because of old grudges and animosities, especially those between Badoglio and Caviglia.

During the trips to Rome, before and after the meetings with the politicians, Croce had discussions with members of the young generation who were active in the underground. In September 1942 a group under the leadership of Leone Cattani and Nicolò Carandini reorganized the Liberal Party and began the publication of a clandestine newspaper. This paper, in the spring of 1943, published Bonomi's editorial calling on all anti-Fascist parties to form a Freedom United Front and urging the king to fire Mussolini and to put an end to the war. During March 1943, Croce travelled several times from Sorrento to Rome for political consultations with Bonomi and Casati. On one of those visits to the capital, more than a hundred people gathered in the apartment of his daughter, where he was staying, and the visitors included not only Liberals but also members of the Party of Action, to which his daughter and her husband also belonged.

At the end of March 1943, the conspirators decided to request a meeting with the king without further delay. Bonomi was given the task of presenting the requests of the group, specifically, for the king to replace Mussolini and to form a new government supported by all the anti-Fascist parties and with the clear mandate to negotiate a separate peace with the Allies. Others tried to enlist the help of key members of the royal entourage to increase pressure on the king. It was for this reason that Croce and his friend Umberto Zanotti Bianco went, in secret, to see Maria José, the wife of Crown Prince Umberto. In the presence of her mother, the queen of Belgium, Croce urged the princess that the time had come 'to compel the King to fire Mussolini, to put an end to the Fascist regime, and to liquidate the alliance with Germany.'[5]

Underground activity and political meetings continued in the following months. In April, in the apartment of Croce's daughter, an eyewitness counted thirty people in the room, talking politics and literature with Croce but also discussing anti-Fascist flyers and their clandestine distribution. However, despite the many efforts and the hopes of the old Liberals, Bonomi and Soleri were not able to obtain an appointment with the king until June, by which time the economic and military situation had further deteriorated. Reluctant by nature to take the initiative, always afraid to make a fatal mistake for the dynasty, the king continued to vacillate, wasting precious time. Nor were the Liberal leaders without faults of their own: even when they were aware of the gravity of the situation and recognized that time was of the essence, they never contemplated a daring action but rather proceeded according to old rules and showed undue deference to the monarch, thereby missing opportunities.[6]

Il Regno del Sud

By the time the king finally did act, the Germans had strengthened their forces in Italy and the Allies had landed in Sicily. Instead of forming a government made up of politicians and supported by the democratic parties, as even Badoglio suggested, the king created a cabinet headed by Badoglio but in the main consisting of uninspiring bureaucrats, unwilling to make a clear break with the old regime and incapable of taking a bold decision about the war. Even worse, amidst fears of a German reaction and hopes of immediate assistance from the Allies, the government entered the peace negotiations without clear ideas and then delayed the conclusion with useless vacillations, dreaming of better terms that were no longer in the cards. When the armistice with the Allies was signed and announced to the nation, the king, Badoglio, and the rest of the cabinet, to avoid capture by the Germans and to ensure the continuity of the state, abandoned the capital for southern Italy, without issuing clear orders to the armed forces. The removal of the government from Rome to Apulia turned into a chaotic and ignominious flight. In the absence of leadership at the top, the authority of the state collapsed and Italy returned to the conditions of the past, invaded by foreign armies, devastated by civil wars, divided into factions, and the achievements of the Risorgimento almost destroyed.[7]

After 8 September 1943, Italy plunged into general chaos, with only the Catholic Church remaining intact. With bold resolution, the Germans invaded Italy and returned a dejected Mussolini to nominal power in northern Italy. But in the north, almost spontaneously, an active resistance arose, later to be bolstered by the adherence of anti-Fascist parties and also, in no small measure, by army officers who had remained faithful to the king and had refused to join Mussolini's new republic. Rome was declared an open city, sheltered in part by Vatican organizations and by the pope's authority but in fact ruled by the German police. There, despite the danger and the repression, the anti-Fascist parties formed a Committee of National Liberation (CLN) under the chairmanship of Bonomi. In southern Italy, the Allies continued their slow advance and allowed the king and Badoglio to set up a rather weak government, first in Brindisi and later in Salerno. Despite Italy's declaration of war against Germany and its status as 'co-belligerent' on the Allied side, the Allies retained full control over Italian affairs by the terms of the armistice, and they acted accordingly.[8]

Leader of the Opposition

In 1942, to avoid the dangers of the Allies' bombs, Croce had moved from Naples to Sorrento; then, in the Fall of 1943, to avoid the danger of being kidnaped by the Germans, he was taken by British and Italian soldiers to Capri, where he would be better protected by the Allied navy. Croce's villa in Capri became a centre of political activity, almost a seat of a virtual government, and there Croce assumed the role of leader of the anti-Fascist opposition to the king. In a time of general disarray, despite old age, he became a political leader and a man of action, and a rather pugnacious one at that. He was in constant touch with political developments in Rome and in southern Italy, through the frequent travels of his son-in-law or other friends. Government ministers as well as other political leaders from Rome and from southern Italy went to Capri to seek his advice, to show their support, or to suggest a different political course. Allied generals, agents of British and American secret services, and war correspondents came to hear his views, to pay respect, or simply out of curiosity. But Croce also had political discussions with the Allied political ministers, and in particular with Harold Macmillan, Robert Murphy, 'the inscrutable' Andrej Vyschinski, and René Massigli, who told Croce and Sforza that 'the Allies were repeating in Italy the same mistakes made in North Africa, where they had favoured Giraud instead of De Gaulle.' Often, among the British and American visiting officers, Croce had the pleasure of meeting sons of old friends, students of his philosophy, readers of his works, or, in Macmillan's case, a publisher of his books.

From the fall of 1943 to the summer of 1944, Croce participated directly in political events. He worked closely with Carlo Sforza, the former and future minister of foreign affairs, who had just returned from exile, and with Enrico De Nicola, the former speaker of the House and a future head of state. During these months, all three rejected invitations to join the Badoglio cabinet as individuals. Instead, they worked together for a clear break with the old regime and for a new course. Croce had three priorities at this time. First, as a condition for his acceptance of a ministerial post, he demanded the immediate abdication of the king and his son Umberto, to be replaced by a regency council. Secondly, he proposed the creation of a new government, made up of democratic politicians and supported by all the anti-Fascist parties. Finally, both Croce and Sforza agreed that the priority of the new government had to be an expanded war effort, in order to hasten the liberation of Italy from the Germans and to improve relations with the Allies.[9]

During those months, Croce showed unusual diplomatic tact and political realism. Unlike other leaders, he soon realized how the nature of the war, the military occupation, and the terms of the armistice greatly curtailed the government's freedom of action. Croce's actions in those months, and in general the position of the democratic forces in southern Italy, were greatly handicapped by British policy and in particular by Churchill's mistrust of anti-Fascist leaders and his preference for elements of the old regime. To address this problem, Croce and Sforza worked on several fronts. They wrote letters, in passable English, to Roosevelt and Churchill, to Cordell Hull and Anthony Eden, to Adolph Berle and Harold Hicks, and to other American and British politicians. The aim was always the same: to allay 'Churchill's fears' of anti-Fascist leaders, to convey 'the deepest dismay' over the Allies' support of the king and 'the present government,' and to explain the need instead for 'the orderly creation of a democratic government,' not only to satisfy Italian aspirations but also to protect more effectively the interests of the Allies, now and in the future. To the same end, Croce also used his international prestige and contacts. He wrote to Walter Lippmann, reminding him of their old friendship and asking for his support against British policies and for a more benevolent attitude towards Italy from the United States. To create a better understanding of Italy's position and to generate sympathy for anti-Fascist political aspirations, he gave press interviews and private talks to his old or new friends working as war correspondents. In this context he met often with Cecil Sprigge of the Manchester Guardian and Reuters, with Herbert Matthews of the New York Times, and also with the Canadian James Minifie, who wrote for American and Canadian newspapers. Finally, as a small gesture designed to create good feelings, in October 1943, Omodeo, as the new president of the University of Naples, with Croce's advice, conferred an honorary degree on General Mark Clark, the commander of the American Fifth Army.

But, for Croce, a bigger war effort remained of paramount importance in the effort to regain support among the Allies. Besides urging

Badoglio's government to increase Italy's military contribution, in October 1943 he and his friends proposed and tried to organize the formation of a military legion made of volunteers, able to fight beside the allies but under the Italian flag. For the occasion, in Capri, Croce, Alberto Tarchiani, and Raimondo Craveri constituted themselves into a local Committee of National Liberation, to give their action more authority. Croce wrote the manifesto, inviting Italian soldiers and civilian young men to join such a legion in the tradition of the Risorgimento and in the spirit of Garibaldi. The flyers were printed, published, and posted in many cities of southern Italy. A general was found who seemed to have the ability and the reputation to organize and to lead such a unit. Croce discussed the initiative with General William Donovan, the head of the Office of Strategic Services, who approved the idea and then urged his superiors to support it. Volunteers began to gather in chosen places. Tarchiani and Craveri made a special trip to Brindisi and informed Badoglio of their new initiative. He praised the plan, made some promises, and spoke well of Croce but in the end did nothing. The initiative of an independent Italian legion remained stillborn, sabotaged by Italian and British generals unwilling to support a military unit created by anti-Fascist parties and organized outside the influence of the regular army.

During this period Croce also took a close interest in the revival of political activity and for this reason maintained close relations with his friends in Naples and in other cities. With his encouragement, in the fall of 1943, the Naples Committee of National Liberation was created, made up of the representatives of all the anti-Fascist parties, led by Vincenzo Arangio Ruiz, a Liberal and Croce's close friend; this was one of the first of such organizations to emerge in Italy. At the same time, Croce helped reorganize the Liberal Party in Naples and southern Italy, 'in the tradition of Cavour' and 'without the degeneration of the past.' He became president of the party but continually urged De Nicola to play a more active role in politics and to assume the leadership of Liberal forces, as heir to Giolitti's tradition. He also encouraged his friend Adolfo Omodeo to be active in the Party of Action. Despite old age and the difficulties of travelling, Croce participated in the first congress of anti-Fascist parties in Bari, in January 1944. With some effort and cajoling, he was able to impose his views on that assembly and to moderate the demands of the radical elements. The left-wing parties wanted the immediate abrogation of the monarchy and the replacement of Badoglio with an anti-Fascist leader; Croce persuaded them to defer the institutional question to a referendum to be held after the end of the war. The assembly elected an executive committee, or *Giunta,* and Croce and Sforza became its spokesmen. In their meetings with Badoglio and the allied military authorities, they could claim with reason that they spoke not only for themselves but for all the other democratic parties.[10]

Croce versus the King

After the Bari congress, Croce and Sforza entered into difficult negotiations with Badoglio and with the Allied authorities to overcome the king's refusal to abdicate and British reluctance to see any political change. For Croce, the king had betrayed the Statuto and bore joint responsibility with Mussolini for the crimes of fascism. After Mussolini's fall, Croce regarded the abdication of the king and his son as a necessary step to achieve a clear break with the past and to give a strong signal of a new beginning, and perhaps as the only way to save the monarchy itself. During this time many people wanted Croce to replace Badoglio as prime minister. The initiative came from Ugo La Malfa of the Party of Action and was encouraged by De Nicola and other political leaders. But Croce refused without hesitation, stating that he did not have the requisite qualifications for such a job. In that period, he made it known that he preferred Sforza to become prime minister.

Croce adopted a different course only when the British government vetoed the replacement of Badoglio and Churchill made clear his personal dislike of Sforza. Confronted by British opposition, and to break a dangerous impasse, Croce and Sforza finally agreed to serve under Badoglio in a new government, provided the new cabinet was made up of anti-Fascist politicians and supported by the democratic parties. Despite his questionable past, they came to accept Badoglio because they had no choice and the marshal, as signatory to the armistice, had the confidence and the support of the Allies. But Croce and Sforza remained adamant in asking for the abdication of the king, prior to the formation of the new government.[11]

Besides the obstacles thrown up by Britain and the stubborn refusal of the king to abdicate, Croce had to deal with the radical demands of Rome's Committee of National Liberation. On 18 March 1944, while he and Sforza were involved in painful and fruitless negotiations in the south, the CLN, at the behest of the Party of Action and supported by the Socialists and the Communists, demanded the immediate abolition of the monarchy, the proclamation of the republic, and the assumption of full powers by the committee itself. Those demands resonated in large sectors of the population in northern and also in southern Italy, stirring enthusiasm and fear at the same time. Croce, however, regarded the demands as not only illegal but also extremely dangerous. He made known to his friends in Rome and especially to the Actionists that the creation of a third government in Rome would only add confusion to an already chaotic situation and further antagonize the Allied authorities.

Faced with a difficult situation and with contrasting demands, in those days Croce showed political realism, combining conciliation and diplomacy with determination. For example, he made a sincere effort, not always successful, to control his visceral resentment against 'the felon king' and to check his animosity towards the Party of Action. He also displayed admirable patience and dignity in dealing with Allied generals and personnel, some of whom did not possess either intelligence or good manners. Particularly timely, and sometimes amusing, were Croce's attempts to appease De Nicola and Sforza, the first being easily offended and the second capable of mercurial outbursts.

In the end, against the backdrop of the continued refusal of the king to abdicate and the opposition of the British government to any institutional change, a typical Italian solution was found to break the impasse and move forward. During the first two weeks of March, in secret and lengthy meetings with the king and with Croce, De Nicola worked out an unusual constitutional arrangement devised by his fertile legal mind and by his insight into the murky psychology of the king. Vittorio Emanuele would remain king until almost the liberation of Rome, then he would retreat to private life and name his son as lieutenant general of the kingdom, exercising royal prerogatives until the Italian people made a final choice through a popular referendum at the end of the war. Thus, the regency had become a lieutenancy, which hardly pleased anybody. This plan was communicated to the government by the king on 16 March, with a statement in key parts dictated or corrected by Croce himself. Croce had accepted the legal arguments of De Nicola, with some reluctance, and then a few days later had the task of convincing an even more sceptical Sforza to accept the plan. With that obstacle cleared, by the end of March 1944 the doors were open for Croce and Sforza to participate in Badoglio's third cabinet and to form the first democratic government of the new Italy supported by all the anti-Fascist parties.[12]

The Svolta of Salerno

The impasse between the king and Croce had already been overcome, and the accord reached but not yet made public, when on 27 March 1944

Palmiro Togliatti, the leader of the Italian Communist Party, returned to Italy from Russia. A few days earlier, Stalin had extended diplomatic recognition to the new Italian government, and now Togliatti imposed on his surprised comrades a different policy, a new turn, which has passed into the history books as the *svolta di Salerno*. Togliatti's offer to serve under the king and to support a Badoglio government without fussy reservations hastened the publication, at the beginning of April, of the accord reached between the king and De Nicola. It did not change the outcome, but as Croce appreciated, it did change the terms of present and future Italian politics. Togliatti's announcement signalled the presence of a *Partito Nuovo* and a new kind of Communist leader, who would be 'able to adjust party tactics to different circumstances, without renouncing, however, its strategic ends,' to use Federico Chabod's words. The initiative offered to left-wing parties a less ideological choice but one more consonant with the tragic necessities of the time. 'To my surprise,' Croce wrote, 'Togliatti has been the most reasonable and the most eager in accepting the new course.' At that moment, moreover, Togliatti's realism, like Croce's moderation, greatly facilitated the formation and composition of the new ministry and compelled the Socialists and the Actionists to accept De Nicola's solution first and then to join the government, despite their reluctance to serve under Badoglio, let alone to swear allegiance to the king.

The intervention of Togliatti also underscored the difference between the new mass party and the Liberal forces. Most Liberal leaders were old men who acted in slow motion, moved according to tradition, and relied on their personal prestige. The much younger Togliatti had been shaped by different experiences; he could act with speed and energy, knowing that his policies were supported by a great power and by a well-disciplined party. It took more than a month for De Nicola, Croce, and Sforza on one side and the king and Badoglio on the other to reach an agreement, writing letters and arranging meetings. In less than a week, Togliatti announced a new policy, called a meeting of the party's national council, and imposed his new program, which then was accepted and defended and spread throughout Italy by Communist militants.[13]

The New Badoglio Government

Despite the presence of Togliatti, Croce was the driving force behind the short life of the new Badoglio government, as 'adviser, persuader and mediator,' in Croce's words. The cabinet was formed and often met in his villa, out of respect for his age and physical condition. Its program was written by Croce and accepted with marginal modifications by all the other members, Togliatti included. Badoglio chose his ministers in consultation with Croce and was always deferential to his authority. It was Croce who pressed successfully for the appointment of the Actionist Omodeo as minister of Education, against the reservations of the Catholics and the indifference of the other parties. Badoglio made Croce privy to state secrets that, in compliance with the clauses of the armistice, he could not share with other leaders. Croce was among the very few who knew the full text of the armistice, when it was still secret; the other politicians and the general public knew only its military terms. Finally, the government's program reflected the ideas and priorities of Croce and Sforza.

Once the new government began operations, Croce remained the chief adviser to Badoglio, who consulted him on all important issues. Often, Croce's wisdom and common sense were employed to smooth relations among different personalities or to achieve a compromise acceptable to all parties. Inside the cabinet, among other initiatives, Croce prepared the bill for the creation of a consultative assembly, made up of outstanding individuals chosen by all the parties, to act as a sort of temporary parliament. After years of authoritarian decisions imposed from above, Croce wanted to recreate an institution where the public and the politicians could regain parliamentary experience and where the actions of the government would be publicly defended, laws debated openly, and financial bills explained and then approved. Croce was not successful, then or later, in persuading the government to implement a cleansing of the civil service, or *epurazione*, moderate and limited in scope but still intended to remove from the administration of the state unrepentant Fascists and other dangerous elements who were or had been in positions of leadership and influence.[14]

In later years, both Croce and Togliatti praised the ability and the dignity, even the loyalty, of Badoglio, the old fox, servant of many masters. Both agreed that Badoglio, with his canny military bearing, had improved relations with the Allies; both also recognized that under his leadership the cabinet worked well and made important decisions. In fact, the last Badoglio government achieved a great deal in its short life and greatly influenced future events. It was the first democratic government of the new Italy; it included all the anti-Fascist parties, was supported in Rome by the CLN, and was recognized in Milan by the forces of the Resistance. Among the chaos and the divisions of the time, Badoglio and Croce, with the help of De Nicola, Sforza, and Togliatti, had been able to form a truly national government, 'strong and authoritative' in Togliatti's words, that healed the split between north and south, recreated national unity, and prepared the ground for peaceful institutional change. Above all, it avoided in Italy a repetition of the recent Spanish and Greek tragedies.[15]

CHAPTER THIRTEEN

The Elder Statesman, 1944–1952

Croce's participation in Badoglio's cabinet represents his most direct role in the political affairs of Italy. Once Rome was liberated from the Germans and returned to Italy, the king retired to private life while Badoglio resigned and without much ceremony was replaced by Bonomi in June 1944. With the formation of the Bonomi cabinet, political power shifted to the CLN, and more precisely to the national mass parties. The influence of independent figures declined and the large political parties reasserted their pre-eminence in national affairs and in the decisions of the government. Croce remained in the Bonomi cabinet without much enthusiasm for a few more months, then he resigned, unwilling to travel often from Naples to Rome. But old age was only one of the reasons for his resignation. He also felt uncomfortable in the new political atmosphere prevailing inside the cabinet.

Croce and the Allies

Inside or outside the government, Croce used his personal prestige to improve the international position of Italy, constantly urging the Western powers to recognize Italy as an ally and reminding them that generous treatment of Italy was in the interests of democratic nations and European reconstruction. In September 1944, during a public gathering in Rome attended by all the major political leaders, he made requests to the British and Americans in the name of what Italians had suffered under Mussolini and the Germans and for what they had done in the Resistance and beside the Allies. In particular, Croce asked for the abolition of the clauses of the armistice that greatly reduced the sovereignty of Italy and allowed the military administrators to interfere in internal affairs, complicating the political process, increasing the financial burdens, and practically reducing Italy to a colony. The speech received a positive response from all quarters. The Socialist leader and future president of the republic, Sandro Pertini, wrote a letter of congratulation to Croce, calling him 'a courageous fighter for Italian freedom.'[1]

A few months later, Croce sent a letter to the British papers in which he lamented the exclusion of Italy from the San Francisco Conference, which had been called for the purpose of establishing the United Nations. Finally, in September 1945, during the London conference that discussed the peace negotiations with Germany's allies, Croce wrote to the Manchester Guardian expressing the hope that the five powers would propose 'a constructive peace' to Italy, not punitive terms, so that the new Italy would not be 'mutilated, humiliated and made impotent.' On various occasions, Croce made known his fears and anxiety about the fate and the future of Trieste and the Italian population of Istria.

In a few cases, Croce, like other old Liberal leaders, weakened his case when he lamented the loss of Italian colonies and asked for their return under Italian administration. Croce was on much better moral ground when he advised Italians to defend the national interest with determination but to avoid nationalistic posturing, cultivating instead 'the sentiment of temperance and humanity' of the Italian Risorgimento. Faithful to the ideas expressed earlier in his *History of Europe*, Croce was among the first to accept the idea of European unification, as it had been conceived in Fascist jails by Altiero Spinelli, Eugenio Colorni, and Ernesto Rossi and written about in their 'Ventotene Manifesto.'[2]

It was in the course of these political interventions that Croce, to attract support from an international audience for the new Italy and to soften the hostility of former enemies, defined fascism as 'a parenthesis in the history of Italy.' On all other occasions, however, fascism remained for Croce 'a moral illness of our time.'

Croce and the Party of Action

In internal affairs, Croce and the Liberal Party encouraged a speedy return to legality and normality as the necessary condition for economic reconstruction. This policy of moderation clashed with the aspirations of the more progressive forces of the anti-fascist movement. Croce's rejection of radical solutions, his desire to limit the functions of the committees of national liberation, and his preference for traditional institutions put him and the Liberals at odds with the Communists and the Socialists but also with the Party of Action, the only new political party born out of the struggle against fascism, heir of Amendola's democracy, Gobetti's liberalism, Rosselli's Giustizia e Libertà, and Calogero's liberalsocialism. The debate between Croce and the 'Actionists' acquired a personal tone and a special bitterness, not unusual among those who happen to have ideological affinities but take separate roads. Many leaders of the new party had been greatly influenced by Croce's writings, some of them had even proposed him to be prime minister, and quite a few were personal friends of long standing, including his two major collaborators during the regime, Adolfo Omodeo and Guido De Ruggiero, not to mention his own daughter and her husband.[3]

Yet, despite friendship and cultural affinities, political collaboration proved impossible and personal relations became strained. The reasons were manifold and rather complicated, reflecting different political experiences and personal backgrounds. There were also philosophical differences that went back to the split between Croce and Gentile. After the war, facing new problems and different challenges, Guido De Ruggiero no longer felt comfortable with past solutions. As a better guide to practical action, he wanted to conciliate 'the recent achievements of Croce's historicism' with the best heritage of the Enlightenment. In a book with the rather expressive title, *Return to Reason*, he proposed in fact a return to 'the general concepts of Illuminism' and to the 'eternal and supreme values of liberty, justice and humanity.' Those were the very goddesses that Croce had once spurned, in favour of Marx's realism. Now, after his discovery of a new 'religion of freedom,' he was protected from their charms even more than before. For Croce, it was this principle that urged man to action and provided him with the light to understand the past and the energy to create a better future and a more equitable society. There was a dispute with Guido Calogero about the relationship between freedom and justice. Calogero seemed to place them on equal pedestals, one reinforcing the other. For Croce, however, freedom was the spring of life and justice was one of its creations; one should not be confused with the other, for if they were, the danger was that both of them would be contaminated. Such disagreements recreated the old conflicts between the moderate and the Jacobin traditions, and between the heritage of Cavour and the legacy of Mazzini. The majority of Actionists were much younger than Croce and had gone through different experiences; many of them had been in jail or in exile during the regime, or had fought in the Resistance of northern Italy, and now were impatient with his moderation, preferring more radical solutions and ready to experiment with new ways. For his part, Croce was suspicious of the Jacobin enthusiasm displayed by 'Actionists' on many occasions and accused them of authoritarian tendencies. Some of them, in fact, were prone 'to dictate' their solutions or their arguments, showing a moralistic attitude typical of enlightened intellectual elites, and were unmoved by the reality of the here and now. Most of the Actionists seemed not to notice the contradiction between the proclamation of a radical revolution, which by necessity requires duress and the use of force, and their goal of an open society. Croce was not against social reforms per se, but he was opposed to their adoption in a hurry and without respecting due process. After the fall of fascism, for Croce the first priority was the restoration of political freedom. As was to be expected, there were also different interpretations of Italian history out of which flowed different assessments of fascism and divergent solutions to the problems of Italian society. Croce continued to defend the achievements of liberal Italy and the permanent value of Risorgimental traditions. Many members of the Party of Action regarded the Risorgimento as a failed revolution, considered fascism as a 'revelation,' and did not share Croce's admiration for Giolitti, or even for Cavour.

Typical of these disagreements was an exchange in June 1945 between Croce and Ferruccio Parri, the leader of the Party of Action and the new prime minister. In the first speech delivered before the Consultative Assembly, Parri, following his moralistic inclinations and Mazzinian heritage, felt compelled to venture a judgment on Italian history, claiming that liberal Italy had never known a true democratic government. Croce immediately came to the defence of liberal Italy, rebutting Parri's argument and defending the heritage of the Risorgimento for the same reasons that he had rejected the Fascist accusations against the *Italietta* of Giolitti. In fact, on this occasion he repeated the arguments that he had used with great force in his *History of Italy*. In the tragic conditions of the time, both Parri's statement and Croce's rebuttal were politically inopportune, fostering unnecessary divisions. Both, however, felt strongly about the matter: 'It is the duty of sons to defend the work of fathers,' Croce claimed. But the authority of the government was certainly not increased by the exchange, even if Croce had no intention of creating difficulty for Parri.

In the campaign against the Parri government, the opposition used Croce's speech in a selective way. To embarrass Parri, the conservative papers emphasized Croce's historical arguments. Nobody noted then or remembered later 'the admiration' and 'the gratitude' that Croce expressed to Parri for his contribution and for his role in the struggle against fascism and in the war against the Germans. At the same time, few seemed to note that Croce expressed agreement with the political and economic program of the government. Nor did many appreciate that Croce's intervention was directed less against Parri than against the intellectuals of the new generation who did not show much admiration, let alone reverence, for the values and traditions of the Risorgimento and were repeating old accusations already used by Fascist writers. These evident links between old and new attitudes prompted Croce to comment in his diaries: 'Under the changed clothes, I feel a persistent fascism in the literary habits, of Italy and Italian intellectuals.'[4]

Croce and Communism

After the end of the war, as Croce had done during the Fascist regime, he continued to fight against the old enemies of Jacobinism, clericalism, and communism: the political forces and the philosophical ideas that he regarded as inimical to a liberal society. But, from 1945 until his death, the criticism of old and new forms of clericalism remained of secondary importance; his greatest efforts were directed against the theory and praxis of the Communist Party, especially after the Party of Action disappeared from the scene. Having rejected the ethical state of Hegel and Gentile, Croce could not accept an ethical party that preached and imposed dogmatic theories and longed for a society without differences and freedom of choice. Unlike many Italian intellectuals of the time, even some of his old friends, Croce never succumbed to the charms of Togliatti, nor did he have any doubt about the totalitarian character of Russian society, and the despotic nature of Soviet communism. Also, in view of the later evolution of Italian communism, it is interesting to note that at this early stage Croce urged the Communist leaders to make a special effort to give an Italian contribution to international communism, instead of offering a pedantic imitation of Russian ideas and repeating 'the lamentable nonsenses' of Lenin and Stalin.[5]

Some years later, when Gramsci's letters were published to great acclaim, Croce praised his personal integrity and intellectual acumen. But when the other writings of Gramsci appeared, many critics inside and outside the Communist Party regarded his ideas as a new philosophical system – a conclusion that Croce could not accept. He argued that Gramsci's efforts had been directed not to the creation of a philosophical system but to the foundation of a political party.[6]

Mussolini's End and the Death of Gentile

In April 1945, while they were trying to escape, often disguised as German soldiers, Mussolini and several fascist leaders were captured and summarily executed by Italian partisans. When the news reached Naples, Croce commented in his diaries that such a violent death 'seemed a rather fitting end.' On 29 April the bodies of Mussolini and the other leaders were hung upside down in Piazzale Loreto in Milan, before jeering crowds. That macabre scene was described by Croce for what it really was: 'a shameful exhibition of corpses' and 'an offence to our humanity.' Yet, though 'the event had produced a painful impression,' Croce's judgment on the victims remained stern: 'Those bad and mean people deserved to be sent to death.'

On this occasion, as on others during that period, Croce expressed a harsh opinion of Mussolini. 'The man was nothing; the end has reconfirmed this judgment. We should forget him, but at the same time we should always remember that many people or the majority regarded him as a genial and beneficial force, and applauded and supported him for many years.' His stark assessment of Mussolini reflected well Croce's mood at that time, when he was still surrounded by the ruin and destruction that Mussolini's policies had brought to Naples, to Italy, and to the Italian people.[7]

But there was more to it. In Croce's vision of politics, Mussolini's complete lack of merit either as a man or as a leader indicated an absence not so much of personal ability as of moral energy. As we have seen before, Croce regarded the determination to be guided by the moral idea as an essential attribute of 'the good political leader.' Vico equated this leadership quality with the constant care of the public good, while the old patriots of the Risorgimento saw it as love of fatherland. In Croce's assessment, then, Mussolini, as a political leader, was driven neither by a concern for the public good nor by love of the fatherland. As a result, his policies had 'destroyed all that our fathers had built.'

Croce's reaction to Gentile's assassination on 17 April 1944 was much different. The news 'deeply upset me,' Croce wrote in his diaries. It was not the end that he had wished or expected for his old friend. After Mussolini's fall in July 1943, he had hoped at least to assure Gentile's physical safety and to make possible his return to studies; he had even urged Badoglio's new minister of education to use tact in dealing with Gentile. The pain of such a cruel end was probably increased by the realization that, in the new and bitter civil war, nobody was secure anymore, not

even an old and unarmed philosopher. Croce wrote three slightly different accounts of this incident for his diaries, a sign, no doubt, of his
greatly perturbed emotions, or *animo perturbato e commosso*, in Vico's classical expression. He repeated his condemnation of Gentile's adherence
to fascism, as well as his negative assessment of Gentile's philosophy and
his cultural and political activities after 1943. But he also expressed a certain restrained pathos. Confronted suddenly by such a dramatic event,
Croce found that 'the colours of the old affections' reappeared, to use
Gennaro Sasso's words. He ended the three accounts with the same
image: the weeping of his wife, as a modern Niobe. Listening to the news
and hearing 'the harsh remarks on Gentile, expressed by the radio com-
mentator ... Adelina ... burst into tears, remembering him as a kind man
and as a friend, always greeted with joy, when he came to Naples as our
guest, during the first years of our marriage.'[8]

The friendship between Croce and Gentile had been deep, born out
of common aspirations and shared values. Fascism had separated them
and destroyed their personal relationship, but political differences
never erased completely the warm feelings they once had for each
other.

The Constituent Assembly

In June 1946 the Italian people were called upon to choose between
monarchy and republic in a referendum, and, in elections held simultaneously, to elect the members of a constituent assembly whose main task
was to draft a new constitution that would replace the old and now dis-
credited Statuto. In the referendum, the monarchy lost and the House
of Savoy came to an inglorious end. In the general elections, Croce was
elected to the assembly but the result was far from a personal triumph –
he came fifth in a list of six. Owing to his efforts, however, for the first
time the various currents of Italian liberalism came together, if a little
too late; Bonomi, Croce, Nitti, and Orlando ran under the same banner, the National Democratic Union. The Union did well nationally, but
its performance was greatly inferior to that of the Christian Democrats,
the Socialists, and the Communists. Liberalism was no longer the dominant force in Italian politics. From then on, Italian politics would be
dominated by large mass parties, inspired by ideals in many ways different from the Risorgimento tradition.

On the institutional question, mainly for sentimental reasons and
without much passion, Croce voted for the monarchy. Yet, when the time

came to elect the new head of state, the Socialist Party officially proposed Croce as the next president of the republic. To assure the acceptance of his nomination, Pietro Nenni, the leader of the Socialists, wrote Croce an eloquent letter that spoke to his standing even among political adversaries and fierce republicans: 'Today nobody better than you can represent Italy before the world, and can assure with more loyalty the life of the Italian republic.' To the appeals of the Socialists, De Nicola himself added his own arguments, urging Croce 'not to refuse his historical duty.' But it was all to no avail; Croce refused to be drafted and made it clear that, if drafted, he was not willing to stand.[8] Croce's refusal, as he knew and hoped, opened the door for the election of Enrico De Nicola, who proved to be an ideal president, always scrupulous and impartial in the exercise of his office. He created the legal framework and the political precedents that were later followed by his successors, or ignored at their peril.

During the life of the Constituent Assembly, Croce was present at the most important sessions, but his participation in the debates was minimal. In 1946 he was eighty years old, and old age had begun to exact its toll. As a member of the assembly, he made only two important speeches, which resonated in the country at large. In the first one, in March 1947, he gave an overview of 'the design of a new constitution of the Italian state,' as presented to the assembly by the special drafting committee that had laboured under the leadership of Meuccio Ruini, Croce's old friend. Croce lamented that 'the work was not fully successful,' 'lacked an original synthesis,' and contained 'incoherences and contradictions.' He argued that the committee had been subject to different influences, had to accept many compromises, and in the end had produced a document 'without conceptual coherence and harmony,' juxtaposing rather than unifying the rights of the individual and the authority of the state, legal protections and social aspirations. Faithful to a unitarian conception of the state, Croce, like the Liberal Nitti and the Communist Togliatti, objected to the increased powers given to the provinces and to 'the creation of complex and untried regional institutions' that weakened 'the unity of the State,' 'the only gift of the Risorgimento still surviving intact,' 'among the ruins created by the war.' Above all, Croce, this time along with the Socialist Nenni and the Actionist Calamandrei, opposed the inclusion of the Lateran Pacts in the new constitution, calling the incorporation of a bilateral treaty between two states into the fundamental law of the nation 'a juridical monstrosity' and 'a logical error and a legal scandal.'[10]

Croce delivered his other great speech during the debate on the ratification of the Peace Treaty in July 1947. On this occasion, he questioned both the legitimacy of the Nuremberg Tribunal and the right of the victors to sit in judgment of the defeated. At the end of the bitter conflict, if the elimination of enemy leaders was deemed necessary to avoid future dangers to peace and to assure the security of Europe, it was preferable to employ 'the old and different practice, exempt from hypocrisy ... when enemy leaders and generals, or some of them ... were quickly sent to death,' 'thus concluding the war.' Croce's speech, as was customary with him, contained practical considerations and philosophical arguments that involved the relationship between morality and politics, national interest and international cooperation; it also reflected on the rights and duties that war imposes on individuals and on nations, in victory or in defeat. With regard to the more pressing question of ratification, Croce began by recognizing that Italy and the Italian people, not only fascism and Mussolini, had lost the war, but then, speaking this time like an old Jacobin, he asked the Constituent Assembly to reject the treaty and to refuse its ratification on the grounds of national dignity and as a protest against the unjust policy of the Allies, who not only were imposing burdens on the Italian people but also pretended to pass 'a moral and legal judgment on Italy and its history.'

Croce expressed the feelings of many Italians, inside and outside the assembly; his speech had been read and approved by De Nicola, the new head of state, and his stand had been discussed with other political leaders as well, such as Orlando and Sturzo. Many had hoped for a more lenient treaty, and they were surprised when presented with a punitive peace which was imposed rather than negotiated, despite the recognized status of Italy as a 'co-belligerent nation.' In fact, unlike the Marshall Plan, the Peace Treaty has to be regarded as an old-fashioned and myopic document of international power politics which saddled republican Italy with moral and material burdens for crimes that Mussolini, the Fascist movement, and the king had committed; the anti-Fascist leaders and the popular parties then in government did not deserve such treatment. For that reason alone, it was necessary, as Luigi Sturzo wrote to Croce, for somebody, 'in this unhappy moment of our history,' to speak against the treaty in the assembly, in order to show 'that England and America do not see the reality' and that 'the ratification of the treaty was not necessary for the results of the Paris conference and was harmful to national and European interests.' Many friends or political adversaries, inside and outside the assembly, expressed 'personal gratitude' to Croce, even those, like Emilio Lussu and Luigi Einaudi, who voted in favour of the treaty for reasons of political necessity.[11]

President of the Liberal Party

Croce's choice of the monarchy over the republic in the referendum of 1946 reflected his natural moderation, but it also showed his attachment to historical tradition. Confronted by a troubling present, Croce often, during the last part of his life, advocated a return to the ways of liberal Italy. No doubt his nostalgia for the past explained his personal sympathy for old Liberal leaders like De Nicola and Orlando. But nostalgia did not preclude him from accepting solutions demanded by the changed conditions of the times. Rather than proposing an impossible return to the ways of the past, he rather lamented the disappearance of the spirit that had animated the Italy of his youth, when political adversaries were not regarded as enemies, and politics did not interfere with personal relationships, party politics had not become an all-embracing passion, and freedom and the liberal institutions were a shared ideal and common faith.[12]

After the war, his nostalgia notwithstanding, Croce was not a conservative, let alone a reactionary, as Alfredo Parente has shown. In judging Croce's position in the last part of his life, one has to make a distinction, as Adolfo Omodeo did then and Gennaro Sasso has done more recently, between Croce's personal views and the policies of the Liberal Party. Moreover, an argument can be made that Croce's presidency of the Liberal Party was not that useful to the party itself and was even harmful to his own political reputation, creating confusion, especially among the new generation, between the conservative policies of the Liberal Party and the liberal ideology represented by Croce. As party president, Croce always stressed first principles but ignored the requirements of modern mass politics. Living in Naples, he delegated the running of the party in Rome to others, who sometimes abused his confidence and often ignored his advice. In short, he did not have the inclination or the requirements for party politics. In the end, despite Croce's efforts, the Liberal Party was not able to remain a party of the centre that provided a synthesis between progress and conservation; instead, it drifted to the right, losing its more progressive elements.

This was a great disappointment to Croce. When he had reorganized the liberal forces in southern Italy, Croce made it clear that conservatives who had been Fascists were not welcome in the Liberal Party. At that time, Croce had hoped that not only Liberals but also Democrats and even reformist Socialists would join the new party. He made constant reference to the progressive heritage of Cavour's liberalism and rejected the conservative tradition of Salandra. In this vein, he advocated radical social change: 'Much needs to be done in the production and distribution of wealth, and in the organization of labour, and all this has to be done in new and different ways than before.' Prior to the elections of 1946, Croce assured Bonomi that 'liberalism and democracy are like two Siamese brothers, two persons joined by one circulatory blood system.' For this reason, Croce rejected any alliance with Uomo Qualunque, the first political movement to reappear on the right after the war, founded by the genial but coarse Guglielmo Giannini. Finally, in his correspondence with Professor Calogero, the theoretician of *Liberalsocialismo*, Croce declared his preference for a liberalism that was democratic and, on the other side, for a socialism that was liberal, and hoped for an alliance between the two movements against clericalism and communism. The frequent references in his diaries to friendly meetings with Pietro Nenni and cordial discussions with Giuseppe Saragat and Rodolfo Morandi are further evidence of Croce's benevolent disposition towards socialism and Socialists, at least toward 'generous Socialists' who defended and promoted a socialism with a human face. He urged Calagero and his friends to work for a reformist socialism, 'of which we all feel the need.'[13]

Even after Croce concentrated his attacks on the Communist Party, and regarded communism as the new challenge of Italian democracy, he remained open to social reforms that favoured 'the creation of new life' and 'the promotion of freedom.' In 1946, speaking to the first national conference of the Liberal Party, Croce stressed that, for him, the Liberal Party was naturally a party of the centre that had to be ready to accept new solutions to old problems and willing to support even radical reforms as long as these increased the freedom of the citizens and were not undertaken out of ideological opposition to a market economy. Unlike Einaudi, who had a stronger preference for the market economy, both for economic and moral reasons, Croce was comfortable with a mixed economy.[14]

Finally, in 1951, in his last message to a congress of the party, Croce urged Liberals to follow the example of the governing Labour Party of Great Britain, recognizing that, in its present circumstances, Italy needed reforms rather than more conservatism. In his old age, then, Croce clearly remained a moderate liberal, and in certain respects he had even returned to the radical aspirations of his youth.[15]

Italian Institute for Historical Studies

In 1947 Croce resigned from the presidency of the Liberal Party, and in 1948, under a special constitutional dispensation, he, like other former parliamentarians, became a member of the new Republican Senate. But Croce did not make public speeches any more. Only once did he leave Naples, when he went to Rome to cast his vote for Italy's participation in NATO. But he continued to write short articles for newspapers that were full of his usual verve, containing political observations and historical judgments which future events would often prove sound. Many of those articles appeared in the periodical *Il Mondo*, one of the most influential post-war weeklies that the more progressive liberals had founded, with Croce's blessing, after they had left the Liberal Party.

Much of Croce's energy in these years was devoted to the affairs of the Italian Institute for Historical Studies, a post-graduate school that he had founded in 1947, with the help of Raffaele Mattioli and Alessandro Casati, and to which he donated his library and a wing of his house. The aim of the school was to teach the unity of history and philosophy, and to offer a place where students could be helped in doing their research and could acquire a deeper familiarity with historical methodology. Directed by Federico Chabod, chosen after the untimely death of Adolfo Omodeo, the institute soon acquired an international reputation, attracting promising Italian historians like Rosario Romeo, Renzo De Felice, Ruggiero Romano, and Gennaro Sasso.

At the institute, for the first time in his life, Croce became a teacher, giving ten lectures, from 1948 to 1950, on historiographical questions. In those lectures, Croce often touched on the genesis and the nature of fascism and on the reasons for its success. He reiterated in one lecture his belief that fascism was a crisis of modern European civilization – 'a lowering of moral energy,' 'a crisis of liberal ideals' – brought about by 'the entire historical process' that began slowly in the second part of the nineteenth century and then accelerated in the first years of the twentieth. In this period, he argued, the idea of individual freedom and personal responsibility, and the rights and duties of man, that had informed the history of Europe from the Renaissance and the Reformation and had been given new vigour by liberal and constitutional movements after the French Revolution were challenged and rejected by new movements appealing to different ideas and inspired by irrational feelings. The result had been 'a weakening in the faith of freedom,' a decline of liberal values, a rejection of constitutional ways, and, at the same time, 'a rising cult of violence,' an 'expectation and preparation of the violent act,' and 'an awaiting of the exceptional and messianic man.' In this 'process of facts and events,' Croce stated that the most 'relevant' of 'the accidents and incidents' and 'historical necessities' that had undermined the spirit of liberty and favoured the rise of irrational forces were the militarism and 'the irrational will to power' of German society, the violent nature of the Russian Revolution and the revival of an authoritarian Marxism, and the passions and turmoil generated by the First World War. The European crisis manifested itself first in Italy in a period when freedom had become devalued and moral and political energy was lacking. Then, to quote from Croce's review of one of Emilio Lussu's books, 'in the confusion of ideas and general weariness,' taking advantage of 'the contrasts and weakness' that were evident in Italian society and among political leaders, it had been possible for a man, 'who was not necessarily a great man,' and a movement, 'not wanted by a single class alone' but 'supported by a new and strange ecclesia,' to achieve power and destroy the liberal system.[16]

In the last of these lectures, Croce offered advice to future historians on how to deal with the history of Italy under the Fascist regime. As he often did in those years, he deeply lamented the damage done to Italian society and the ruin brought to the nation by the Fascist dictatorship. He left no doubt of his negative judgment on the whole period and on Mussolini and on the other leaders of that time. But, in accordance with his historical theories, Croce also urged historians to refrain, when dealing with the years of fascism, from painting 'a canvas all black' or making a catalogue 'full of crimes and shame.' Instead, historians should look more deeply and widely at the whole society and reality and make an effort to discover the good things that were also done in that time, or continued to be done, for the benefit of both the present or the future. Moreover, Croce advised future historians 'to give justice openly to those who had joined the Fascist regime not for base passion but moved by generous aspirations, though they were not sustained by critical reason, as happens to immature and youthful spirits.' For his part, he had done just that in a newspaper article published in 1944, both in Rome and Naples. Reading letters written by young Fascists 'who had worn the black shirt' and then had volunteered and died in Mussolini's wars, Croce confessed to have found in the words of those young men, 'despite mental blindness,' 'sincere enthusiasm' and 'devotion to the fatherland.' But, in those letters, Croce had also seen 'the proof of the treasury of moral energies that the oppressive regime misguided, exploited and wasted and at the end had betrayed.'[17] For Croce, the true positive aspect of that tragic period was the struggle for freedom and the example of men who opposed the dictatorship and fought against fascism, all of them suffering and many dying for their ideals. 'If for nothing else, fascism will be remembered for this: for the adversaries that it generated and encountered; for the many who suffered inside the jails, in the places of confinement and in exile; for those who died of privations and did not surrender; for those who died fighting against the Fascists and the invading Germans.' 'All of these,' Croce wrote on another occasion, 'though they belonged to different parties,' deserved to be placed 'with reverence and gratitude' in a common 'spiritual pantheon of the nation,' because they fought and died 'not for a party but for mankind' and 'for a moral ideal that purified their hearth.' In the conclusion of his lecture, among the most important results of fascism, Croce counted the tremendous shock that compelled Italians to 'rid themselves of illusions' and to rediscover and 'to love with more passion' the value of freedom and the ideals of democracy. On a personal level, Croce also confessed that the struggle against the dictatorship had given him a new vigour and 'almost a second youth,' 'filling me with increased activity and with fighting spirits'; it also compelled him 'to rethink with more intensity political ideas and philosophical concepts,' and above all 'made me realize that the work of the thinker and the writer has to be in harmony with the duties of the man and the citizen.'[18]

The Last Years

Croce's career in the classroom did not last long. In 1950 he suffered a stroke that immobilized his right side for a few days. After that incident, Croce's physical activity and writing ability were greatly reduced. Yet, despite this, he was able to continue his intellectual work until the last days of his life, helped by the devotion of his daughters, who read books to him and wrote from his dictation. From 1940, even though he continued to be actively involved in politics, Croce's literary production remained as remarkable as before. His intellectual interests were still wide-ranging. Some of his best philosophical essays and some of his most moving soliloquies were written in this period. In the philosophical essays, Croce dealt especially with the origin of the dialectic and with the troubling category of vitality and its dialectical relation with morality, trying to reconcile the voracious appetites of the individual with the ethical demands of the universal.

The tragic events of recent European history – the wanton destruction caused by the war, the sufferings imposed on innocent peoples – affected Croce's vision of history and found reflections in his philosophy. His earlier optimism was toned down and at times gave way to pessimism. The dialectical conception of life acquired a more dramatic sequence, and it no longer guaranteed the triumph of the good or social progress. The events of the war had shown that freedom and morality are continually challenged by adverse elements, that man is surrounded by dangers and temptation from every side and at all times. Croce even began to sense that the rhythm of life can be broken and that barbarism can destroy civilization. Finally, he now came to the realization that Europe's mission had come to an end. The old certainties had disappeared, leaving man to contemplate a tottering world, continually menaced by the violence of elemental forces.

Still, certain themes remained as tenacious as before in Croce's life and thought: the power of reason, the freedom of the human spirit, the ability of man to choose good, history as an act of human creation. Besides freedom, Croce's philosophy now included a religion of work, which stressed the primacy of *doing* and the responsibility of the individual. In this world of ours, 'in which we are at risk of losing ourselves at any moment,' we have to do as best as we can, 'fulfilling with zeal all our duties as human beings and as good citizens,' and continuing 'to perform our work and tasks,' 'because death cannot find us in stupid idleness.'[19]

Death found Croce on 20 November 1952. The family refused a state funeral, but the nation naturally turned the event into an occasion of remembrance. The government proclaimed a day of mourning and the schools remained closed. From all over Italy, public authorities, political leaders, exponents of anti-fascism, and simple friends went to Naples, as on a pilgrimage. The city came to a standstill and the streets were lined with thousands of people. No official speeches were made on the day of the funeral, and there was no religious ceremony, but Croce's wife made known that she and two of her daughters had remained at home to pray.

The most appropriate eulogy was delivered years later, on 25 February 1966, by an old friend and comrade of Gobetti and Rosselli, Matteotti and Turati, as part of the official ceremonies to mark the centennial year of Croce's birth. That day in Naples, Giuseppe Saragat, speaking as president of the republic, reminded the old and the new generations what Croce's books and example had meant to those who suffered persecution, jail, and exile in the struggle against fascism and in the defence of freedom.[20]

Conclusion

Recently released and newly discovered documents have clarified Croce's political actions and revealed new aspects of his personality. After reading his diaries, one can no longer view Croce as an Olympian philosopher, serenely contemplating the unfolding of the universe, indifferent to political events. The diaries have shown a complex man, subject to bouts of depression but tenacious in his determination, constant in his beliefs, full of fighting spirit, and deeply involved with the general welfare of the country and the personal situation of his friends.

The letters so far published show that, in his personal relationships, Croce was a man of many facets, frequently writing to his friends to give or to ask for information but also to console or to encourage and, during the Fascist regime, to urge them to continue the good fight. His presence at critical moments, in personal affairs or political events, is now attested by the accounts written by those who had close relations with him, and at one time or another experienced directly his assistance or generosity.

The police files in the National Archives leave no doubt that, under the Fascist regime, Croce was willing to take risks and was not afraid to face dangers. He received in his residences or visited in other cities notorious anti-Fascists, was involved with members of the underground, and even maintained relations with the exiles in France. The Fascist authorities regarded Croce as an adversary of the regime and kept his house, his movements, and mail under close and constant police scrutiny. To pry into Croce's inner feelings, the police recruited special informers, able to gain his confidence and to discuss political affairs without arousing his suspicion.

Despite police and political harassment, Croce continued to live a

normal life during the Fascist regime, taking only some elementary precautions and not departing much from his routines of previous years.
But his personal feelings and social environment changed completely. A
joyful disposition towards life and work was supplanted by an outlook of
gloom and doom; old friends deserted his house and were replaced by
new friends of the young generation. Cultural activities remained of paramount importance, but, under the pressure of political events, Croce's
interests moved from literary matters to historical and political ones.
Philosophical essays and historical books were the occasions for political
interventions and were employed as tools to celebrate freedom, to
defend the ideals of the Risorgimento, and to condemn authoritarian
rule. These works found faithful readers throughout the country, inspiring young people to join the opposition or strengthening the old politicians to continue the resistance, creating a sort of ideal 'Italian Family'
dispersed in various Italian cities and made up of small but influential
groups.

Croce's opposition was slow to materialize and took some time before
manifesting itself publicly. During the turmoil that followed the end of
the First World War, he shared the anxieties of other Italians and was
annoyed by the frequent strikes and by the chaos they created in the
public services; however, unlike many others, he never feared the immi-
nence of a revolution in Italy comparable to what had happened in Russia, nor did he show any enthusiasm for the Dalmatian adventure of
D'Annunzio. Before the March on Rome, there is no praise or approval
in his writings or public statements for Fascist violence.

When Mussolini achieved power in 1922, Croce shared the illusion,
common to all other Liberal and some Democratic leaders, that Italy
would soon return to normality, enjoying a period of social peace. Like
Giolitti, he hoped that the new government would restore law and order
and give a new vigour to the liberal state, bringing into the mainstream
the young generations that had fought in the war. He never feared that
the government would change the fundamental nature of the constitution and destroy the heritage of the Risorgimento. The support given to
the coalition government by all the Liberal and Democratic parties, as
well as the presence of trusted generals in key positions, offered the
assurance that the nation's institutions were in no danger and that, in
the last analysis, the king had the situation under control.

In these conditions, from the fall of 1922 to the summer of 1924,
Croce showed a benevolent disposition towards the government and
Mussolini. In the Senate he voted for the government after the March

on Rome and, after the murder of Matteotti, supported a motion of confidence in July 1924. In the press, he defended the reform of education sponsored by Gentile, praised the policies of the government, and, during the elections of 1924, expressed his desire for the victory of the government list, as the necessary condition for a return to constitutional ways. But, even in this period, Croce never joined the cheering crowds, maintaining instead an open mind and showing independence of judgment. He publicly defended the political reputation of Nitti against the attacks of the Fascist press, and he expressed solidarity with Gobetti and Amendola, the leader of the opposition, when both became victims of Fascist violence.

Above all, Croce, unlike many others, never denied his liberal ideas and never confused liberalism with fascism. Instead, in private letters and public discussions, he rejected the claim of Gentile and nationalist historians that fascism was the offspring of idealistic philosophy and the heir of the Italian Risorgimento. Croce's support for the Mussolini government came to an end in the aftermath of the Matteotti affair, though not without some hesitation and persisting illusions. In that time of confusion, Croce's desire to put an end to Mussolini's experiment and to replace him with another leader at the appropriate moment was strong enough that, on political grounds, he broke off his long friendship with Gentile.

When in 1925 Mussolini began the destruction of the liberal state, and Rocco started to lay the foundations of the authoritarian regime, Croce went into opposition immediately. He came forward and assumed a position of intransigent opposition at a time when other liberals and Democrats became frightened, abandoned the struggle, or joined the Fascists. In this period of general disarray, Croce became a member of the Liberal Party, participated in its national meetings, and made public speeches on his behalf, in a last attempt to galvanize its membership.

At the invitation of Giovanni Amendola, he wrote the 'Anti-Fascist Manifesto' and then helped to turn the collection of signatures in its support into a resounding success. As long as freedom of the press remained in place, Croce did not hesitate to criticize government policy, or to poke fun at Mussolini and other Fascist leaders, revealing their cultural shortcomings. From this point on, coherent in his political position, he refused any collaboration with the cultural institutions that the regime was creating to enlarge its appeal among intellectuals.

In a short while, Croce became one of the leaders of the anti-Fascist opposition and was regarded as an enemy of the regime. As a result, during the violence that followed the Zamponi attempt against the life of Mussolini in the fall of 1926, his house was invaded and damaged by Fascist thugs. Significantly, during that night of violence, the residences of a Liberal senator, a Communist leader, and two members of Parliament, a Democrat and a Socialist, were assaulted at the same time. The regime tried to intimidate all its opponents, hoping to cow each of them into submission. It succeeded with some, but not with Croce.

When political parties were banned and freedom of the press came to an end, Croce used his periodical, the republication of old books, and finally the writing of new works to promote liberal ideals and to condemn the new authoritarian practices. In 1928 he published the *History of Italy*, which immediately became a best-seller and also took on the function of a political manifesto. The book offered a defence of liberal Italy and showed the beneficial effects produced by free institutions, offering at the same time a veiled, but unmistakable criticism of Mussolini's leadership.

Never a great parliamentarian, Croce seldom spoke in the Senate but rather supported the leaders of the opposition and then voted against all the new laws that destroyed personal freedom, changed the nature of the liberal state, and created the Fascist regime and the dictatorship of Mussolini. Finally, in 1929, Croce himself was chosen to be the spokesman of the opposition, and he was the only member of Parliament who dared to speak against the Lateran Pacts, defending the separation of church and state and condemning the new alliance between the throne and the altar.

The years that followed the Lateran Pacts were gloomy ones for antifascism. Those who still dared to oppose the regime and carried on the good fight had to be willing to face persecution and to confront harassment, living for years the life of social outcasts. Croce was expelled or was compelled to resign from national academies and learned societies of which he had been a member for a long time. From 1930 until 1943, the government regarded Croce as a political adversary of the first order, and one who warranted close scrutiny. Policemen monitored his house, opened his mail, and reported his movements.

Despite police harassment, Croce refused to be intimidated and continued to carry on a spirited opposition to fascism, first of all by writing books and publishing his periodical with his usual zeal. During 'the years of consensus,' Croce's opposition remained active also in the political field. He kept in touch with his political and academic friends by a constant stream of mail and by undertaking, at regular intervals, trips to

Italian cities. The house in Naples and the summer residence in Piedmont became places of pilgrimage, where visitors went to give and to receive information, or to find words of advice and encouragement.

Croce also maintained contacts with the young people who were involved in underground activities, and he did not abandon them when they were caught by the police and ended up in jail or were sent to *confino*. He also made several trips abroad and on those occasions had meetings and long conversations with anti-Fascist exiles, including Sturzo, Sforza, Nitti, and Carlo Rosselli. During this period, too, Croce helped some of his anti-Fascist friends in more concrete ways. He made financial loans to promising young men in difficulty and helped young scholars to publish their books or to find translation work. He asked Laterza, his publisher, to pay some anti-Fascist writers more than the current commercial rate and to charge the difference to his account.

Croce's willingness to challenge official policies and his readiness to help friends in political difficulty became more evident after the adoption of racial laws in Italy. As he had done with German scholars, Croce provided letters of reference for Italian Jews who decided to emigrate, while also helping in various ways those who remained in Italy. At the same time, he joined Laterza to fight against the confiscation of old or new books written or translated by Jewish authors, writing letters to the authorities praising the books and their authors.

Finally, with Laterza, Croce mobilized liberal and democratic culture, creating an intellectual front of resistance against fascism. During the Fascist regime, Croce experienced almost a second intellectual youth and wrote some of his best political essays and historical books. All these writings were inspired by liberal ideas and motivated by a rejection of authoritarian rule. A few became best-sellers, and all of them generated a great deal of interest and discussion. They were read in schools, at home, in jail, or in exile and helped to undermine the authority of the regime by providing the critical tools to challenge its ideological foundations. His books sustained the members of the resistance while also inspiring many young people to join the ranks of the opposition or to question anew the policies of Mussolini and the ideas of fascism. In the end, Croce's writings of this period constitute a body of ideas and ideals contrary to the ideology of fascism and of the other authoritarian regimes of the times. Without a doubt, these writings were one of the most significant contributions to the struggle against Mussolini and fascism.

Because of his moral authority as well as literary and political activities, Croce became the head of an ideal 'Italian Family' with connections in various Italian cities. This family in fact was a widespread anti-Fascist network, kept together by moral ties but without any formal structure, made up of Liberals, Democrats, and Socialists, people of different classes and professions but all united against the Fascist regime and working for the return of political freedom.

From 1942 to 1943, when the fortunes of the war changed and the invasion of national territory became imminent, Croce played an active part in the civilian conspiracy, that urged the king to fire Mussolini and put an end to fascism. After the fall of Mussolini and the division of Italy into two warring camps, Croce's villas in Capri and in Sorrento became centres of political activity, and he assumed almost the functions of a leader of the official opposition against the king and his government.

Among the first to realize the limitations imposed by war on Italy's freedom of action, Croce used his international reputation and his personal prestige to improve relations with the Allies and collaboration among Italian politicians. From the fall of 1943 until the spring of 1944, Croce played a pivotal role in the so-called Kingdom of the South, showing common sense and determination together with unsuspected political ability and diplomatic skills in dealing with Italian politicians and Allied figures alike.

With De Nicola first and Togliatti later, Croce was instrumental in devising a temporary compromise that broke a dangerous impasse with the king and made possible the formation of the third Badoglio government. Supported by all the anti-Fascist parties, it became a truly national government. Croce wrote the program of the government and remained its driving force, always consulted by Badoglio. In its short life, that cabinet re-established national unity between north and south, assured a peaceful resolution of the monarchical question, and laid the foundations for the democratic evolution of Italian politics.

During the chaos that followed the fall of Mussolini, Croce's reputation was one of the few remaining assets left to the Italian people, and he used his prestige wisely and in the national interest. Until his death, respect for Croce remained universal and, in the main, transcended the differences of political parties. During and after the war, several of his books were republished and enjoyed solid success. Every time a position of national importance had to be filled, the name of Croce was suggested immediately. Had he been a man of political ambition, he could have been prime minister in 1944 and he would have had a good chance to become the first president of the republic in 1946. When Croce died in 1952, the mourning was general, heartfelt, and publicly expressed by all parties, in Parliament, in the mass media, and in the streets of Naples.

In trying to assess Croce's contribution to modern Italian history, we should remember the passionate feelings that he generated in his life, in friends and foes alike; we should also keep in mind the political nature and the partisan origin of those sympathies or animosities. In this respect, to appreciate fully the unique role that Benedetto Croce played under the Fascist regime, and to reach a balanced historical judgment on his life, we must take note of the friendship that Croce enjoyed, while the struggle was under way, with Amendola and Gobetti, Rosselli and Ginzburg, Gramsci and Sturzo, Nitti and Turati, and all those others who suffered persecution, jail, and exile for their love of freedom. The admiration that such men and women felt for Croce is the best testimony to his anti-Fascist and liberal credentials and to his central place in the history of modern Italy.

Tanto Nomini Nullum Par Elogium.

Notes

Introduction

1 Carlo Antoni, *Commento a Croce* (Venice: Neri Pozza, 1955); Eugenio Garin, *Cronache di Filosofia Italiana,* 2 vols. (Bari: Laterza, 1975); Gennaro Sasso, *Benedetto Croce: La Ricerca della Dialettica* (Naples: Morano, 1975).

2 Antonio Gramsci, *Lettere dal Carcere* (Turin: Einaudi, 1965), 612–13; Giuseppe Saragat, 'Nel Primo Centenario della Nascita di Benedetto Croce,' *Rivista di Studi Crociani* 3 (March 1966): 83–93.

3 Renzo De Felice, *Rosso e Nero* (Milan: Baldini and Castoldi, 1995).

4 Palmiro Togliatti, in Presidenza del Consiglio dei Ministri, *Verbali del Consiglio dei Ministri, Governo Bonomi, 18 Giugno–12 Dicembre 1945,* vol. 3, 8–9; Emilio Sereni in Piergiovanni Permoli, *Lezioni su l'Antifascismo* (Bari: Laterza, 1962), 285–8; Nello Ajello, *Intellettuali e PCI, 1944–1948* (Bari: Laterza, 1979).

5 Michele Abbate, *La Filosofia di Benedetto Croce e la Crisi della Società Italiana* (Turin: Einaudi, 1966); Emilio Agazzi, 'Benedetto Croce e l'Avvento del Fascismo,' *Rivista Storica del Socialismo* 9 (September 1966): 76–103; Emilio Agazzi, 'Benedetto Croce: dalla Revisione del Marxismo al Rilancio dell'Idealismo,' *Storia della Società Italiana,* vol. 19, ed. I. Barbadoro (Milan: Teti, 1980), 279–330; Emilio Agazzi, 'Croce e l'Antifascismo Moderato: fra Ideologia Italiana e Ideologia Europea,' *Storia della Società Italiana* vol. 22, ed. I. Barbadoro (Milan: Teti, 1983), 259–339; Carlo Carini, *Benedetto Croce e il Partito Politico* (Florence: Olschki, 1975); Corrado Ocone, *Bibliografia Ragionata degli Scritti su Benedetto Croce* (Naples: ESI. 1993).

6 Gaetano Salvemini, 'La Formazione della Filosofia Politica di Benedetto Croce,' *Il Ponte* (May 1954): 810–812; Gaetano Salvemini, 'La Politica di Benedetto Croce,' *Il Ponte* (November 1954): 1728–43; Mario Vinciguerra, 'Di Croce e dell'Equità,' *Il Ponte* (July–August 1954): 1251–53; Gaetano

Salvemini, *Opere VI, Scritti sul fascismo* vol. 3 (Milan: Feltrinelli, 1974), 353–86, 440–65. For other Democratic views, see Arrigo Cajumi, 'Benedetto Croce Precursore del Fascismo,' *Occidente* 2, no. 4 (1955): 325–31; Renato Treves, 'A Proposito di Cajumi e di Croce,' *Occidente* 6 (1957): 539–44; Paolo Vita Finzi, *Le Delusioni della Libertà* (Florence: Vallecchi, 1961), 141–179. For a filofascist view, see Ulisse Benedetti, *Benedetto Croce e il Fascismo* (Rome: Volpe, 1967).

7 Chester McArthur Destler, 'Some Observations on Contemporary Historical Theory,' *American Historical Review* 55, no. 1 (October 1949): 503–29; James Moceri, 'Communications to the Editor,' *American Historical Review* 56, no. 3 (April 1951): 453–60; Chester McArthur Destler, 'Benedetto Croce and Italian Fascism: A Note on Historical Reliability!' *Journal of Modern History* 24 (March–December 1952): 382–90; Scott H. Lyttle, 'Croce, il Metodo Storico e lo Storico,' *Nuova Antologia*, no. 465 (1955): 29–44.

8 Denis Mack Smith, 'The Politics of Senator Croce. I. 1866–1915: The Philosophic Preparation,' *Cambridge Journal* 1 (October 1947–September 1948): 28–42; Denis Mack Smith, 'The Politics of Senator Croce. II. 1915–1922: War and revolution,' *Cambridge Journal* 1 (October 1947–September 1948): 279–91; Denis Mack Smith, 'Croce and Fascism,' *Cambridge Journal* 2, no. 6 (March 1949): 343–56; Denis Mack Smith, 'Benedetto Croce: History and Politics.' *Journal of Contemporary History* 8 no. 1 (January 1973): 41–62.

9 Michele Biscione, 'Benedetto Croce nella Interpretazione di Denis Mack Smith,' *Clio* 14, no. 1 (January–March 1978): 35–61; Walter Maturi, *Interpretazioni del Risorgimento* (Turin: Einaudi, 1962), 673–696; Rosario Romeo, *Il Giudizio Storico sul Risorgimento* (Palermo: Bonanno, 1978); Rosario Romeo, *L'Italia Unita e la Prima Guerra Mondiale* (Bari: Laterza, 1978).

10 Norberto Bobbio, *Autobiografia* (Bari: Laterza, 1997); Norberto Bobbio, *Dal Fascismo alla Democrazia* (Milan: Baldini and Castoldi, 1997); Norberto Bobbio, *Cultura e Politica* (Turin: Einaudi, 1956); Eugenio Garin, *Intellecttuali del XX Secolo* (Rome: Editori Riuniti, 1987).

11 Corrado Ocone, *Bibliografia Ragionata*; Augusto Guerra, 'Vent'anni di Studi sul Croce Politico (1944–1964),' *De Homine* 11–12 (December 1964): 287–340; Vittorio Stella, 'Il Giudizio e la Prassi: Studi su Croce dal 1971 al 1975,' *La Cultura* 16 (1975): 313–51; Vittorio Stella, Il Giudizion su Croce: Consuntivo di un Centario,' *Giornale di Metafisica* (1967): 643–712.

1. The Background to National Politics, 1866–1920

1 Benedetto Croce, *Contributo alla Critica di Me Stesso* (Milan: Adelphi, 1989), 13–27; Benedetto Croce, *Memorie della Mia Vita* (Naples: Istituto Italiano per gli Studi Storici, 1992), 5; Benedetto Croce, *Storia del Regno di Napoli* (Bari:

Laterza, 1958), 317–426; Fausto Nicolini, *Croce* (Turin: UTET, 1962). Raffaele Colapietra, *Benedetto Croce e la Politica Italiana* (Bari: Centro Librario, 1969).

2 Croce, *Contributo*, 17–20; Croce, *Memorie*, 6–9; Raffaello Franchini. *Note Biografiche di Benedetto Croce* (Turin: ERI, 1953).

3 Croce, *Contributo*, 20; Croce, *Memorie*, 9–10.

4 Croce, *Contributo*, 22; Croce, *Memorie*, 10–11; Franchini, *Note Biografiche*, 16.

5 Croce, *Contributo*, 22–6; Croce, *Memorie*, 12–14; Elena Croce and Alda Croce, 'Lettere di Silvio Spaventa a Benedetto Croce,' in Various Authors (henceforth AA.VV.), *Un Augurio a Raffaele Mattioli* (Florence: Sansoni, 1970), 246–81.

6 Croce, *Contributo*, 26–9; Croce, *Memorie*, 14–17; Benedetto Croce, *Scritti e Discorsi Politici*, vol. 2 (Bari: Laterza, 1967), 287–8; Franchini, *Note Biografiche*, 18–24.

7 Croce, *Memorie*, 14; Elena Croce, *Ricordi Familiari* (Florence: Vallecchi, 1962); Alfredo Parente, *Croce per Lumi Sparsi* (Florence: La Nuova Italia, 1975), 229–56.

8 Croce, *Contributo*, 31–5; Benedetto Croce, *Lettere a Giovanni Gentile* (Milan: Mondadori, 1981), 11, 25, 34, 57, 69; Benedetto Croce, *Materialismo Storico ed Economia Marxistica* (Bari: Laterza, 1951), 271–316; Croce, *Memorie*, 17–21; Labriola, Antonio, *Lettere a Benedetto Croce. 1895–1904* (Naples: IISS, 1975).

9 Croce, *Memorie*, 22–3, 31; Benedetto Croce, *Pagine Sparse*, vol. 2 (Bari: Laterza, 1960), 44–9; Labriola, *Lettere*, 53, 58, 94, 167–70, 238–41, 267–270, 272–6, 291–7, 329, 335–8; Filippo Turati e Benedetto Croce, *Carteggio* (Naples: Bibliopolis, 1998), 70–1, 80–1.

10 Labriola, *Lettere*, 272–4, 278–9; Antonio Cordeschi, *Croce e la Bella Angelina* (Milan: Mursia, 1994).

11 Croce, *Contributo*, 46–65; Croce, *Memorie*, 25–39; Franchini, *Note Biografiche*, 25–34. Carlo Antoni, *Commento a Croce* (Venice: Neri Pozza, 1955); Gennaro Sasso, *Benedetto Croce. La Ricerca della Dialettica* (Naples: Morano, 1975).

12 Croce, *Contributo*, 40–2; Croce, *Lettere a Gentile*, 122, 132, 156; Benedetto Croce, *Nuove Pagine Sparse*, vol. 1 (Naples: Ricciardi, 1948), 3–11; Benedetto Croce, *Cultura e Vita Morale* (Bari: Laterza, 1955), 143–59, 161–98; Daniela Coli, *Croce, Laterza e la Cultura Europea* (Bologna: Il Mulino, 1983), 15–60; Gabriele Turi, *Giovanni Gentile* (Florence: Giunti, 1995).

13 Benedetto Croce, *Carteggio Croce–Prezzolini*. vol. 2, ed. E. Giammattei (Rome: Istituto Storico della Letteratura, 1990), 340–2; Croce, *Cultura e Vita Morale*, 139–200; Benedetto Croce, *Lettere a Giovanni Castellano, 1908–1949*, ed. P. Fontana (Naples: IISS, 1985), 44–5; Benedetto Croce, *Pagine Sparse*, vol. 1 (Bari: Laterza, 1960), 100–25;

14 Salvemini, *Scritti sul Fascismo*, vol. 3, 440–62; Vinciguerra, 'Di Croce e dell'Equità,' 444–5.

15 Benedetto Croce, *I Taccuini di Lavoro*, vol. 1 (Naples: Arte Tipografica, 1986), 188–98; Giustino Fortunato, *Carteggio*, vol. 1, 1865–1932 (Bari: Laterza, 1978), 188–9, 192, 194, 195.

16 Croce, *Pagine Sparse*, vol. 1, 535–43; Croce, *Taccuini*, vol. 1, 42, 53, 83, 88, 403–7.

17 Benedetto Croce, *Carteggio Croce–Prezzolini*, vol. 2, 433–51; Benedetto Croce, *Carteggio Croce–Vossler* (Bari: Laterza, 1988), 184–93; Benedetto Croce, *Epistolario*, vol. 1, *Scelta di Lettere a Cura dell'Autore, 1914–1935* (Naples: IISS, 1967), 3–4; Benedetto Croce, *L'Italia dal 1914 al 1918* (Bari: Laterza, 1956), 50–1; Croce, *Lettere a Giovanni Gentile*, 476–84, 488–94; Croce, *Taccuini*, vol. 1, 412–24, 429, 437, 439, 441, 445–8; Benedetto Croce, *Storia d'Italia dal 1871 al 1915* (Bari: Laterza, 1959), 293–312, 300.

18 Croce, *Carteggio Croce–Vossler*, 209, 227, 228; Croce, *Epistolario*, vol. 1, 411; Croce, *L'Italia dal 1914 al 1918*, 51–218; Croce, *Lettere a Giovanni Gentile*, 495–8, 530; Croce, *Taccuini*, vol. 1, 449–54.

19 Croce, *Epistolario*, vol. 1, 11, 20–1, 32; Croce, *L'Italia dal 1914 al 1918*, 151, 214, 218, 283; Croce, *Taccuini*, vol. 1, 495, 500, 521; Benedetto Croce, *I Taccuini di Lavoro*, vol. 2 (Naples: Arte Tipografica, 1987), 29, 32, 33, 67.

20 Croce, *L'Italia dal 1914 al 1918*, 229; Croce, *Lettere a Giovanni Gentile*, 546–7; Croce, *Taccuini*, vol. 2, 38–44.

21 Croce, *L'Italia dal 1914 al 1918*, 278, 296; Croce, *Lettere a Giovanni Gentile*, 565; Croce, *Taccuini*, vol. 2, 89.

22 Croce, *Carteggio Croce–Vossler*, 198, 210, 211–213, 236, 249, 259; Croce, *Epistolario*, vol. 1, 34–5; Croce, *L'Italia dal 1914 al 1918*, 283, 290; Croce, *Lettere a Giovanni Gentile*, 566, 567, 569, 579, 594; Croce, *Taccuini*, vol. 2, 110–12, 119, 123, 135, 137, 143, 153.

23 Croce, *Carteggio Croce–Vossler*, 198–210, 211–13, 236, 249–59.

24 Ibid., 32–3; Croce, *Epistolario*, vol. 1, 33–4; Croce, *L'Italia dal 1914 al 1918*, 214–18, 250–5, 255–63, 263–70, 287–90, 331–2; Croce, *Lettere a Giovanni Gentile*, 577, 566; Benedetto Croce, *Nuove Pagine Sparse*, vol. 1 (Naples: Ricciardi, 1949), 331–2; Benedetto Croce, *Carteggio (Croce–Prezzolini*, vol. 1, ed. E. Giammattei (Rome: Istituto Storico della Letteratura, 1990), 461; Denis Mack Smith, 'Benedetto Croce: History and Politics,' 41–61 (esp. 45).

25 Croce, *Carteggio Croce–Vossler*, 236; Croce, *Storia del Regno di Napoli*, 356.

26 Croce, *Una Famiglia di Patrioti* (Bari: Laterza, 1949), 21–42, 1–98.

2. From Giolitti to Mussolini, 1920–1922

1 Pietro Nenni, *Storia di Quattro Anni* (Turin: Einaudi, 1946).

2 Croce, *Taccuini*, vol. 2, 26, 162–3; Croce, *Nuove Pagine Sparse*, vol. 1, 63–79; Croce, *Contributo*, 83–7; Archivio Centrale dello Stato (henceforth ACS). *Presidentza del Consiglio dei Ministri*. 1920, Busta 585.

3 Croce, *Carteggio Croce–Vossler*, 265, 284.

4 Croce, *Taccuini*, vol. 2, 170–4; ACS, *Verbali del Consilio dei Ministri*, March 1920–July 1921, vol. 14, 46–186; Benedetto Croce, *Discorsi Parlamentari* (Rome: Bardi, 1966), 50–60, 63–4.

5 Croce, *Taccuini*, vol. 2, 222–9; Croce, *Nuove Pagine Sparse*, vol. 1, 75–6; ACS, *Verbali del Consiglio dei Ministri*, March 1920–July 1921, vol. 14, 169–71; ACS, *Carte Bonomi*, Buste 1, 4.

6 Croce, *Nuove Pagine Sparse*, vol. 1, 56–8, 59, 69–70; Croce, Taccuini, vol. 2, 197; Franchini, *Note Biografiche*, 34–5; Croce, *Discorsi Parlamentari*, 50–60, 63–4; Croce, *Contributo*, 86.

7 Croce, *Nuove Pagine Sparse*, vol. 1, 429–31.

8 Nicolini, *Croce*, 311–422, 338; Croce, *Epistolario*, vol. 1, 90; Benedetto Croce, *Epistolario*, vol. 2, *Lettere ad Alessandro Casati, 1907–1952* (Naples: IISS, 1969), 97.

9 Ibid.

10 Croce, *Nuove Pagine Sparse*, vol. 1, 71–5.

11 Croce, *Lettere a Giovanni Castellano*, 115–17; Croce, *Epistolario*, vol. 2, 61; Benedetto Croce, *Carteggio Croce–Amendola*, ed. Roberto Pertici (Naples: IISS, 1982); Giorgio Candeloro, *Storia dell' Italia Moderna*, vol. 9, 1922–39 (Milan: Feltrinelli, 1981), 343–70; Luigi Salvatorelli, *Storia d'Italia nel Periodo Fascista* (Turin: Einaudi, 1964), 166–92; Nino Valeri, *Giolitti* (Turin: UTET, 1971), 287–320; Roberto Vivarelli, *Storia delle Origini del Fascismo*, vol. 2 (Bologna: Il Mulino, 1991), 569–883.

12 Croce, *Nuove Pagine Sparse*, vol. 1, 60–1; Renato Treves, 'Enrico Bassi Socialista e Antifascista a Bologna,' *Nuova Antologia*, no. 561 (1989): 159–61.

13 Croce, *Taccuini*, vol. 2, 292–3; Croce, *Nuove Pagine Sparse*, vol. 1, 80–95; Luigi Russo, 'Benedetto Croce,' *Belfagor* 2 (1953): 1–15.

14 Benito Mussolini, *Opera Omnia*, vol. 12 (Florence: La Fenice, 1952–63), 453–60; Raffaele Colapietra, *Napoli tra Dopoguerra e Fascismo* (Milan: Feltrinelli, 1962), 204–208.

15 Mussolini, *Opera Omnia*, vol. 12, 461.

16 Renzo De Felice, *Mussolini il Fascista*, vol. 1, *La Conquista del Potere, 1921–1925* (Turin: Einaudi, 1966), 253–71, 286–94.

17 Valeri, *Giolitti*, 350–6.

18 Palmiro Togliatti, *Lezioni sul Fascismo* (Rome: Editori Riuniti, 1970); Leo Valiani, 'Lenin, Hitler, Mussolini. Tre Vie alla Dittatura,' *Nuova Antologia*, no. 552 (October–December 1983): 11–19.

19 Croce, *Contributo*, 99.

20 Ibid.

21 Croce, *Pagine Sparse*, vol. 2, 475; Nino Valeri, *La Lotta Politica in Italia: Dall' Unità al 1925; Idee e Documenti* (Florence: Le Monnier, 1973), 610; Valiani, 'Lenin, Hitler, Mussolini.' 11–19; Croce, *Contributo*, 62, 95–6.

22 Croce, *Taccuini*, vol. 2, 295–8; Nicolini, *Croce*, 342–3; Quirino Piras, *Battaglie Liberali* (Novara: Gaddi, 1926), 15–16.
23 Colapietra, *Benedetto Croce*, vol. 1, 210.
24 Giustino Fortunato, *Carteggio*, vol. 2, *1912–1922* (Bari: Laterza, 1979), 416–18, 417.
25 Russo, 'Benedetto Croce,' 1–15; Giustino Fortunato, *Carteggio*, vol. 3, *1923–1926* (Bari: Laterza, 1980), 123, 156.
26 Luigi Russo, 'Nuove Conversazioni con Benedetto Croce,' *Belfagor* 4 (1953): 560–71.
27 Russo, 'Benedetto Croce,' 1–15.
28 Croce, *Nuove Pagine Sparse*, vol. 1, p 61.
29 Ibid., 61.
30 Ibid., 62–3.
31 Croce, *Lettere a Giovanni Gentile*, 612; Croce, *Epistolario*, vol. 2, 68; Croce, *Carteggio Croce–Vossler*, 281.
32 Croce, *Nuove Pagine Sparse*, vol. 1, 62.
33 Ibid., 62–3.
34 Mussolini, *Opera Omnia*, vol. 12, 453–61.

3. From Critical Benevolence to Opposition, 1923–1924

1 Candeloro, *Storia dell' Italia Moderna*, vol. 9, 26–7.
2 Croce, *Pagine Sparse*, vol. 2, 439; Croce, *Carteggio Croce–Amendola*, 77.
3 Croce, *Taccuini*, vol. 2, 333; Aldo Garosci, 'Benedetto Croce Antifascista,' *Resistenza*, vol. 20, no. 4 (January 1966): 3; Paolo Spriano, *Storia del Partito Comunista Italiano*, vol. 1 (Turin: Einaudi, 1967), 235.
4 Croce, *Carteggio Croce–Amendola*, 78–9; Eva Kuhn Amendola, *Vita con Giovanni Amendola*, 491.
5 Croce, *Nuove Pagine Sparse*, vol. 1, 63.
6 Ibid.; Croce, *Taccuini*, vol. 2, 339–40.
7 Bruno Villabruna, 'Il Discorso del Bivacco e le Elezioni del 1924,' in *Trent' Anni di Storia Italiana*, ed. Franco Antonicelli (Turin: Einaudi, 1975), 65–6.
8 Croce, *Lettere a Giovanni Gentile*, 655–9.
9 Croce, *Pagine Sparse*, vol. 2, 443–5; Croce, *Taccuini*, vol. 2, 339–40, 343.
10 Croce, *Pagine Sparse*, vol. 2, 475–8.
11 Croce, *Nuove Pagine Sparse*, vol. 1, 64.
12 Croce, *Pagine Sparse*, vol. 2, 475–8.
13 Ibid., 475–8. See also Benedetto Croce, *Conversazioni Critiche*, vol. 3 (Bari: Laterza, 1932), 342.
14 Croce. *Pagine Sparse*, vol. 2, 475–8.

15 Croce, *Epistolario*, vol. 1, 100; Croce, *Pagine Sparse*, vol. 2, 475–8.
16 Turi, *Giovanni Gentile*, 304–67.
17 Fortunato, *Carteggio*, vol. 3, 35–7; Antonio Salandra, *Memorie Politiche 1916–1925* (Reggio Calabria: Parallelo, 1975), 53.
18 Fortunato, *Carteggio*, vol. 3, 37; Croce, *Epistolario*, vol. 1, 118–21.
19 Ibid., 100.
20 Croce, *Cultura e Vita Morale*, 244–7.
21 Ibid.
22 Ibid.
23 Croce, *Epistolario*, vol. 1, 98.
24 Ugo Spirito, *Critica della Democrazia* (Milan: Rusconi, 1976), 21–7; Turi, *Giovanni Gentile*, 313–14; Croce, *Cultura e Vita Morale*, 245–7.
25 Ibid., 268–9, 292.
26 Croce, *Epistolario*, vol. 2, 69.
27 Croce, *Storia del Regno di Napoli*, 285, 279–301.
28 Fortunato, *Carteggio*, vol. 3, 38, 91.
29 Croce, *Nuove Pagine Sparse*, vol. 2, 203–226; Croce, *Taccuini*, vol. 2, 321–2.
30 Croce, *Pagine Sparse*, vol. 2, 475–8.
31 Ibid.; Candeloro, *Storia dell' Italia Moderna*, vol. 9, 33–57.
32 Colapietra, *Napoli tra Dopoguerra e Fascismo*, 263–81.
33 Croce, *Pagine Sparse*, vol. 2, 479–82.
34 Ibid.
35 Ibid.
36 Benedetto Croce, *Etica e Politica* (Bari: Laterza, 1956), 363–9; Croce, *Taccuini*, vol. 2, 246, 352, 356, 360, 257, 368–9.
37 Simona Colarizi, *Dopoguerra e Fascismo in Puglia* (Bari: Laterza, 1977), 200–5.
38 Candeloro, *Storia dell' Italia Moderna*, vol. 9, 58–68; Salvatorelli, *Storia d'Italia nel Periodo Fascista*, 312–18.
39 De Felice, *Mussolini il Fascista*, vol. 1, 619–26; Leo Valiani, 'La Storia del Fascismo nella Problematica della Storia Contemporanea e nella Biografia di Mussolini,' *Rivista Storica Italiana* 79 (1967): 459–81.
40 Alberto Giovannini, *Il Rifuto dell'Aventino* (Bologna: Il Mulino, 1966); Candeloro, *Storia dell'Italia Moderna*, vol. 9, 68–90.
41 Luigi Einaudi, 'Ricordi e Divagazioni sul Senato Vitalizio,' *Nuova Antologia* 467 (1956): 173–208.
42 Nicolini, *Croce*, 339–50; Croce, *Taccuini*, vol. 2, 371; Russo, 'Benedetto Croce,' 1–15; Benito Mussolini, *Opera Omnia*, vol. 20 (Florence: La Fenice, 1952–63) 307–25.
43 Croce, *Nuove Pagine Sparse*, vol. 1, 65.
44 Benito Mussolini, *Opera Omnia*, vol. 21 (Florence: La Fenice, 1952–63), 12–17.

45   Candeloro, *Storia dell'Italia Moderna*, vol. 9, 75; Salvatorelli, *Storia d'Italia nel Periodo Fascista*, 336–8; Croce, *Taccuini*, vol. 2, 373.

46   Giorgio Levi Della Vida, *Fantasmi Ritrovati* (Venice: Neri Pozza, 1966), 195.

47   Croce, *Pagine Sparse*, vol. 1, 67; Croce, *Taccuini*, vol. 2, 374; Mario Vinci-guerra, 'Vita Interiore di Alessandro Casati,' *Nuova Antologia*, no. 471 (1957): 497–504; Levi Della Vida, *Fantasmi Ritrovati*, 184–99; Umberto Zanotti Bianco, *Carteggio 1919–1928* (Bari: Laterza, 1989), 571–2; Salandra, *Memorie Politiche*, 66; Croce, *Nuove Pagine Sparse*, vol. 1, 75.

48   Levi Della Vida, *Fantasmi Ritrovati*, 195.

49   Croce, *Pagine Sparse*, vol. 2, 482–6; Croce, *Taccuini*, vol. 2, 375.

50   Croce, *Pagine Sparse*, vol. 2, 482–6.

51   Ibid.

52   Ibid.

53   Ibid.

54   Ibid.

55   Croce, *Epistolario*, vol. 1, 102.

56   Ibid.

57   Giorgio Amendola, *Una scelta di vita* (Milan: Rizzoli, 1981), 104; Candeloro, *Storia dell'Italia Moderna*, vol. 9, 72–8.

58   Croce, *Epistolario*, vol. 1, 103, 105; ibid., vol. 2, 74–5, 76, 81; Croce, *Taccuini*, vol. 2, 381, 388, 398.

59   Piras, *Battaglie Liberali*, 20–2.

60   Croce, *Pagine Sparse*, vol. 2, 449–50; Croce, *Taccuini*, vol. 2, 384; Eva Kuhn Amendola, *Vita con Giovanni Amendola*, 549–50.

61   Giovanni Gentile, *Lettere a Benedetto Croce*, vol. 5 (Florence: Le Lettere, 1990), 444–6.

62   Croce, *Lettere a Giovanni Gentile*, 670; Croce, *Epistolario*, vol. 1, 107.

63   Gentile, *Lettere a Benedetto Croce*, vol. 5, 254–9, 430–2; Croce, *Lettere a Giovanni Gentile*, 668–70; Fortunato, *Carteggio*, vol. 3, 111.

64   Giovanni Gentile, *Epistolario. vol. 9. Carteggio Gentile–Omodeo* (Florence: Sansoni, 1974), 318–29; Turi, *Giovanni Gentile*, 337–53.

65   Croce, *Epistolario*, vol. 1, 118–21.

66   Ibid., vol. 2, 84–85; ibid., vol. 1, 121; Gennaro Sasso, *Per Invigilare Me Stesso* (Bologna: Il Mulino, 1989), 61–76; Gennaro Sasso, *Filosofia e Idealismo*, vol. 1 (Naples: Bibliopolis, 1994), 467–544; Mauro Visentini, 'Croce–Gentile. La Fine del Sodalizio,' *La Cultura* vol. 31, no. 2 (1993): 317–42.

67   Croce, *Nuove Pagine Sparse*, vol. 1, 65–6; Fausto Nicolini, *Croce Minore* (Naples: Ricciardi, 1963), 100.

68   Croce, *Taccuini*, vol. 2, 352–63; Croce, *Etica e Politica*, 213–83, 353–7; Norberto Bobbio, *Politica e Cultura* (Turin: Einaudi, 1955), 211–68; Giuseppe

Galasso, *Croce e lo Spirito del Suo Tempo* (Milan: Mondadori, 1990), 311–51; Aldo Garosci, 'Il 1924,' *Rivista di studi Crociani* 3 (1966): 137–50, 304–15; Aldo Garosci, *Il Pensiero Politico di Benedetto Croce* (Turin: Cheroni, 1961); Garosci, 'Croce e La Politica'; Giovanni Sartori, *Studi Crociani*, vol. 2, *Croce Etico Politico e Filosofo della Libertà* (Bologna: Il Mulino, 1997); Sasso, *Per Invigilare Me Stesso*, 61–76; Sasso, *Benedetto Croce*, 425–605.

69 Croce, *Nuove Pagine Sparse*, vol. 2, 228.
70 Croce, *Etica e Politica*, 231–37.
71 Garosci, 'Il 1924', 145; Aldo Garosci, 'Sul Concetto di Borghesia,' in AA.VV., *Miscellanea Walter Maturi* (Turin: Giappicelli, 1966), 437–76.
72 Croce, *Taccuini*, vol. 2, 363, 364, 379; Benedetto Croce, *Storia dell'Età Barocca in Italia* (Bari: Laterza, 1957), x; Sasso, *Per Invigilare Me Stesso*, 96–7; Garosci, 'Il 1924,' 311; Sasso, *Benedetto Croce*, 505–35.
73 Croce, *Nuove Pagine Sparse*, vol. 2, 227–30.
74 Croce, *Memorie*, 39; Croce, *Contributo*, 89, 100, 117; Piero Gobetti, *Scritti Politici* (Turin: Einaudi, 1969), 876–81.
75 Croce, *Epistolario*, vol. 1, 140; ibid., vol. 2, 127.

4. 'Continuous and Resolute Opposition,' 1925

1 Croce, *Contributo*, 87–9.
2 Croce, *Epistolario*, vol. 2, 87–8.
3 Luigi Russo, *Il Dialogo dei Popoli* (Florence: Parenti, 1955), 239.
4 Croce, *Epistolario*, vol. 1, 111.
5 Colapietra, *Benedetto Croce*, vol. 2, 556, 559–70.
6 Croce, *Taccuini*, vol. 2, 411–26; Croce, *Epistolario*, vol. 2, 89.
7 Croce, *Taccuini*, vol. 2, 421; Piras, *Battaglie Liberali*, 23–9.
8 Croce, *Epistolario*, vol. 1, 117.
9 Piras, *Battaglie Liberali*, 35–7.
10 Croce, *Pagine Sparse*, vol. 2, 493–6.
11 Ibid.
12 Ibid.
13 Ibid.
14 Ibid.
15 Ibid.
16 Ibid.
17 Croce, *Epistolario*, vol. 1, 115–16.
18 Ibid., vol. 2, 89, 91–2, 106; Croce, *Taccuini*, vol. 2, 418; F. Margiotta Broglio, 'Travaglio e Crisi dello Stato Liberale nelle Lettere di Benedetto Croce a Francesco Ruffini,' *Nuova Antologia*, no. 556 (1986): 408–36.

19 Croce, *Contributo*, 87–8.

20 Croce, *Pagine sparse*, vol. 2, 450–4.

21 Croce, *Pagine Sparse*, vol. 2, 496–7.

22 Ibid., 502–3; Croce, *Taccuini*, vol. 2, 448; Piras, *Battaglie Liberali*, 81–102.

23 Raffaele Emidio Papa, *Fascismo e Cultura* (Padua: Marsiglio, 1974); Valeri, *Lotta Politica in Italia*, 585–91, 681–5.

24 Croce, *Carteggio Croce–Amendola*, 83–6; Croce, *Epistolario*, vol. 1, 108; ibid., vol. 2, 89; Croce, *Taccuini*, vol. 2, 416–17; Raffaele Colpietra, 'Lettere inedite di Benedetto Croce a Guiseppe Lombardo Radice,' *Il Ponte*, vol. 2 (1968): 992.

25 Croce, *Pagine Sparse*, vol. 2, 487–91.

26 Ibid.

27 Ibid.

28 Ibid.

29 Ibid.

30 Ibid.

31 Ibid.

32 Ibid.

33 Croce, *Carteggio Croce–Amendola*, 82–90; Croce, *Epistolario*, vol. 1, 111–14.

34 Giovanni Gentile, *Politica e Cultura*, vol. 2 (Florence: Sansoni, 1971), 251, 279, 341; ACS, Segreteria Particalare Del Duce, Carteggio Riservato, RSI., Busta 15.

35 Croce, *Pagine Sparse*, vol. 2, 492–3; Croce, *Nuove Pagine Sparse*, vol. 1, 67–8; Croce, *Epistolario*, vol. 1, 98–9; Croce, *Taccuini*, vol. 2, 425.

36 Croce, *Pagine Sparse*, vol. 2, 458–62; Croce, *Taccuini*, vol. 2, 433; Gaetano Brescia, *Croce Inedito* (Naples: Società Editrice Napoletana, 1986), 396–401.

37 Croce, *Carteggio Croce–Amendola*, 80–1.

38 Ibid., 90–2; Croce, *Taccuini*, vol. 2, 429.

39 Croce, *Carteggio Croce–Amendola*, 92.

40 Ibid., 93–4.

41 Ibid.; Levi Della Vida, *Fantasmi Ritrovati*, 174–84; Simona Colarizi, *Democratici all'Opposizione. Giovanni Amendola e l'Unione Nazionale* (Bologna: Il Mulino, 1977), 113–41; Croce, *Nuove Pagine Sparse*, vol. 1, 55–6.

42 Croce, *Epistolario*, vol. 1, 124–5; Croce, *Taccuini*, vol. 2, 442–9; Turati e Croce, *Carteggio*, 57–8.

43 Gabriele Turi, *Il Fascismo e il Consenso degli Intellettuali* (Bologna: Il Mulino, 1980), 40–1.

44 Croce, *Epistolario*, vol. 2, 89; ibid., vol. 1, 108.

45 Colpietra, 'Lettere Inedite,' 992–3; Croce, *Epistolario*, vol. 2, 96.

46 Turi, *Giovanni Gentile*, 359–67.

47 Giovanni Gentile, *Carteggio Gentile–Omodeo* (Florence: Sansoni, 1974), 434–6; Levi Della Vida, *Fantasmi Ritrovati*, 230, 211–50.

48 Croce, *Cultura e Vita Morale*, 283–9.
49 Ibid., 283–288.
50 Ibid.
51 Ibid.
52 Ibid.
53 Croce, *Pagine Sparse*, vol. 2, 454–7, 498–502.
54 Croce, *Carteggio Croce–Vossler*, 319; Croce, *Contributo*, 75–6.
55 Croce, *Carteggio Croce–Omodeo*, 5.
56 Luigi Albertini, *Epistolario*, vol. 4 (Milan: Mondadori, 1968), 1899–1903; Nicolini, *Croce*, 359–60.
57 Gobetti, *Scritti Politici*, 876–81.
58 Croce, *Contributo*, 87–88.
59 Benedetto Croce, *Lettere a Vittorio Enzo Alfieri* (Milazzo: Sicilia Nuova, 1976), 5.
60 Sasso, *Per Invigilare Me Stesso*, 99–100.
61 Croce, *Taccuini*, vol. 2, 441–2; Nicolini, *Croce*, 355.
62 Croce, *Taccuini*, vol. 2, 452.

5. New Forms of Opposition, 1926

1 Croce, *Taccuini*, vol. 2, 469–70.
2 Ibid., 470–1; V. Castronovo and N. Tranfaglia, *La Stampa Italiana nell'Età Fascista* (Bari: Laterza, 1980), 29.
3 Croce, *Pagine Sparse*, vol. 2, 463–7.
4 Ibid.
5 Ibid.
6 Ibid., 467–71.
7 Ibid.
8 Croce, *Epistolario*, vol. 1, 126; Croce, *Taccuini*, vol. 2, 490–502.
9 Croce, *Epistolario*, vol. 1, 127; Sasso, *Per Invigilare Me Stesso*, 130; Garin, *Cronache di Filosofia Italiana*, vol. 2, 447; Croce, *Taccuini*, vol. 2, 470.
10 Croce, *Taccuini*, vol. 2, 463.
11 Croce, *Epistolario*, vol. 1, 126–7.
12 Ibid., vol. 1, 128–9.
13 Lelio Basso and L. Anderlini, *Le Riviste di Piero Gobetti* (Milan: Feltrinelli, 1961), 439–56.
14 Croce, *Epistolario*, vol. 1, 125.
15 Ibid., 131–2.
16 Ibid.
17 Fortunato, *Carteggio*, vol. 3, 222.

18 Gaetano Salvemini, *Carteggio, 1894–1926*, vol. 4 (Bari: Laterza, 1985–8), 536.
19 Croce, *Epistolario*, vol. 2, 95; Croce, *Taccuini*, vol. 2, 471.
20 Arturo Carlo Jemolo, *Anni di Prova* (Venice: Neri Pozza, 1969), 248–51.
21 Salvatorelli, *Storia d'Italia nel Periodo Fascista*, 379–85.
22 Amendola, *Una Scelta di Vita*, 164–7; Salvatorelli, *Storia d'Italia nel Periodo Fascista*, 459.
23 Croce, *Taccuini*, vol. 2, 503.
24 Nicolini, *Croce*, 362–6.
25 Fortunato, *Carteggio*, vol. 3, 249–52.
26 Croce, *Taccuini*, vol. 2, 503–5.
27 Croce, *Epistolario*, vol. 1, 133.
28 Ibid., vol. 2, 102.
29 Croce, *Lettere a V.E. Alfieri*, 16; Russo, *Il Dialogo dei Popoli*, 335.
30 Croce, *Epistolario*, vol. 2, 102.
31 Croce, *Carteggio Croce–Vossler*, 323–4.
32 Vito Galati, *Colloqui con Benedetto Croce* (Brescia: Morcelliana, 1957), 50–2.
33 Sasso, *Per Invigilare Me Stesso*, 139–40; Parente, *Croce Per Lumi Sparsi*, 270–85.
34 Croce, *Epistolario*, vol. 1, 133–4; Fortunato, *Carteggio*, vol. 3, 251–2.
35 Parente, *Croce Per Lumi Sparsi*, 255–6; Amendola, *Una Scelta di Vita*, 164–7.
36 Croce, *Epistolario*, vol. 1, 134; Croce, *Taccuini*, vol. 2, 506–7.
37 Croce, *Nuove Pagine Sparse*, vol. 1, 68–9; Croce, *Taccuini*, vol. 2, 507.
38 Croce, *Nuove Pagine Sparse*, vol. 1, 69.
39 Elena Croce, *Ricordi Familiari*, 17–25.
40 Croce, *Contributo*, 90; Benedetto Croce, *Storia d'Europa nel Secolo Decimonono* (Bari: Laterza, 1957), 209–11.
41 Croce, *Contributo*, 90–1; Croce, *Nuove Pagine Sparse*, vol. 1, 71.
42 Russo, *Il Dialogo dei Popoli*, 302; Garin, *Cronache di Filosofia Italiana*, vol. 2, 406–7.
43 Benedetto Croce, *Storiografia e Idealità Morale* (Bari: Laterza, 1950), 115–16.

6. Towards a New Definition of Liberalism, 1927–1928

1 Croce, *Scritti e Discorsi Politici*, vol. 2, 301; Benedetto Croce and Luigi Einaudi, *Carteggio Croce–Einaudi*, ed. Luigi Firpo (Turin: Fondazione Luigi Einaudi, 1988), 149; Mimmo Franzinelli, *I Tentacoli dell' Ovra* (Turin: Bollati, 1999).
2 Benedetto Croce, *Taccuini*, vol. 3 (Naples: Arte Tipografica, 1987), 4.
3 ACS, Segreteria Particolare del Duce, Carteggio Ordinario, Pubblica Sicurezza 1929, Categorie AI, Busta 10, Fascicolo Croce Benedetto.
4 ACS, Carte Reale, Busta 2; Amendola, *Una Scelta di Vita*, 184–5.
5 ACS, Car. Ris. RSI., Busta 15; ACS, Ministero degli Interni, Direzione della

Pubblica Sicurezza, Divisione Polizia Politica, Fascicoli Personali e Risevati, Fascicolo Croce Benedetto, Busta 348; ACS, Pub. Sic. 1929, Busta 10. Croce, *Taccuini*, vol. 3.

6 Croce, *Taccuini*, vol. 3, 105.
7 ACS, Pub. Sic. 1929, Busta 10; ACS, Car. Ris. RSI, Busta 15; ACS, Fas. Per, Busta 348.
8 Croce, *Taccuini*, vol. 3, 71, 87, 88, 94–5.
9 Ibid., 88, 94–5.
10 Benedetto Croce, 'Esuli,' *Rivista Abruzzese* 30, no. 2 (1977): 85–95.
11 Giustino Fortunato, *Carteggio*, vol. 4, 1927–32 (Bari: Laterza, 1981), 10–28, 38, 63; Amendola, *Una Scelta di Vita*, 185–6.
12 Benedetto Croce e Ada Gobetti, *Carissima Ada–Gentilissimo Senatore. Carteggio Ada Gobetti–Benedetto Croce, 1928–1952*, ed. S. Caprioglio (Turin: Franco Angeli, 1990).
13 ACS. Fas. Per, Busta 359.
14 Croce, *Taccuini*, vol. 3, 70, 123.
15 Croce, *Lettere a V.E. Alfieri*, 24–26, 30–1.
16 ACS. Fas. Per, Busta 358; Alfieri, *Nel Nobile Castello*, 17–18.
17 B. Marinelli, 'L'Esperienza Provinciale di Domenico Petrini nel Carteggio con Benedetto Croce,' *Belfagor* 4 (1986): 180–96.
18 Croce, *Taccuini*, vol. 3, 77.
19 Ibid., 103–4.
20 Ibid., 51, 76.
21 ACS, Pol. Pol, Materie, Busta 101; Croce, *Taccuini*, vol. 3, 86.
22 Croce, *Nuove Pagine Sparse*, vol. 1, 72–7; Croce, *Taccuini*, vol. 3, 25.
23 ACS, Car. Ris. RSI, Busta 15; ACS, Pub. Sic, 1929. Busta 10; Toni Iermano, *Lo Scrittoio di Croce* (Naples: Fausto Fiorentino, 1992), 279–81.
24 Armando Gavagnin, *Vent'Anni di Resistenza al Fascismo* (Turin: Einaudi, 1957), 253–61, 262–7.
25 ACS, Pub. Sic, 1929, Busta 10; ACS, Casellario Politico Centrale, Buste 64, 396, 5429; Elena Croce, *Ricordi Familiari*, 23; Amendola, *Una Scelta di Vita*, 184–5.
26 Croce, *Contributo*, 88, 94–5.
27 Croce, *Scritti e Discorsi Politici*, vol. 2, 300–2.
28 Croce, *Materialismo Storico*, xiv–xv.
29 Croce, *L'Italia dal 1914 al 1918*, 3–4.
30 Croce, *Etica e Politica*, 290–300.
31 Ibid.
32 Ibid. See also, Benedetto Croce, *Conversazioni Critiche*, vol. 5 (Bari: Laterza, 1939), 202–29.

33 Croce, *Etica e Politica*, 290–300.
34 Ibid.
35 Croce, *Etica e Politica*, 321–7.
36 Ibid.
37 Nicola Tranfaglia, *Carlo Rosselli, dall'Interventismo a Giustizia e Libertà* (Bari: Laterza, 1968), 168.
38 Croce, *Etica e Politica*, 328–46.

7. The Defence of Liberal Italy, 1926–1928

 1 ACS, Car. Ris, RSI, Busta 15; ACS, Fas. Per, Busta 348; Croce. *Taccuini*, vol. 3, 2, 29, 53.
 2 Gennaro Sasso, *La 'Storia d'Italia' di Benedetto Croce Cinquant'Anni dopo* (Naples: Bibliopolis, 1979); Sasso, *Benedetto Croce*, 349–424, 425–608.
 3 Croce, *Contributo*, 88, 89.
 4 Sasso, *La 'Storia d'Italia' di Benedetto Croce*.
 5 ACS, Car. Ris, RSI, Busta 15; Croce, *Storia d'Italia*, 67–114, 213–33.
 6 ACS, Pub. Sic. 1929, Busta 10; ACS, Fas. Per, Busta 348; Croce, *Storia d'Italia*, 179–212.
 7 Ibid., 233–58.
 8 Ibid., 230–1.
 9 Ibid., 159–78, 238–9.
10 Sasso, *La 'Storia d'Italia' di Benedetto Croce*.
11 Croce, *Etica e Politica*, 309–22.
12 Croce, *Storia d'Italia*, 259–78.
13 Ibid., 293–312.
14 Ibid., 290–1.
15 Sasso, *La 'Storia d'Italia' di Benedetto Croce*.
16 Croce, *Memorie*, 27, 29; Croce, *Taccuini*, vol. 2, 183; Croce, *Contributo*, 76.
17 Croce, *Nuove Pagine Sparse*, vol. 1, 324.
18 Ibid., vol. 1, 332; Croce, *Storia d'Italia*, vii.
19 Croce, *Nuove Pagine Sparse*, vol. 1, 333–7.
20 Croce, *Taccuini*, vol. 3, 28.
21 Croce, *Carteggio Croce–Vossler*, 327–30; Croce, *Epistolario*, vol. 2, 88, 106–7.
22 Fortunato, *Carteggio*, vol. 4, 56–8, 67–9, 70–7; Croce, *Lettere a Giovanni Castellano*, 151.
23 Croce, *Taccuini*, vol. 3, 6; Croce, *Epistolario*, vol. 1, 88, 135–9.
24 Ibid., 88, 140–1; Croce, *Lettere a Giovanni Castellano*, 150.
25 Sasso, *La 'Storia d'Italia' di Benedetto Croce*, 59–60.
26 Croce, *Taccuini*, vol. 3, 50; Nicolini, *Croce*, 382–3; Nicolini, *Croce Minore*, 167–9; Fortunato, *Carteggio*, vol. 4, 75.

27 Renzo De Felice, *Mussolini il Fascista. 2 L'Organizzazione dello Stato Fascista 1925–29.* (Turin: Einaudi, 1968); Giovanni Belardelli, preface to *Italia in Cammino* by Gioacchino Volpe (Bari: Laterza, 1991), xxviii–xxxv.

28 ACS, Pub. Sic. 1929, Busta 10; ACS, Car. Ris. RSI., Busta 15; ACS, Fas. Per, Busta 348; Iermano, *Lo Scrittoio di Croce*, 268–9.

29 ACS, Pub. Sic. 1929, Busta 10; ACS, Car. Ris. RSI. Busta 15; De Felice, *Mussolini il Fascista*, vol. 2, 480–1; ACS, Pub. Sic. 1929, Busta 10; Croce, *Nuove Pagine Sparse*, vol. 1, 334.

30 Croce, *Nuove Pagine Sparse*, vol. 1, 326–30; G.B. Gifuni, *Salandra Inedito* (Milan: Pan, 1973), 119–20; Fortunato, *Carteggio*, vol. 4, 88–94, 103; Ottavio Barié, *Luigi Albertini* (Turin: UTET, 1972), 524–6.

31 Croce, *Nuove Pagine Sparse*, vol. 1, 325–6; Croce, *Epistolario*, vol. 1, 147–8; Gaetano Salvemini, *Opere 6 Scritti sul Fascismo*, vol. 2 (Milan: Feltrinelli, 1966), 357–9; Amendola, *Una Scelta di Vita*, 221; Sasso, *La 'Storia d'Italia' di Benedetto Croce*, 59–60.

32 Croce, *Nuove Pagine Sparse*, vol. 1, 336.

33 Gioacchino Volpe, *Nel Regno di Clio. (Nuovi 'Storici e Maestri')* (Rome: Volpe, 1977), 87–8.

34 Fortunato, *Carteggio*, vol. 4, 96–8; Giovanni Belardelli, *Il Mito della Nuova Italia* (Rome: Edizioni Lavoro, 1980), 158; Giovanni Belardelli, foreword to *Italia in Cammino* by G. Volpe, xxiii–xxiv.

35 Fortunato, *Carteggio*, vol. 4, 137, 147.

36 Gioacchino Volpe, *L'Italia in Cammino*, 13–16. For Gentile's reactions, see Coli, *Croce, Laterza*, 46–52; Gentile, *Epistolario*, vol. 9, 397–400; Turi, *Giovanni Gentile*, 373–7.

37 ACS, C.P.C. Busta 64; ACS, C.P.C. Busta 396; ACS, C.P.C. Busta 5929; Vittorio Enzo, Alfieri, *Nel Nobile Castello* (Milazzo: Edizioni Spes, 1986), 28; Croce, *Lettere a V.E. Alfieri*, 22–6; Croce, *Taccuini*, vol. 3, 75; Croce, *Lettere a Giovanni Castellano*, 154–7; Turi, *Giovanni Gentile*, 379.

38 Giuseppe Marcenaro, ed. *Pietre. Antologia di una Rivista 1926–1928* (Milan: Mursia, 1973), 8–37; Gavagnin, *Vent'anni*, 268.

39 ACS, C.P.C. Busta 64; ACS, C.P.C. Busta 396; ACS, C.P.C. Busta 5929.

40 ACS, Fas. Per. Busta 348.

8. The Lateran Pacts, 1929

1 Candeloro, *Storia d'Italia*, vol. 9, 233–50; De Felice, *Mussolini, il Fascista*, vol. 2, 382–436; Arturo Carlo Jemolo, *Chiesa e Stato negli Ultimi Cento Anni* (Turin: Einaudi, 1963), 431–506.

2 Adolfo Omodeo, *Libertà e Storia* (Turin: Einaudi, 1960), 496.

3 Croce, *Taccuini*, vol. 3, 118.

4 Amendola, *Una Scelta di Vita*, 240.
5 ACS, Polizia Politica, Associazioni, Busta 224, Fas. 466; De Felice, *Mussolini, il Fascista*, vol. 2, 437–83.
6 Croce, *Taccuini*, vol. 3, 124.
7 ACS, Pol. Pol. Materie, Busta 132; De Felice, *Mussolini, il Fascista*, vol. 2, 477–83; Aldo Forbice, *La Forza Tranquilla. Bruno Buozzi, Sindacalista Riformista* (Turin: Franco Angeli, 1984), 74–7; Gavagnin, *Vent'Anni*, 457.
8 Jemolo, *Chiesa e Stato*, 431–506; Benito Mussolini, *Opera Omnia*, vol. 24, (Florence: La Fenice, 1952–63) 43–98.
9 Croce, *Taccuini*, vol. 3, 125, 131, 132, 133; Margiotta Broglio, 'Travaglio e Crisi dello Stato,' 13–40, 207–27.
10 Croce, *Taccuini*, vol. 3, 133.
11 Croce, *Pagine Sparse*, vol. 2, 504–9.
12 Ibid.
13 Ibid.
14 Ibid.
15 Ibid.
16 Colapietra, 'Lettere Inedite,' 997; Mussolini, *Opera Omnia*, vol. 24, 98; Guido Calogero, 'Ricordi e Riflessioni. 1. Benedetto Croce,' *La Cultura* 4, no. 1 (1966): 145–78.
17 ACS, Car. Ris., RSI, Busta 15; ACS, Pub. Sic. 1929, Busta 10; ACS, Fas. Per. Busta 348.
18 ACS, Pub. Sic. 1929, Busta 10; ACS, Fas. Per. Busta 348.
19 ACS, Pub. Sic. 1929, Busta 10; Barbara Allason, *Memorie di un'Antifascista* (Florence: Vallecchi, 1946), 83–90; ACS, Fas. Per. Busta 348; Benedetto Croce–Pietro Pancrazi, *Caro Senatore. Epistolario 1913–1952* (Florence: Passigli, 1989), 44; Ugo Ojetti, *Taccuini 1914–1943* (Florence: Sansoni, 1954), 319–26, 355; Francesco Margiotta Broglio, *Italia e Santa Sede dalla Grande Guerra alla Conciliazione* (Bari: Laterza, 1966), 530; De Felice, *Mussolini, il Fascista*, vol. 2, 422.
20 Vittorio De Caprariis, E. Montale, and L. Valiani, *Benedetto Croce* (Milan: Comunità, 1963), 60–1; Giancarlo Pajetta, *Il Ragazzo Rosso* (Milan: Rizzoli, 1976), 206.
21 ASC, Carte Reale, Busta 2; Amendola, *Una Scelta di Vita*, 229.
22 Pietro Scoppola, *La Chiesa e il Fascismo, Documenti e Interpretazioni* (Bari: Laterza, 1971), 241–4; ACS, Pol. Pol. Associazioni. Busta 224, Fasc. 466; ACS, Car. Ris., RSI, Busta 15; ACS, Pub. Sic. 1929, Busta 10; ACS, Carte Reale, Busta 2.
23 Scoppola, *Chiesa e Fascismo*, 215–17; ACS, Pub. Sic. 1929, Busta 10; ACS, Car. Ris., RSI, Busta 15; ACS, Fas. Per. Busta 348.

24 ACS, Pub. Sic. 1929, Busta 10; ACS, Car. Ris., RSI, Busta 15; Augusto Monti, *I Miei Conti con la Scuola* (Turin: Einaudi, 1988), 243–4; Croce, *Pagine Sparse*, vol. 1, 70.

25 ACS, Fas. Per. Busta 348; Croce, *Taccuini*, vol. 3, 152, 153, 155, 141, 148.

26 Paolo Treves, *What Mussolini Did to Us* (London: Gollancz, 1940), 153.

27 Ibid., 156–7, 290, 351.

28 ACS, Fas. Per. Busta 348; ACS, Fas. Per. Busta 366; Vinciguerra, 'Di Croce e dell'Equità,' 443–5; Croce, *Epistolario*, vol. 1, 163; ACS, C.P.C. Busta 5429; ACS, Pol. Pol. Materie, Busta 105; Salvemini, *Scritti sul Fascismo*, vol. 2, 441, 434–53; Gavagnin, *Vent'Anni*, 318–25; Mario Vinciguerra, 'L'Alleanza Nazionale e Lauro De Bosis,' in *Trent'Anni di Storia Italiana*, ed. Franco Antonicelli, 170–3; Croce, *Taccuini*, vol. 3, 161, 179, 180, 205, 228.

29 ACS, Fas. Per. Busta 348; ACS, Carte Reale, Busta 2; ACS, Fas. Per. Busta 366.

30 ACS, Fas. Per. Busta 348.

31 Livia Tilgher, 'Ricordo di Mario Vinciguerra,' *Rivista di Studi Crociani* 7 (1970): 70–4.

32 Russo, *Il Dialogo dei Popoli*, 355–6.

33 Roberto Pertici, 'Benedetto Croce Collaboratore Segreto della "Nuova Italia" di Luigi Russo,' *Belfagor* 36 (1981): 187–206; Antonio Resta, 'La Nuova Italia nella Firenze di Alessandro Pavolini,' *Belfagor* 384 (1983): 309–22.

34 Croce, *Taccuini*, vol. 3, 137–8.

35 ACS, Fas. Per. Busta 348; Croce, *Taccuini*, vol. 3, 137–40, 149.

36 ACS, Pub. Sic. 1929, Busta 10; ACS, Car. Ris., RSI, Busta 15; ACS, Fas. Per. Busta 348; Iermano, *Lo Scrittoio di Croce*, 276; Croce, *Taccuini*, vol. 3, 135.

37 Ibid., 130, 140.

38 Colapietra, 'Lettere Inedite,' 996.

9. 'Faith in the Future and Courage in the Present,' 1930–1940

1 Croce, *Scritti e Discorsi Politici*, vol. 2, 46–7, 361–2.

2 Ibid., 298–311, esp. 301.

3 Barié, *Albertini*, 524; Croce e Einaudi, *Carteggio Croce–Einaudi*; Vittorio Enzo Alfieri, *Maestri e Testimoni di Libertà* (Milazzo: Sicilia Nuova Editrice, 1976) 36–59, 60–73; Alfieri, *Nel Nobile Castello*, 3–34, 36–58; Giorgio Amendola, *Storia del Partito Communista Italiano* (Rome: Editori Riuniti, 1978), 430–3; Luigi Salvatorelli, 'L'Opposizione Democratica Durante il Fascismo,' in AA.VV., *Il Secondo Risorgimento* (Rome: Istituto Poligrafico Dello Stato, 1955), 98–180; ACS, Fas. Per. Buste 348, 351, 359; Antonio Gramsci, *Il Materialismo Storico e la Filosofia di Benedetto Croce* (Turin: Einaudi, 1955), 179.

4 ACS, Fas. Per. Buste 348–67; ACS, Car. Ris., RSI, Busta 15; ACS, Pub. Sic. 1929, Busta 10.

5 ACS, Fas. Per. Busta 348; ACS, Car. Ris., RSI, Busta 15; ACS, Pub. Sic. 1929, Busta 10.

6 Ibid.

7 ACS, Fas. Per. Busta 348; ACS, Fas. Per. Busta 358.

8 Ibid.

9 ACS, Fas. Per. Buste 348–67; ACS, Car. Ris., RSI, Busta 15; ACS, Pub. Sic. 1929, Busta 10.

10 ACS, Fas. Per. Busta 348; ACS, Car. Ris., RSI, Busta 15; ACS, Pub. Sic. 1929, Busta 10.

11 Croce, *Contributo*, 92; Croce, *Storiografia e Idealità Morale*, 115.

12 Gramsci, *Lettere dal Carcere*, 612–614; Gramsci, *Il Materialismo Storico*, 179.

13 Elena Croce, *Ricordi Familiari*, 23; Bianca Ceva, *Storia di una Passione: 1919–1943* (Milan: Garzanti, 1948); Alfieri, *Maestri e Testimoni*; Alfieri, *Nel Nobile Castello.*

14 Allason, *Memorie*; Giuliana Benzoni, *La Vita Ribelle* (Bologna: Il Mulino, 1985); Nina Ruffini, 'Ricordi Crociani,' *Nuova Antologia*, vol. 526 (1976): 333–41; Croce e Ada Gobetti, *Carissima Ada*; E. Croce, *Ricordi Familiari*, 27; Gaetano De Sanctis, Ricordi (Florence: La Nuova Italia, 1970), 143–57.

15 ACS, Fas. Per. Busta 348; ACS, C.P.C. Busta 64.

16 ACS, Fas. Per. Busta 348.

17 Vinciguerra, 'Di Croce e dell'Equità,' 443–5; ACS, Fas. Per. Busta 348; Croce e Gobetti, *Carissima Ada*, 24–5, 42; Amendola, *Una Scelta di Vita*, 185.

18 Giorgio Amendola, 'Il Tribunale Speciale e l'Antifascismo all'Interno,' in AA.VV., *Fascismo e Antifascismo*, vol. 2 (Milan: Feltrinelli, 1974), 217–46; ACS, Fas. Per. Busta 348; Croce, *Epistolario*, vol. 1, 164; Spriano, *Storia del Partito Communista Italiano*, vol. 1, 197; Lucio Lombardo Radice, *Fascismo e Anticomunismo* (Turin: Einaudi, 1947), 84; Sergio Bertelli, *Il Gruppo. La Formazione del Gruppo Dirigente del PCI. 1936–1948* (Milan: Rizzoli, 1980).

19 ACS, Fas. Per. Buste 348, 351, 363; ACS, Car. Ris., RSI, Busta 15.

20 Stefan Zweig, *The World of Yesterday* (Lincoln: University of Nebraska Press, 1950), 342–3; Croce, *Taccuini*, vols. 3 and 4.

21 ACS, Fas. Per. Buste 348, 358.

22 Allason, *Memorie*; Bobbio, *Dal Fascismo alla Democrazia*, 215–36; Bobbio, *Autobiografia*; Leone Ginzburg, *Scritti* (Turin: Einaudi, 1964); Mario Fubini, *Saggi e Ricordi* (Naples: Ricciardi, 1960), 181–95; ACS, Fas. Per. Busta 348; Giovanni De Luna, 'Una Cospirazione alla Luce del Sole,' in *L'Itinerario di Leone Ginzburg*, ed. Nicola Tranfaglia (Turin: Bollati, 1996), 12–39; E. Croce, *Ricordi Familiari*, 34; Carlo Dionisotti, *Ricordi della Scuola Italiana* (Rome: Edizioni di

Storia e Letteratura, 1998), 493–503; Carlo Dionisotti, *Natalino Sapegno* (Turin: Bollati, 1994), 80.

23 Croce, *Taccuini*, vols. 3 and 4; Alfieri, *Maestri e Testimoni*; Alfieri, *Nel Nobile Castello*.
24 ACS, Fas. Per. Buste 348, 351, 358; Croce, *Taccuini*, vol. 5, 286.
25 ACS, Fas. Per. Buste 348, 351.
26 Croce, *Taccuini*, vol. 4, 70.
27 Russo, *Il Dialogo dei Popoli*, 282–361, esp. 336–37.
28 Croce, *Nuove Pagine Sparse*, vol. 1, 453; Croce, *Taccuini*, vol. 3, 320–1.
29 Iermano, *Lo Scrittoio di Croce*, 285–346; Croce, *Taccuini*, vol. 5, 329.
30 ACS, Fas. Per. Buste 348, 363.
31 Galati, *Colloqui con Croce*, 51; ACS, Fas. Per. Busta 365.
32 Benedetto Croce, *Vite di Avventure, di Fede, e di Passione* (Milan: Adelphi, 1989), 199–297, esp. 214–20.
33 ACS, Fas. Per. Busta 348.
34 Croce, 'Esuli,' 85–95; Croce, *Taccuini*, vol. 3.
35 Croce, 'Esuli'; ACS, Fas. Per. Buste 348, 365.
36 Garosci, 'Benedetto Croce Antifascista,' 3; ACS, C.P.C. Buste 2293, 5029.
37 Croce, 'Esuli'; Croce, *Taccuini*, vols. 3 and 4; Croce, *Nuove Pagine Sparse*, vol. 2, 274–5; Salvemini, *Scritti sul Fascismo*, vol. 3, 451; ACS, Fas. Per. Buste 348, 360, 363; ACS, Car. Ris., RSI, Busta 15; Carlo Rosselli, *Dall'Esilio. Lettere alla Moglie, 1929–1937* (Florence: Passigli, 1927), 100.
38 Croce, *Taccuini*, vol. 3, 186–7, 205–11, 251, 268–9, 272–5, 310–12, 332, 396–400; vol. 4, 43–4; ACS, C.P.C. Busta 5929; Croce, 'Esuli.'
39 Croce, *Epistolario*, vol. 1, 162–3; Croce, *Carteggio Croce–Vossler*, 310; Benedetto Croce, *Ultimi Saggi* (Bari: Laterza, 1963), 251–64; Concetto Marchesi, *40 Lettere a Manara Valgimigli* (Milan: Pesce D'Oro 1979), 38; Russo, *Dialogo dei Popoli*, 332–3.
40 Croce, 'Esuli'; Croce, *Taccuini*, vol. 4, 104, 124; ACS, Fas. Per. Busta 351; Joyce Lussu, *Lotte, Ricordi e Altro* (Rome: Biblioteca del Vascello, 1992), 81.
41 Croce, *Contributo*, 88; ACS, Fas. Per. Busta 348.
42 Croce, *Contributo*, 88; Tilgher, 'Ricordo di Mario Vinciguerra,' 70–4; ACS, Fas. Per. Busta 348; Mario Vinciguerra, *Croce: Ricordi e Pensieri* (Naples: Vajro, 1957), 17.
43 Giorgio Agosti, *Rodolfo Morandi* (Bari: Laterza, 1971), 92, 102, 104; ACS, Fas. Per. Busta 352; Garosci, 'Benedetto Croce Antifascista,' 3.
44 ACS, Fas. Per. Busta 348; Ceva, *Storia di una passione*.
45 Michele Giua, letter in Salvemini, *Scritti sul Fascismo*, vol. 3, 449–50; Garosci, 'Benedetto Croce Antifascista'; Carlo Ludovico Ragghianti, *Disegno Storico della Resistenza Italiana* (Florence: Nistri Lischi, 1962) 296; Tristano Codi-

gnola, 'GL e il Partito d'Azione,' in AA.VV., *Giustizia e Libertà nella Lotta Anti-fascista* (Florence: La Nuova Italia, 1978), 423–36.

46 Ragghianti, *Disegno Storico*, 384; Mario Sansone, 'La Lezione di Croce,' in AA.VV., *Benedetto Croce 40 Anni Dopo* (Pescaro: Ediars, 1993), 11; Carlo Rosselli, *Dall'Esilio*, 102.

47 Calogero, 'Ricordi e Riflessioni. 1', 145–78, esp. 158–61; Guido Calogero, *Difesa del Liberalsocialismo* (Rome: Atlantica, 1945); Aldo Capitini, *Uno Schedato Politico* (Perugia: Ed. Perugia, 1988); ACS, Fas. Per. Busta 351.

48 Ragghianti, *Disegno Storico*, 296.

10. Cultural Activity as Political Opposition, 1930–1940

1 Croce, *Contributo*, 75–6, 88–9; Adolfo Omodeo, 'La Collaborazione con Benedetto Croce durante il Ventennio,' *La Rassegna d'Italia*, nos. 2–3 (1946): 266–73.

2 Parente, *Croce per Lumi Sparsi*, 573–96.

3 Salvemini, *Scritti sul Fascismo*, vol. 3, 361–4; Renzo De Felice, *Mussolini il Duce. 1 Gli Anni del Consenso. 1929–1936* (Turin: Einaudi, 1974), 112–23; AA.VV., *Cento Anni Laterza* (Bari: Laterza, 1985), 122–4, 226–7; Antonio Giolitti, *Lettere a Marta. Ricordi e Riflessioni* (Bologna: Il Mulino, 1990), 15–25.

4 Antonio Jannazzo, *Croce e il Comunismo* (Naples: ESI, 1982); Coli, *Croce, Laterza*, 158–70; Bertelli, *Il Gruppo*; ACS, Fas. Per. Busta 348; Benedetto Croce, *Conversazione Critche*, vol. 5 (Bari: Laterza, 1939).

5 Croce, *Storia d'Europa nel Secolo Decimonono*, 209, 236, 361–72; Croce, *Epistolario*, vol. 2, 124–5, 131–3, 135; Sasso, *Benedetto Croce*, 425–608; Gramsci, *Lettere*, 607–10, 612–13, 631–4; AA.VV., *Cento Anni Laterza*, 36, 122–4, 178, 224; Aldo Capitini, *Nuova Socialità e Riforma Religiosa* (Turin: Einaudi, 1950), 15; Ernesto Rossi, *Elogio della Galera* (Bari: Laterza, 1968), 71, 169, 397–9; Enrico Alpino, 'Una Conversazione con Benedetto Croce nel 1932,' *Rivista di Studi Crociani* 3 (1966): 218; Croce, *Contributo*, 76–7; Croce, *Storiografia e Idealità Morale*, 105–6; Eugenio Garin, *Intervista Sull'Intellettuale* (Bari: Laterza, 1997), 19; Carlo Azeglio Ciampi, 'Io, Croce e Giamburrasca', *La Repubblica* (2/2/02): 18.

6 Nicolini, *Croce*, 384–5; Croce, *Epistolario*, vol. 2, 131–5; ACS, Fas. Per. Buste 348, 358; Croce, *Taccuini*, vol. 3, 277–86; Benedetto Croce, *Carteggio Croce–Omodeo*, ed. M. Gigante (Naples: IISS, 1978), 49; ACS, Car. Ris., RSI, Busta 15.

7 ACS, Fas. Per. Buste 348, 358, 363, 366; ACS, C.P.C. Busta 2293; AA.VV., *Cento Anni Laterza*, 226.

8 ACS, Fas. Per. Busta 348; ACS, Ministero Della Cultura Popolare, Gabinetto,

Busta 117; Benedetto Croce, *Il Carattere della Filosofia Moderna* (Bari: Laterza, 1945), 104–74; Croce, *La Storia Come Pensiero e Come Azione* (Bari: Laterza, 1954).

9 Benedetto Croce, *Orientamenti: Piccoli Saggi di Filosofia Politica* (Milan: Gilardi e Noto, 1934); Croce, *Epistolario*, vol. 2, 160–3; Croce, *Taccuini*, vol. 3, 420, 427, 433, 435, 443; ACS, Fas. Per. Buste 348, 351, 358; Rossi, *Elogio della Galera*, 255.

10 Nicolini, *Croce*, 356–7; Parente, *Croce per Lumi Sparsi*; Croce, *Nuove Pagine Sparse*, vol. 2, 1–11; Croce, *Taccuini*, vol. 3, 405–6, 414; De Felice, *Mussolini il Duce 1929–1936*, 112–23; Jemolo, *Anni di Prova*, 146, 155; AA.VV., *Cento Anni Laterza*, 178.

11 See: *La Critica* (1930–40); Croce, *Conversazioni Critiche*, vols. 4 and 5.

12 ACS, Fas. Per. Buste 348, 350, 351, 358, 366; ACS, Min. Cul. Pop, Gabinetto, Busta 117; ACS, Seg. Par. Duce. Carteggio Ordinario, Busta 637; Croce, *Epistolario*, vol. 2, 214, 220–1.

13 Coli, *Croce, Laterza*, 15–59; ACS, Fas. Per. Buste 348, 358; AA.VV., *Cento Anni Laterza* (Bari: Laterza, 1985), 19; Croce, *Scritti e Discorsi Politici*, vol. 2, 105–9; Elena Croce, *Ricordi Familiari*, 20; Eugenio Garin, *La Cultura Italiana Fra '800 e '900* (Bari: Laterza, 1976), 159–77.

14 Croce, *Contributo*, 90–2; ACS, Fas. Per. Buste 348, 351, 358; Croce, *Scritti e Discorsi Politici*, vol. 2, 105–19.

15 De Felice, *Mussolini il Duce. 1929–1936*, 107–109; Giuseppe Bottai, *Diario 1935–1944* (Milan: Rizzoli, 1989), 355; De Begnac, *Taccuini Mussoliniani*, 303, 283–371.

16 Ernesto Ragionieri, *Storia d'Italia*, vol. 4, *Dall'Unità a Oggi* (Turin: Einaudi, 1976), 2196; Croce, *Contributo*, 91.

11. Difficult Choices, 1930–1940

1 De Felice, *Mussolini il Duce, 1929–1936*, 109–10; Benedetto Croce, *Conversazioni Critiche*, vol. 4 (Bari: Laterza, 1951), 319–20; Levi Della Vida, *Fantasmi Ritrovati*, 238–44; ACS, Fas. Per. Busta 348.

2 Calogero, 'Ricordi e Riflessioni. 1,' 151; Croce, *Conversazioni Critiche*, vol. 4, 319–20, 297–341.

3 Croce, *Taccuini*, vol. 3, 171–72, 181; ibid., 247–57, 279–85; ACS, Fas. Per. Busta 348; De Sanctis, *Ricordi*, 143–57.

4 Gennaro Sasso, 'Visitando una Mostra,' *La Cultura* (January–June 1986): 5–37, esp. 10; Levi Della Vida, *Fantasmi Ritrovati*, 211–50; Gaetano De Sanctis, *Ricordi*, 143–57; Croce e L. Einaudi, *Carteggio Croce–Einaudi*, 7–9, 62–5; Augusto Monti, letter in G. Salvemini, *Scritti sul Fascismo*. vol. 3, 477–8.

5 Rossi, *Elogio della Galera*, 95–8; Salvatore Luria, *A Slot Machine, a Broken Test Tube* (New York: Harper and Row, 1984).

6 Croce, *Epistolario*, vol. 1, 175.
7 Croce, *Carteggio Croce–Omodeo*, 64–6.
8 Croce, *Epistolario*, vol. 1, 183–4; ACS, Fas. Per. Busta 348; De Sanctis, *Ricordi*, 143–57.
9 Croce, *Epistolario*, vol. 1, 186; ACS, Fas. Per. Busta 348.
10 Croce, *Taccuini*, vol. 3, 171, 247, 257, 482; ACS, Fas. Per. Busta 348.
11 Croce, *Taccuini*, vol. 3, 511, 534, 536, 543, 560, 562, 567; ACS, Fas. Per. Busta 348; ACS, Pol. Pol. Materie, Busta 132.
12 Croce, *Epistolario*, vol. 1, 187; Croce, *Taccuini*, vol. 3, 512; Parente, *Croce per Lumi Sparsi*, 262–5; ACS, Fas. Per. Busta 348.
13 Bianca Ceva, 'Una Testimonianza su Benedetto Croce,' *Nuova Antologia*, vol. 530 (June–August 1977): 143–5; Vittorio Foa, *Il Cavallo e la Torre* (Turin: Einaudi, 1991), 93.
14 Croce, *Taccuini*, vol. 3, 543; Einaudi, 'Ricordi e Divagazioni,' 175–208; Croce, *Lettere a Giovanni Castellano*, 211; Aldo Capitini, *Elementi di un'esperienza Religiosa* (Bari: Laterza, 1947), 5; ACS, Fas. Per. Busta 351.
15 Croce, *Epistolario*, 187–8; Aldo Garosci, 'In un Giorno d'Estate, a Grenoble Croce si Fermò dal Giovane Fuoruscito,' *Resistenza*, vol. 22, no. 1 (1966): 3; Croce, *Pagine Sparse*, vol. 2, 520–5.
16 Renzo De Felice, *Storia degli Ebrei sotto il Fascismo*, 2 vols. (Milan: Mondadori, 1978), 287–407; Renzo De Felice, *Mussolini il Duce*, vol. 2, 1936–40 (Turin: Einaudi, 1981), 3–330, 466–625, 866–77, esp. 487–500; Candeloro, *Storia dell'Italia Moderna*, vol. 9, 447–62; Galeazzo Ciano, *Diario 1937–1943* (Milan: Rizzoli, 1980), 95, 193; Benito Mussolini, *Opera Omnia*, vol. 29, (Florence: La Fenice, 1957), 185–96; Croce, *Scritti e Discorsi Politici*, vol. 2, 323–6; Angelo Ventura, 'La Persecuzione Fascista contro gli Ebrei nell'Università Italiana,' *Rivista Storica Italiana* 109 (January 1987): 121–97; Angelo Ventura, 'La Svolta Antiebraica nella Storia del Fascismo Italiano', *Rivista Storica Italiana* 113 (2001): 36–65.
17 Benedetto Croce, *Pagine Sparse*, vol. 3 (Bari: Laterza, 1960), 174–99; Benedetto Croce, *Terze Pagine Sparse* (Bari: Laterza, 1955), vol. 1, 195, 249–51; Sasso, *Per Invigilare Me Stesso*, 179–210; Croce, *Conversazioni Critiche*, vol. 5, 186–97, 294–8, 362–3.
18 Croce, *Epistolario*, vol. 1, 173–4.
19 Croce, *Pagine Sparse*, vol. 2, 525–7.
20 Croce, *Pagine Sparse*, vol. 2, 510–20.
21 Croce, *Pagine Sparse*, vol. 2, 527–8; Croce, *Carteggio Croce–Vossler*, 379; Croce, *Taccuini*, vol. 4, 119; Croce, *La Storia*, 314–18.
22 Croce, *Epistolario*, vol. 1, 171–2; Croce, *Carteggio Croce–Vossler*, 353–5, 358.
23 Einaudi, 'Ricordi e Divagazioni.'

24 ACS, Fas. Per. Buste 360, 365, 358, 366.
25 Croce, *Nuove Pagine Sparse*, vol. 1, 32–7; ACS, Fas. Per. Busta 358.
26 ACS, Fas. Per. Buste 365, 366; Sandro Gerbi, *Raffaele Mattioli e il Filosofo Donato* (Turin: Einaudi, 2002), 89–91.
27 ACS, Fas. Per. Buste 348–67; Gerbi, *Raffaele Mattioli*, 89–91.
28 Giorgio Falco, *La Santa Romana Repubblica* (Naples: Ricciardi, 1958), vii; AA.VV., *Cento Anni Laterza*, 8–11.
29 Croce, *Scritti e Discorsi Politici*, vol. 2, 111–13; Croce, *Taccuini*, vol. 4, 131, 132–3, 140–1; ACS, Fas. Per. Busta 358.
30 Croce, *Taccuini*, vol. 4, 22, 93–7, 103–4.
31 Arnaldo Momigliano, *Pagine Ebraiche* (Turin: Bollati, 1987), 147.
32 Croce, *Taccuini*, vol. 4, 127–9, 93, 95, 97–9, 101, 103–5, 107, 115, 117–20, 122–4, 127–9, 131, 134–7, 140–1, 149, 160–1, 193, 196.
33 Croce, *Contributo*, 93–4, 101; Benedetto Croce, *Scritti e Discorsi Politici*, vol. 1 (Bari: Laterza, 1963), 49–58, 95–7; Ruffini, 'Ricordi Crociani,' 333–41; Renzo De Felice, *Mussolini l'Alleato. 2 L'Italia in Guerra 1940–1943. Crisi e Agonia del Regime* (Turin: Einaudi, 1990), 671–959; Rosario Romeo, *Dal Piemonte Sabaudo all'Italia Liberale* (Turin: Einaudi, 1963), 250–86.

12. The Fall of Mussolini and the Kingdom of the South, 1940–1944

1 Giorgio Candeloro, *Storia dell'Italia Moderna*, vol. 10, 1939–45, (Milan: Feltrinelli, 1984), 13–103; De Felice, *Mussolini il Duce. 1936–1940*, 626–793, 794–846; De Felice, *Mussolini l'Alleato. 2*, 671–958, 959–1098; Salvatorelli, *Storia d'Italia nel Periodo Fascista*, 1008–86.
2 Croce, *Taccuini*, vol. 4, 1942, 1943; Ivanoe Bonomi, *Diario di un Anno* (Milan: Garzanti, 1946); Arnaldo Ciani, *Il Partito Liberale Italiano* (Naples: ESI, 1968), 27–85; Sante Marelli, *Storia dei Liberali da Cavour a Zanone* (Pesaro: Panozzo, 1981); Parente, *Croce per Lumi Sparsi*, 286–313; Nicolini, *Croce*, 378–98; Partito Liberale Italiano, *Il PLI dal XII al XIV Congresso Nazionale, 1971–1973*, vol. 2 (Rome: Ferri, 1973), 63–90; Ragghianti, *Disegno Storico*; Marcello Soleri, *Memorie* (Turin: Einaudi, 1946).
3 Croce, *Taccuini*, vol. 4, 432; ACS, Fas. Per. Busta 348; Turi, *Giovanni Gentile*, 490–500.
4 Croce, *Taccuini*, vol. 4, 1941, 1942, 1943; Benzoni, *La Vita Ribelle*, 148; Fubini, *Saggi e Ricordi*, 181–96; Ruffini, 'Ricordi Crociani,' 333–41.
5 Croce, *Taccuini*, vol. 4, see 1943; Ruffini, 'Ricordi Crociani'; Benzoni, *La Vita Ribelle*; Galati, *Colloqui con Croce*, 117–23; Bonomi, *Diario di un Anno*, xxxvii.
6 Bonomi, *Diario di un Anno*; Soleri, *Memorie*; De Felice, *Mussolini l'Alleato*, vol. 2, 1089–1412; Candeloro, *Storia dell'Italia Moderna*, vol. 10, 104–229.

7 Candeloro, *Storia dell'Italia Moderna*, vol. 10, 230–346; Salvatorelli, *Storia d'Italia nel Periodo Fascista*, 1087–1164; Renzo De Felice, *Mussolini l'Alleato. 3 La Guerra Civile, 1943–45* (Turin: Einaudi, 1997).

8 Silvio Bertoldi, *Vittorio Emanuele* (Turin: UTET, 1970), 420–67; Roberto Battaglia, *Storia della Resistenza Italiana* (Turin: Einaudi, 1964); Piero Pieri, *Badoglio* (Turin: UTET, 1974), 771–866.

9 Croce, *Taccuini*, vol. 4, 435–81; ibid., vol. 5, 1–68; Croce, *Scritti e Discorsi Politici*, vol. 1, 85–141, 171–356; Benedetto Croce, *Quando l'Italia Era Tagliata in Due,* July 1943–June 1966 (Bari: Laterza, 1948); Nicolini, *Croce*, 399–416; Franchini, *Note Biografiche*, 46–8; Harold Macmillan, *War Diaries 1940–1943* (London: Macmillan, 1985), 270, 355, 368, 427, 450, 711; Parente, *Croce per Lumi Sparsi*, 286–313; Leo Valiani, *Tra Croce e Omodeo* (Florence: Le Monnier, 1984), 60–85; Lino Zeno, *Ritratto di Carlo Sforza* (Florence: Le Monnier, 1975); Enzo Santarelli, *Mezzogiorno. 1943–1944* (Milan: Feltrinelli, 1999); Maurizio Griffo (a cura), *Dall'"Italia Tagliata in Due' all'Assemblea Costituente.* (Bologna: Il Mulino, 1998).

10 Croce, *Taccuini*, vols. 4 and 5, 1943–45; Croce, *Scritti e Discorsi Politici*, vol. 1, 81–141; Raimondo Craveri, *La Campagna d'Italia e i Servizi Segreti* (Milan: La Pietra, 1980), 19–31; Alessandro Casati, *Saggi, Postille e Discorsi* (Milan: Mondadori, 1957), 289–91; Griffo, *Dall'"Italia Tagliata in Due,'* 61–88.

11 Croce, *Taccuini*, vol. 5 (Naples: Arte Tipografica, 1987), 1944; Parente, *Croce per Lumi Sparsi*; Ugo La Malfa, 'La Lotta per la Repubblica,' in *Lezioni sull'Antifascismo*, ed. Piergiovanni Premoli (Bari: Laterza, 1962), 255–82; Pieri, *Badoglio*; Valiani, *Tra Croce e Omodeo*.

12 Croce, *Taccuini*, vol. 5, 1944; Griffo, *Dall'"Italia Tagliata in Due'*.

13 Croce, *Taccuini*, vol. 5, 1944; Giorgio Bocca, *Palmiro Togliatti* (Bari: Laterza, 1973), 361–90; Paolo Spriano, *Storia del Partito Comunista Italiano*, vol. 5 (Turin: Einaudi, 1967–75), 282–337; Bertelli, *Il Gruppo*, 211–13; Griffo, *Dall'"Italia Tagliata in Due.'*

14 Benedetto Croce, *Taccuini*, vol. 5, 1944; Croce, *Epistolario*, vol. 2, 257; Croce, *Scritti e Discorsi Politici*, vol. 1, 44–9; Croce, *Carteggio Croce–Omodeo*, 235; Griffo, *Dall'"Italia Tagliata in Due.'*

15 P. Togliatti, 'Il Governo di Salerno,' in *Trent'Anni di Storia Italiana*, 365–77; Croce, *Taccuini*, vol. 5, 1944, 1945.

13. The Elder Statesman, 1944–1952

1 Croce, *Taccuini*, vol. 5, 1944; Bonomi, *Diario di un Anno*; ACS, Carte Orlando, Busta 8, Carteggio. Fasc. 383; Croce, *Scritti e Discorsi Politici*, vol. 2, 87–104; Griffo, *Dall'"Italia Tagliata in Due,'* 211–12.

2 Croce, *Scritti e Discorsi Politici*, vol. 2, 260–2, 263, 264–7, 354–6.

3 Ragghianti, *Disegno Storico*, 297; Giovanni De Luna, *Storia del Partito d'Azione* (Milan: Feltrinelli, 1984); Valiani, *Tra Croce e Omodeo*, 196–220; Gennaro Sasso, *Filosofia e Idealismo*, vol. 3 (Naples: Bibliopolis, 1997), 301–414; Gennaro Sasso, *La Fedeltà e l'Esperimento* (Bologna: Il Mulino, 1992), 119–72; Guido de Ruggiero, *Il Ritorno alla Ragione* (Bari: Laterza, 1946), 3–41.

4 Croce, *Scritti e Discorsi Politici*, vol. 2, 199–202.

5 Croce, *Scritti e Discorsi Politici*, vol. 1, 304–5; vol. 2, 67–71, 177–81, 182–8, 231–4; Croce, *Taccuini*, vol. 5, see:1945; Leo Valiani, *L'Avvento di De Gasperi* (Turin: De Silva, 1949).

6 Croce, *Terze Pagine Sparse*, vol. 2 (Bari: Laterza, 1955) 166–8, 276–81. vol. 1, 137–9, 252–3, 254–6; Croce, *Taccuini*, vol. 5, 1944, 125–8; Croce, *Scritti e Discorsi Politici*, vol. 1, 334–6; Presidenza del Consiglio dei Ministri, *Verbali del Consiglio dei Ministri. Governo Bonomi. 18 Giugno–12 Dicembre 1945*, vol. 3, 8–9; Emilio Sereni, 'La Lotta per La Repubblica. Testimonianze,' in *Lezioni sull'Antifascismo*, ed. Piergiovanni Permoli (Bari: Laterza, 1962), 288; Sasso, *La Fedeltà e l'Esperimento*, 215–34.

7 Croce, *Taccuini*, vol. 5, 278.

8 Sasso, *Per Invigilare me Stesso*, 40–60.

9 Croce, *Taccuini*, vol. 6, 1946, 46–50; Griffo, *Dall''Italia Tagliata in Due,'* 265–6.

10 Croce, *Scritti e Discorsi Politici*, vol. 2, 365–72, 394–5; Croce, *Taccuini*, vol. 6 (Naples: Arte Tipografica, 1987), 1947, 108–9, 111; ACS, Carte Orlando, Busta 8, Carteggio, Fasc. 383.

11 Croce, *Scritti e Discorsi Politici*, vol. 2, 404–11, 401–3; Croce, *Taccuini*, vol. 6, 1949, 94–5, 136, 139, 141–4; Griffo, *Dall''Italia Tagliata in Due,'* 302.

12 Croce, *Epistolario*, vol. 2, 250–1; Croce, *Scritti e Discorsi Politici*, vol. 2, 199–201; Croce, *Storiografia e Idealità Morale*, 113; ACS, Carte Orlando, Busta 8–Carteggio, Fasc. 383. See also Croce, *Conversazioni Critiche*, vol. 3, 342.

13 Calogero, 'Ricordi Crociani'; Croce, *Carteggio Croce–Omodeo*, 205–14; Sandro Setta, *Croce, il Liberalismo e l'Italia Postfascista* (Rome: Bonacci, 1979); Parente, *Per Lumi Sparsi*.

14 Benedetto Croce, *I Taccuini di Lavoro*, vol. 6 (Naples: Arte Tipografica, 1987), 290–2, 293–5, 296–8; Croce, *Scritti e Discorsi Politici*, vol. 1, 140; Croce, *Epistolario*, vol. 2, 269–75.

15 Croce, *Terze Pagine Sparse*, vol. 1, 308–10, 298–308, 289–97, 291–3; Croce, *Scritti e Discorsi Politici*, vol. 2, 212–30, 298–310, 311–15, 357–365, 435–43, 453–63; Ciani, *Il Partito Liberale Italiano*, 27–85; Garosci, 'Croce e la Politica,' 163–98.

16 Gennaro Sasso, *Filosofia e Idealismo*, vol. 1, (Naples: Bibliopolis, 1994), 545–606; Croce, *Scritti e Discorsi Politici*, vol. 2, 172–7; Croce, *Storiografia e Idealità Morale*, 55–67.

17 Croce, *Scritti e Discorsi Politici*, vol. 2, 64–6; Croce, *Storiografia e Idealità Morale*, 107–16.
18 Ibid., 115–16.
19 Sasso, *Per Invigilare me Stesso*; Parente, *Croce per Lumi Sparsi.*
20 Saragat, 'Nel Primo Centenario della Nascita di Benedetto Croce,' 83–93; Parente, *Croce per Lumi Sparsi.*

Bibliography

Archival Sources

Archivio Centrale dello Stato, Rome

Carte Bonomi Ivanoe
  Buste 1, 2, 4
Carte Casati Alessandro
  Buste 3, 4
Carte Nitti Francesco Saverio
  Busta 86, Fascicolo Croce Benedetto
Carte Orlando Vittorio Emanuele
  Busta 3, Carteggio
  Fascicolo 383, Croce Benedetto
Carte Reale Eugenio
  Busta 2, Scritti Editi e Inediti
Casellario Politico Centrale
  Busta 64, Fascicolo Alfieri Vittorio Enzo
  Busta 98, Fascicolo Amendola Giorgio
  Busta 396, Fascicolo Basso Lelio
  Busta 417, Fascicolo Bauer Riccardo
  Busta 1422, Fascicolo Colorni Eugenio
  Busta 2293, Fascicolo Garosci Aldo
  Busta 3390, Fascicolo Morandi Rodolfo
  Busta 5029, Fascicolo Tarchiani Alberto
  Busta 5541, Fascicolo Vinciguerra Mario
Ministero della Cultura Popolare, Gabinetto
  Busta 117, Fascicolo 7981, Rivista *La Critica*, Croce Benedetto

Ministero dell'Interno, Direzione Pubblica Sicurezza
  Divisione Polizia Politica, Fascicoli Personali e Risevati
    Fascicolo Croce Benedetto
      Buste 348–67
      Busta 70, Fascicolo Casati Alessandro
      Busta 561, Fascicolo Garosci Aldo
      Busta 563, Fascicolo Ginzburg Leone
      Busta 712, Fascicolo Laterza Giovanni
      Busta 998, Fascicolo Parente Alfredo
      Busta 1129, Fascicolo Ragghianti Carlo Ludovicio
      Busta 1480, Fascicolo Vinciguerra Mario
  Divisione Polizia Politica, 1927–44, Materie
      Buste 101, 105, 132
  Divisione Affari Generali e Riservati, 1927–44, G.I. Associazioni
      Busta 224
      Fascicolo 466, Relazioni Trimestrali
Presidenza del Consiglio dei Ministri, 1920
    Fascicolo 1–4
    Busta 585
Presidenza del Consiglio dei Ministri, 1921
    Fascicolo 1–4, 1–5, 1–6
    Busta 616
Presidenza del Consiglio dei Ministri, 1944–7
    Fascicolo 1-4-1, 12001–14644.
    Fascicolo Personale 12508, S.E. Senatore Benedetto Croce
Segreteria Particolare del Duce, Carteggio Ordinario, 1922–43
    Busta 10, Fascicolo Croce Benedetto Senatore
    Busta 637, Fascicolo 204553 Croce Benedetto (1940)
    Segreteria Particolare del Duce, Carteggio Ordinario, Pubblica Sicurezza
      1929, Categorie A1
Segreteria Particolare del Duce, Carteggio Riservato RSI
    Busta 15, Fascicolo 77, Croce Benedetto
    Sottofascicolo 1, Carte from 26/6/1925 to 17/4/1943
    Sottofascicolo 2, Carte from 16/9/1943 to 28/4/1944
Verbali del Consiglio dei Ministri, 14 March 1920–27 July 1927; vol. 14. 46–186,
    22 June 1920–1 July 1921

Books by Croce

Croce, Benedetto. *Il Carattere della Filosofia Moderna*. Bari: Laterza, 1945.

– *Contributo alla Critica di Me Stesso*. Milan: Adelphi, 1989.
– *Conversazioni Critiche*. 5 vols. Bari: Laterza, 1932–9.
– *Cultura e Vita Morale*. Bari: Laterza, 1955.
– *Dieci Conversazioni*. Bologna: Il Mulino, 1993.
– *Discorsi Parlamentari*. Rome: Bardi, 1966.
– *Discorsi di Varia Filosofia*. 2 vols. Bari: Laterza, 1945.
– *Due Anni di Vita Politica Italiana (1946–47)*. Bari: Laterza, 1948.
– *Esuli*. Pescara: Rivista Abruzzese. Anno. 30, no. 2 (1977): 85–95.
– *Eternità e Storicità della Filosofia*. Rieti: Petrini, 1930.
– *Etica e Politica*. Bari: Laterza, 1956.
– *Una Famiglia di Patrioti*. Bari: Laterza, 1949.
– *Filosofia e Storiografia*. Bari: Laterza, 1949.
– *L'Italia dal 1914 al 1918*. Bari: Laterza, 1950.
– *La Letteratura della Nuova Italia*. vol. 4. Bari: Laterza, 1955.
– *Materialismo Storico ed Economia Marxistica*. Bari: Laterza, 1951.
– *Memorie della Mia Vita*. Naples: Istituto Italiano per gli Studi Storici, 1966.
– *La Mia Filosofia*. Milan: Adelphi, 1993.
– *Nuove Pagine Sparse*. 2 vols. Naples: Ricciardi, 1949.
– *Orientamenti: Piccoli Saggi di Filosofia Politica*. Milan: Gilardi e Noto, 1934.
– *Pagine Politiche*. (July–December 1944). Bari: Laterza, 1945.
– *Pagine Sparse*. 3 vols. Bari: Laterza, 1960.
– *Pensiero Politico e Politica Attuale. Scritti e Discorsi Politici* (1945). Bari: Laterza, 1946.
– *Per la Nuova Vita d'Italia. Scritti e Discorsi*. (1943–44). Naples: Ricciardi, 1944.
– *La Poesia*. Bari: Laterza, 1963.
– *Quando l'Italia Era Tagliata in Due*. (July 1943–January 1944) Bari: Laterza, 1948.
– *Scritti e Discorsi Politici*. 2 vols. (1943–47). Bari: Laterza, 1963.
– *La Storia come Pensiero e come Azione*. Bari: Laterza, 1954.
– *Storia del Regno di Napoli*. Bari: Laterza, 1958.
– *Storia dell'Età Barocca in Italia*. Bari: Laterza, 1957.
– *Storia d'Europa nel Secolo Decimonono*. Bari: Laterza, 1957.
– *Storia d'Italia dal 1871 al 1915*. Bari: Laterza, 1959.
– *Storiografia e Idealità Morale*. Bari: Laterza, 1950.
– *I Taccuini di Lavoro*. 6 vols. Naples: Arte Tipografica, 1987.
– *Terze Pagine Sparse*. 2 vols. Bari: Laterza, 1955.
– *Ultimi Saggi*. Bari: Laterza, 1948.
– *Vite di Avventure, di Fede e di Passione*. Milan: Adelphi, 1989.
– and Luigi Einaudi. *Liberismo e Liberalismo*. Ed. Paolo Solari. Naples: Ricciardi, 1957.

Croce's Letters and Correspondence

Colapietra, Raffaele. 'Lettere Inedite di Benedetto Croce a Giuseppe Lombardo Radice.' *Il Ponte* (Florence), (1968): 976–97.

Croce, Benedetto. *Carteggio Croce–Amendola*. Ed. Roberto Pertici. Naples: IISS, 1982.

– *Carteggio Croce–Antoni*. Ed. Marcello Musté. Bologna: Il Mulino, 1996.

– *Carteggio Croce–Omodeo*. Ed. M. Gigante. Naples: IISS, 1978.

– *Carteggio Croce–Prezzolini*. 2 vols. Ed. E. Giammattei. Rome: Istituto Storico della Letteratura, 1990.

– *Carteggio Croce–Torraca*. Ed. F. Guerriero. Galatina: Congedo, 1979.

– *Carteggio Croce–Vossler*. Bari: Laterza, 1988.

– *Epistolario 1. Scelta di Lettere a Cura dell'Autore*. 1914–35. Naples: IISS, 1967.

– *Epistolario 2. Lettere ad Alessandro Casati*. 1907–52. Naples: IISS, 1969.

– *Lettere a Giovanni Castellano*. 1908–49. Naples: IISS, 1985.

– *Lettere a Giovanni Gentile*. Milan: Mondadori, 1991.

– *Lettere a Giuseppe Prezzolini*. Ed. O. Besomi. Bellinzona: Archivio Storico Ticinese, 1981.

– *Lettere a Vittorio Enzo Alfieri*. 1925–52. Milazzo: Sicilia Nuova, 1976.

– and Ada Gobetti. *Carissma Ada–Gentilissimo Senatore. Carteggio Ada Gobetti–Benedetto Croce*. Ed. S. Caprioglio. (1928–52). Turin: Franco Angeli, 1990.

– and Luigi Einaudi. *Carteggio Croce–Einaudi*. Ed. Luigi Firpo. Turin: Fondazione Luigi Einaudi, 1988.

– and Pietro Pancrazi. *Caro Senatore. Epistolario 1913–1952*. Florence: Passigli, 1989.

Croce, Elena and Alda. 'Lettere di Silvio Spaventa a Benedetto Croce.' In AA.VV., *Un Augurio a Raffaele Mattioli*. Florence: Sansoni, 1970, 246–81.

Fucinese, Damiano. 'Dieci Lettere Inedite di Croce.' *Dimensioni* (Lanciano), nos. 5–6. (December 1966): 6–18.

Ginzburg, Leone. 'Lettere a Benedetto Croce', 1930–42. *Il Ponte* (Florence), 1977, 1153–83.

Griffo, Maurizio, ed. *Dall''Italia Tagliata in due' all'assemblea Costituente*. Documenti e Testimonianze dai Carteggi di Benedetto Croce. Bologna: Il Mulino, 1998.

Margiotta Broglio, F. 'Travaglio e Crisi dello Stato Liberale nelle Lettere di Benedetto Croce a Francesco Ruffini.' *Nuova Antologia* 556 (1986): 408–36.

Turati, Filippo, and Benedetto Croce. *Carteggio*. Naples: Bibliopolis, 1998.

Zucaro, Domenico. 'Il caso Germani. Diciotto Lettere di Benedetto Croce.' *Il Ponte* (1968): 51–66.

Biographies of Croce

Borsari, Silvano. *L'Opera di Benedetto Croce.* Naples: IISS, 1964.
Boulay, Charles. *Benedetto Croce jusqu'en 1911.* Geneva: Librairie Droz, 1981.
Brescia, Giuseppe. *Croce Inedito.* Naples: Società Editrice Napoletana, 1986.
Castellano, Giovanni. *Benedetto Croce. Il Filosofo, il Critico, lo Storico.* Bari: Laterza, 1936.
Colapietra, Raffaele. *Benedetto Croce e la Politica Italiana.* 2 vols. Bari: Edizioni del Centro Libraio. 1969.
Croce, Elena. *Ricordi Familiari.* Florence: Vallecchi, 1962.
De Feo, Italo. *Benedetto Croce e il Suo Mondo.* Turin: ERI, 1966.
– *Croce: L'Uomo e L'Opera.* Milan: Mondadori, 1975.
Franchini, Raffaello. *Intervista su Croce.* Naples: Sen, 1978.
– *Note Biografiche di Benedetto Croce.* Turin: ERI, 1953.
Nicolini, Fausto. *Croce.* Turin: UTET, 1962.
– *Il Croce Minore.* Naples: Ricciardi, 1963.
– *L'Editio ne Varietur dell'Opera di Benedetto Croce.* Naples: IISS., 1960
Sasso, Gennaro. *Per Invigilare Me Stesso.* Bologna: Il Mulino, 1989.

Memoirs, Letters, and Contemporary Sources

AA.VV. [Various Authors.] *Cento Anni Laterza, 1885–1985. Testimonianze degli Autori.* Bari: Laterza, 1985.
Albertini, Luigi. *Epistolario.* 5 vols. Milan: Mondadori, 1968.
Allason, Barbara. *Memorie di un'Antifascista.* Florence: Vallechhi, 1946.
Alpino, Enrico. *Colloqui con Croce.* Genoa: Tolozzi, 1970.
Amendola, Giorgio. *Un'Isola.* Milan: Rizzoli, 1980.
– *Una Scelta di Vita.* Milan: Rizzoli, 1981.
Basso, L., and L. Anderlini, ed. *Le Riviste di Piero Gobetti.* Milan: Feltrinelli, 1961.
Bauer, Riccardo. *Quello Che Ho Fatto.* Bari: Laterza, 1971.
Benzoni, Giuliana. *La Vita Ribelle.* Bologna: Il Mulino, 1985.
Bonomi, Ivanoe. *Diario di un Anno.* Milan: Garzanti, 1946.
Bottai, Giuseppe. *Diario 1935–1944.* Milan: Rizzoli, 1989.
Burzio, Filippo. 'Croce e gli Italiani durante il Fascismo.' *La Rassegna d'Italia* 2, no. 3 (1946): 135–44.
Calogero, Guido. *Difesa del Liberalsocialismo.* Rome: Atlantica, 1945.
Capitini, Aldo. *Elementi di un'Esperienza Religiosa.* Bari: Laterza, 1947.
– 'Sull'Antifascismo dal 1932 al 1943. *Il Ponte* 11 (1955): 848–54.
Casati, Alessandro. *Saggi, Postille e Discorsi.* Milan: Mondadori, 1957.

Ceva, Bianca. 'Immagini della Memoria.' *Nuova Antologia* no. 548 (1982): 174–8.
– *Storia di una Passione*. Milan: Garzanti, 1948.
– 'Una Testimonianza su Benedetto Croce.' *Nuova Antologia*. no. 530 (1977): 142–5.
Ciano, Galeazzo. *Diario. 1937–1943*. Milan: Rizzoli, 1980.
Codignola, Ernesto. 'Pagine di Diario,' in AA.VV., *Ernesto Codignola in 50 Anni di Battaglie Educative*. Florence: La Nuova Italia, 1967, 177–88.
De Begnac, Ivon. *Taccuini Mussoliniani*. Bologna: Il Mulino, 1990.
Del Secolo, Floriano. 'Croce e la Sua Casa nel Ventennio.' *La Rassegna d'Italia* 2, no. 3 (1946): 274–80.
De Sanctis, Gaetano. *Ricordi*. Florence: La Nuova Italia, 1970.
Dionisotti, Carlo. *Ricordi della Scuola Italiana*. Rome: Edizioni di Storia e Letteratura, 1998.
Einaudi, Luigi. 'Ricordi e Divagazioni sul Senato Vitalizio.' *Nuova Antologia* no. 467 (1956): 173–208.
Flora, Francesco, ed. *Benedetto Croce*. Milan: Malfasi, 1954.
Foa, Vittorio. *Il Cavallo e la Torre*. Turin: Einaudi, 1991.
– *Lettere della Giovinezza. Dal Carcere 1935–1943*. Turin: Einaudi, 1998.
Fortunato, Giustino. *Carteggio*. 4 vols., 1865–1932. Bari: Laterza, 1978–81.
– *Scritti politici*. Bari: Laterza, 1981.
Fubini, Mario. *Saggi e Ricordi*. Naples: Ricciardi, 1968.
Galati, Vito. *Colloqui con Benedetto Croce*. Brescia: Morcelliana, 1957.
Garosci, Aldo. 'Benedetto Croce Antifascista.' *Resistenza* 20, no. 4 (1966): 7–8.
– 'In un Giorno d'Estate, a Grenoble Croce si Fermò dal Giovane Fuoruscito.' *Resistenza* 20, no. 1 (1966): 3.
Gavagnin, Armando. *Una Lettera al Re*. Florence: La Nuova Italia, 1951.
– *Vent'Anni di Resistenza al Fascismo. Ricordi e Testimonianze*. Turin: Einaudi, 1957.
Gentile, Giovanni. *Epistolario 7. Lettere a Benedetto Croce*. Vol. 5. Florence: Le Lettere, 1990.
– *Epistolario 9. Carteggio Gentile–Omodeo*. Florence: Sansoni, 1974.
– *Epistolario 13. Carteggio Gentile–Calogero*. Florence: Le Lettere, 1998.
– *Lettere a Benedetto Croce*. 4 vols. Florence: Sansoni, 1972–80.
– *Politica e Cultura*. 2 vols. Florence: Sansoni, 1971.
Giua, Michele. Letter to Gaetano Salvemini. *Scritti sul Fascismo*. Vol. 3, 449. Milan: Feltrinelli, 1974.
Gobetti, Piero. *Scritti Politici*. Ed. Paolo Spriano. Turin: Einaudi, 1969.
Gramsci, Antonio. *Lettere dal Carcere*. Turin: Einaudi, 1965.
– *Il Materialismo Storico e la Filosofia di Benedetto Croce*. Turin: Einaudi, 1955.
Jemolo, Arturo Carlo. *Anni di Prova*. Venice: Neri Pozza, 1969.
Kuhn Amendola, Eva. *Vita con Giovanni Amendola*. Florence: Parenti, 1960.

Labriola, Antonio. *Lettere a Benedetto Croce. 1895–1904.* Naples: IISS, 1975.

La Malfa, Ugo. *Scritti 1925–1953.* Milan: Mondadori, 1988.

Leonetti, Alfonso. *Un Communista.* (1895–1930). Milan: Feltrinelli, 1977.

Levi Della Vida, Giorgio. *Fantasmi Ritrovati.* Venice: Neri Pozza, 1966.

Luria, S.E. *A Slot Machine, a Broken Test Tube.* New York: Harper and Row, 1984.

Lussu, Joyce. *Lotte. Ricordi e altro.* Rome: Biblioteca del Vascello, 1993.

Marcenaro, Giuseppe, ed. *Pietre. Antologia di una Rivista.* 1926–28. Milan: Mursia, 1973.

Marchesi, Concetto. *40 Lettere a Manara Valgimigli.* Milan: Pesce d'Oro, 1979.

Momigliano, Arnaldo. 'La Critica.' *La Rassegna d'Italia* 2, no. 3 (1946): 234–6.

Monti, Augusto. *I Miei Conti con la Scuola.* Turin: Einaudi, 1988.

Mussolini, Benito. *Opera Omnia.* Vol. 12. Florence: La Fenice, 1952–63.

– *Opera Omnia.* Vol. 17. Florence: La Fenice, 1952–63.

– *Opera Omnia.* Vol. 20. Florence: La Fenice, 1952–63.

– *Opera Omnia.* Vol. 21. Florence: La Fenice, 1952–63.

– *Opera Omnia.* Vol. 24. Florence: La Fenice, 1952–63.

– *Opera Omnia.* Vol. 29. Florence: La Fenice, 1952–63.

Ojetti, Ugo. *I Taccuini.* 1914–43. Florence: Sansoni, 1954.

Omodeo, Adolfo. 'La Collaborazione con Benedetto Croce durante il Ventennio.' *La Rassegna d'Italia* 2, no. 3 (1946): 266–73.

– *Lettere.* Turin: Einaudi, 1963.

– *Libertà e Storia.* Turin: Einaudi, 1960.

– *Momenti della Vita di Guerra.* Bari: Laterza, 1934.

– *Scritti e Discorsi Politici.* Turin: Einaudi, 1960.

Pajetta, Giancarlo. *Il Ragazzo Rosso.* Milan: Rizzoli, 1976.

Piras, Quirino. *Battaglie Liberali.* Novara: Gaddi, 1926.

Rosselli, Carlo. *Dall'Esilio. Lettere alla Moglie. 1929–1932.* Florence: Passigli, 1997.

Rossi, Ernesto. *Elogio della Galera.* Bari: Laterza, 1968.

Ruffini, Nina. 'Ricordi Crociani.' *Nuova Antologia* no. 526 (1976): 333–41.

Russo, Luigi. 'Benedetto Croce.' *Belfagor* 2 (1953): 1–15.

– *Il Dialogo dei Popoli.* Florence: Parenti, 1955.

– 'Nuove Conversazioni con Benedetto Croce.' *Belfagor* 4 (1953): 158–71.

Salandra, Antonio. *Memorie Politiche.* 1916–25. Reggio Calabria: Parallelo, 1975.

Salvemini, Gaetano. *Carteggio.* (1894–1926). 4 vols. Bari: Laterza, 1985–8.

Soleri, Marcello. *Memorie.* Turin: Einaudi, 1946.

Tilgher, Livia. 'Ricordo di Mario Vinciguerra.' *Rivista di Studi Crociani* 7 (1970): 70–4.

Togliatti, Palmiro. 'Il Governo di Salerno.' In *Trent'Anni di Storia Italiana.* Ed. Franco Antonicelli, 365–77. Turin: Einaudi, 1975.

– In Presidenza del Consiglio dei Ministri. *Verbali del Consiglio dei Ministri. Governo Bonomi.* 18 June–12 December 1945, vol. 3. 8–9.

Treves, Paolo. *What Mussolini Did to Us.* London: Victor Gollancz, 1940.

Villabruna, Bruno. 'Il Discorso del Bivacco e le Elezioni del 1924.' In *Trent'Anni di Storia Italiana.* Ed. Franco Antonicelli, 62–7. (1915–45). Turin: Einaudi, 1975.

Vinciguerra, Mario. 'L'Alleanza Nazionale e Lauro De Bosis.' In *Trent'Anni di Storia Italiana.* Ed. Franco Antonicelli, 170–3. Turin: Einaudi, 1975.

– *Croce. Ricordi e Pensieri.* Naples: Vajro, 1957.

Zanotti Bianco, Umberto. *Carteggio.* 1919–28. Bari: Laterza, 1989.

Zweig, Stefan. *The World of Yesterday.* Lincoln: University of Nebraska Press, 1950.

Books

AA.VV. *Croce Quarant'Anni dopo.* Pescara: Ediars, 1993.

AA.VV. *Fascismo e Antifascismo.* 2 vols. Milan: Feltrinelli, 1974.

AA.VV. *Giustizia e Libertà nella Lotta Antifascista.* Florence: La Nuova Italia, 1978.

AA.VV. *Omaggio a Benedetto Croce. Saggi sull'Uomo e sull'Opera.* Turin: ERI, 1953.

AA.VV. *Il Secondo Risorgimento.* Rome: Istituto Poligrafico dello Stato, 1955.

Abbate, Michele. *La Filosofia di Benedetto Croce e la Crisi della Società Italiana.* Turin: Einaudi, 1967.

Agazzi, Emilio. 'Benedetto Croce: dalla Revisione del Marxismo al Rilancio dell'Idealismo.' In *Storia della Società Italiana.* Vol. 19. Ed. I. Barbadoro, 279–30. Milan: Teti, 1980.

– 'Croce e l'Antifascismo Moderato: fra Ideologia Italiana e Ideologia Europea.' In *Storia della Società Italiana.* Vol. 22. Ed. I. Barbadoro, 259–339. Milan: Teti, 1983.

– *Il Giovane Croce e il Marxismo.* Turin: Einaudi, 1962.

Agosti, Giorgio. *Rodolfo Morandi.* Bari: Laterza, 1971.

Ajello, Nello. *Intellettuali e PCI. 1944–8.* Bari: Laterza, 1979.

Albertini, Alberto. *Vita di Luigi Albertini.* Milan: Mondadori, 1945.

Alfieri, Vittorio Enzo. *Maestri e Testimoni di Libertà.* Milazzo: Sicilia Nuova Editrice, 1976.

– *Nel Nobile Castello.* Milazzo: Edizioni Spes, 1986.

Amendola, Giorgio. *Intervista sull'Antifascismo.* Bari: Laterza, 1994.

– *Storia del Partito Communista Italiano.* Rome: Editori Riuniti, 1978.

– 'Il Tribunale Speciale e L'Antifascismo all'Interno.' In AA.VV., *Fascismo e Antifascismo. (1918–36),* 217–46, esp. 225–6. *Lezioni e Testimonianze.* Milan: Feltrinelli, 1974.

Antoni, Carlo. *Commento a Croce.* Venice: Neri Pozza, 1955.
- *La Restaurazione del Diritto di Natura.* Venice: Neri Pozza, 1959.
- *Lo Storicismo.* Turin: ERI, 1957.
Antonicelli, Franco, ed. *Trent'Anni di Storia Italiana.* (1915–1945). Turin: Einaudi, 1961.
Aquarone, Albero. *L'Organizzazione dello Stato Totalitario.* Turin: Einaudi, 1995.
Barié, Ottavio. *Luigi Albertini.* Turin: UTET, 1972.
Battaglia, Roberto. *Storia della Resistenza Italiana.* Turin: Einaudi, 1964.
Bazoli, Maurizio. *Fonti del Pensiero Politico di Benedetto Croce.* Milan: Marzorati, 1971.
Belardelli, Giovanni. *Il Mito della Nuova Italia. Gioacchino Volpe tra Guerra e Fascismo.* Rome: Edizioni Lavoro, 1980.
Benedetti, Ulisse. *Benedetto Croce e il Fascismo.* Rome: Volpe, 1967.
Bertelli, Sergio. *Il Gruppo. La Formazione del Gruppo Dirigente del PCI. 1936–1948.* Milan: Rizzoli, 1980.
Bertoldi, Silvio. *Vittorio Emanuele.* Turin: UTET, 1970.
Biscione, Michele. *Interpreti di Croce.* Naples: Giannini, 1968.
Bobbio, Norbetto. *Autobiografia.* Bari: Laterza, 1997.
- *Politica e Cultura.* Turin: Einaudi, 1956.
- *Dal Fascismo alla Democrazia.* Milan: Baldini and Castoldi, 1997.
- *Italia Fedele. Il Mondo di Gobetti.* Florence: Passigli, 1986.
- *Maestri e Compagni.* Florence: Passigli, 1984.
- *Profilo Ideologico del Novecento Italiano.* Turin: Einaudi, 1986.
Bocca, Giorgio. *Palmiro Togliatti.* Bari: Laterza, 1973.
Bonetti, Paolo. *Introduzione a Croce.* Bari: Laterza, 1996.
Bruno, Antonino, ed., *Benedetto Croce.* Catania: Giannotta, 1974.
Burks, Richard. 'Benedetto Croce.' In *Some Modern European Historians.* Ed. Bernadotte Schmitt, 66–99. Chicago: University Press of Illinois, 1942.
Camurani, Ercole. *Il Partito Liberale nella Resistenza.* Rome: Bonacci, 1971.
Candeloro, Giorgio. *Storia dell'Italia Moderna. 1700–1950.* 11 vols. Milan: Feltrinelli, 1976–86.
Capitini, Aldo. *Nuova Socialità e Riforma Religiosa.* Turin: Einaudi, 1950.
Carr, Edward H. *What Is History?* New York: Knopf, 1962.
Caserta, G. Ernesto. *Croce and Marxism.* Naples: Morano, 1987.
Castronovo, A., and N. Tranfaglia. *La Stampa Italiana nell'Età Fascista.* Bari: Laterza, 1980.
Chabod, Federico. *A History of Italian Fascism.* New York: Fertig, 1975.
- *Lezioni di Metodo Storico.* Bari: Laterza, 1969.
Ciani, Arnaldo. *Il Partito Liberale Italiano.* Naples: ESI, 1968.
Colapietra, Raffaele. *Napoli tra Dopoguerra e Fascismo.* Milan: Feltrinelli, 1962.

Colarizi, Simona. *Democratici all'Opposizione. Giovanni Amendola e l'Unione Nazionale.* Bologna: Il Mulino, 1977.
– *Dopoguerra e Fascismo in Puglia.* Bari: Laterza, 1977.
– *L'Italia Antifascista dal 1922 al 1940.* 2 Vols. Bari: Laterza, 1974.
Coli, Daniela. *Croce, Laterza e la Cultura Europea.* Bologna: Laterza, 1983.
Cordeschi, A. *Croce e la Bella Angelina.* Milan: Mursia, 1994.
Corsi, Mario. *Le Origini del Pensiero Politico di Benedetto Croce.* Naples: Giannini, 1974.
Craveri, Raimondo. *La Campagna d'Italia e i Servizi Segreti.* Milan: La Pietra, 1980.
De Caprariis, Vittorio, E. Montale, and L. Valiani. *Benedetto Croce.* Milan: Comunità, 1963.
De Felice, Renzo. *Il Fascismo e i Partiti Politici Italiani del 1921–1923.* Bologna: Cappelli, 1966.
– *Il Fascismo. Le Interpretazioni dei Contemporanei e degli Storici.* Bari: Laterza, 1970.
– *Intellettuali di Fronte al Fascismo.* Rome: Bonacci, 1985.
– *Le Interpretazioni del Fascismo.* Bari: Laterza, 1970.
– *Intervista sul Fascismo.* Bari: Laterza, 1975.
– *Mussolini il Duce.* 1. *Gli Anni del Consenso. 1929–1936.* Turin: Einaudi, 1974.
– *Mussolini il Duce.* 2. *Lo Stato Totalitario. 1936–1940.* Turin: Einaudi, 1981.
– *Mussolini il Fascista.* 1. *La Conquista del Potere. 1921–25.* Turin: Einaudi, 1966.
– *Mussolini il Fascista, 2 L'Organizzazione dello Stato Fascista. 1925–1929.* Turin: Einaudi, 1968.
– *Mussolini. Il Mito.* Bari: Laterza, 1983.
– *Mussolini il Rivoluzionario. 1883–1920.* Turin: Einaudi, 1965.
– *Mussolini l'Alleato.* 1. *L'Italia in Guerra 1940–1943. Dalla Guerra Breve alla Guerra Lunga.* Turin: Einaudi, 1990.
– *Mussolini l'Alleato.* 2. *L'Italia in Guerra 1940–1943. Crisi e Agonia del Regime.* Turin: Einaudi, 1990.
– *Mussolini l'Alleato.* 3. *La Guerra Civile 1943–1945.* Turin: Einaudi, 1997.
– *Rosso e Nero.* Milan: Baldini and Castoldi, 1995.
– *Storia degli Ebrei sotto il Fascismo.* 2 vols. Milan: Mondadori, 1978.
De Frede, Carlo. *Benedetto Croce, il Fascismo e la Storia.* Naples: De Simone, 1981.
De Luna, Giovanni. *Storia del Partito d'Azione.* Milan: Feltrinelli, 1984.
Delzell, Charles P. *Mussolini's Enemies: The Italian Anti-fascist Resistance.* Princeton: Princeton University Press, 1961.
De Marzi, Giacomo. *Piero Gobetti e Benedetto Croce.* Urbino: Quattro Venti, 1996.
De Ruggiero, Guido. *Ritorno alla Ragione.* Bari: Laterza, 1946.
– *Storia del Liberalismo Italiano.* Bari: Laterza, 1959.
Di Lalla, Manlio. *Storia del Liberalismo Italiano.* Florence: Sansoni, 1976.
Dionisotti, Carlo. *Natalino Sapegno.* Turin: Bollati, 1994.

Falco, Giorgio. *La Santa Romana Repubblica.* Naples: Ricciardi, 1958.

Forbice, A. *La Forza Tranquilla. Bruno Buozzi, Sindacalista Riformista.* Turin: Franco Angeli, 1984.

Fornaca, Remo. *Benedetto Croce e la Politica Scolastica in Italia nel 1920–1921.* Rome: Armando, 1968.

Franzinelli, Mimmo. *I Tentacoli dell OVRA.* Turin: Bollati, 1999.

Galasso, Giuseppe. *Croce e lo Spirito del Suo Tempo.* Milan: Mondadori, 1990.

– *Croce Gramsci e Altri Storici.* Milan: Mondadori, 1978.

Garin, Eugenio. *Cronache di Filosofia Italiana.* 2 vols. Bari: Laterza, 1975.

– *La Cultura Italiana fra '800 e '900.* Bari: Laterza, 1976.

– *Intellettuali Italiani del XX Secolo.* Rome: Editori Riuniti, 1987.

– *Intervista sull'Intellettuale.* Ed. Mario Ajello. Bari: Laterza, 1997.

Garosci, Aldo. 'Croce e la Politica.' in AA.VV., *L'Eredità di Croce,* 163–72. Naples: Guida, 1985.

– 'Gli Ideali di Libertà dal Risorgimento alla Crisi Fascista.' In AA.VV., *Il Secondo Risorgimento,* 1–94. Rome: Istituto Poligrafico dello Stato, 1955.

– *Il Pensiero Politico di Benedetto Croce.* Turin: Cheroni, 1961.

– *Pensiero Politico e Storiografia Moderna.* Pisa: Nistri-Lischi, 1954.

– *Storia dei Fuoriusciti.* Bari: Laterza, 1953.

– *La Vita di Carlo Rosselli.* 2 vols. Florence: Vallecchi, 1975.

Gentile, Emilio. *La Grande Italia.* Milan: Mondadori, 1999.

– *Le Origini dell'Ideologia Fascista. (1918–1925).* Bologna: Il Mulino, 1996.

Gerbi, Sandro. *Raffaele Mattioli e il Filosofo Domato.* Turin: Einaudi, 2002.

Gifuni, G.B. *Salandra Inedito.* Milan: Pan, 1973.

Giovannini, Alberto. *Il Rifiuto dell'Aventino.* Bologna: Il Mulino, 1966.

Hughes, Henry Stuart. *Consciousness and Society: The Reorientation of European Thought, 1890–1930.* New York: Alfred A. Knopf, 1958.

Iermano, Toni. *Lo Scrittoio di Croce.* Naples: Fausto Fiorentino, 1992.

Jacobelli, Jader. *Croce Gentile. Dal Sodalizio al Dramma.* Milan: Rizzoli, 1989.

Jabobitti, Edmund E. *Revolutionary Humanism and Historicism in Modern Italy.* New Haven: Yale University Press, 1981.

Jannazzo, Antonio. *Croce e il Communismo.* Naples: ESI, 1982.

– *Croce e il Prepartito della Cultura.* Rome: Carucci, 1987.

Jemolo, Arturo Carlo. *Chiesa e Stato in Italia negli Ultimi Cento Anni.* Turin: Einaudi, 1963.

La Malfa, Ugo. 'La Lotta per la Repubblica.' In *Lezioni sull'Antifascismo.* Ed. Piergiovanni Permoli, 255–84. Bari: Laterza, 1962.

Lombardo, Radice Lucio. *Fascismo e Anticomunismo.* Turin: Einaudi, 1947.

Lyttelton, Adrian. *The Seizure of Power: Fascism in Italy, 1919–1929.* London: Weidenfeld and Nicolson, 1973.

Mack Smith, Denis. *Da Cavour a Mussolini*. Catania: Bonanno, 1968.

Macmillan, Harold. *War Diaries, 1940–1943*. London: Macmillan, 1985.

Maggi, Michele. *La Filosofia di Benedetto Croce*. Florence: Ponte alle Grazie, 1989.

Marelli, Sante. *Storia dei Liberali da Cavour a Zanone*. Pesaro: Panozzo, 1981.

Margiotta Broglio, Francesco. *Italia e Santa Sede dalla Grande Guerra alla Conciliazione*. Bari: Laterza, 1966.

Matteucci, Nicola. *Il Liberalismo in un Mondo in Trasformazione*. Bologna: Il Mulino, 1967.

Maturi, Walter. *Interpretazioni del Risorgimento*. Turin: Einaudi, 1962.

Mautino, Aldo. *La Formazione della Filosofia Politica di Benedetto Croce*. Bari: Laterza, 1953.

Momigliano, Arnaldo. *Pagine Ebraiche*. Turin: Bollati, 1987.

Musté, Marcello. *Benedetto Croce*. Naples: Morano, 1990.

Nenni, Pietro. *Storia di Quattro Anni*. Turin: Einaudi, 1946.

Ocone, Corrado. *Bibliografia Ragionata degli Scritti su Benedetto Croce*. Naples: ESI, 1993.

Omodeo, Adolfo. *Difesa del Risorgimento*. Turin: Einaudi, 1951.

– *Il Senso della Storia*. Turin: Einaudi, 1959.

Papa Emidio Raffaele. *Fascismo e Cultura*. Padua: Marsiglio, 1974.

Parente, Alfredo. *Croce per Lumi Sparsi*. Florence: La Nuova Italia, 1975.

Partito Liberale Italiano. *Il PLI dal XII al XIV Congresso Nazionale*. 2 vols. Rome: Ferri, 1973.

Patuzzi, Claudia. *Laterza*. Naples: Liguori, 1982.

Pellegrini, Alessandro, ed. *Tre Cattolici Liberali*. Milan: Adelphi, 1973.

Permoli, Piergiovanni, ed. *Lezioni sull'Antifascismo*. Bari: Laterza, 1962.

Pezzino, Giuseppe. 'L'Intellettuale e la Politica in Croce Attraverso *La Critica*.' In *Benedetto Croce*. Ed. Antonino Bruno. Catania: Giannotta, 1974.

– *Morale e Società in Benedetto Croce*. Catania: CUECM, 1998.

Pieri, Piero, and Giorgio Rochat. *Badoglio*. Turin: UTET, 1974.

Quazza, Guido, ed. *Fascismo e Società Italiana*. Turin: Einaudi, 1973.

Ragghianti, Carlo Ludovico. *Disegno Storico della Resistenza Italiana*. Florence: Nistri Lischi, 1962.

Ragionieri, Ernesto. *Storia d'Italia*. Vol. 4, no. 3. *Dall'unità a Oggi*. Turin: Einaudi, 1976.

Roberts, David D. *Benedetto Croce and the Use of Historicism*. Berkeley: University of California Press, 1987.

Romeo, Rosario. *Il Giudizio Storico sul Risorgimento*. Palermo: Bonanno, 1978.

– *Italia Moderna tra Storia e Storiografia*. Florence: Le Monnier, 1977.

– *L'Italia Unita e la Prima Guerra Mondiale*. Bari: Laterza, 1978.

– *Dal Piemonte Sabaudo all'Italia Liberale*. Turin: Einaudi, 1964.

Rosa, Alberto Asor. *Storia d'Italia*. Vol. 4, no. 2. *Dall'unità a Oggi*. Turin: Einaudi, 1975.

Salvatorelli, Luigi. 'Il Delitto Matteotti e la Crisi del 1924–26.' In AA.VV., *Fascismo e Antifascismo*, 148–68. Milan: Feltrinelli, 1967–8.

– *Nazionalfascismo*. Turin: Einaudi, 1975.

– 'L'Opposizione Democratica durante il Fascismo.' In AA.VV., *Il Secondo Risorgimento*, 98–100. Rome: Istituto Poligrafico dell Stato, 1955.

– *Storia d'Italia nel Periodo Fascista*. Turin: Einaudi, 1964.

Salvemini, Gaetano. *Opere VI. Scritti sul Fascismo*. 3 vols. Milan: Feltrinelli, 1966–76.

Santarelli, Enzo. *Mezzogiorno 1943–1944. Uno Sbandato nel Regno del Sud*. Milan: Feltrinelli, 1999.

Saragat, Giuseppe. *Nel Primo Centenario della Nascita di Benedetto Croce*. Naples: Ricciardi, 1966.

Sarfatti, Michele. *Gli Ebrei nell' Italia Fascista*. Turin: Einaudi, 2000.

Sartori, Giovanni. *Stato e Politica in Benedetto Croce*. Naples: Morano, 1966.

– *Studi Crociani*. 2 vols. Bologna: Il Mulino, 1997.

Sasso, Gennaro. *Benedetto Croce. La Ricerca della Dialettica*. Naples: Morano, 1975.

– *Le Due Italie di Giovanni Gentile*. Bologna: Il Mulino, 1998.

– *La Fedeltà e l'Esperimento*. Bologna: Il Mulino, 1993.

– *Filosofia e Idealismo*. 3 vols. Naples: Bibliopolis, 1994.

– *La 'Storia d'Italia' di Benedetto Croce Cinquant'Anni Dopo*. Naples: Bibliopolis, 1979.

Scoppola, Pietro. *La Chiesa e il Fascismo. Documenti e Interpretazioni*. Bari: Laterza, 1971.

– *La Repubblica dei Partiti*. Bologna: Il Mulino, 1997.

Sereni, Emilio. 'La Lotta per la Repubblica. Testimonianze.' In *Lezioni sull'Antifascismo*. Ed. Piergiovanni Permoli, 285–8. Bari: Laterza, 1962.

Setta, Sandro. *Croce, il Liberalismo e l'Italia Postfascista*. Rome: Bonacci, 1979.

Spadolini, Giovanni. *Il Debito con Croce*. Florence: Le Monnier, 1990.

Spirito, Ugo. *Critica della Democrazia*. Milan: Rusconi, 1976.

– *Memorie di un Incosciente*. Milan: Rusconi, 1977.

Spriano, Paolo. *Storia del Partito Comunista Italiano*. 5 vols. Turin: Einaudi, 1967–75.

Sprigge, Cecil. *Benedetto Croce, Man and Thinker*. Cambridge: Bowes and Bowes, 1952.

Stella, Vittorio. *Il Giudizio su Croce. Momenti per una Storia delle Interpretazioni*. Pescara: Trimestre, 1971.

Tasca, Angelo. *Nascita e Avvento del Fascismo*. 2 vols. Bari: Laterza, 1972.

Togliatti, Palmiro. *Lezioni sul Fascismo*. Rome: Editori Riuniti, 1970.

Tranfaglia, Nicola. *Carlo Rosselli, dall'Interventismo a 'Giustizia e Libertà.'* Bari: Laterza, 1968.
- *La Prima Guerra Mondiale e il Fascismo.* Turin: UTET, 1995.
- ed. *L'Itinerario di Leone Ginzburg.* Turin: Bollati Boringhieri, 1996.
Tranfaglia, N., and A. Vittoria. *Storia degli Editori Italiani.* Bari: Laterza, 2000.
Turi, Gabriele. *Il Fascismo e il Consenso degli Intellettuali.* Bologna: Il Mulino, 1980.
- *Giovanni Gentile.* Florence: Giunti, 1995.
Valeri, Nino. *Da Giolitti a Mussolini. Momenti della Crisi del Liberalismo.* Florence: Parenti, 1956.
- *Dalla 'Belle Epoque' al Fascismo.* Bari: Laterza, 1975.
- *Giolitti.* Turin: UTET, 1971.
- *La Lotta Politica in Italia. Dall'Unità al 1925; Idee e Documenti.* Florence: Le Monnier, 1973.
- *Tradizione Liberale e Fascismo.* Florence: Le Monnier, 1972.
Valiani, Leo. *L'Avvento di De Gasperi.* Turin: De Silva, 1949.
- *Dall'Antifascismo alla Resistenza.* Milan: Feltrinelli, 1959.
- *Il PSI nel Periodo della Neutralità 1914–1915.* Milan: Feltrinelli, 1977.
- *Tra Croce e Omodeo.* Florence: Le Monnier, 1984.
Vigezzi, Brunello. *L'Italia di Fronte alla Prima Guerra Mondiale.* Milan: Ricciardi, 1966.
Vita-Finzi, Paolo. *Le Delusioni della Libertà.* Florence: Vallecchio, 1961.
Vivarelli, Roberto. *Il Fallimento del Liberalismo.* Bologna: Il Mulino, 1981.
- *Storia delle Origini del Fascismo.* 2 vols. Bologna: Il Mulino, 1991.
Volpe, Gioacchino. *L'Italia in Cammino.* Ed. Giovanni Belardelli. Bari: Laterza, 1991.
- *Nel Regno di Clio.* (Nuovi 'Storici e Maestri'). Rome: Volpe, 1977.
Ward, David. *Antifascism: Cultural Politics in Italy 1943–1946.* Toronto: Ars Un. Press, 1996.
Zangrandi, Ruggero. *Il Lungo Viaggio Attraverso il Fascismo.* 2 vols. Milan: Garzanti, 1971.
Zeno, Lino. *Ritratto di Carlo Sforza.* Florence: Le Monnier, 1975.
Zunino, Pier Giorgio. *Interpretazione e Memoria del Fascismo.* Bari: Laterza, 1991.

Articles

Agazzi, Emilio. 'Benedetto Croce e l'Avvento del Fascismo.' *Rivista Storica del Socialismo* 9 (September 1966): 76–103.
Alfieri, Vittorio Enzo. 'I Presupposti Filosofici del Liberalismo Crociano.' *La Rassegna d'Italia* 1, no. 2. (1946): 118–34.

Alpino, Enrico. 'Una Conversazione con Benedetto Croce nel 1932.' *Rivista di Studi Crociani* 3 (1966): 218–22.

Arton, Eugenio. 'Tre Cattolici Liberali.' *Nuova Antologia* no. 518 (1973): 451–90.

Biscione, Michele. 'Benedetto Croce nella Interpretazione di Denis Mack Smith.' *Clio* 14, no. 1 (January–March 1978): 35–61.

Bobbio, Norberto. 'Il Mondo di Antonicelli: Fra Croce e Gobetti.' *Nuova Antologia* no. 561. (1989): 103–8.

Busino, C. 'Croce, il Marxismo e Pareto.' *Rivista Milanese di Economia* 21 (1987): 47–73.

Cajumi, Arrigo. 'Benedetto Croce Precursore del Fascismo.' *Occidente* 2, no. 4 (1955): 325–31.

Calogero, Guido. 'Ricordi e Riflessioni. 1. Benedetto Croce.' *La Cultura* 4, no. 1 (1966): 145–78.

– 'Ricordi e Riflessioni. 4. Postilla ai Ricordi Crociani.' *La Cultura* 5, no. 1 (1967): 166–79.

Camurani, Ercole. 'Benedetto Croce nelle Carte del Ministero della Cultura Popolare.' *Rivista di Studi Crociani* 14 (1977): 133–48.

Capanna, Francesco. 'Croce di Fronte al Fascismo.' *Nuova Rivista Storica* (1964): 579–637.

Caserta, C.F. 'Primi Passi di Croce Letterato.' *Rivista di Studi Crociani* (1972): 44–63.

Ceva, Bianca. 'Aspetti della Crisi della Cultura Italiana Attraverso le Lettere di Adolfo Omodeo, 1910–1946.' *Il Movimento di Liberazione in Italia* 80, no. 3 (1965): 3–36.

– 'Benedetto Croce e l'Antifascismo.' *Il Movimento di Liberazione in Italia* 75, no. 2 (1964): 99–108.

– 'Benedetto Croce e le Vicende Politiche Italiane fra il 1915 e il 1935 Attraverso l'Epistolario.' *Il Movimento di Liberazione in Italia* 20, no. 91 (1960): 103–15.

– 'Lettere di Benedetto Croce ad Alessandro Casati.' *Il Movimento di Liberazione in Italia* 22, no. 98 (1970): 102–10.

Ciampi, Carlo Azeglio. 'Io, Croce e Giamburrasca.' *La Repubblica* (2 Feb. 2002): 18.

Colombo, Arturo. 'Bobbio Racconta Quegli Anni Bui Rischiarati da Croce.' *Nuova Antologia* no. 562. (1989): 185–203.

Craveri, Piero. 'La Fedeltà Risorgimentale di Casati.' *Nuova Antologia* no. 509 (1970): 499–518.

Destler, Chester McArthur. 'Benedetto Croce and Italian Fascism: A Note on Historical Reliability!' *Journal of Modern History* 34 (March–December 1952): 382–90.

– 'Some Observations on Contemporary Historical Theory.' *American Historical Review* 55, no. 1 (1949): 503–29.

Di Lalla, Manlio. 'Croce tra Fascismo e Antifascismo.' *Nord e Sud* (1972): 68–115.

Dionisotti, Carlo. 'Arnaldo Momigliano e Croce.' *Belfagor* (1988): 317–41.

Farnetti, Cristina. 'L'Enciclopedia Italiana e Croce: una Fallita Richiesta di Adesione.' *La Cultura* 23, no. 2 (1995): 297–303.

Felici, Lucio. 'Gli Anni Romani di Benedetto Croce.' *Il Palatino* (1967): 35–41.

Garibbo, R. 'Le Alleanze Politico-Culturali di Benedetto Croce nel Periodo Precedente la Prima Guerra Mondiale.' *Rivista di Studi Crociani* 6 (1969): 38–49, 193–204.

Garosci, Aldo. 'Il 1924.' *Rivista di Studi Crociani* 3 (1966): 137–52, 304–15.

– 'Sul Concetto di Borghesia. Verifica di un Concetto Crociano.' In AA.VV., *Miscellanea Walter Maturi*, 437–76. Turin: Giappicelli, 1966.

Guerra, Augusto. 'Vent'anni di Studi su Croce Politico.' (1944–64). *De Homine* 11, no. 12 (December 1964): 287–340.

Hartmut, Ullrich. 'La Campagna per il Divorzio nella Napoli Inizio Secolo e l'Atteggiamento di Benedetto Croce.' *Rivista di Studi Crociani* 7 (1970): 320–44.

– 'Croce e la Neutralità Italiana.' *Rivista di Studi Crociani* 6 (1969): 11–28, 155–72.

Jacobitti, Edmund E. 'Hegemony before Gramsci: The Case of Benedetto Croce.' *Journal of Modern History* 52, no. 1 (1980): 66–84.

Jannazzo, Antonio. 'Croce e la Corsa verso la Guerra.' *Rivista di Studi Crociani* 12 (1975): 256–76.

– 'Croce e il Prepartito della Cultura.' *Rivista di Studi Crociani* 10 (1973): 189–243.

Lapi, Nazareno. 'Croce, Togliatti e l'Operazione Gramsci.' *Rivista di Studi Crociani* 21 (1982): 171–91.

Little, Scott H. 'Croce, il Metodo Storico e lo Storico.' *Nuova Antologia* no. 465 (1955): 29–44.

Lonne, Karl Egon. 'Benedetto Croce e Heinrich von Treitschke.' *Rivista di Studi Crociani* 7 (1970): 35–55.

Mack Smith, Denis. 'Benedetto Croce: History and Politics.' *Journal of Contemporary History* 8, no. 1 (1973): 41–62.

– 'Croce and Fascism.' *The Cambridge Journal* 2, no. 6 (March 1949): 343–56.

– 'The Politics of Senator Croce. 1. 1866–1915: The Philosophic Preparation.' *Cambridge Journal* 1 (October 1947–September 1948): 28–42.

– 'The Politics of Senator Croce. 2. 1915–1922: War and Revolution.' *Cambridge Journal* 1 (October 1947–September 1948): 279–91.

Marinelli, B. 'L'Esperienza Provinciale di Domenico Petrini nel Carteggio con Benedetto Croce.' *Belfagor* (1986): 180–96.

Moceri, James. 'Communications to the Editor.' *American Historical Review* 56, no. 3 (1951): 453–60.

Parente, Alfredo. 'Vinciguerra e Croce.' *Rivista di Studi Crociani* 7 (1970): 74–7.

Pertici, Roberto. 'Benedetto Croce Collaboratore Segreto della Nuova Italia di Luigi Russo.' *Belfagor* 36 (1981): 187–203.

Perticone, Giacomo. 'Croce Uno e Due.' *Storia e Politica* (1958): 219–25.

Pieri, Piero. 'Fascismo e Resistenza.' *Itinerari* (1966): 577–602.

Pontieri, Ernesto. 'Una Baruffa Letteraria tra Giustino Fortunato e Gaetano Salvemini a Proposito della Nomina a Senatore di Benedetto Croce.' *Rivista di Studi Crociani* 7 (1970): 208–18.

Ragionieri, Ernesto. 'Rileggendo la Storia d'Italia di Benedetto Croce.' *Belfagor* 21 (1966): 125–49.

Resta, Antonio. 'La Nuova Italia nella Firenze di Alessandro Pavolini.' *Belfagor* 38, no. 4 (1983): 308–22.

Roberts, David D. 'History as Thought and as Action,' in Jack D'Amico, Dain A. Trafton, and Massimo Verdicchio, *The Legacy of Benedetto Croce: Contemporary Critical Views* (Toronto: University of Toronto Press, 1999), 196–230.

Romeo, Rosario. 'Croce e l'Europa.' *La Cultura* (1978): 444–58.

Ruffini, Nina. 'Zanotti Bianco e il Mezzogiorno.' *Nuova Antologia* no. 511 (1971): 500–508.

Ruggiero, Edoardo. 'Coerenza Etica del Croce Politico (1943–1952).' *Rivista di Studi Crociani* 16 (1979): 323–41.

Salvemini, Gaetano. 'La Formazione della Filosofia Politica di Benedetto Croce.' *Il Ponte* (1954): 810–12.

– 'La Politica di Benedetto Croce.' *Il Ponte* (1954): 1728–43.

Saragat, Giuseppe. 'Nel Primo Centenario della Nascita di Benedetto Croce.' *Rivista di Studi Crociani* 3 (1966): 83–93.

Sasso, Gennaro. 'Croce e la Storia.' *La Cultura* (1983): 341–55.

– 'Due Variazioni Polemiche nell'interpretazione di Croce.' *La Cultura* (1968): 260–76.

– 'A Proposito di un Libro su Croce.' *La Cultura* (1967): 437–69.

– 'Visitando una Mostra.' *La Cultura* (1986): 5–37.

Setta, Sandro. 'Benedetto Croce e la Sinistra Liberale nel Carteggio con Leone Cattani.' *Storia Contemporanea* 19 (1988): 115–42.

Stella, Vittorio. 'Il Giudizio su Croce: Consuntivo di un Centenario.' *Giornale di Metafisica* (1967): 643–712.

– 'Il Giudizio e la Prassi: Studi su Croce dal 1971 al 1975.' *La Cultura* 16 (1975): 313–51.

Togliatti, Palmiro. Review of 'Benedetto Croce, per la storia del comunismo in quanto realtà politica. Bari: Laterza, 1943.' *La Rinascita* 1, no. 1 (1944).

Treves, Renato. 'Enrico Bassi Socialista e Antifascista a Bologna.' *Nuova Antologia* 561, no. 3 (1989): 159–61.

– 'A Proposito di Cajumi e di Croce.' *Occidente* 6 (1957): 539–44.

Valiani, Leo. 'Croce Filosofo della Libertà.' *Nuova Antologia* no. 552 (1983): 61–100.

– 'Lenin, Hitler, Mussolini. Tre Vie alla Dittatura.' *Nuova Antologia* no. 552 (October–December 1983): 11–19.

– 'Il Liberalsocialismo.' *Rivista Storica Italiana* 1 (1969).

– 'La Storia del Fascismo nella Problematica Contemporanea e nella Biografia di Mussolini.' *Rivista Storica Italiana* 79 (1967): 459–81.

Ventura, Angelo. 'La Persecuzione Fascista contro gli Ebrei nell'Università Italiana.' *Rivista Storica Italiana* 109 (1997): 121–97.

– 'La Svolta Antiebraica nella Storia del Fascismo Italiano.' *Rivista Storica Italiana* 113 (2001): 36–65.

Vinciguerra, Mario. 'Di Croce e dell'Equità.' *Il Ponte* (July–August 1954): 1251–53.

– 'Il Gruppo di Italia Nostra.' *Studi Politici* 4 (1954): 640–65.

– 'Vita Interiore di Alessandro Casati.' *Nuova Antologia* no. 471 (1957): 497–504.

Visentin, Mauro. 'Croce e Gentile: La Fine del Sodalizio.' *La Cultura* 31, no. 2 (1993): 317–42.

Zucaro, Domenico. 'Benedetto Croce e i Patti Laterani.' *Mondo Operaio* (1968): 31–6.

– 'Croce clandestino.' *Il Mondo* (26 Feb. 2002): 11.

Index

Abbiate, Mario, 73
Academy of Italy, 76, 108, 158
Accademia dei Lincei, 218
Accademia Pontaniana. *See* Pontanian Academy
Alatri, Paolo, 229
Albertini, Leonardo, 194
Albertini, Luigi, 38, 73, 85, 90, 104, 112, 130, 159, 168, 170, 181, 194, 219, 227
Albertini, Piera, 100
Alfieri, Vittorio Enzo, 101–2, 117, 129, 152–3, 183–4
Allason, Barbara, 163, 177–8, 181
Ambrosini, Luigi, 72
Amendola, Antonio, 186
Amendola, Giorgio, 118, 124, 164, 175, 179–80, 186, 192, 207
Amendola, Giovanni, 51, 65, 69, 72–4, 87–90, 92–4, 112, 175, 186, 248, 263, 267
American and Jewish Tribune, 224
Andreotti, Giulio, 226
Ansaldo, Giovanni, 127–8
Anti-Fascist Manifesto, 87–91
(*L*) *Anti-Fascista*, 164
Antoni, Carlo, 9–10, 21

Antonicelli, Franco, 181–2
Arangio Ruiz, Vincenzo, 240
Archivio Centrale dello Stato (ACS). *See* National Archives
Argan, Giulio Carlo, 208
Attila, 190
'Autobiographical Notes,' 43, 101, 121–2, 133, 141, 146, 208
Avanti!, 19, 166
Aventine Secession, 65–9, 113, 157

Badoglio, Pietro, 127, 188, 218, 220, 233–4, 236–8, 240–1, 243–4, 246, 251, 266
Balbo, Italo, 227
Barres, Maurice, 99
Barth, Karl, 205
Basso Lelio, 153
Bauer, Riccardo, 193, 201, 205, 220
Beard, Charles, 6, 224
Becker, Charles, 6
Benda, Julien, 29
Benes, Edvard, 178
Benzoni, Giuliana, 177–8
Berenson, Bernard, 226
Bergamini, Alberto, 24, 109, 159, 219
Bergson, Henri, 145

Berle, Adolph, 239
Bernstein, Eduard, 17
Bianchi, Michele, 63
Biblioteca di Cultura Moderna, 134
Bismarck, Otto von, 199
Bissolati, Leonida, 129
Bobbio, Norberto, 9, 64, 198
Bocchini, Arturo, 124, 126, 149, 162,
    174, 179, 187–8, 202, 206
Boethius, Anicius Severinus, 190
Bonomi, Ivanoe, 9, 41, 64, 129, 163,
    234–6, 246, 252, 256
Bordiga, Amadeo, 114
Bottai, Giuseppe, 71, 206, 211
Boulay, Charles, 10
Bourgeoisie, 139
Bracco, Roberto, 110–11, 114, 158, 203
Brosio, Manlio, 182
Buozzi, Bruno, 158
Butler, Nicholas M., 225

Calamandrei, Piero, 183, 253
Caldara, Emilio, 158
Calogero, Guido, 194, 201, 203, 215,
    248, 256
Calosso, Umberto, 51
Calvino, Italo, 128
Candeloro, Giorgio, 72, 50
Capitini, Aldo, 194, 221
Caporetto, 30–1, 46, 234
Caracciolo, Galeazzo, 187
Caradonna, Giuseppe, 209
Carandini, Nicolò, 183, 136
Carattere della Filosofia Moderna, 203–4,
    230
Carducci, Giosuè, 12, 28
Casati, Alessandro, 69, 73–4, 76, 79,
    81, 84, 87, 96–7, 105–7, 112, 116–17,
    168, 172, 178, 180, 184, 191, 193–4,
    219–20, 227, 235–6, 257, 445, 481

Casellario Politico Centrale, 176
Cassiser, Ernst, 215
Castellano, Giovanni, 106, 220–1
Castelli, Michele, 124, 169
Cattani, Leone, 183, 236
Caviglia, Enrico, 181, 236
Cavour, Camillo Benso, 15, 159, 199,
    240, 248–9, 256
Censorship, 174–5
Centro Interno, 193
'Cesare,' 178, 203
Ceva, Bianca, 178, 193, 220
Ceva, Umberto, 193
Chabod, Federcio, 9, 77, 152, 243, 257
Charles V, 187
Churchill, Winston, 239, 241
Ciampi, Carlo Azeglio, 201
Ciarlantini, Franco, 91–3
Cifarelli, Michele, 184
Cittadella, Maria, 178
Clark, Mark, 239
Codignola, Ernesto, 185, 210
Colapietra, Raffaele, 10
Collingwood, Robert, 6, 190, 228
Colonna Di Cesarò, Giovanni Anto-
    nio, 178
Colorni, Eugenio, 124, 193, 247
Communism, 137, 192, 198–9, 250–1
Communist Party, 216, 243, 250
Constituent Assembly, 252–5
Consulta (Consultative Assembly),
    224
Contini, Gianfranco, 200
Coppola, Francesco, 32–3
Corriere Italiano, 62–4
Corriere della Sera, 38, 100, 104–5, 151
Cosmo, Umberto, 31, 165, 180–1
Counter-Reformation, 78
Craveri, Raimondo, 240
Crispi, Francesco, 17, 142, 151, 219

(*La*) *Critica*, 22–3, 104–7, 204–7
Croce, Adelina, 115–17, 251
Croce, Benedetto: Anti–Fascist Manifesto, 87–91; break with Gentile, 74–6; collaboration with *Il Giornali d'Italia*, 24–5; Constituent Assembly, 253–5; correspondence as resistance, 109–13, 185–6; cultural activity as resistance, 133–6; disagreement with Gentile, 57–60; expulsion from academies, 217–18; fall of Mussolini, 233–7; family tragedy, 12–13; Fascist congress in Naples, 41–43; First World War, 27–31; on fascism, 143–5, 257–9; Gentile's reform of education, 52–4; Giolitti's influence, 39; help to anti-Fascists, 127–30; influence under fascism, 196–9; invasion of his house, 114–22; Italian Encyclopedia, 95–7; Labriola's influence, 17–20; last years, 259–60; Lateran Pacts, 155–64, 253; leader of opposition, 238–41; life under fascism, 173–5; March on Rome, 41–3, 47–9; Marxism and socialism, 17–20; Matteotti Affair, 67–9; member of Liberal Party, 81–4; minister with Badoglio, 243–5; minister of education, 35–43; nationalism, 33–4; newspaper interviews, 54–6, 62–4, 70–2; Party of Action, 247–50; philosophy, 21–2, 259–60; police surveillance, 123–4; president of Liberal Party, 255–6; Racial Laws, 221–31; relations with the exiles, 125–7, 186–91; relative freedom under fascism, 208–12; religious crisis, 12; Roman period, 13–14; Second World War, 231–2; solidarity with Jews, 227–31; Spaventa's influence, 13–15; travels in Italy and abroad, 124–7, 182–5, 186–91; underground organizations, 132–3, 167–8, 191–5, 250; Vittorio Emanuele, 131–2, 238–42; wealth, 16–17
Croce, Elena, 126, 178, 203
(*La*) *Cultura*, 182
Cultura e Vita Morale, 58, 97

D'Annunzio, Gabriele, 23, 28, 32, 38, 145, 262
De Begnac, Ivon, 211–12
De Bosis, Lauro, 167
De Caprariis, Vittorio, 9
De Felice, Renzo, 197, 257
De Gasperi, Alcide, 235
De Gaulle, Charles, 238
Del Croix, Carlo, 74
De Lollis, Cesare, 210
De Nicola, Enrico, 238, 240–4, 253–5, 266
Depretis, Agostino, 14, 61, 141
De Ruggiero, Guido, 135, 148, 150–1, 169, 180, 183, 206–7, 215, 248
De Sanctis, Francesco, 12, 47, 98, 105–6
De Sanctis, Gaetano, 178, 183, 202, 210, 214–15, 217
De Stefani, Alberto, 51
Destler, Chester McArthur, 6–7
De Viti De Marco, Antonio, 216
Diaz, Armando, 32, 48
Di Robilant, Irene, 167, 178
Donovan, William, 240
Dorso, Guido, 185, 186
Dulbecco, Renato, 216

Eden, Anthony, 239
Einaudi, Giulio, 172, 198, 210

Einaudi, Luigi, 97, 138, 172, 182, 210, 215–16, 226–7, 255
Einaudi publishing house, 172, 182, 198, 210
Einstein, Albert, 190
Elections: 1919, 35–6; 1921, 40–1; 1924, 62–5; 1929, 157–8; 1946, 252
Elementi di Politica, 77
Enciclopedia Italiana. See Italian Encyclopedia
Engels, Friederich, 17
Epurazione, 224
Ercole, Francesco, 175
Esame di Stato, 37, 53, 54
Ethiopian war, 218–222
Etica e Politica, 136
Exiles, 186–91

Fabbri, Luigi, 41
Facta, Luigi, 63
Falco, Giorgio, 229
(*La*) *famiglia italiana*, 134–5, 177–9, 265
(*Una*) *Famiglia di patrioti*, 33
Farinacci, Roberto, 57, 63, 71, 93
Fascism, 40–3, 59, 65, 83–4, 143–5, 257–9
Fascist Party: 1922 Congress in Naples, 41–3; elections in 1921, 40–1; elections in 1924, 64–5; March on Rome, 44–5; strength in 1922, 42–4
Fedele, Pietro, 131, 218
Federzoni, Luigi, 25, 60, 219
Ferrara, Mario, 172, 209, 226
Ferrero, Guglielmo, 119
Fiore, Tommaso, 184
First World War, 27–31
Fisher, Herbert A.L., 129

Flora, Francesco, 104, 184
Foa, Vittorio, 192, 205
Fortunato, Giustino, 16, 20, 25, 46–7, 56, 75, 100, 109, 111–12, 115, 125, 127–8, 147–8, 150, 152, 168
Franchini, Raffaello, 9
Frassati, Alfredo, 102, 105, 181
Fuoriusciti, 108–9. *See also* Exiles
Fusco family, 170

Galante Garrone, Alessando, 197
Galasso Giuseppe, 9
Galati, Vito, 118
Gallarati Scotti, Tommaso, 184
Gandhi, Mohandás K., 221
Garibaldi, Giuseppe, 28, 240
Garin, Eugenio, 9, 122, 200, 207
Garosci, Aldo, 9, 76, 124, 139, 188–9, 203
Gasparri, Pietro, 156
Gavagnin, Armando, 132–3
Gentile, Giovanni, 9, 22–4, 32, 37, 48, 51–2, 56, 59–60, 69, 73, 77, 79, 81, 85, 87–91, 95–7, 100, 107, 116, 119, 136, 142, 146, 162, 168, 191, 203, 205, 212, 248, 250–2, 263; adhesion to fascism, 56; Anti-Fascist Manifesto, 87–90; break with Croce, 74–6; collaboration with Croce, 22; death, 251–2; Italian Encyclopedia, 95–7; minister of education, 52–4
Gerbi, Antonello, 228–9
German Social Democratic Party, 18, 30, 34
Giannini, Guglielmo, 256
Ginzburg, Carlo, 181
Ginzburg, Leone, 181–2, 193–4, 210, 216–17, 230, 267
Ginzburg, Natalia, 181
Gioberti, Vincenzo, 57, 59

Giolitti, Antonio, 198
Giolitti, Giovanni, 4, 7, 20, 23–7, 34, 35–41, 43, 45, 49, 66, 72, 81–3, 85, 94, 105, 116, 126–7, 131, 141–4, 146, 150, 155, 157, 181, 188, 198, 213–15, 223, 229, 234–5, 240, 260, 262; Aventine Secession, 66; Croce's judgment, 141–4; elections of 1924, 63–4; influence on Croce, 39; last cabinet, 35–41; March on Rome, 43
Giolittian era, 20–2
Giornale d'Italia, 24–5, 51–2, 53, 54–6, 70–2, 81, 90–2
Giovane Italia. *See* Young Italy
Giraud, Henri, 238
Giua, Michele, Mrs, 230
Giunta, Francesco, 63
Giustizia e Libertà, 6, 172–3, 182–3, 187–94, 197, 216
Gobetti, Ada, 126–9, 175, 178, 181
Gobetti, Piero, 51, 73–4, 79, 100–1, 112, 126, 128, 182, 211, 248, 263, 267
Goethe, J.W., 231
Gorky, Maxim, 180
Gramsci, Antonio, 5, 22, 32, 51, 165, 169, 172–3, 177, 182, 209, 250, 267
Grand Council of Fascism, 130, 131, 157, 227
Grandi, Dino, 71, 233
Groethuisen, Bernhard, 139

Halevy, Daniel, 190
Hegel, Georg Wilhelm Friedrich, 12, 224, 250
Heidegger, Martin, 205
Hicks, Harold, 239
History of the Baroque Age in Italy, 77, 99–100
History of Europe, 199–202
History of Italy, 140–52

History of the Kingdom of Naples, 60–1
History as Thought and as Action, 203, 225, 230
Hitler, Adolf, 184
Hull, Cordell, 239
Huxley, Aldous, 190

Iermano, Toni, 185
Institutional question, 252–3
Invasion of Croce's house, 114–22
Ischia, 13
Italia Nostra, 27
Italian Encyclopedia, 95–7
Italian family. *See* (La) famiglia Italiana
Italian Institute for Historical Studies (IISS), 257–9
Italy from 1914 to 1918, 29, 135–6

Jacini, Stefano, 184
Jews, 221–6, 227–31

Kant, Immanuel, 223
Kautsky, Karl, 17
Keynes, John Maynard, 172
Klibansky, Raymond, 215
Kuliscioff, Anna, 143

Labour Party, 256
Labriola, Antonio, 14, 16, 17, 19, 207
Labriola, Arturo, 114
La Malfa, Ugo, 184, 235, 241
Lateran Pacts, 155–64, 253, 264
Laterza, Giovanni, 22, 119, 126, 129, 130, 134, 140, 149–50, 158, 174–5, 185, 197–8, 202, 210, 214, 229, 265
Laterza publishing house, 129, 134, 149, 174–5, 197, 206–8
Law of the Guarantees. *See* Lateran Pacts

Lenin, Vladimir I., 199, 206
Leonardo, 168
Lessing, Gotthold E., 226
Levi, Alessandro, 182–3, 228
Levi, Carlo, 182
Levi, Giuseppe, 216
Levi Della Vida, Giorgio, 68–70, 94, 97
Levi Montalcini, Rita, 216
Liberal Party, 45, 73, 81–4, 171–3, 182–3, 235–6, 240, 247–8, 255–7
Liberalism, 15, 26, 57–8, 60–1, 97–9, 133–4, 136–9, 183
Liberalsocialism, 194
Liberismo, 138–9. *See also* Liberalism
Library of Modern Culture, 193, 207
Licitra, Carmelo, 59
Lippmann, Walter, 180, 239
Lombardo Radice, Giuseppe, 54, 87, 96–7, 170, 175
Lucetti, Gino, 108
Lucretia, 57
Ludwig, Emile, 222
Luria, Salvatore, 216
Lusignoli, Alfredo, 68
Lussu, Emilio, 191, 255, 258
Lussu, Joyce, 191
Luther, Martin, 83

Machiavelli, Niccolò, 76, 78
Mack Smith, Denis, 5, 7–10, 32, 152, 208
Macmillan, Harold, 238
Manifesto Antifascista. See Anti-Fascist Manifesto
Mann, Thomas, 190, 221
Manzoni, Alessandro, 91
March on Rome, 43–9
Marchesi, Concetto, 191, 216
Maria José, Princess, 132, 236

Marinetti, Filippo, 59–60, 223
Martini, Ferdinando, 178
Marx, Karl, 7, 17, 19, 23 46, 120, 135, 205, 248
Marxism, 17–19, 135, 137, 250–1
Masaryk, Tomas, 178
Masonic Order, 85–6
Massigli, Renè, 238
Materialismo Storico ed Economia Marxistica, 135
Matteotti, Giacomo, 7, 65, 67, 71, 75–6, 79–80, 95, 260, 263
Matteotti Affair, 65–74
Matthews, Herbert, 239
(*Il*) *Mattino*, 86
Mattioli, Raffaele, 172, 184, 229, 235, 257
Maturi, Walter, 9, 152
Maurras, Charles, 99
Mazzini, Giuseppe, 57, 59, 112, 129, 132, 221
Meinecke, Friedrich, 190
Mesmil, Jacques, 41
Messalina, 57
(*Il*) *Mezzogiorno*, 93
Mila, Massimo, 201, 205
Minifie, James, 239
Missiroli, Mario, 110
Momigliano, Arnaldo, 228, 230
Momigliano, Attilio, 228
Mondadori publishing house, 184
(*Il*) *Mondo*, 89, 93, 257
Mondolfo, Rodolfo, 229
Montenerodomo, 34
Monti, Augusto, 165–6
Morandi, Rodolfo, 193, 256
Morelli, Domenico, 110
Mosca, Gaetano, 61, 84, 109
Movimento di Rinnovamento Politico e Sociale Italiano, 194

Murphy, Robert, 238
Mussolini, Benito, 3–4, 9–10, 30, 32, 40–50, 53–7, 59–61, 74, 76, 79–83, 90–1, 94–5, 98, 101–2, 105–6, 108–10, 113–17, 121, 123–4, 127, 130–3, 142–3, 145, 149–51, 156–9, 162–6, 171, 173–7, 180, 183, 187, 189–90, 193, 196, 199, 206, 208, 212, 213, 216, 218, 220–3, 231, 233–7, 241, 246, 251, 254, 258, 263–6; Croce's relative freedom, 208–23; death, 251; elections of 1921, 40–1; fall in 1943, 233–7; Lateran Pacts, 162–6; March on Rome, 44–7; Matteotti Affair, 65–9; Racial Laws, 220–3; Zamboni assassination attempt, 113–14

Naples, 41–3, 179–81
Napoleon, Louis, 121
(*Die*) *Nation*, 224
National Alliance, 167–8, 193
National Archives, 176–7
National Democratic Union, 252
National Liberal Party, 83
National Liberation Committee (CLN), 237, 240–1
Nationalism, 32–3, 60–1, 84, 89
NATO, 182, 257
Nenni, Pietro, 253, 256
Neri, Mario, 133
(*The*) *New Republic*, 221
Newspaper interviews, 54–6, 62–4, 70–2
Nicolini, Fausto, 10, 119
Niobe, 252
Nitti, Francesco Saverio, 16, 26, 34, 41, 112, 125–6, 188, 202, 252–3, 263, 265, 267
(*La*) *Nuova Italia*, 168–9

Nuova Politica Liberale, 17, 59

Oath of loyalty, 213–16, 217–18
Ojetti, Ugo, 105, 183
Omodeo, Adolfo, 75, 97, 100, 135, 156, 159, 175, 179, 184, 205–6, 213, 217, 239–40, 244, 248, 255, 257
Ordine Nuovo, 51
Orientamenti, 204
Orlando, Vittorio Emanuele, 31, 34, 252, 254–5
Ossietzhy, Carl von, 221

Pajetta, Giancarlo, 192
Pancrazi, Pietro, 163
Parente, Alfredo, 9, 255
Parri, Ferruccio, 143, 182, 209, 235, 248–9
Party of Action, 128, 165, 172, 184, 195, 197, 207, 235, 236, 240, 241, 247–50
Party membership, 216–17
Paul, Saint, 217
Pavolini, Alessandro, 203–4
Peace Treaty, 254–5
Pellico, Silvio, 154
Pertini, Sandro, 143, 247
Perugini, Gaetano, 185–6
Petrini, Domenico, 130
Pietre, 152–3
Pirandello, Luigi, 76
Pistelli, Ermenegildo, 91
Pius XI, Pope, 91, 156
Plato, 396
plebiscite of 1929, 157–8
Poerio brothers, 33–4, 39
Politica, 7, 32–3
Pontanian Academy, 108, 218
(*Il*) *Popolo D'Italia*, 72
Popular Party, 35–6, 40, 49, 54, 188

Preziosi, Giovanni, 93
Prezzolini, Giuseppe, 24–5

Racial Laws, 221–31
Ragghianti, Carlo Ludovico, 180, 186, 195
Ragionieri, Ernesto, 212
Reale, Eugenio, 124, 164, 167–8
Referendum of 1946, 252–3
Reform of education, 52–4
Regno del Sud, 237–45
(*Il*) *Resto del Carlino*, 110
Ricciardi, Riccardo, 129
Rinascita, 5
Risorgimento, 60–1, 106–7, 231–2
Rivista di Studi Crociani, 10
Rivoluzione Liberale, 73
Rizzoli publishing house, 184
Rocco, Alfredo, 32, 60, 66, 80, 85, 107, 142, 163, 209, 212
Rockefeller Foundation, 172
Romano, Ruggiero, 257
Romeo, Rosario, 152, 232, 257
Roosevelt, Franklin Delano, 239
Rosenberg, Alfred, 223–4
Rosselli, Carlo, 139, 143, 151, 168, 183, 186–90, 193–4, 209, 230, 248, 260, 265, 267, 369, 396, 466, 487, 496; meetings with Croce, 188–90, 193–4
Rosselli, Nello, 74, 127, 183, 186, 189, 193
Rossi, Ernesto, 172, 192–3, 201, 204, 216, 247
Rossi Doria, Manlio, 207
Ruffini, Francesco, 52, 73, 84–5, 97, 105, 108, 120, 130 133, 159–60, 181–2, 215
Ruffini, Nina, 178
Ruini, Meuccio, 129, 235

Russo, Luigi, 46, 67, 81, 117, 122, 168–9, 180, 183–5, 203, 210, 215

Saitta, Armando, 198, 203
Salandra, Antonio, 14, 20, 24–6, 46, 50, 64, 83, 150, 256
Salvadori, Max, 191
Salvatorelli, Luigi, 105
Salvemini, Gaetano, 5–6, 24, 42, 56, 90, 100, 111–12, 164–5, 167, 189, 197, 212, 216
Sapegno, Natalino, 139, 256, 260
Saragat, Giuseppe, 139, 256, 260
Sarfatti, Margherita, 222
Sarocchi, Gino, 73
Sartori, Giovanni, 9
Sasso, Gennaro, 9, 10, 140, 255, 257
Scaglione, Emilio, 93
Scialoja, Vittorio, 159
Scorza, Carlo, 234
Segre, Umberto, 166
Semeria, Giovanni, 178
Senate, 25–6, 66–9, 84–6, 155–64, 225–7
Sereni, Emilio, 5
Second World War, 231–2
Sforza, Carlo, 36, 38, 126, 163, 187–8, 238–9, 241–4, 265
Shaw, George Bernard, 190,
Socialism, 19–20, 35–6, 64, 193
Socialist Party, 17, 19, 30, 35–6, 40, 42, 64, 143, 145
Solari, Giole, 181
Soleri, Marcello, 131, 234
Sombart, Werner, 139
Sonnino, Sidney, 20, 23–6
Sorel, Georges, 17, 145
Spaventa, Silvio, 14–16, 47, 105–7, 156, 229
Special Tribunal, 114

Spinelli, Altiero, 247
Spirito, Ugo, 58
Spitzer, Leo, 226
Sprigge, Cecil, 9, 219, 239
Springarn, Joel Elias, 118
Sraffa, Piero, 172
Stael, Anne Louise Mdme de, 129
Stalin, Joseph, 198, 205, 243
(*La*) *Stampa*, 31, 72, 102, 105
Sturzo, Luigi, 42, 49, 127, 188, 254, 265, 267
Suardo, Giacomo, 226
Survey Graphic, 109
Svolta of Salerno, 242–3

Taccuini di Lavoro, 45–6, 102–3, 127, 131, 147, 157–8, 159–60, 164
Tagliacozzo, Enzo, 228
Tarchiani, Alberto, 240
(*Il*) *Tevere*, 64, 149
Thaon de Revel, Paolo, 32, 47
Tilgher, Livia, 168
Timpanaro, Sebastiano, 56
Tino, Adolfo, 184
Tittoni, Tommaso, 115
Togliatti, Palmiro, 5, 43, 208, 243–5, 250, 253, 263, 266
Torraca, Francesco, 47
Toscanini, Arturo, 193
Totila, 190
Tranfaglia, Nicola, 138
Treves, Claudio, 127, 166–7, 183, 188
Treves, Paolo, 166–7, 202, 208, 228
Treves, Pietro, 167
Treves, Renato, 229
Treves publishing house, 149
Turati, Augusto, 151–2
Turati, Filippo, 19, 30, 36, 46, 66, 94, 127–8, 143, 188, 216, 236, 260, 267
Turin, 181–2

Umberto 1, King, 142
Umberto, Prince, 131–2, 239
Underground organizations, 132–3, 167–8, 191–5, 250
(*L'*) *Unità*, 25
Unitary Socialist Party, 86
Uomo Qualunque, 256

Valery, Paul, 190
Valiani, Leo, 9, 139, 163, 192
Venturi, Franco, 188
Venturi, Lionello, 188, 215
Vico, Giambattista, 12, 21
Vinciguerra, Mario, 153, 167–8, 179, 190, 193
Vittorio Emanuele, III, King, 20, 131, 142–3, 242
(*La*) *Voce*, 24, 25
Volpe, Gioacchino, 79, 87, 96, 151–2, 191
Vossler, Karl, 32, 36, 117–18
Vyschinski, Andrej, 238

Webb, Sidney, 190
Wilson, Woodrow, 31–2

Young Italy, 132–3, 192

Zamboni, Anteo, 113–14, 264
Zampanelli, Angelina, 20
Zanardelli, Giuseppe, 24
Zaniboni, Tito, 86
Zanotti Bianco, Umberto, 34, 173, 183, 236
Zweig, Stefan, 180